World Politics: The Global System

THE DORSEY SERIES IN POLITICAL SCIENCE

EDITOR NORTON E. LONG *Brandeis University*

World Politics:
The Global System

by

HERBERT J. SPIRO
Professor of Political Science
University of Pennsylvania

Foreword by Ernest A. Gross

1966

THE DORSEY PRESS — HOMEWOOD, ILLINOIS

First Printing, August, 1966
Second Printing, May, 1967

Library of Congress Catalog Card No. 66–24620

Printed in the United States of America

To

HOWARD C. and ELIZABETH W. PETERSEN

Preface

This book grew out of my course on World Politics at Amherst College. I approached this subject as I had previously approached the comparative study of politics at lower levels, national or subnational, in western countries or in the "developing areas." This choice of method was deliberate, because I had been concerned for some time about the old gulf between studies—and students—of international relations and of comparative politics and government, and the new, widening gap between political scientists working on western and nonwestern countries.

The old cleavage resulted from the assumption of a qualitative difference between national and international politics, both of which were being studied with inadequate tools. The technological revolution through which we are living has brought about a qualitative transformation of conventional international relations into world politics. The possessors of a plethora of power are inhibited in its use, so that the old assumption of the qualitative difference between national and international politics is no longer tenable, and power is only one of several dimensions of the process of politics, be it global or local. All political systems today are, ultimately, subsystems of the worldwide system of politics. The universality of politics must yield universals of politics that are, at least in their rock-bottom fundamentals, susceptible to study through the rules of valid analogy.

For the first time in human history, all men everywhere are within potential reach of each other's voice and vision. The whole world has become the *agora* of the *polis*, the marketplace of Aristotle's city-state. Mankind possesses the means not only of global communication, but also of total human destruction. Both contribute to the growing feelings of belonging to a community of mankind. The human community can develop itself or destroy itself only through politics, which Aristotle called the queen of the sciences long before these ultimate possibilities arose. The problems given to political science have never been as weighty as they are today, and the tasks for the study of world politics may be considered the most difficult and consequential tasks to which any intellectual discipline has ever addressed itself—or ever will.

Acknowledgements

I should like to acknowledge my thanks to the following for their permission to quote passages from the indicated publications:

The President and Fellows of Harvard College—*World Peace through World Law* by Grenville Clark and Louis B. Sohn; The Twentieth Century Fund—*Strategy and Arms Control* by Thomas C. Schelling and Morton H. Halperin; Alfred A. Knopf—*Politics among Nations* by Hans J. Morgenthau; Frederick A. Praeger—*The Soviet Union at the United Nations* by Alexander Dallin; Stevens and Sons, Ltd., London, and Frederick A. Praeger—*The Common Law of Mankind* by C. Wilfred Jenks; John Wiley & Sons, Inc.—*The Political Foundations of International Law* by Morton A. Kaplan and Nicholas deB. Katzenbach; Prentice-Hall, Inc.—*A Framework for Political Analysis* by David Easton; the Editors of the *Indiana Law Journal*—"Structuring Impartiality in International Third-Party Lawmaking" by Thomas M. Franck; the Associated Press—"Eden Sees Munich as Lasting Lesson" by the Earl of Avon; Games Research, Inc.—Rules of the game *Diplomacy*.

I am grateful also to the University of Pennsylvania for a faculty research grant, and to Miss Susanne D. Mueller and Mr. Robert R. Benedetti, whose thorough research assistance was made possible by this grant.

Early in this book, a distinguished student of international politics is quoted asserting that "the typical conflict between the mother-in-law and her child's spouse is in its essence a struggle for power, . . . [and] foreshadows the conflict on the international scene between the policies of the status quo and the policies of imperialism." I am dedicating this book to my parents-in-law not only because of their constructive involvement in world politics, but also in order to test Professor Morgenthau's analogy. At this point, I can only conclude either that its applicability is far from universal, or that relations between my parents-in-law and myself have been very atypical.

Philadelphia   HERBERT J. SPIRO
August, 1966

Foreword

By Ernest A. Gross

The world to which this book addresses itself—the world of today—
is characterized by two facts of decisive relevance to proper understanding of world politics. One of these concerns the nature of power
in the Age of the Atom; the other, the interdependence of mankind
in the Age of the Individual.

In his first address to the Congress of the United States, November
27, 1963, President Johnson summed up the significance for world
politics of the nuclear deadlock and the capacity for "overkill":

> In this age, when there can be no losers in peace and no victors in war,
> we must recognize the obligation to match national strength with national
> restraint. We must be prepared at one and the same time for both the con-
> frontation of power and the limitation of power.

It might have been more accurate to speak of the "imperative" of
exercising national restraint, rather than the "obligation" to do so. The
latter term implies an option, which in truth is not really open. Nor
can moral credit or virtue be attributed to a course for which there is
no feasible alternative. Translated into the vernacular, acceptance of
"the limitation of power" merely recognizes the stark and simple fact
that the atomic giants are musclebound.

The fallacy of the so-called "doctrine of massive retaliation" was
that it confused the *existence* of nuclear capability with the wholly
different issue of its *utility*. Although avowedly intended to demonstrate our national will, so that "aggressors might not act through
miscalculation," it failed of this purpose for at least two reasons: first,
because it is impossible to codify or define the conduct which would
trigger its use, and secondly, because it is not, in practical fact, use-
able. The deterrent value of nuclear might inheres in its very existence,
and it exists on several sides.

This is not to say that a show of national determination—as in the Cuban missile crisis—is irrelevant to the resolution of a particular conflict. In fact, no one can say what the outcome in fact might have been, had the Soviet government not corrected its error of setting in motion a chain of events, the consequences of which it could neither foresee nor control. This is the real lesson of Cuba. Similar considerations must have governed the decision of the United States Government to deny air cover or other support to the invasion of the Bay of Pigs which, like the "missile sneak," had been surreptitiously mounted with American assistance.

In Vietnam, likewise, we have confronted the same dilemma to which President Johnson referred in his message to Congress: the need to "match national strength with national restraint."

Professor Spiro's analysis of the character and requirements of world politics proceeds from the undeniably sound premise of "the illimitable, global character of virtually all international violence today." It is precisely such "illimitable effects" which underly and account for the strategies of insurgency, "national liberation war," or "Special Warfare"—all synonyms describing efforts to attain political ends without recourse to full (and suicidal) use of available national strength in the Age of the Atom.

Moreover, as Professor Spiro points out, "the qualitative transformation of power combines with other revolutionary factors to erode and destroy the old consensus on the procedures of conventional diplomacy and warfare that used to provide a . . . framework for international relations before World War I."

The nature of the "other revolutionary factors," referred to in the preceding quotation, leads us to the second fact, mentioned at the outset, which likewise has decisive relevance to proper understanding of world politics: the interdependence of mankind in the Age of the Individual.

At the time of the "great debate" between General MacArthur and his government, a cartoon by Herblock was widely published. It showed the General standing alongside a map of the world, in the shape of a thin rectangle, the upper surface of which carried the map of Asia. Near him stood President Truman, standing next to a world globe. The caption represented the President as saying simply: "Mine is round."

The forces of rapid social change, of accelerated demands for human rights, and of aspirations for national or other institutional means of self-expression, all move in global orbits. Failure to accept and act upon this premise leads to a double illusion: one is that the limits of political problems are coterminous with the geographical limits of the area in which such problems arise; the other is that solutions are to be found within the isolated confines of the problems themselves.

Such an illusion is reminiscent of medieval maps of the then-known world, the edges of which were marked by the rim of the void. Political problems, like the globe itself, have no edges or rims; they move in concentric and overlapping circles.

If common interests and a common destiny confront mankind, is it delusive to speak of a "community of mankind"? Here we come up against the conflict of political theory marked by the opposing extremes of "power realists" and exponents of "world government." The essence of the question tends to become submerged in a verbal flood.

What does the concept of "community" signify?

Professor Spiro defines his notion of community as one which "requires as a minimum only awareness of the pursuit of common goals, and of members' inability to solve alone the problems arising out of these goals." The indispensable ingredient, accordingly, is "awareness."

A "community" may be said to exist whenever a group (or groups) think that it exists, or are impelled to act as if it existed. Such an impulse may be generated from within, reflecting a spontaneously perceived necessity or advantage. Or, it may be imposed from without, with dictated goals and coerced means. It may, indeed, be a product of both internal and external stimuli, as in the case of a community of individuals composing an army at war, which is united by a common tradition and a common danger, and unified by an enforced discipline.

A major contribution which Professor Spiro's book makes to an understanding of "politics"—which he defines as "more or less deliberate efforts to bring about change"—is his emphasis on *process* and *method,* as distinguished from *substance.* Starting from the premise that there is "a basic resemblance, if not identity, between the making of decisions in the smallest and the largest of human communities," he searches out common denominators of principle and practice which mark a "conception of politics that is truly universal." Indeed, Professor Spiro describes this as the "basic search conducted in this book."

If there is any master key to the riddles and locks of contemporary problems of peace and power, it is that fashioned by Professor Spiro's insight into the lesson taught by all political experience: *The greater the limitation upon the uses of force to gain political ends, the higher the premium upon processes necessary to achieve just and peaceful change.*

As he demonstrates, the "power realists," or *Realpolitiker,* commit the error of analyzing the nature and requirements of world politics on the basis of an obsolete approach to international relations, which, in essence, "was one-dimensional (power) or, at best, two-dimensional (power and law)."

At the other extreme, exponents of world government tend to prescribe new institutional correctives for political ills, in preference to less dramatic methods of exercising and nourishing the organisms with which world politics already is endowed.

The quest for "an analytical category more helpful than 'power'" —as well as for a map more helpful than a blueprint of Utopia—involves analysis of the basic goals of any political system, including a universal one. Professor Spiro finds, and defines, such goals in procedural, rather than substantive, terms: "stability, flexibility, efficiency, and effectiveness." Unless there is some measure of "dynamic equilibrium among the four basic goals," a political system cannot be regarded as a "success." It is only too painfully obvious that the "international community" is not a "success"; indeed, it does not even qualify as a rudimentary "system." The point, however, is that inasmuch as the central problems for mankind are how to prevent universal extermination and how to achieve generally shared aspirations, lessons derived from the workings of political systems in smaller communities must be applied to the development of world politics for the community of mankind.

It is inherent in the concept of "community," that there must always coexist opposing tendencies of integration or cohesion, and fragmentation or fission. In all social processes, varied and shifting views are held regarding goals, as well as methods and priorities for achieving agreed goals.

When diversity and dissent are kept within the "foul lines" of an ordered society, they are accepted as essential attributes of a dynamic order. Democratic systems, indeed, with intuitive insight, hail diversity and dissent as civic virtues and find in this the major distinction be-

tween libertarian and authoritarian approaches. It is a major premise
of the former that forces of cohesion and stability within a community
are strengthened, to the extent that the individuals comprising the
community are informed with a capacity for *self*-discipline. Education
and persuasion in a libertarian system therefore are directed toward
the end of fostering an increased public ability to take enlightened decisions and to make wise choices. The key is *understanding*, and this
is an attribute of the mind of the individual, as distinguished from
consensus, which is a group quality.

The objective always must be to achieve, or approach, consensus
upon the basis of what de Tocqueville described as "self-interest
rightly understood." How does a community go about the awesome
task of defining and pursuing its true self-interest, with understanding
of the conflicting claims and interests which always must arise within
and between communities of men?

Lessons of experience, from the Greek *polis* to the New England
town meeting—either in micro- or macrocosmic units—show that
community consensus upon "self-interest rightly understood" can best
be achieved through general participation in conflict resolution and
decision making. This, of course, does not mean that a community can,
or should, resolve all issues of common concern by a show of hands.
In all advanced societies participation includes extensive delegation
of authority, always, however, with the reservation of the requirements of disclosure and accountability.

Thus interpreted, general participation in the political process is
essential to the development of a sense of shared responsibility. And
such a sense, in turn, is an indispensable ingredient of the capacity for
self-discipline, which is the prerequisite of a dynamic political system,
able to pursue effectively the four goals of "stability, flexibility, efficiency, and effectiveness," as formulated by Professor Spiro in this
book.

The authoritarian outlook—often shared by the elite-minded "power
realists"—tends to deride the libertarian emphasis upon collective participation in decision making. It is pointed out that a decision is not
valid merely because it is the product of a collective judgment. Indeed, the device of checks and balances is built into our own system
to guard against collectively inspired mischief as much as against executive abuse. And the derision of a parliamentary system as a "*gou-
vernement qui parle*" often is applied to the United Nations General

Assembly as well—at its best, a "debating society"; at its worst, a "forum of irresponsibility."

Such criticisms of the libertarian or shared-responsibility emphasis, however, ignore the human experience that decisions imposed upon a community from above or outside are much less likely to reflect "self-interest rightly understood," than decisions emanating from within an informed and self-disciplined society. This is, no doubt, why de Tocqueville, with characteristic insight, declared that such self-interest was men's "chief remaining security against themselves." No autocrat ever has lived who possessed sufficient wisdom, compassion, and humility rightly to understand the self-interest of the community, or to sort out that self-interest from his own. If ever such a paragon should emerge, he would feel compelled by these very qualities to promote the capacity of his fellows to participate more responsibly in the politics of the society. In other words, he would be diligently working toward his own early retirement.

If one accepts the validity—as I do—of Professor Spiro's thesis of "the universality of basic political processes, no matter when or where they are taking place," the experience of political systems throughout history is highly relevant to the requirements of world politics.

What are the major impediments to achievement of a "dynamic equilibrium" among the goals of a universal political system? It is no answer to point out that no such system exists; this merely begs the question by posing it in different form.

While World War II was still being waged, high hopes were held that such a system would follow in the wake of battle. Such hopes were not a monopoly of the starry-eyed few. In February, 1943, the late Sir Winston Churchill addressed a message to President Roosevelt, which he entitled "Morning Thoughts: a Note on Post-war Security."

The great British leader expressed his conviction that, in view of the

certainty that a third struggle will destroy all that is left of the culture, wealth, and civilization of mankind and reduce us to the level almost of wild beasts, the most intense effort will be made by the leading powers to prolong their honorable association and, by sacrifice and self-restraint, win for themselves a glorious name in human annals.

Analysis of the reasons for the failure of so realistic a vision does not now focus as sharply as it did formerly upon Soviet intransigeance and ambition as the sole causes of frustration. Experience with such intransigeance at and after the end of the war did indeed impel Churchill to transform his "Morning Thoughts" of 1943 into the second thoughts of his celebrated speech of March 5, 1946, at Fulton, Missouri.

Nevertheless, objective appraisal of the current and continuing impediments to the "honorable association" predicted by Churchill does not find the lack of requisite "sacrifice and self-restraint" to be confined to any one nation or group. Nor does any one State—not even the United States—have title to claim a monopoly of the "political faculty," which Professor Spiro describes as "the faculty of deliberation about disagreement, with an eye to its purposive resolution."

Far from demonstrating a highly developed "faculty of deliberation about disagreement," we—scarcely less than the other great powers—incline toward a style of world politics which, in the view of the author of this book, "is more pathological now than it was at the end of World War II."

The United States has shared in a general reluctance to have recourse to processes of peaceful, i.e., "third-party" settlement. By the Connally amendment, we have shown distrust for the International Court of Justice, verging on contempt. We speak of the "Rule of Law," but keep the key to the courthouse in our own pocket.

When conflicts arise between those who demand revision, particularly in the areas of social change and human rights, and those who seek to maintain the *status quo,* we almost invariably tend to support the latter by our actions, even while eloquently professing our sympathies for the former.

International agreements for the protection and promotion of human rights are pigeonholed, or killed, in the Senate by a leadership (largely from southern states) which applies one standard in judging the political behavior of this and other nations, while reserving a lower standard by which to measure advancement of civil rights at home or abroad.

Above all, we tend to combine piety with hypocrisy when we profess deep loyalty to the peace-keeping processes of the United Nations, while at the same time harboring a suspicion, close to fear, of the judgments of other nations and leaders. It is an attitude which runs deep in the strain of American tradition, attributable in some measure to our history of isolation fostered by the geography of a preatomic age, combined with the self-righteousness of power. The attitude is not confined to political leadership; it appears in surprising places, such as derision by Walter Lippmann of

the myth, propagated since the first world war by the naive and idealistic followers of Wilson, that all sovereign states, whether big or small, are not only alike in their human rights, but alike also in their *rights* to exercise influence in the world.

The self-betrayal is implicit in the choice of the word "right," instead of "capacity"; it is explicit in falsely equating naiveté with idealism.

Might does not determine the ability to *influence*, although it does, of course, enlarge the capacity to *control*. When Jefferson said "opinion is power" he reminded us that mankind responds to pressures other than force.

Repudiation of the hollow and misnamed "doctrine of massive retaliation"—which rested on a false analogy to the prenuclear concept of maintaining a balance of power through preponderance of strength —has helped to restore another kind of "balance," that of a balanced judgment concerning the limitation of power. But it is one thing to comprehend that we are in, or at the threshold of, an era in which no retaliation could be "massive" enough to forestall devastating reprisal. It is quite another thing to find and employ political process by which the nuclear-power void can be bridged. As Professor Spiro reminds us, the network of treaty organizations to which we are party cannot adequately serve that objective. The principal reason this is so is because the treaties are "insufficient for purposes of drawing territorial or qualitative 'lines' whose crossing by the other side would set off 'defensive' action."

In our domestic system, "aggressions" against the public peace are punishable crimes only when they are codified as such and defined with reasonable specificity. In the rudimentary and chaotic international order, this is not generally true. Practice of civilized nations has produced general consensus that piracy, slavery, and now, genocide, are punishable delicts. But the concept of "aggression" has defied efforts of codification. Instead, judgments must be made in the context of specific situations. And if chaos is to be abated, and the international "code duello" abandoned, such judgments must be *collectively* made. The United Nations Charter preserves the right of self-defense as an inherent element of the right of survival. The right of self-defense, however, is envisaged as a limited remedy, a mere stopgap, "until the

Security Council (i.e., the appointed agency of the organized international community) has taken the measures necessary to maintain international peace and security." (Article 51.) The breakdown, or by-passing, of this fundamental concept should not be allowed to obscure its imperative character.

In the age of overkill, marked by the "illimitable global character" of violence anywhere, the processes of collective judgment and collective action must be seen as essential elements of *universal self-defense.*" This is the not-so-deeply buried "secret" of the United Nations Charter.

No matter from what point of view, therefore, one approaches *the* problem of "how to prevent the extermination of mankind," one must affirm the indispensability of a system of world politics in the sense defined by Professor Spiro—that is, a universal concern about common problems, accompanied by cooperation *and conflict* in efforts directed toward their purposive resolution. The question is not *whether* such a system of world politics is essential, but, rather, *how* viably, and within what predictable limits of form and time, such a system can be nurtured to maturity.

The concluding chapter of this book, "Ideological Conciliation," suggests ways in which the processes of world politics could be helped toward relative effectiveness, if not maturity. Some common denominators of mutual concern and interest, especially those relevant to survival, transcend ideological lines. A nascent "community," accordingly, is discernible.

Notwithstanding a prevalent tendency to overstate the "détente" between the major protagonists, there is little room for doubt that in recent years, the concept of "coexistence" has lost some of its sterility. During the Stalin era, it was little more than a cover plan for communist probing and prowling; at best it was a synonym for abstention from mischief which might spin out of control. More recently, "coexistence" has acquired a more positive content: a sporadic and selective collaboration, even though systematic cooperation is denied. Hence, there is room and ground for the creation of what Professor Spiro terms "sound situations of responsibility." As in the case of all political systems, the ingredients, which are enumerated in his analysis, must be blended through general participation, which means affording to the participants "opportunities to contribute to those central decisions whose consequences will affect themselves."

Above all, as this book makes crystal clear, it is impossible to stabilize procedures unless such procedures are effectively and consistently used. No system can grow unless there is repeated recourse to available institutions and, as Professor Spiro points out, "the greater the volume of substantively varied issues that are fed into the world political system, the better are chances for growth of consensus upon one common procedural law of mankind."

The translation of the "rule of law" from a slogan to a process requires vision without which, as was said long before the dawn of the nuclear age, "the people perish."

Table of Contents

Chapter 1

Introduction

The Novelty of World Politics

"WORLD POLITICS" is a novel title for this kind of book. In the 1950's, and for many decades before, "international relations" was the most common description of our subject. Only slowly was *politics* substituted for *relations,* most notably and influentially by Professor Hans J. Morgenthau in his *Politics among Nations,* which first appeared in 1948. The replacement of *international* by *world* began much more recently and has gained a much narrower acceptance.

Why these changes? This question is significant in the sense that it is not "merely academic," because the changes in terminology reflect changes in the reality which the words seek to describe. More important, these changes reflect changes in our perception of that reality. Until roughly the end of World War II, there *was* no world politics. Instead there were relations among a limited number of sovereign national states. These relations, to be sure, had their effects upon many parts of the world, as indicated by the fact that people spoke of the "World War" almost from the beginning of the first of the two great military conflicts to have borne that designation so far. But World War I was fought overwhelmingly in Europe. And even World War II, some of whose most important theaters of operations were in the Pacific area, in Asia, and in Africa, was importantly focused upon Europe. Though the United States was a reluctant and therefore late-starting participant in both World Wars; though Canada and many Latin American countries were members of both alliances against Germany; and though Japan was a minor belligerent in World

1

War I and a major belligerent in World War II, neither World War was understood as affecting as large a proportion of the surface or the population of the globe as is expected of a possible World War III in the future.

The main reason for taking a global perspective upon what used to be called "international relations" is that, today for the first time in history, a global community of mankind exists or, at any rate, is coming into existence in the consciousness of human beings. This change is being produced by related positive and negative causes. The chief positive cause consists of rapidly and radically improving technology, especially of transportation and communication. The chief negative cause of the growing awareness of the existence of the world-wide community of mankind is the expanding scope of the destructiveness of weapons. Politically conscious people in the most remote and exotic backwaters of the earth—Nepal, Yemen, or the Central African bush—are aware of the rivalries of the Cold War, and the masses in the most advanced countries recognize the danger to their own security from "escalating" conflicts that begin as petty internecine rivalries in the most backward countries. Moreover, as the risks of nuclear world war mount and the density of global communications networks grows, the proportion of the population that must be described as "politically conscious" is also increasing to the point where, before long all over the world, it will include virtually all adults.

If these factors can give us a brief explanation of the substitution of *world* politics for *international* relations, how can we account for the substitution of world *politics* for international *relations?* Conventional international relations was confined, as already mentioned, to a few sovereign nation states. Membership in this exclusive "club" of active "powers" varied from time to time. Before World War I, it included Great Britain, France, Germany, Russia, Austria-Hungary, perhaps Italy, and peripherally the United States of America. Before World War II, the club of powers consisted of Great Britain, France, Germany, the Soviet Union, the United States, Japan, and again perhaps Italy. These powers conducted active relations among themselves and also acted upon the other more or less passive states that were involved in international relations. These activities among the great powers and by them toward less powerful states were not described as "politics" for one basic reason:

Ever since the forging of the modern state as both a theoretical concept and a practical institution, in the sixteenth century, politics has generally been regarded as concerned essentially with the establishment, transmission, and control of centralized power within the state. These power "processes" were viewed as taking place within a territory with clearly defined boundaries and within a framework of law backed up ultimately by the sovereign state with its "monopoly of legitimate physical violence" (to use Max Weber's definition of the state). On the other hand, relations *among* sovereign states operated neither within clearly defined territorial boundaries, nor under a final enforcement agency, even when they conformed strictly to international law. Though the study of both national politics and international relations thus focused upon power, the power processes involved in these two activities were believed to be qualitatively so different, that neither practitioners nor students of international relations could conceive of them as a mere extension of national politics.

The facts of the period, as distinguished from people's understanding of these facts, support the distinction between national politics and international relations. In democratic states at least, all citizens participated in politics more or less directly. International relations, on the contrary, were handled by specialists: diplomats in peacetime and the military in war. Today, however, these professional specialists have in large measure been displaced by an odd assortment of people whose domestic political activities "spill over," as it were, into the world arena, and vice versa. In both democratic and nondemocratic states, ordinary citizens can contribute to and are affected by world politics much more directly and more frequently than in the bygone era of international relations. Qualitative differences between domestic politics and world politics are therefore evaporating and, as a result, a comparative approach to the study of domestic politics that yields good results can be expected to prove equally useful in the study of world politics.

The Study of International Relations

Since international relations was believed to differ qualitatively from the domestic politics of national states, these two sets of phenomena were studied by two sets of scholars who used different methods. Even today, many American universities still reflect this differentiation by having separate departments and degree programs for political science and international relations. Today there may be even less intellectual exchange and agreement upon method between students of international politics and other political scientists than prevails, for example, between students of international economics and other economists.

During the period between the two World Wars, when international relations were being conducted by professional specialists who were either diplomats or military men, international relations were being studied mainly by the scholarly counterparts of these two professions, that is, the diplomatic historian and the "professor of military science and tactics." Jurists—students of international law—addressed themselves to the study of the loose general framework within which "war is nothing but a continuation of political intercourse with an admixture of other means," in the classic formulation of the Prussian military theorist Karl von Clausewitz.[1]

This meant that two approaches which were considered mutually exclusive predominated in the study of international relations. On the one hand, jurists and their followers used an institutionalist or legalistic approach that concentrated on international law and international organization. On the other hand, those who were more interested in what happened when international law was ineffective—as they believed it to be most of the time—concentrated their attention upon the use of organized force. In Germany, where prominent founders of both schools worked, adherents of the latter approach were fond of describing it as *Realpolitik,* i.e., realistic politics. A similar division between institutionalists and realists existed also within the ranks of students of national and comparative politics. However, a majority of these scholars, during the decades that ended with the outbreak of World War II, tended to be institutionalists, whereas the *Realpolitiker* dominated the study of international relations. This difference further contributed to the methodological gulf that separated students of international relations from students of "lower levels" of politics.

The approach of this book is based upon the thesis that the conditions which once brought about this divorce between the study of

---

[1] Karl von Clausewitz, "War as an Instrument of Policy," *On War,* trans. O. J. Matthijs Jolles (New York: Modern Library, 1943), Book VIII, chap. vi, b, p. 596.

the internal politics of states and the study of relations among states have evaporated. Today there is one global political system of which all national and other smaller political systems are component parts. No qualitative or "essential" difference in political processes can be found between lower political systems and the all-encompassing global system to warrant the study of the two different levels of politics by different methods.

This basic thesis about the unity of politics and the fundamental resemblance of politics at all levels is by no means original. In a later section on the "Sociology of Knowledge" of the study of world politics, we will have occasion to take a close look at the many and varied new professional specialists who have all but replaced conventional diplomatic and military historians, jurists, and old-fashioned military scientists and *Realpolitiker*. Among them are students of various aspects of decision making, including psychologists, economists, theoretical physicists and mathematicians, game theorists, computer engineers, and others. Most of these contemporary professional students of international politics started their careers as specialists in their respective nonpolitical fields and disciplines. They transferred their attention to world politics on the explicit or implicit assumption of a basic resemblance, if not identity, between the making of decisions in the smallest and the largest of human communities.

While the thesis of the basic unity of all kinds of politics is therefore not original, it seems to be acknowledged more widely outside than inside of political science. Indeed, the influx of other professions into the study of world politics must have been caused in large part by the intellectual vacuum left by the methodological and geographical divisions among political scientists themselves. By now, however, most political scientists are reconciled to the proposition that politics—whether conducted in a municipality, a member state of a federal system, a large nation, an international alliance, or the United Nations—involves qualitatively similar or even identical processes. Gabriel A. Almond, for example, speaks of the universality of political functions. These "functions," however, still betray a continuing preoccupation with power in the sense of force or organized means of violence, so that one can easily gain the impression that *Realpolitik* has won the battle. Nowadays even students of various aspects of national politics focus upon power processes, though they frequently do so with a considerably modernized vocabulary.

Most contemporary political scientists compare political systems with respect to power: the concentration of power, the direction of its use, the controls upon its wielders, and so forth. The functionalist approach to comparative politics, for example, distinguishes "input" and "output" functions. The input functions are (1) political socialization and recruitment, (2) interest articulation, (3) interest aggregation, and (4) political communication. The output functions are (1) rule making, (2) rule application, and (3) rule adjudication. These output functions are clearly a reformulation of the three "functions" of the American separation of powers—legislation, execution, and adjudication. The input functions refer to the mobilization of power within the political system, and the output functions to the uses that are made of this power. A straightforward comparison, employing these categories, between a national system like the United States and the global political system of world politics would have to conclude that the main difference between the two is to be found in the much poorer performance of the output functions in the world system. And this brings us back to the original cause of the divorce between the study of domestic politics and international relations. Either the thesis about the unity of all politics is wrong, or the focus upon power, no matter how reworded, yields unsatisfactory results. Since we accept the unity of politics, we must find an analytical category more helpful than "power."

The Study of World Politics as Politics

Any claim to originality that can be advanced on behalf of the method used in this book arises from neither the substitution of *world* for *international*, nor the replacement of *relations* with *politics*. It must rather be based upon our conception or our understanding of all politics, anywhere and at any time. The conceptions of politics upon which most contemporary studies are based today still stand in the heavy shadow of the state-centered and, therefore, power-centered approach that prevailed generally until World War II—and which made perfectly good sense during that period because it corresponded, by and large, to the realities of that time. Even an innovator like Professor Almond, though he was not primarily concerned with international politics at all, but with the "politics of the developing areas," concedes that he casts his focus upon "legitimate physical compulsion."[2] One can question the adequacy and the accuracy of this focus for the study of those political systems for which it was immediately intended, but that lies beyond our interests here. When applied to world politics, this method would simply have to conclude that there is no global political system:

> What we propose is that the political system is that system of interactions to be found in all *independent societies* which performs the functions of integration and adaptation (both internally and vis-à-vis other societies) by means of the employment, or threat of employment, of more or less legitimate physical compulsion. The political system is the legitimate, order-maintaining or transforming system in the society.[3]

This shortcoming would still permit comparison of different international systems—say, the contemporary one and that of the 1930's—in terms of their approximation, low in both these cases, to this "definition" of a political system. However, this approach, because it is too one-dimensional, would yield inadequate and distorted results.

For example, if we concentrate on the effectiveness of "legitimate" power, how can we explain the role played by states that wield very little power within the contemporary international system? Indeed, how can we explain the attainment of independence and statehood by (relatively speaking) utterly powerless communities that were previously colonial dependencies of some of the most powerful Powers in the world? This approach may have yielded some useful insights when applied to the limited international relations of the decades before the global political system came into being. Even if we concede that much, however, its utility ceased with the acquisition of nuclear weapons by the United States and the Soviet Union.

One unprecedented fact of the present has brought about such radical changes from the immediate as well as the older past, that the exclusive focus upon means of force has lost its relevance. This fact is the virtually unlimited destructiveness of nuclear weapons. Conventional international relations were characterized by a scarcity of power. Contemporary world politics is characterized by a plethora of power. This radical change is reflected in the following paradox: Comparison of these two periods shows that, while a scarcity of power

---

[2]Gabriel A. Almond, "Introduction: A Functional Approach to Comparative Politics," *The Politics of the Developing Areas,* Almond and James S. Coleman, eds. (Princeton: Princeton University Press, 1960), p. 7.

[3]*Loc. cit.* Italics supplied.

prevailed, major participants in international relations were much readier to use violence than are the possessors of the plethora of nuclear power today. The "Great Powers" of international relations were quite willing to use their limited power, while the so-called "Super Powers" of present-day world politics have, until now, been so inhibited by the overabundance of the means of destructive force at their disposal, that they have made no use of nuclear weapons in military conflicts. The use of two atomic bombs by the United States against Japan at the end of World War II was the concluding act of the earlier era and, therefore, constitutes no exception to this statement; and the deliberate detonation of nuclear weapons as part of the bargaining process between the United States and the Soviet Union, because it stopped short of the eruption of military violence, corroborates the statement.

This radically novel element in world politics makes obsolete the one-dimensional approach that concentrates on power. This element accounts for the inadequacy of this approach even when it is balanced by the other focus of conventional studies of international relations, upon the procedures of international law and the institutions of international organization. This counterbalance would, in effect, make the approach two-dimensional, again on the classical Clausewitzian assumption that war is the continuation of diplomacy by other, that is, violent, means. There is simply more to politics—any kind of politics—than *either* peaceful bargaining within a framework of institutionalized law, *or* efforts to impose one's will by means of organized violence. In this sense, all approaches to the study of politics which (in the words of some college catalogue descriptions of the scope and purpose of political science) identify politics with the "use of power in human relations," are unsatisfactory in general, and more unsatisfactory than usual when applied to contemporary world politics in particular. The conception of politics and the approach to its study upon which this book is based result from the foregoing critique.

Politics and Power

Some scholars and many laymen consider the ubiquity of "power" in politics so obvious, and find this ubiquity of such central importance, that they use power as the sole focus for the study and analysis of international politics. This is true even of those few scholars who neither recognize practical nor create intellectual barriers between the fields of national and international politics. Hans J. Morgenthau, for example, concludes his description of the school of political realism, of which he is the most influential contemporary exponent, by writing:

> Intellectually, the political realist maintains the autonomy of the political sphere, as the economist, the lawyer, the moralist maintain theirs. He thinks in terms of interest defined as power, as the economist thinks in terms of interest defined as wealth; the lawyer, of the conformity of action with legal rules; the moralist, of the conformity of action with moral principles. The economist asks: "How does this policy affect the wealth of society, or a segment of it?" The lawyer asks: "Is this policy in accord with the rules of law?" . . . And the political realist asks: "How does this policy affect the power of the nation?" (Or of the federal government, of Congress, of the party, of agriculture, as the case may be.)[4]

Later in his book, Professor Morgenthau gives power a narrower meaning:

> When we speak of power . . . we have in mind not man's power over nature, or over an artistic medium, such as language, speech, sound, or color, or over the means of production or consumption, or over himself in the sense of self-control. When we speak of power, we mean man's control over the minds and actions of other men. By political power we refer to the mutual relations of control among the holders of public authority and between the latter and the people at large.[5]

Moreover, the minds whose control is achieved by means of power belong to human beings whose "nature" has remained unchanged "since the classical philosophies of China, India, and Greece endeavored to discover" the laws of politics that "have their roots in human nature."[6] One final quotation from Morgenthau's influential work shows how ubiquitous he believes politics, and with it the use of power, to be in human relations:

> The tendency to dominate, in particular, is an element of all human associations, from the family through fraternal and professional associations and local political organizations, to the state. On the family level, the

---

[4]Hans J. Morgenthau, *Politics among Nations: The Struggle for Power and Peace* (3rd ed., New York: Alfred A. Knopf, 1960), pp. 11 f. Quoted by permission of Alfred A. Knopf.

[5]*Ibid.*, p. 28.

[6]*Ibid,* p. 4.

typical conflict between the mother-in-law and her child's spouse is in its essence a struggle for power, the defense of an established power position against the attempt to establish a new one. As such it foreshadows the conflict on the international scene between the policies of the status quo and the policies of imperialism.[7]

Morgenthau's identification of politics with power, as applied to the study of "politics among nations," has been criticized from a variety of viewpoints, as both a tool of analysis and a guide to policy in the "national interest." Inis L. Claude, Jr., for example, in his definitive critique of the concept of the balance of power, shows the several, often contradictory meanings in which this term has been used.[8] Stanley H. Hoffmann finds the "realist" approach too static:

> The price one has to pay for identifying the "timeless features" of the political landscape is the sacrifice of understanding the process of change in world affairs. The theory stresses the autonomy of international relations to the point of leaving outside its pale the forces which work for change and which, cutting across the states, affect the states' behavior.[9]

One could expand this particular criticism by noting the possibility—it has already become a fact—that units other than states act in international politics. Even if human nature were constant and unchanging, the use of power in international politics would manifest itself differently from time to time, as human beings combined in different types of political units for purposes of acting in international politics. Adherents of the school of *Realpolitik* treat the nineteenth century, the classical age of the European balance of power, as a normative model, sometimes to the extent that they criticize any political conduct that deviates from nineteenth century practices, even though the conditions of that epoch obviously no longer obtain today. In other words, the power approach to the study of politics, because it is grounded in the assumed constancy of human nature and institutions, leaves insufficient room for changes in the substance of power through invention, other innovation, or unwilled changes in the "human condition."

The identification of politics with power is open to another criticism, arising from a difficulty of which Morgenthau himself seems to

---

[7] *Ibid.*, p. 34.

[8] Inis L. Claude, Jr., *Power and International Relations* (New York: Random House, 1962), chap. 2 and *passim.*

[9] Stanley H. Hoffmann (ed.), *Contemporary Theory in International Relations* (Englewood Cliffs, N. J.: Prentice-Hall, Inc., 1960), p. 35.

be aware. This conception of politics is simply too broad to make it useful as a "precision tool." For example, Morgenthau provides his readers with an inventory of the "elements of national power": geography, natural resources (food, raw materials), industrial capacity, military preparedness (technology, leadership, quantity and quality of armed forces), population (distribution, trend), national character, national morale, the quality of diplomacy, and the quality of government.[10] This broad meaning assigned to the concept of power makes it virtually meaningless. The relative power of two states, for instance, can hardly be compared unless the analyst could assign values to the many ingredients that are said to make up the total national power of actors in international politics. These difficulties lead Morgenthau in the end to advocate reliance upon intuition "in order to reduce to the minimum the unavoidable errors in the calculations of power. . . ."[11] Even where no artificial barriers are erected between international and other "lower" kinds of politics, power remains an unsatisfactory because unrefined and excessively static concept for description and analysis.

---

[10]Morgenthau, *op. cit.*, chap 9.
[11]*Ibid.*, p. 157.

Chapter 2

The Old and the New

The Game of Diplomacy

FOR PURPOSES of describing old-fashioned international relations, the power approach was quite satisfactory. For purposes of comparing international relations of the earlier period with world politics of the contemporary period, this approach is unsatisfactory. The radical differences between these two periods can be contrasted from a variety of viewpoints. Here we shall examine them under four main headings:

1. *The Change in Units*
   from a few, mainly European, sovereign national states as the major actors in international relations
   to the so-called "blocs" consisting of former sovereign national states that combined together in looser or tighter treaty organizations; plus the poorly defined new states, formerly colonial dependencies of the great powers; plus genuinely international participants in world politics, like the Secretariat of the United Nations.
2. *The Change in Force*
   from its scarcity, accompanied by its widespread use
   to the overabundance of force, which is accompanied by its infrequent use among the major actors in global politics.
3. *The Change in Goals*
   from the pursuit of limited goals, with limited means, according to procedures of negotiation that commanded wide and strong consensus
   to the pursuit of unlimited goals, in both their substance and geo-

graphical scope, in the face of the virtual disappearance of the old procedural consensus and the slow and painful evolution, by a method of trial and error, of new procedures of negotiation.

4. *The Change in the Personnel of International Politics*
   from professional diplomats and military men, most of whom had similar and even related backgrounds
   to the participation of entire populations and the replacement of the old professionals by new specialists in propaganda and subversion, by amateurs, professional revolutionaries, businessmen, party hacks, and others who lack both similar substantive experience and common procedural commitments.

Though these four major changes are radical, their effects have been neither complete nor even. *In international politics, the old and the new still continue to coexist.* The difficulties for an accurate understanding of the new realities arise from the fact that most practitioners and students of the subject still try to grasp the new by means of concepts, that is, "handles," that were originally forged in order to understand the old and by now obsolescent.

To become aware of the changes that have occurred and that are still going on today, we should first get a clear picture of international relations as it was "played" in the period between the Congress of Vienna and World War I. The parlor game *Diplomacy* provides such a picture.[1] The game is played by seven players: England, Germany, Russia, Turkey, Austria-Hungary, Italy, and France. The game begins in the spring of 1901, when each player has three "units," i.e., armies and/or fleets, except Russia, which has four: two armies and two fleets. The object of the game, according to the rules, is to dominate Europe. "This occurs when one country has eighteen supply centers." For every supply center. i.e., province, that the player loses to another country, he has to give up one of his armies or fleets to the particular "enemy" who took the province. Each spring and fall, each country may move any, all, some, or none of its forces on a turn. Moves are made when players write down secretly the orders for their forces, which are then made public by all players at the same time.

Diplomacy. This is the most important rule of the game. Before each move the countries negotiate with each other. They may agree on moves each will make, attacks they will carry out, support they will give each

---

[1] *Diplomacy* (Boston, Mass.: Games Research, Inc., copyright, 1960).

other, and spaces they will or will not invade, and they may conduct propaganda or espionage. Any agreement is possible. The rules impose no sanction for failure to carry out an agreement. Negotiations may be secret or public. They may take place at the playing table or in another part of the room or house.

The game *Diplomacy* gives a fairly realistic picture of old-fashioned European international relations. Diplomatic and military officers of the "old school" tended to look upon their activities as a game. Among them, a strong consensus prevailed upon the rules of their game. These rules were continuous from diplomacy to warfare, in keeping with the dictum of von Clausewitz. Moreover, it was considered a continuing game. This meant that players did not want to liquidate other players or to alienate them too much. Clear distinctions prevailed between war and peace and, in wartime, between the status of belligerent and neutral. There was constant awareness of the possibility, indeed the probability, of the use of force, and this awareness made for continuous "plays" with threats of force.

While the object of diplomacy may have been to dominate Europe, this was not understood in the same sense in which Nikita Khrushchev said, "We will bury you," to his capitalist opponents. To be sure, even Khrushchev, we trust, did not mean that the Soviets literally intended to bury the West in the debris caused by nuclear world war, but rather that communism would replace capitalism and that, as he told President Eisenhower, the generation of Eisenhower's grandchildren would be communists.

The difference between the contemporary goal of dominating the world and the older goal of dominating Europe can best be brought out by comparing two German international politicians, Hitler and Bismarck. After the conquest of France in the summer of 1940, Hitler's soldiers sang: *"Heute gehört uns Europa, morgen die ganze Welt!"* ("Today we own Europe, tomorrow we will own the whole world!") Hitler's war goals were unlimited. By contrast, his predecessor Bismarck, the founder and chancellor of the Second German Reich, did not want to liquidate France after its defeat at the hands of the Prussian and other German armies in 1871. Bismarck did impose a very high war indemnity upon France which the latter, however, was able to pay off years before it was finally due. Germany also annexed two French provinces, Alsace and Lorraine, but these contained a largely German-speaking population. The newly founded German national state, in 1871, was as strongly committed to the rules of European diplomacy as the defeated older national state of France. This was not due to unusually high standards of morality or chivalry on the part of the Germans. It did not even involve any high degree of awareness of the rules and procedures to which diplomats and rulers of that period were committed, though Bismarck himself had served successfully as Prussian ambassador to St. Petersburg and Paris. But all the participants in European diplomacy and power politics at least sensed that they favored the continuation of the game, to be played among the same major players, most of whom had been playing it at least since the Congress of Vienna. Whatever their motives may have been—and we will examine the motives later—they did not conduct international war for total, unlimited goals, like the war aim of "unconditional surrender," with which Winston Churchill and Franklin D. Roosevelt countered Hitler's war aim of world domination during World War II.

In the older period of international relations, the big powers did not pursue unlimited goals. What set the limits to the goals which they did pursue? What defined the content of their limited goals?

Sovereign National States

The content of the limited goals pursued by members of the old European state system was defined by the character of its members. They were sovereign national states. The concept is a triple one. It implies the territoriality of statehood, the desirability of homogeneous nationality, and the independence from external or internal control of the sovereign power within each national territory. From this triple concept, we can deduce the major goals pursued by the European powers that played important roles in conventional international relations.

Territoriality was crucial to statehood. It meant that the sovereign had exclusive control of the state's territory. Like sovereignty and nationality, territoriality was an innovation, as both concept and fact. During the Middle Ages, exclusive control of real estate was not considered an essential prerequisite for the existence of an organized community. For example, it was said of the Germanic tribes that they "carried their law with them" wherever they went in the course of the great migrations. Each of these tribes thought of itself, and was

thought of by others, as a permanent community despite the fact that
that it did not permanently and habitually inhabit, or exercise exclusive control over, a clearly defined territory. There are some parallels between these medieval Germanic tribes and tribes in Africa at
the beginning of the "scramble for Africa" in the nineteenth century.
At that time, with the exception of the Muslim communities, most
African tribes had very poorly defined notions of territoriality. The
new territorial frontiers were drawn by the European colonial powers,
and to this day these borders constitute much lower barriers in the
minds—and to the movement—of most Africans than in the minds of
their former rulers, who have meanwhile become their partners in
world politics.

Territoriality as both a theoretical concept and an institutional
fact came into being partly in response to technological innovation.
The technology of armaments, transportation, and communications
let territoriality appear as feasible, desirable, and perhaps necessary.
Similarly, in our own age, technological innovation has contributed
importantly to theoretical and institutional developments that threaten
to throw territoriality upon the "trash-heap of civilization." Contemporary states and the larger "blocs" that are superseding them in world
politics simply cannot maintain the "hard-shelled" boundaries through
which neither weapons nor communications can penetrate.[2]

As long as territoriality remained an essential ingredient of statehood, one of the main goals of diplomacy and of its continuation, war,
consisted of the defense or acquisition of territory. In the parlor game
of *Diplomacy*, the players seek to win provinces as supply centers for
their armies and fleets. In other words, territory was considered desirable for its own sake *and* as a source of military power. But land
was sought as a source of power in this military sense for the sake of
not only supply, but also of population, including the human resources
with which armies and navies were manned. Before the rise of cultural
nationalism, rulers frequently sought to augment their population for
purely military purposes. Frederick William I of Prussia had his re-
cruiting officers "kidnap" men tall enough to serve as his grenadiers
from the territory of neighboring princes. At this time, the cultural
homogeneity of the population living under a single sovereign was
not considered either necessary or desirable. People of diverse ethnic

---

[2]See John H. Herz, *International Politics in the Atomic Age* (New York: Columbia University Press, 1959), *passim*.

and cultural affinities lived under one ruler, because they owed loyalty to him and his royal dynasty.

By 1871, when both Italy and Germany had achieved national unification, *nationality* had become an essential ingredient of a community's claim to organize itself as an independent state. This principle was carried to its logical conclusion, when President Woodrow Wilson included the right to national self-determination in the philosophy of his Fourteen Points. Now *any* community that was culturally homogenous could lay legitimate claim to independent statehood, and *any* minority living under a culturally different majority government could legitimately demand its "reunification" with its cultural brethren in a neighboring state in which they constituted the majority. After World War I, several plebiscites were conducted in order to ascertain the wishes of minority populations living in such situations.

The theory and institutionalization of nationality, like that of territoriality, had important technological causes. Aristotle gave as his criterion of the ideal size of the *polis* (the Greek city-state), the possibility of assembling the male citizen members of the community on the market place within the reach of a single speaker's voice. He naturally took it for granted that all citizens spoke the same language. By the time that nationality had become an essential ingredient of statehood, communications technology and the beginnings of mass literacy let the inclusion, within the boundaries of one sovereign state, of all people who spoke and read the same language appear as convenient and desirable. Again, however, more recent—and more radical—advances in the technology of communications are tending to make the principle of cultural nationality as obsolescent as that of territoriality. Soon all human beings everywhere will be within the reach of a single speaker's voice and image anywhere upon earth, with the help of television, communications satellites, and the technique of simultaneous translation.

At the time of its introduction, the principle of nationality served as a limiting factor for diplomacy-warfare. States in conflict could lay *legitimate* claim only to territory that was inhabited by a culturally related population: witness the case of Alsace-Lorraine cited above.

Sovereignty was the most important component of statehood throughout this period which began roughly in the sixteenth century. States continued to exist and to be recognized as major powers throughout these centuries even if, like Austria-Hungary, they were multinational "plural" societies, so long as they were in demonstrable possession of the paraphernalia of sovereignty. That is why an understanding of the concept of sovereignty is most important for the understanding of conventional international relations.

The concept was forged by political theorists of the period in which the most pressing problem to be solved was that of conflicting loyalties. During the Middle Ages, Christian political philosophers had worked out sophisticated theories concerning relations between spiritual and temporal authorities—relations that caused theoretical concern only in Western Christendom, because only there did a conflict arise between Church and Empire. Individuals could rely upon these theories when faced with problems of conflicting loyalties. The Reformation destroyed the world for which these loyalty-defining theories had been forged. To whom did a community or an individual owe loyalty now, to church or state, to a Roman Catholic or a Protestant prince who claimed to be legitimate ruler of the territory in which one lived? This was the question to which theorists like Jean Bodin and Thomas Hobbes addressed themselves. Their answer was that the individual owed ultimate obedience to his sovereign:

And in him consisteth the Essence of the Commonwealth; which (to define it,) is 'One Person, of whose Acts a great Multitude, by mutuall Covenants one with another, have made themselves every one the Author, to the end he may use the strength and means of them all, as he shall think expedient, for their Peace and Common Defence.'

And he that carryeth this Person, is called SOVERAIGNE, and said to have *Soveraigne Power;* and every one besides, his SUBJECT.[3]

Hobbes also said that sovereigns in their relations with one another were in a perpetual state of war, because each was the equal of every other one, and none recognized a common superior on earth that could settle disputes among them. The concept and institution of sovereignty, therefore, must be understood against this specifically western background, into which it was introduced deliberately as an innovation designed to put an end to chaos, anarchy, and war.

The Shift of Motives

We have seen that the content of the limited goals pursued by the major actors in the period of conventional international relations was

---

[3]Thomas Hobbes, *Leviathan,* chap. xvii.

defined by the character of these actors as sovereign national states. Sovereignty, nationality, and territoriality each had ordering, stabilizing, limiting consequences for the goals that states could legitimately pursue in European international relations. But these concepts had not existed for all time and though they did have the limiting consequences over the long run that have just been described, both concepts and institutions were innovations when first introduced—and they were widely regarded as disruptive and subversive in their immediate effects. After all, even when the concept of sovereignty was presented by someone other than Bodin, who quite obviously was working for his master the King of France, it offered clear competition to ancient principles of loyalty that enjoyed the support of "vested interests." A somewhat similar process may be occurring in our own time, when global loyalities, and thought about international political problems in terms of a global community of all mankind, are beginning to compete with national loyalties. *If* mankind survives without a nuclear world war, then our successors one hundred years or more from now may say that these novel concepts and institutions incorporating global loyalties also had an ordering, stabilizing, limiting effect. Meanwhile, however, a majority of international politicians and political theorists considers these global concepts as destructive and subversive.

The ordering consequences of concepts initially considered subversive can be illustrated by way of the transformation which the notion of *honor* has undergone since the time of Edmund Burke. In his *Reflections on the Revolution in France,* he used the execution of Queen Marie Antoinette of France on the guillotine to bemoan the disappearance of honor from Europe. "But the age of chivalry is gone," he wrote, to have been replaced by "that of sophisters, œconomists, and calculators."[4] Actually, the age of chivalry was not yet quite gone, or, at any rate, there were still men in Europe who owed their primary loyalty to dynastic rulers in terms of an only slowly dying code of chivalry. Honor was still *individual* in this sense. During the next fifty years, honor was to be "nationalized."

A most dramatic instance of the operation of national honor as a *motive* of foreign policy occurred during the so-called "Don Pacifico incident" in 1849–50. Don Pacifico was a Moroccan Jew who happened

---

[4]Edmund Burke, *Reflections on the Revolution in France* (London: J. Dodsley, 1790), p. 113.

to be a British subject. He held money claims against the government of Greece, which he pressed until his home in Athens was looted by a Greek mob. Lord Palmerston, the British Foreign Secretary, thereupon sent the British fleet to blockade the Piraeus, the port of Athens, in order to compel the Greek government to comply with British demands for the payment of an indemnity to Don Pacifico. The maneuver succeeded, and Palmerston was attacked for his policy in the British House of Commons. Palmerston defended himself in his greatest speech, and one of the greatest in the history of parliamentary government:

He opened with a deft denial of the proposition . . . that "British subjects abroad must not look to their own country for protection, but must trust to that indifferent justice which they may happen to receive at the hands of the Government and tribunals of the country in which they may be." . . . Then he dealt with the argument of false chivalry. "Does the smallness of the country justify the magnitude of its evil acts? . . . We are to be generous to those who have been ungenerous to you; and we cannot give you redress because we have such ample and easy means of procuring it.[5]

Palmerston's peroration follows:

I do not complain of the conduct of those who have made these matters the means of attack upon Her Majesty's Ministers. The Government of a great country like this, is undoubtedly an object of fair and legitimate ambition to men of all shades of opinion. It is a noble thing to be allowed to guide the policy and to influence the destinies of such a country; and, if ever it was an object of *honourable* ambition, more than ever must it be so at the moment at which I am speaking. For while we have seen, as stated by the Right Honourable Baronet the Member for Ripon, the political earthquake rocking Europe from side to side—while we have seen thrones shaken, shattered, levelled; institutions overthrown and destroyed—while in almost every country of Europe the conflict of civil war has deluged the land with blood from the Atlantic to the Black Sea, from the Baltic to the Mediterranean; this country has represented a spectacle *honourable* to the people of England, and worthy of the admiration of mankind.

We have shown that liberty is compatible with order; that individual freedom is reconcilable with obedience to the law. We have shown the example of a nation, in which every class of society accepts with cheerfulness the lot which Providence has assigned to it; while at the same time every individual of each class is constantly striving to raise himself in the

[5]Phillip Guedalla, *Palmerston 1784–1865* (New York: G. P. Putnam's Sons, 1927), pp. 330 f.

social scale—not by injustice and wrong, not by violence and illegality—but by persevering good conduct, and by the steady and energetic exertion of the moral and intellectual faculties with which his Creator has endowed him. To govern such a people as this, is indeed an object worthy of the ambition of the noblest man who lives in the land; and therefore, I find no fault with those who may think any opportunity a fair one, for endeavouring to place themselves in so distinguished and *honourable* a position. But I contend that we have not in our foreign policy done anything to forfeit the confidence of the country. . . . I maintain that the principles which can be traced through all our foreign transactions, as the guiding rule and directing spirit of our proceedings, are such as deserve approbation. I therefore fearlessly challenge the verdict which this House, as representing a political, a commercial, a constitutional country, is to give on the question now brought before it; whether the principles on which the foreign policy of Her Majesty's Government has been conducted, and the sense of duty which has led us to think ourselves bound to afford protection to our fellow subjects abroad, are proper and fitting guides for those who are charged with the government of England; and whether, as the Roman, in days of old, held himself free from indignity, when he could say *Civis Romanus sum;* so also a British subject, in whatever land he may be, shall feel confident that the watchful eye and the strong arm of England will protect him against injustice and wrong.[6]

Palmerston's speech suggests that *national* honor was very much an operative motive of British foreign policy. The contrasts between Great Britain in the mid-nineteenth century and her successor, the United States of America, in the mid-twentieth century are many and profound. United States citizens today cannot safely "look to their own country for protection, but must trust to that indifferent justice which they may happen to receive at the hands of the Government and the tribunals of the country in which they may be." Often since then end of World War II, American citizens have been robbed, expropriated, attacked, arrested, tortured, and killed in foreign countries, many of them relatively as weak vis-à-vis the United States as Greece was vis-à-vis the United Kingdom. The United States has concluded "Status of Forces Agreements" with many of its allies, under which American military and civilian personnel assigned to these countries is subjected to the jurisdiction of their courts. The inhibitions upon the use of the illimitable nuclear power at the disposal of the United States are so strong, that even the threat to use this power has not been invoked except in the most critical confrontations with

---

[6]*House of Commons, Debates,* 3rd series, Vol. CXII (1850), pp. 443-44. Italics supplied.

the Soviet Union itself over an issue like Cuba, not the fate of individual American citizens who were unjustly victimized in foreign countries. And even when the United States used the pretext of protecting its citizens against injury in internal rebellions in order to rescue them or to introduce its own armed forces into another country, as in the Congo in November, 1964, and in the Dominican Republic in May, 1965, its operative motive, admitted soon after intervention, was neither the protection of its individual citizens, nor the assertion of national honor, but the prevention of increased Communist intervention.

However, from the time of Palmerston onward, national honor continued to be an operative motive, as distinguished from mere pretext used in propaganda, of foreign policy for the major European powers. For example, Britain and France "honored" their treaty obligations to Poland at the outbreak of World War II. In this context, we can also recall the anachronism of "chivalrous" cavalry charges by Polish troops against German tanks at the outbreak of that conflict. (The words *cavalry, chivalry*, and the terms for "horse" in the Romance languages are obviously related, because it was the knight—in German, *Ritter*, from *Reiter* or rider—on horseback who was the bearer of the code of chivalry—in German, *Ritterlichkeit*.)

By the end of World War II, which had been fought for unlimited war aims, national honor had largely disappeared as an operative motive of foreign policies. This disappearance manifested itself in a number of ways, among them the crumbling of consensus upon the procedures of their profession that had previously facilitated relations among professional soldiers. For example, American generals frequently refused to return the military salute and handshake proffered by surrendering German generals at the end of the war. Whereas they would previously have recognized their enemies as brother officers and fellow professionals who, in the changing fortunes of war, happened to be on the losing side, the Americans now regarded the Germans as accomplices in mass murder, and they did not want to shake hands that they believed to be sullied with the blood of millions of innocent nonmilitary victims. The war crimes trials that were held after the war, in Nuremberg and Tokyo, further contributed to the destruction of the older concept of national honor and, along with it, of transnational consensus on professional ethics among both military and diplomats.

Today, national honor is still often appealed to in speeches and in the official proclamations of policies issued by states acting in international politics. But these same states, and especially the "superpowers," in fact tolerate multiple violations of their national honor which, in the earlier period, would have been regarded as causes of war, and to which they would then have responded with a variety of forceful punitive measures as reprisals. To restrict our illustrations to the United States alone, we could cite the shooting down of unarmed, in some cases civilian, airplanes, not only by the Soviet Union, but also by Yugoslavia, during a period which would formerly have been called "peacetime." Deprivations of life, liberty, or property of American citizens by the governments or mobs of other countries, both strong and weak, have already been mentioned. Commercial American airplanes have been hijacked. American politicians, from the President, the head of state, on down, have been insulted by officials of other governments. The most that the United States has done in reprisal has been to protest, or to reduce or cancel foreign aid.

As an operative motive of foreign policy, national honor has been replaced by "prestige." This was revealed, for instance, during the American presidential campaign of 1960, when Senator John F. Kennedy, the successful Democratic candidate, charged that opinion polls taken by the United States Information Agency in various foreign countries had shown a serious decline in American prestige there as a result, he alleged, of the ineffective policies of President Eisenhower's expiring Republican Administration. Many official State Department communiqués, as well as presidential speeches, assert that American prestige abroad, which is related to the "credibility" of the nuclear deterrent of the United States, is an important consideration of policy.

Some readers will object to this low value assigned to national honor as an operative factor in foreign policy. They will tell us that they still have strong feelings about the national honor of the United States, like President Lyndon B. Johnson who defended his policy in Vietnam on such grounds during the years 1965 and 1966. However, closer questioning of these patriots would probably reveal that even they also hold other commitments to political units larger than their "nation," like the "Free World." In any case, objections like these show that it is just as difficult to draw an exact dividing line between the period of national honor and the period of prestige, as it was earlier to draw an exact dividing line between the era of chivalry and the era of national honor. These objections also again demonstrate the coexistence of the old and the new in contemporary world politics.

Emerging Loyalties

If national honor is no longer operative, what is replacing it? This question is particularly important since sovereign states are still the most efficient ultimate enforcers of loyalty: The sovereign state levies taxes, conscripts, jails, and executes individuals, and it can now threaten the extermination of millions and hundreds of millions of human beings.

Our everyday language reveals that broader, more encompassing loyalties are emerging. As just mentioned, even highly "nationalistic" American patriots often speak of their commitment to the Free World or the "West." These are obviously internationalist term. Indeed, the phrase "Free *World*" suggests a global intent. The Communists are even more explicitly internationalist in their orientation and have been so ever since their founding fathers, Karl Marx and Friedrich Engels, exclaimed: "Workers of the *world,* unite! You have nothing to lose but your chains! You have a *world* of freedom to gain!" Their current disciples in both the Soviet Union and Communist China openly espouse internationalist goals and, at least in their dealings with foreign opponents, avow their eagerness to subvert existing national loyalties.

The new states, many of which are self-styled members of the "uncommitted," "nonaligned," "neutralist" camp, and many of which have never been *national* states, also assert their internationalist aspirations and loyalties. Even the fascists, once regarded as extreme prototypes of chauvinistic nationalism under Mussolini and Hitler, nowadays, hold international conventions that suggest that they, too, have reluctantly come to accept as inevitable the antinationalist trend toward internationalism.

Analysis of the emergence of new global loyalties is made more difficult by the fact that the two superpowers, the United States and the Soviet Union, are themselves not typical national states on the European pattern of the nineteenth century. In everyday language, neither citizens of these two states, nor outsiders, use the national labels when they refer to these two political entities. We speak of the Soviet Union more than we speak of Russia, and of the United States more often than of America. In the Soviet Union, a phrase like "Soviet man" has become a part of ordinary parlance, and national traits and Russian loyalties must be of lower importance for a political system whose ideology looks forward eagerly to the transformation not of *national* character but of *human* nature itself. In the United States, people are probably more conscious of their nationality than in the Soviet Union, partly as a result of the "melting pot" aspects of the society, which also help explain the "superpatriotism" of so-called "hyphenated" Americans, that is, citizens of the first or second generation and, usually, of European descent.

However, compared with the old national states of Europe, neither the United States nor the Soviet Union is culturally exclusive. Both eagerly welcome newcomers. Both naturalize newcomers easily. And both have been successful in generating new loyalties among both recent immigrants and foreign admirers. Countries like Germany or Great Britain, by contrast, are culturally exclusive in the sense that they usually continue to regard as "foreigners" citizens even of the third or fourth generation, so long as these display culturally distinctive traits.

Even the great powers of the earlier period of European international relations are now being transformed. The European Union movement combined France, Germany, Italy, Belgium, the Netherlands, and Luxemburg in several common supranational enterprises. Though France under President De Gaulle appeared at times to be trying to reassert the older form of nationalism, France continued as a member of the European Common Market. French nationalism, at least since the French Revolution, has always contained strong elements of cultural internationalism, as implied by a notion of *la mission civilisatrice.* Germany, because it is located on one of the focal points of the Cold War, is no longer the national state that it was from 1871 to 1945. Where do ultimate loyalties lie in that kind of situation? Should a young German be ready to die for the *Vaterland,* which no longer exists as a sovereign state; or for the Federal Republic of Germany; or for the German Democratic Republic in the Soviet Zone? Opinion polls taken among young West Germans have shown that very few of them are ready to die for their fatherland, certainly a much lower proportion than before either World War. They frequently cite as objects of their loyalties larger entities, like a united Europe or even mankind.

The problem of ultimate loyalties is becoming more difficult for two related reasons: first, the change in the actors from national states to bloc-sized units and beyond; and second, the change in the technology at the disposal of these actors in world politics. The technology of communications and of force which they control is global in its effects, and unlimited in space and time. These changes, in turn, cast doubt upon the efficiency and the effectiveness of national units as important participants in world politics and as objects of the ultimate loyalties of individuals.

False Analogies

The substance of international politics has been transformed as a result of the positive and negative changes in technology. It has been transformed to such an extent, that the relations between actors, their goals, and the means they use in pursuit of these goals have also undergone a radical, qualitative alteration. Nevertheless, both practitioners and scholars continue to treat many contemporary situations in world politics as though they were analogous to situations in the period before World War I. Upon examination, most of these analogies turn out to be false. Many of the worst troubles of world politics may be attributed in large measure to the misunderstanding of current realities that results from attempts to "grasp" them by means of analogies to apparently similar circumstances in the earlier period.

Genius has been identified as the capacity to make original analogies, that is, to be first in recognizing the analogous in two sets of circumstances that seem off-hand to be different. We could extend this notion of genius to its opposite by saying that action based upon completely false analogies constitutes madness. In the middle ground between these two extremes of genius and madness, we would find mediocrity in the thoughtless acceptance of routine. Between the middle and the pole of madness would be the area where one acts "thoughtfully" on the basis of erroneous analogies and consequently gets into trouble.

Before we can apply this suggestion about the harmful consequences of action upon false analogies to world politics, we should be quite clear about the meaning of "analogy." According to the Oxford English Dictionary, *analogy* is "Equivalency or likeness of relations; . . . a name for the fact, that, the *relation* borne to any object by some attribute or circumstance, corresponds to the *relation* existing between another object or circumstance pertaining to it."[7] According to Webster's, *analogy* is "A relation of likeness, *between* two things . . ., consisting in the resemblance not of the things themselves, but of two or more attributes, circumstances, or effects. . . . Similarity or essential resemblance, but its specific meaning is a similarity of relations."[8]

What are some of the analogies between postwar and prewar international situations, whose validity we can test by reference to this definition? They are analogies between situations, crises, institutions, and personalities, and they are being made practically every day by both politicians and observers of international affairs. One of the most frequent of these analogies is to the "appeasement" of Adolf Hitler that was attempted at Munich in 1938, by the British and French Prime Ministers, Neville Chamberlain and Edouard Daladier. Hardly a crisis of the Cold War has occurred, hardly a dispute between the white and colored worlds, which someone has not referred to as another "Munich." To mention only a few, this analogy was applied to each of the crises over West Berlin, in 1948, 1958, and 1961; to the confrontation between the United States and Communist China in Korea, to the Hungarian uprising of 1956, to United States relations with Dr. Castro's Cuba, to the sale of wheat by the United States and some of its allies to the Soviet Union, to the various crises in Vietnam, and to many other events in which it appeared, at least for a time, that the Communists were going to gain while the Western parties to the particular dispute were going to lose territory, population, or prestige. Similarly, in relations between the white states and the colored, "underdeveloped" areas of the world, frequent analogies with Munich are common. For instance, the term has been applied to the nationalization of the Suez Canal by President Nasser of the United Arab Republic, to the "surrender" by the European colonial powers of their possessions in Africa and Asia to "powerless" independence movements, to the pressure applied by the United States to the Netherlands during its dispute with Indonesia over West New Guinea, and to the attacks by President Sukarno of Indonesia upon the Federation of Malaysia that was founded in 1963.

Other prewar events are also used to provide analogies by means

---

[7]*Oxford English Dictionary* (1888). Italics supplied.
[8]*Webster's New International Dictionary* (2nd ed., 1937).

of which current events are to be made more easily comprehensible. For example, just as the Spanish Civil War was said to be a great rehearsal for World War II, so the Korean and Vietnamese conflicts and the disorders in the Congo are said to be great rehearsals for World War III.

The problems of the United Nations are treated as though they were analogous to the problems of the League of Nations which failed so disastrously during the interwar period. Sometimes an individual is pointed to as playing not only an analogous, but an identical role within these two international organizations and situations. Thus, when Emperor Haile Selassie of Ethiopia addressed the General Assembly of the United Nations in New York, in 1963, some observers remembered his dramatic and vain appearance before the General Assembly of the League of Nations in 1936, after his country had been invaded by Mussolini's Italian army. Occasionally analogies are made between the failure to use poison gas in World War II and the failure, so far, to use nuclear weapons in the period since 1945. Again, the several disarmament conferences that were held between the two World Wars and which, in retrospect, must be regarded as unsuccessful, are nowadays cited by analogy with the conferences that have been held in order to reduce nuclear weapons, control them, prevent their proliferation, or ban their testing. Because the earlier conferences turned out to be failures, it is asserted that the later, allegedly analogous conferences are doomed to fail as well.

Occasionally, world politics is analyzed by analogy to even earlier eras of history. For instance, the inability of the Greek city-states to form viable larger federations capable of resisting the great empires of the Mediterranean world is pessimistically adduced by way of analogy to the apparent inability of contemporary nation states to form larger federations in their confrontation with the great Communist bloc. Optimists, on the other hand, sometimes see the Cold War by analogy to the religious wars between Islam and Christianity, or between Catholicism and Protestantism during the Reformation. Other optimists think of current efforts to construct either an Atlantic alliance or world government by analogy to the earlier process of "nation building" in European countries or to the construction of the American federal union in 1788.

Easier to understand—and more tempting to make—are the analogies made between two apparently similar situations within the postwar period, for example, the Berlin crisis of 1948 and that of 1961, aspects of Soviet-United States relations before and after the death of Joseph Stalin, or the Cold War before and after China's emergence as a challenger within the communist camp to the previously undisputed preeminence of the Soviet Union.

Our contention here is that all of these analogies are false. They are false because—even if the *substance* of the power used between, say, Nazi Germany and its adversaries in the 1930's were similar to the substance of power used between the two nuclear blocs in the 1960's (and it is in fact quite dissimilar)—the *relations* among component parts of the earlier and the later situations that are treated as analogous are not similar in fact. Transformations have occurred in the principal actors, from sovereign national states to larger and looser aggregates; and in their goals, which used to be limited and are now unlimited. These transformations by themselves reduce the similarity that can exist in the *relations* among the components of any two situations, one before, the other after these transformations had occurred.

The shortcomings of thought about the present by way of analogy to the prewar past are revealed by an article written by Lord Avon who, as Anthony Eden, served as British Foreign Secretary and Prime Minister. The article was published on the occasion of the twenty-fifth anniversary of the signing of the Munich Pact in 1938.

From the day when the Munich agreement was signed 25 years ago, argument about it has been bitter and confused. A pretext can be made for Munich as a desperate expedient to gain time; it was never a constructive act of statesmanship heralding peace.

Unfortunately, it was as peace in our time that its authors sought to defend it. These illusions, misplaced as they were, can hardly be understood unless they can be traced to their source.

Mr. Neville Chamberlain [British Prime Minister, 1937–40] and those who thought like him, whether in Britain, France or the United States, did not see the Czech crisis as a further step in the aggrandizement policy of a dictatorship avid for conquest. On the contrary, they placed themselves in the position of the men they were facing and concluded that they had some grievances.

The Czech rule, it was argued, had not been uniformly considerate to the German minority. Czechoslovakia was a recent creation and something of a polyglot state; it was not so extraordinary that the Nazi rulers should be impatient.

A neutral disposition, to be fair to the point of being blind, had its inevitable consequence, that the British Government approached the crisis as an honest broker instead of an honest facer of truths. This stemmed from a failure to read the character and intentions of the dictatorships of Hitler and Mussolini, whether in Abyssinia or Czechoslovakia, or, later, Albania.

As a consequence the unfortunate Lord Runciman was sent upon a mission to find a reasonable solution between two parties, one of whom, the Czechs, was prepared to accept any concession which still allowed of national survival, while the other, on Hitler's instructions, was always to ask that amount more than President Benes could give, to keep ahead in the bidding, but not too far ahead all at once.

The consequence was inevitable. The Czechs were asked by those to whom they looked for support and understanding to yield more than their country's safety permitted, and they were doomed.

Yet, up until the hour of the Nazi invasion in March, 1939, there were apologists defending the Munich settlement as compatible with the survival of Czechoslovakia. Sir Winston Churchill and I, then of course out of office, were sitting together discussing a cartoon which derided as scaremongers those who held opinions such as ours, when the news of the German entry into Prague was brought to us.

It should be worthwhile to probe how these mistaken thoughts could have grown so strongly and to have a care lest they should thrive again.

Fundamentally it was the fault of "appeasement", of cherishing the illusion that to buy a little time, even at the expense of the security of an ally at second remove, was to contribute to peace, whereas it was in truth a surrender to the threat of force, laying the paving stones to war.

The distinction should always be recognizable, if often unwelcome. I tried to define it in a speech in the House of Lords two years ago:

"It is whether the agreement for which they [the Government] are working will serve only to relax tension for a while, or whether it is in the true interests of lasting peace. We must not perpetrate an injustice in order to get a little present ease; and the Government has to consider whether its decision gives peace, not just for an hour or a day or two, but in its children's time. That is the difference between appeasement and peace."

There have been some modern applications of appeasement and, as always, they are catching. From the Middle East with [Gamal Abdel] Nasser [President of the United Arab Republic] they spread to the Far East with Sukarno [President of Indonesia], and then across to the Caribbean where Castro, encouraged by the success of his predecessors in seizing foreign national or international property with impunity, laid hands on many million dollars' worth of American commercial enterprises in Cuba.

Castro's career being unruffled by protests, he tempted fate too far by inviting or allowing deadly Soviet weapons of attack upon his soil. The American riposte was salutary and effective. Its nearest parallel in the thirties was when, in conditions of less danger, Anglo-French naval action, sustained by the smaller Mediterranean powers, sent Mussolini's pirate submarines hastily home to base. Yet the tendency to "perpetrate an injustice in order to get a little present ease" persists now as then.

Southeast Asia presents some disturbing recent examples.

When Indonesia's demand for Western New Guinea rose to a crescendo two years ago, no pretense was made that the population of Papuans had any affinity with their would-be annexers. On the contrary, the summons was just a new piece of colonialism made all the more blatant by Indonesia's own pledges towards Western New Guinea when she became a state in 1949.

Yet, when Indonesia took physical action against the territory by parachute landings and other means, the request of the Netherlands Government to the United Nations for observers to view and report upon these events was refused by the Acting Secretary General.

The pretext was extraordinary: that to do so would be to depart from neutrality unless both parties agreed to their presence. It can hardly be accepted that the alleged aggressor and the victim must agree before the United Nations can inform itself on events in response to an appeal from one of its members.

When I read of these happenings, the memory of the well-intentioned Runciman mission came back to me with its inevitable failure, and inescapable sequel. The wolf and the lamb having been cautioned in the same terms, the wolf is not the least bit embarrassed and only craves permission to approach its jaws within striking distance of the victim's throat, which being granted, the final meal is simply delayed a while. So it was that Munich settled nothing except the fate of Czechoslovakia, just as the heralded agreement about Western New Guniea settled nothing except the fate of the Papuans, behind the facade of a plebiscite after the event [which had not been held by the time of publication of this book].

The predictable sequence has followed with Indonesian clamor for Borneo and Sarawak, coupled with a denunciation of the new federation of Malaysia. If Indonesia is once again appeased, it is doubtful that she will be the final beneficiary. The Chinese Communists are more likely to figure in that part.

But it is to be hoped that the lesson of Munich will be in the minds of those with whom the responsibility lies to give guidance and to say "No." They should, above all, remember that after the Munich agreement, as in every other instance of surrender for appeasement's sake, the appetite of the demanding power had grown with what it fed upon and soon returned for more, to be satisfied either by persuasion or by force; or to be resisted with greater difficulty than before.

The 25 years which have passed since Munich have seen many attempts to overthrow or subvert the ideas and practices of freedom, and they have not all failed. Some nations now behind the Iron Curtain might have been saved their fate if the West had been united and alert to the danger in time. No such experience must be allowed to befall the countries of Southeast Asia, particularly those whose wise statemanship has led them to form

Malaysia, where a rising standard of living contrasts sharply with the mounting poverty of their heavily armed southern neighbor, Indonesia.

The message of September 1938 stands clear for everyone to read. Never try to satisfy greedy appetites by concessions that are in themselves unjust.[9]

Lord Avon's many analogies made in this article rest upon one fundamental analogy between international relations at the time of the Munich agreement in 1938, and in the years leading up to 1963. He suggests that diplomats should always be pursuing the same basic goals, the "true interests of lasting peace." The fact is, however, that the clear distinction between "peace" and "war," which could be made before World War II, is no longer valid. It is for this very reason that a new term like the *Cold War* has crept into our vocabulary. To be sure, the only analogy between Nazi-Allied relations and Soviet-United States relations that Eden makes involves the Cuban missile crisis of 1962. This analogy is false in all particulars, beginning with the relations between the Czech and Cuban governments and their respective populations, passing on to the relations between these two governments and the foreign governments that appeared to be threatening the "peace" in both situations, and ending with the means of force whose use was threatened in Czechoslovakia and Cuba. Eden himself admits the weakness of the "parallel" between the Cuban crisis and the Anglo-French naval action, "in conditions of less danger," which was mounted against Mussolini's "pirate submarines."

Most of his analogies are between Munich, and crises involving European colonial powers on the one hand and their excolonies on the other. These again are false. President Nasser, when he seized the Suez Canal, was doing something quite different from Chancellor Hitler, when he incorporated into the German Reich the German populated sections of Czechoslovakia. And the reactions of the Western powers to these two threats were also quite different. In the case of Munich, Britain and France urged the Czechoslovak government to cede the demanded territory to Germany, whereas in the case of the Suez Canal, which had been operated by an internationally owned company, Britain and France dispatched troops to the Canal Zone, after Israel had launched an invasion of Egypt. All three states then

---

[9]"Eden Sees Munich as Lasting Lesson," New York *Times*, September 29, 1963, p. 32. Copyright 1963 by the AP. Quoted by permission of Associated Press Newsfeatures.

withdrew their forces under open pressure from the United States, which insisted upon literal observance of the Charter of the United Nations. Within a year after Munich, Hitler had absorbed all of Czechoslovakia and started World War II. Neither Nasser nor anyone else has launched World War III, and Nasser has been unable to absorb any new territory in the area immediately concerned, since the United Arab Republic and Israel have been kept at arm's length by a United Nations peace force. Moreover, the position of President Eisenhower of the United States during the Suez crisis was shaped not only by his genuine support for the principles of the United Nations, but also by the fear of Soviet intervention in the Middle East, which had been threatened by Premier Khrushchev of the Soviet Union and which might have involved the use of nuclear weapons.

The analogy between Munich and the acquisition by Indonesia of West New Guinea from the Netherlands, under United States pressure and United Nations supervision, is similarly false. This was only the final act in the process of the liquidation of the Dutch colonial empire, and President Sukarno's claim to Papua was not based, and could not be based, upon feelings of cultural and racial identity between the Papuans and Indonesians analogous to such feelings between Sudeten Germans and other Germans.

Again, Indonesia's attack upon the Federation of Malaysia, even *before* the Federation came into existence in 1963, is not analogous to Hitler's attack upon the multinational state of Czechoslovakia almost two decades *after* it had come into existence. Sukarno himself described the creation of the Federation as an exercise in British "neocolonialism." In 1963, he committed very few troops to this struggle, as he had few efficient troops to commit. Intermittently between threats and actual small scale guerrilla conflicts, Sukarno and the heads of the governments of the Federation of Malaysia and of the Philippines held conferences to try to resolve the controversy. All of this took place with British involvement and under the shadow of possible Communist Chinese and Soviet involvement, at least until the great anti-Communist purge conducted under leadership of the Indonesian military in 1965-66. Consequently, there existed some danger of "escalation" into a war not confined to Southeast Asia (where the Vietnamese struggle was taking place simultaneously) and not fought with the limited weapons available to Southeast Asian states. Far from being a "further step in the aggrandizement policy of a dictatorship avid for conquest," these conflicts were manifestations of the simultaneous processes of decolonization and the Cold War. The analogies do not hold, and action based upon them, where attempted, has brought results the opposite of those intended. Thus even Indonesia's withdrawal from the United Nations, in January, 1965, differed fundamentally from the withdrawals from the League of Nations, throughout its existence, of many member states, including those branded as aggressors. Indonesia was the first member to leave the United Nations, after two decades of its life, and against the strongly expressed advice of Western states, many uncommitted Asian and African members, and the Soviet Union. Characteristically, though the withdrawal was occasioned by Malaysia's election to temporary membership of the Security Council, Indonesia did not force a vote on that issue during the moratorium on contentious issues in the Nineteenth General Assembly, that was observed in connection with the question of nonpayment of dues by the Soviet Union—although such a move by Indonesia would have dramatized her protest against Malaysia much more effectively than her subsequent withdrawal, and it might have wrecked the United Nations.

Lord Avon made his analogy in retrospect, after he had already "retired" to the House of Lords. However, active international politicians justify or explain their policies on the basis of similar analogies. For example, President Lyndon B. Johnson discussed United States involvement in Vietnam as follows:

Three times in my lifetime—in two world wars and in Korea—Americans have gone to far lands to fight for freedom. We have learned at a terrible and a brutal cost that retreat does not bring safety, and weakness does not bring peace. . . .

We did not choose to be the guardians at the gate, but there is no one else. Nor would surrender in Vietnam bring peace, because we learned from Hitler at Munich that success only feeds the appetite of aggression. The battle would be renewed in one country, and then another country, bringing with it perhaps even larger and crueler conflict, as we have learned from the lessons of history.[10]

Secretary of State Dean Rusk tried to refute criticism of such analogies:

I have noted criticism of the so-called analogy between Hitler and Mao Tse-tung. I am perfectly aware of the important differences between

_____
[10]"Opening Statement," President Johnson's News Conference of July 28, 1965. New York *Times,* July 29, 1965, p. 12.

these two and the countries in which they have exercised power. The seizure of Manchuria by Japanese militarists, of Ethiopia by Mussolini, and of the Rhineland, Austria, and Czechoslovakia by Hitler were laboratory experiments in the anatomy and physiology of aggression. How to deal with the phenomenon of aggression was the principal problem faced in drafting the United Nations Charter, and the answer was collective action. We do ourselves no service by insisting that each source of aggression or each instance of aggression is unique. My own view is that we have learned a good deal about this phenomenon and its potentiality for leading into catastrophe if the problem is not met in a timely fashion.[11]

The popularity of the Munich analogy has not been confined to Western politicians. For example, in March 1966, the official newspaper of the Chinese Communist Party charged that Soviet Russian leaders "wanted 'by hook or by crook' to lead Vietnamese Communists to the conference table 'so as to bring about another Munich.' "[12]

Power as Analogy

Power as the central focus of conventional studies of international relations is itself a concept based upon a false analogy. This is true even where the substance of power, as used in contemporary international politics, is similar to, or identical with, the substance of power used in international relations before World War II. For example, there may be a substantive identity of power between two crises in Latin American international politics during these two periods. However, because of the much greater current global-international involvements of all states, including Latin American ones, this otherwise identical power functions within a context which is relationally quite different. Since power itself is a relational concept, such analogies cannot stand up to criticism.

To make the target of the foregoing critique quite clear, we should emphasize again that the dissimilarities are not necessarily in the "things" of Webster's definition *themselves*, that is, not in the substance of power used in international politics, but these dissimilarities are in the *relations among* the users of power. For example, the very

---

[11]"Text of Rusk's Statement to House Panel on U. S. Policy Toward Communist China," New York *Times*, Sunday, April 17, 1966, p. 34 (from a statement before the Far East Subcommittee of the House Foreign Affairs Committee, delivered on March 16, 1966).

[12]"China Denounces Soviet on Vietnam," New York *Times*, March 7, 1966, p. 1.

fact that, in the Orient, Western notions of sovereignty were not indigenously developed and have usually not been received in the same sense in which they are understood in the originating Occident, means that politicians acting on behalf of states may conceive of their own "power playing" roles, in both internal and international politics, in different terms from those of Western politicians. Again, two African politicians, even in the unlikely event that they think of their international "power" in entirely Western terms, would be employing it against one another in African regional politics in a nonanalogous way, because territoriality and cultural nationalism play a different, less important role in their thinking.

This critique, therefore, aims basically at the conventional conception of *all* politics, that is, at the conventional answer to the question, "What is politics all about?" or, "What goes on in the political process?" Any approach to the study of international politics is based upon an answer to these questions. The standard answer is "Power." Because we find this answer misleading, the basic search conducted in this book is for a conception of politics that is truly universal, in the sense that it can be applied to (because it is derived from) politics no matter where or when or at what level it may be carried on.

This search is neither unique nor original. For instance, Thomas C. Schelling, whose application of bargaining theory to the study of international politics we will have occasion to consider later in Chapter 7, sees analogous elements in all bargaining situations, regardless of the items which are put on the counter to be bargained with, and regardless of the issue over which the bargaining occurs. Schelling sees analogies between the bargaining that goes on among small children and their parents over the consumption of candy and hours of sleep, criminal blackmail exerted by kidnapers, and test explosions of nuclear bombs.[13] These analogies seem to make better sense than those cited above, between situations before and after World War II, because of the very obvious relational dissimilarities between the conditions described as "peace," "war," "appeasement," and even between the entities described as "states," in these two periods of time. The substantive, quantitative transformation of power has been so vast, that it has also brought about qualitative differences. And the change in the principal actors from sovereign national states into units much

---

[13]Thomas C. Schelling, *The Strategy of Conflict* (Cambridge: Harvard University Press, 1960).

larger than states, and much less clearly defined, has further contributed to a condition that makes it very difficult, if not impossible, to find sufficient similarity in the relations among the components of any two situations, to warrant the making of valid analogies.

Earlier, we offered a critique of the conception of politics that finds power at its essential core. Now, we should be able to extend that critique to assert that the concept of power, as used by the school of *Realpolitik,* is not only too broad to have sufficient precision, and too static to allow for the rapid and radical change occurring in international politics today, but that it is altogether inapplicable if understood in the meaning which the term "power" necessarily acquired in the period of conventional international relations. The impact of this critique can be brought out in one final way:

Thomas Hobbes defined "power" as "present means to obtain some apparent future good."[14] Hobbes forged this definition in an age which was extremely conscious of power and its importance, but which was relatively poor in the power actually at its disposal. So, at least, it appears to us in retrospect, although to Hobbes's contemporaries, when they compared themselves with *their* forerunners, theirs was a power-rich age. That is why men like Hobbes, Bodin, and Grotius tried to give clear meaning to power as it related to sovereignty, another concept coined by them in their quest for clarity. However, their notion of power was mercantilist. That is, just as the economists of the period conceived of the total amount of wealth available on earth in fixed, static terms, so these political theorists thought of the total amount of power available on earth in fixed, static terms. International relations was, therefore, looked upon as a "zero sum game." This concept of game theory, applied to the seventeenth century, simply means that, if England gained in wealth or other power, then some other state, like France or Spain, had to lose an equal quantum of wealth or power. They thought it inconceivable that all major participants in international relations could gain at the same time, because the new power acquired by some members had to be lost by others.

Today, however, there is a surfeit of power in the international economy of power. It is possible for one unit to gain without another losing power. In fact, both parties to a major conflict may gain and, as some recent crises have demonstrated, the entire international com-

---

[14]Hobbes, *op. cit.,* chap. x.

munity may benefit from the consequences of an averted nuclear clash, as in the case of the Cuban missile crisis of 1962.

The economist J. K. Galbraith has shown that members of his profession, whose main problem always used to be scarcity, are applying categories to present problems of affluence that are quite unsuited to understanding these problems.[15] Similarly, the international power economy is no longer one of scarcity, but has become one of overabundance. That is why students of world politics would do well to try to refashion their tools of analysis for reasons similar to those urged upon his economist colleagues by Professor Galbraith.

Hobbes's definition of power as applied to the actual use of hydrogen bombs illustrates the point. H-bombs cannot be used as "means to obtain some apparent future good." This is so, because of their side effects. Suppose, for instance, that the United States dropped several H-bombs on the Soviet Union. Even if the Soviet Union did not retaliate—and retaliation would make the operation self-defeating for the United States—radioactive fall-out and other side effects would have undesirable consequences for the allies of the United States in western Europe and, probably, also for the United States itself. And even if these effects of a nuclear explosion could be kept confined to the Soviet Union—and they cannot—what would the United States do with an adversary that had been completely obliterated through the use of nuclear weapons? This question can, of course, also be turned around: What would the Soviet Union do with a United States that it had obliterated through nuclear attack?

Two related answers can be offered to this critique of the power approach. They are related through their common affinity to the conventional equilibrium or balance-of-power theory which, in the nuclear context, is often referred to as the "balance of terror." The first answer rests on the assertion that the use of nuclear weapons may be limited or, in other words, that "limited nuclear war" is possible. This assertion was first put forward in relatively clear terms by Henry A. Kissinger, who suggested that an absolute distinction could be made between tactical and strategic nuclear weapons, and that rules could be worked out between the United States and the Soviet Union, designed to limit the theater of operations within which these tactical nuclear weapons should be used.[16] However, official Soviet publica-

---

[15]J. K. Galbraith, *The Affluent Society* (Boston: Houghton Mifflin, 1958).

[16]Henry A. Kissinger, *Nuclear Weapons and Foreign Policy* (New York: Harper & Bros., 1957).

tions immediately rejected the distinction between tactical and strategic weapons, and since it certainly requires the agreement of both parties to make such distinctions and such a set of rules effective, the theory was impracticable from the very outset.

The second rebuttal of the critique of the power approach claims that there is no essential difference between the contemporary balance of terror, in the "age of overkill," and the old-fashioned balance of power. As proof of their argument, these theorists of power point to the fact that nuclear weapons have not been used since 1945. The existence of the balance of terror means that the overabundance of power available to the United States and the Soviet Union restrains its actual use, except for purposes of threatening or bargaining. It thereby simply returns the actual employment of force to its former, conventional, lower levels.

This kind of argumentation provides the basis for much of the application of game theory to international politics. Test explosions, for example, are seen as blackmail, as already mentioned. The overabundance of force at the disposal of the major nuclear powers is used as much to demonstrate resolution and purpose to one's own population, as to intimidate one's opponent. From this kind of thinking one can also derive the suggestion of installing a so-called "doomsday machine." Such a device would have the capacity to destroy the entire earth if it were triggered by certain events like a full-scale nuclear attack upon the state that had installed it. The particular advantage of a doomsday machine is supposed to be the fact that it restricts the flexibility of the state that built the device. This state would previously have announced publicly to its potential opponents and to the world at large that if a certain "line" is crossed, then—quite beyond its own control—the doomsday machine will be triggered into action. The fact that the state itself has put control of this device beyond its own reach enhances the "credibility" of this particular form of deterrence.

This rebuttal of the critique seems insufficient, because the very need to demonstrate one's own resolution to use these "ultimate weapons," which would entail the destruction of the political system resorting to their use, shows that the content of power has undergone a qualitative transformation and that the power that goes into the contemporary balance of terror is not being used as present means to obtain some apparent future good. This is true even of conventional power, like ground troops with nonatomic weapons, because of the constant danger of "escalation." This danger exists almost every-where, even in remote and backward areas like Indonesia and Ma-laysia, or Yemen and Saudi Arabia, because of the possibility of the involvement of nuclear powers through the ramifications of networks of treaty organizations and ideological alignments that have grown up around the Cold War.

The focus upon power, especially when it is understood in the sense of a zero sum game, tends to distort our perception of the realities of international politics and, indeed, of all politics. It also leads us to overlook many other components that together make up any situation in international politics. Other organizing concepts are needed, which have to be universal in their applicability and capable of passing the test of valid analogies. To provide such concepts—such "handles" by means of which to grasp reality—is the purpose of the next chapter.

Chapter 3

Systematic Politics

Systems Theory*

Students of politics, in their efforts to make their discipline more "scientific," have in recent years been turning to systems theory. In other words, they have made deliberate efforts to look upon politics as though it were going on within a "system of action." Professor Samuel H. Beer has suggested that,

> The idea of a system has been taken over from biological theory and adapted by some social scientists to the study of their subject matter. In biological theory it has been given a fairly complex and technical meaning.[1]

Beer may or may not be right about the biological origins of some contemporary systems theory in political science, but the following citation suggests that *all* good modern political theory has been systems theory, at least implicitly:

> By *systems* I understand any number of men joined in one interest. Some are *regular* and some *irregular*. Of the regular ones, some are absolute and *independent*, others are dependent, that is to say *subordinate*. Of the latter, some are *political* and some *private*. Of private systems, some are *lawful*, some *unlawful*.

This definition and classification of political systems (slightly emended and orthographically updated) was advanced more than three cen-

---

*This section appears in another version as "An Evaluation of the Utility of Systems Theory" in *Contemporary Political Analysis*, James C. Charlesworth, ed. (New York: Free Press, 1966).

[1]Samuel H. Beer, "The Analysis of Political Systems," in S. H. Beer and Adam B. Ulam (eds.), *Patterns of Government: The Major Political Systems of Europe* (2nd ed.; New York: Random House, 1962), p. 25.

turies before the current preoccupation with systems theory, in 1651, by the founder of modern political theory, Thomas Hobbes, at the beginning of chapter 22 of his *Leviathan,* which he entitled "Of Systems, Subject, Political, and Private."

This early use of systems theory is mentioned, not in order to demonstrate that "everything has been said before," but rather in order to emphasize that *anyone* who attempts to study politics scientifically must at least implicitly think of politics as though it were functioning as some sort of system. That is, he must assume that more or less regular relationships can be discerned among various aspects of politics, and between the phenomena he describes as political and certain other phenomena not so described. Professor Morton A. Kaplan expressed this thought in a rather more comprehensive way:

> It is the thesis of this volume that a scientific politics can develop only if the materials of politics are treated in terms of systems of actions. A system of actions is a set of variables so related, in contradistinction to its environment, that describable behavioral regularities characterize the internal relationships of the variables to each other and the external relationships of the set of individual variables to combinations of external variables.[2]

Professor Kaplan would probably disagree with the judgment that what he calls "a scientific politics" has been steadily developing at least since the time of Hobbes. Indeed, a convincing case could be made for Aristotle as the first systems theorist about politics, among other reasons because his four "causes"—material, efficient, formal, and final—foreshadowed the "functional requisites" of some contemporary systems theorists in the science which he founded.[3] The point here is simply that the novelty in political science is not systems theory as such, but the tremendous self-consciousness about systems theory.

This self-consciousness has been very productive for the obvious reason that, whatever our central focus of inquiry, we can best approach answers to the questions we are asking by conceiving of politics in terms not only systematic but also systemic. We may address

---

[2]Morton A. Kaplan, *System and Process in International Politics* (New York: John Wiley & Sons, Inc., 1957), p. 4.

[3]See, e.g., Robert T. Holt, "A Proposed Structural-Functional Framework for Political Science," in *Functionalism in the Social Sciences: The Strength and Limits of Functionalism in Anthropology, Economics, Political Science, and Sociology,* Don Martindale (ed.) (Philadelphia: American Academy of Political and Social Science, 1965), pp. 84–110.

ourselves to very broad questions—What types of institutions and procedures are best designed to insure that policy corresponds to its makers' intentions? Are there criteria for evaluating political philosophies? How can we explain variations in the incidence of international violence? Or we may address ourselves to very narrow questions—why was John Lindsay elected Mayor of New York? How can we explain recent ideological changes in the Roman Catholic Church? Will the military of Black Africa play a role similar to that of their counterparts in Latin America? Regardless of the thrust and scope of our questions, they can best be answered through the comparison of analogous events, processes, and values, when these are viewed within the context of systems.

However, though systems theory as such may be regarded as indispensable to political science, not all systems theories are equally useful. Some contribute to the development of a "scientific politics" while others contribute confusion. Contemporary systems theory— largely because of the very self-consciousness with which it (quite unnecessarily) borrowed its concepts from biology, physics, and even economics and sociology, as sciences generally believed to be "harder" than politics—tends to lure political scientists into traps that are often camouflaged by misplaced analogies.

The chronologically first of these traps is disguised by the term *system* itself. Biological and physical systems at least *seem* to the observer to have an "objective" coherence. They appear as "natural" systems, though appearances may be deceptive. A single human body, for example, can "naturally" be perceived and analyzed as a system. The same is true of the solar system. Similarly, but with less clarity, most societies, especially premodern ones existing in isolation from other societies, seem to the observer to have the "given" characteristics of a system, including coherence, endurance, internal interdependence. They can be defined in terms of such "natural" features shared by their members as common language and customs, which distinguish their members from those of other societies. All these systems share both naturalness and givenness, though to varying degrees. They were not deliberately created by men to serve certain purposes and to perform certain functions (except for some social systems, of which more later). Those systems most frequently designated as political systems, on the other hand, were brought into being, or are being affirmed and reaffirmed, by acts of human will, to serve certain purposes and to perform certain functions. The imperfections in the analogy between "natural" and "artificial" or "voluntary" systems imply that teleological systems analysis is in fact more warranted for political than for other types of systems.

Most political scientists who use systems theory nowadays identify the political system with the state, as it was conceived of by Max Weber, no matter what language they may employ in order to synchronize this concept with their particular brand of systems theory. For example, Professor David Easton asserts that "what distinguishes political interactions from all other kinds of social interactions is that they are predominantly oriented toward the authoritative allocation of values for a society.[4] . . . Thus, we establish the two essential variables for all and any kinds of political system as 'the making and execution of decisions for a society' and 'their relative frequency of acceptance as authoritative or binding by the bulk of the society.'"[5] We saw earlier that, for Professor Gabriel A. Almond, "The political system is the legitimate, order-maintaining or transforming system in the society."[6]

If the political system is thought of in this narrow sense, i.e., basically as the state (almost as "The State," in the Hegelian sense), then all political systems extant today were founded and/or are being maintained, by acts of human will, to serve more or less clearly specified purposes and to perform more or less clearly defined functions, for the society or societies that accept their allocation of values as "authoritative" or their physical compulsion as "legitimate." They can, in other words, be studied as systems precisely because they were set up to be systems. On the other hand, nonpolitical systems, including societies—except for politically created, i.e., "artificial" social systems— are always being anthropomorphized to some extent by systems analysis that ascribes or assumes functional requisites, goals, and the like. In this sense, the political system has served more often as a model for nonpolitical congeries of phenomena described as systems, than "natural systems" have served as models for the political system. This appears to have been true from the beginnings of Western philosophizing and psychologizing in classical Greece. Plato divided individual

---

[4]David Easton, *A Framework for Political Analysis* (Englewood Cliffs, N.J.: Prentice-Hall, Inc., 1965), p. 50.

[5]*Ibid.*, pp. 96 f.

[6]See page 7 above.

man up into three "elements," which might be in harmony or in conflict with each other. Analogously, other political categories, like the legal term "cause" (*aitía*), were projected unto nature and the universe.[7] These projections were made by the early political and natural philosophers, for whom the most important entity was not the individual but the *polis*. They projected both upward and downward from their image of the political system, because man became conscious of it, before he became conscious of himself as an individual, and of nature, as entities distinguishable from the undifferentiated political system.[8]

Similarly today, the by now highly differentiated political system is more easily accessible to analysis than more natural systems. This suggests the possibility that the political system is still (or again) *the* archetype, even when scholars explicitly assert the opposite. However, the fact that all extant political systems conventionally studied as such are more or less "willed" systems does *not* mean that they actually perform the functions which either their founders and elites, or their observers have "built into" or "read out" of them. Nor does it mean that such functions, however described, are "universal political functional requisites." Most obviously, the "output functions" adapted from the American version of the separation of powers (or differentiation of functions)—rule making, rule application, and rule adjudication—are not performed universally, in all systems and at all times, in this particular differentiated form. On the other hand, functions that are read into the political system by false analogy from biological systems (which may in turn originally have been modeled upon earlier concepts of the political system, thereby compounding the analogical error) are likely to lead to even greater confusion. This applies with special force to the function of "boundary maintenance."

Boundary Maintenance

Systems theory distinguishes between external and internal boundaries and their maintenance. One would think, offhand, that political systems are very much concerned with maintaining the integrity of their

---

[7]See Werner Jaeger, *Paideia: Ideals of Greek Culture* (New York: Oxford University Press, 1944), Vol. I, pp. 160 ff.

[8]See Herbert J. Spiro, *Government by Constitution: The Political Systems of Democracy* (New York: Random House, 1959), pp. 28 f.

external boundaries, i.e., if we drop the jargon, that sovereign states protect and defend their frontiers, in ways analogous to the body's defenses against penetration from outside it. However, as Professor Easton has pointed out, "even geographic boundaries" have a "deceptive character," though this "does not weaken the utility of the concept 'boundaries' as an *analytical tool*."[9] *If* we use the concept of the political system by analogy to biological systems and think of the United States of America or Ghana as a political system, we should bear in mind what Professor Easton has to say about the apple:

> An apple is an organic system isolated from its environment by a skin. We take it for granted that if our task is to understand the processes occurring within the apple itself as it matures and decays, we need to take into consideration factors outside of the skin itself. The soil in which the apple tree grows, the nature of the tree itself, and when parted from this, the humidity, temperature, and circulation of the atmosphere in which the apple is stored are all of decisive importance for the life of the apple as a system. Yet, from the point of view of the horticulturalist, these elements are variables external to the apple as an organic system. The boundary is well defined by the skin.[10]

Similarly *and* analogously, sovereign states, even at the height of the bygone period when sovereignty was the most important fact of international relations, were also subsystems—at any rate, components—of more encompassing international political systems. Today, states frequently set themselves goals involving the elimination rather than the protection of their boundaries—like a merger with another political system in a federation, or a sloughing-off of territory formerly within the state's territory. Tomorrow, conceivably, political systems may be able and willing to transfer themselves from one territory and population to another. The conceptual feasibility of such a transfer again suggests that external boundary maintenance is not a universal function of political systems. It also raises some questions about the scope of the political system in relation to the social system and other overlapping nonpolitical systems, and about the function of internal boundary maintenance.

While political systems theorists generally tend to be horizontal "imperialists," most of them are at the same time vertical "mice." They claim a horizontal, i.e., geographical, monopoly of legitimate

---

[9] Easton, *op. cit.*, pp. 67 and 68; italics supplied.
[10] *Ibid.*, p. 64.

physical compulsion for their political system, but vertically they look upon the political system as a *sub*system of the social system. According to various systems theories, the political system must perform the function of maintaining its own internal boundaries against penetration or overflow from and into the social system, and against the economic, cultural, and other less comprehensive differentiated subsystems within the society. Or the political system performs this function and, in addition, those of drawing, maintaining, and redrawing all internal boundaries between the various subsystems of the social system.

The organic analogy seems particularly evident in this concept of internal boundary maintenance, since boundaries can be perceived between the various organs and other components of internally differentiated bodies. In contemporary as in classical Greek political systems, however, no such internal boundaries between "society" and "polity" exist. Nevertheless, much systems theory, forgetting what David Easton calls the "analytic character of *all* systems,"[11] classifies and evaluates political systems according to their performance of this function of maintaining the boundary between the social and the political systems. For example, so-called "totalitarian" systems are said to be directed deliberately by their rulers toward the destruction of this boundary, so that politics becomes "total," with the result that the "society" is "destroyed," or at least "atomized." The roots of this ideological notion of internal boundary maintenance, apart from the relatively recent misleading analogy from biology, must go back to the peculiarly Western Christian experience of the struggle between temporal and spiritual authorities, and the social contract theories formed and informed by this experience. These theories usually— though not in the case of Thomas Hobbes—assumed the pre-existence of society as the condition for the founding of "civil society," "civil government," or the "sovereign." The fact that contemporary sociologists turned to self-conscious systems theory before political scientists did so undoubtedly also contributed to the prevailing narrow view of the political system as a subsystem of the society.

This approach mistakes the greater for the lesser, the more encompassing for the less encompassing, and the more significant for the less significant. The political system is, in the view of this book, more

---

[11]*Ibid.*, p. 42; italics supplied.

important, more comprehensive, and "greater" than the social system. Many political systems in the world today consist of several societies that were joined together deliberately in order to achieve common goals, often newly forged. The patterns of social interaction in most, if not all, modern social systems have been transformed as a result of deliberate political action (which is not to say that the effects of such action upon social patterns are usually the intended effects). Societies —and, as for that matter, economies, cultures, personality systems— "just grow" and therefore deserve the designation of *system* less than political systems. Moreover, the moment that more or less deliberate efforts are made to change society, including the family, economy, culture, or personality systems, the given raw material of these "levels" of human existence is taken up by the political system and the political process. In this sense, the political system is the only "existential" system among the so-called "social systems." The others are merely analogic systems or anthropomorphized systems—unless their raw material is being absorbed by the political system, and then they may be looked upon and analyzed as subsystems of the political system.

In order to avoid confusion, however, society, economy, and similar subordinate sets of relationships should be analyzed as political subsystems only to the extent that the political system treats them as such. This *caveat* is of relatively little practical importance *today,* because all contemporary political systems do in fact treat these patterns of other aspects of their members' lives as political subsystems. The *caveat* may be of slightly greater importance for the historical analysis of periods in which political, economic, spiritual, cultural, and other activities were believed to be carried on in separate compartments, as it were; e.g., when philosophers spoke of "economic man." But even for such periods, we must not overlook that this belief in compartmentalization was the result of more or less deliberate decisions made in the political system—at least if we think of the scope of the political system in terms broader than the conventional ones cited above (on page 44).

The utility of systems theory, as of all else in political science, depends upon the understanding of politics with which it works, upon the notion of "the political" upon which it is based. Most systems theorists still identify politics ultimately with power, compulsion, violence, force, binding decisions, and the like. Many but not all identify the political system ultimately with the state in the Weberian sense. Even when they admit that a kind of politics goes on within families, firms, and churches, including communities of supranational scope that are not continuously or importantly affected by the actions of states, they prefer to focus upon the state as the political system. Sometimes they do so explicitly for reasons of analytical convenience and economy.

This focus tends to distort. It tends to distort the internal analysis of political systems, because it either leaves out of account too much of the allegedly "nonpolitical," or it takes for granted a causal sequence in which political phenomena are viewed as secondary or tertiary effects of "primary" economic, geographical, or social factors. For example, such an approach studies the impact *upon* politics of economic, social, and cultural change in the politics of the developing areas, and thereby neglects the possibility that more or less deliberate efforts to bring about change—that is, politics—have more important consequences for the substantive conditions of life in these areas than vice versa.[12] Or it urges that "governmental authority patterns" be made congruent with social authority patterns in order to promote "stable democracy," without much attention to the possibility that government is more likely to reform social authority patterns than vice versa.[13] It could be argued that one way to avoid this type of distortion would be to consider politics coextensive with all human relations, but this would be tantamount to the surrender of all focus in order to eliminate the distortions engendered by a particular, mistaken focus.

The focus upon the state as *the* political system tends to distort the analysis of international politics, by leading to the qualitative distinction between national and international politics criticized earlier. Professor Kaplan avoids this kind of distortion by explicitly rejecting the focus upon power and by denying that the political system "is the coercive subsystem in the social system."[14] Instead, he focuses upon a political system whose geographical scope is defined by the purposes of a particular analysis. In his view, the main difference between conventional national systems and the global political system is that

---

[12]See "The Primacy of Political Development," in *Africa: The Primacy of Politics,* H. J. Spiro (ed.) (New York: Random House, 1966), chap. 5.

[13]See Harry Eckstein, *A Theory of Stable Democracy* (Princeton: Center of International Studies, 1961).

[14]Kaplan, *op. cit.,* p. 12.

the former are "system dominant," while the latter is "subsystem dominant."[15] "Politics is the contest to fill decision-making roles, to choose alternate political objects, or to change the essential rules of the political system."[16] But even this view of politics seems less than satisfactory, partly because of its definitional nature, partly because it does not entirely overcome the dangers of compartmentalization: "A political system exists when its constitution and laws are communicated successfully *within* a social system."[17]

Universals of Politics

How can we overcome these various disadvantages of systems theory, without moving in the other direction of focuslessness? Simply by remembering the classical statement that politics is the affairs— all the common affairs—of the *polis* and consists of the concerns of the citizens. This means that a political system can exist wherever people are concerned about common problems and are engaged in cooperation *and* conflict in efforts to solve these problems. The scope of a particular political system is defined by the extent of the population so engaged, not only by the scope of power or of authority or of the successfully communicated constitution, and not at all by the scope of a particular social system. Individuals or groupings—"units"—are involved in politics with one another when they are trying to solve their several problems together, because each recognizes that it cannot solve its particular problems alone, without interaction with the others—even though each may be pursuing different goals.

The political process itself begins, not with the *recognition* of problems, but with the *formulation of issues* arising out of the problems. It continues with the *deliberation* of issues, which normally phases over into the *resolution* of the issue which, in turn, is normally followed by the *solution* of the problem that originally gave rise to the issue. Whether or not a political system exists depends not upon acceptance as legitimate or authoritative of the same goals by all, or by some proportion of, the participants; nor upon the capacity of any of the participants to compel others; nor upon the stability over a prolonged period of time of the essential rules governing the process. It

---

[15]*Ibid.*, p. 16.
[16]*Ibid.*, p. 14.
[17]*Loc. cit.*; italics supplied.

depends, rather, upon the participants' awareness of their participation in the political process. The point here is that the participants through their consciousness impose upon their interactions the characteristics of a system. This means that a set of interactions of only brief duration not only can be analyzed as a political system, but may actually be a political system.

The irreducible "existential" functions of political systems are the same as the four phases of the political process seen from another angle: (1) formulation, (2) deliberation, and (3) resolution of issues, and (4) solution of problems. They are irreducible in the sense that all are performed in all political systems (and, incidentally, by analogy to the model of the political system, in all personality systems). Wherever there is human awareness of cooperation and conflict in the solution of problems, these phases of the process are in fact performed. But they are performed in a vast variety of ways, sequences, and combinations of relative attention paid to each. This range of differences among systems can be systematically described by a typology of *political style,* which is in turn derived from the *basic goals* to the pursuit of which political systems are more or less deliberately directed, again in a wide variety of possible combinations. These four basic goals are *stability, flexibility, efficiency,* and *effectiveness.* Individual human beings as such, and as members who "belong" to a multiplicity of political systems—at various "horizontal" levels and crisscrossing these in "vertical" associations—assign different and changing importance to these basic goals in their pursuit of less basic goals (life, liberty, prosperity, or defense) and in their pursuit of circumstantial goals (like the implementation of a particular policy). This means that, in addition to conventionally defined "national" political systems and the "cosmically" defined global system, there exists also at any moment a series of complex, intricate, overlapping networks of political systems that are brought into being as a result of efforts, by units, to solve problems together. Men and political systems change their perspectives upon and their perceptions of problems and goals, partly because they solve some of their problems and therefore approach closer toward their goals. Consequently, a moving picture—as distinguished from the snapshot—taken of political systems would show kaleidoscopic patterns of expanding and contracting political systems that overlap with one another, and whose styles, as well as the styles of their "intersystems" politics with one another, are forever changing except in the rare and pathological case of the exclusive pursuit of stability.

This last-mentioned exception points to a shortcoming of much of the literature on political systems: an excessive preoccupation with stability, as though it were the only, or at least the most important, basic goal which is pursued by men engaged in politics. But political systems also pursue flexibility, efficiency, and effectiveness, in addition to stability. The combinations forever change, but this dynamism is rarely captured by systems theory with its frequently built-in bias toward stability. This bias can be detected even in some systems theories that favor a "dynamic equilibrium," because they fail to take into account the very element which makes political systems not merely analogic but existential systems: human consciousness.

Human beings are aware of discrepancies between their present and some wished-for future condition. They try to work toward the future goals which they invent and set for themselves. On the road toward these goals, they encounter obstacles. In order to overcome these obstacles, to solve these problems, they engage themselves in politics, and they form and dismantle political systems. Sometimes they approach closer toward their goals, sometimes they move or are moved farther away from them, sometimes they forget about them as a result of changes in the perspective of their consciousness, and sometimes they substitute new goals for old ones. Usually all of this is going on simultaneously, all over the earth. And as men are engaged in all these many simultaneous political processes, they change their consciousness of the possible. Often they expand their awareness of that which they recognize as possible. In recent centuries, since the time of Thomas Hobbes, they have increasingly recognized the converse, namely, that whatever may be possible can be achieved ultimately only through politics. We might paraphrase the advertising slogan of a chemical corporation: "Better things for better living through politics!"

Political systems are brought into being as direct or indirect results of more or less deliberate human actions upon nonpolitical reality (which may, in its various given aspects, be conceived of for analytical purposes as composed of systems). Political systems reflect man's consciousness of the possible. The expansion of political systems—of the capacity to generate new goals and issues, to increase participation, and to carry the increased volume of politics—normally contributes to the further expansion of consciousness. From this viewpoint, the continuous development of politics, both within and among systems, can be considered as the human goal of highest priority.

Only systems theory can understand this, because only systems theory can understand politics in this existential sense. Systems theory has been understanding politics in this sense for some centuries.

The Political System*

Politics is the process by which a community deals with its problems. A *community* exists among people who are aware of pursuing common goals. *Problems* are obstacles perceived on the road toward goals. Problems must therefore be recognized in order to become politically relevant or alive. But recognition of a problem by itself does not lead to the generation of politics about it. When there is complete consensus in the community on the solution of a problem, after it has been recognized, no politics concerning this problem takes place. In this sense, a community whose members always agree on solutions to their problems is not a political system. Since there are few (if any) such communities—and the international community is certainly not one of these few—virtually all communities are, for our purposes, political systems. In almost all communities, disagreements occur. Disagreements present *issues*. A *political system,* therefore, is a community that is processing its issues. While the basic prerequisite of community is *consensus,* though minimally only on common goals (which may be negative, like prevention of the extermination of the community of mankind), the basic prerequisite of a political system is dissensus, disagreement. Politics arises out of disagreements within a network, wide or narrow, loose or tight, of agreement.

A problem enters politics once members of the community recognize it *and* disagree about it. A problem leaves politics when it has been "solved," *and* the solution has been recognized. Between the beginning and the end of this process, the issue(s) generated by a problem passes through four *phases* of the "flow of policy":

1. Formulation of the issue.
2. Deliberation of the issue.

*Parts of this Chapter are adapted with permission from Herbert J. Spiro, "Comparative Politics: A Comprehensive Approach," *American Political Science Review,* Vol. LVI, No. 3, (September 1962) pp. 577–595.

3. Resolution of the issue.
4. Solution of the problem.

Since the problems are recognized as obstacles on the road to goals, and goals can have substantive or procedural content, disagreements may arise as *substantive* or *procedural* issues. In either case, the issue may be perceived as involving a long-term, *fundamental* matter, or a short-term, *circumstantial* matter. A political system may be described, and two or more systems may be compared, by "plotting" the incidence of issues with reference to two intersecting axes. The vertical axis runs from the procedural to the substantive extreme, the horizontal from the fundamental to the circumstantial (Figure 1).

(This diagram and those that follow can safely be ignored by readers who object to diagrammatic representations of political realities. They are not meant to suggest the imposition upon the facts of a precision greater than these facts, and our understanding of them, warrant. They do not "prove" anything. The figures may, however, be helpful in suggesting certain patterns of relationships among various aspects and dimensions of political systems. This advantage seems to outweigh the risks of reification of the merely graphic, especially when awareness of these risks reduces them—as in this book.)

FIGURE 1.

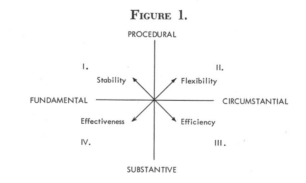

In every political system, some issues arise and are perceived under each of the four combinations. (I) Fundamental procedural issues are generated by problems arising out of the basic goal of *stability*, e.g., by constitutional problems. (II) Procedural circumstantial issues are generated by problems arising out of the basic goal of *flexibility*, i.e. typically, by economic problems in modern or modernizing communities. (III) Circumstantial substantive issues are generated by problems arising out of the basic goal of *efficiency*, e.g., by power problems.

And (IV) substantive fundamental issues are generated by problems arising out of the basic goal of *effectiveness*, e.g., by cultural problems.

The relative *success* of political systems (or of one system at different times) can be gauged by the degree to which they manage to sustain a dynamic equilibrium among the four basic goals. If problems are thought of as the input and solutions as the output of the political system, efficiency measures the output-input ratio. If the system solves none of its problems, it is unsuccessful. But the problems it recognizes for processing, the process itself, and the solutions, also have to be considered effective or acceptable by at least those members of the system whose opposition could put an end to it. Moreover, at least some procedures used for the handling of problems have to remain stable over time, otherwise the system will lose its identity vis-à-vis itself and its basic goals. These procedures, and even more the policies (or solutions) worked out by means of these procedures must be sufficiently flexible to adjust to changes in the content of the community's problems; otherwise stagnation will set in. Stability and effectiveness are concerned with the long run; flexibility and efficiency with the short run. Each of these basic goals needs to be counterbalanced by its temporal opposite. Stability and flexibility are concerned with the procedures used for handling issues; effectiveness and efficiency with the content of problems and their solutions. Each procedural goal should be balanced by its substantive opposite.

Political Style

None of the four basic goals is sufficient by itself for the success of a political system. Exclusive concern with stability is shown by legalistic attempts to foreorder the entire future by means of comprehensive, detailed, and consistent regulation. This is designed to preclude the need for any future choices, to prevent changes in values and goals, and to keep efficiency at its current level, since no novel substantive problems will be allowed to come up. In international politics, an illustration of this tendency is provided by the efforts, since World War II, to give permanent stability to the western camp in the face of the communist threat by means of the vast, comprehensive, and intricate network of treaty organizations, of which the North Atlantic Treaty Organization (NATO), the Central Treaty Organization (CENTO), and the Southeast Asian Treaty Organization (SEATO) are only a few component parts. The final goal pursued here is a kind of regimented bureaucratism. Within one more or less well-balanced political system, members who are overly committed to bringing about only stability will raise a disproportionate number of issues under (I). Their political style is *legalistic* (Fig. 2).

FIGURE 2.

Pathological Style, I.

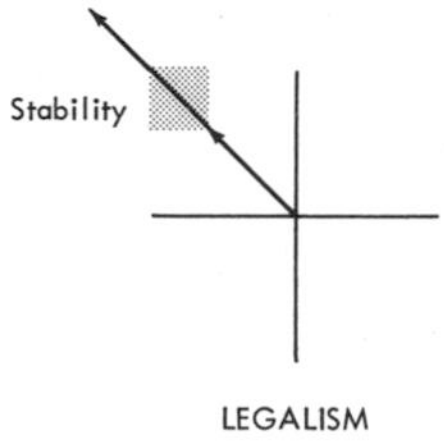

LEGALISM

FIGURE 3.

Pathological Style, II.

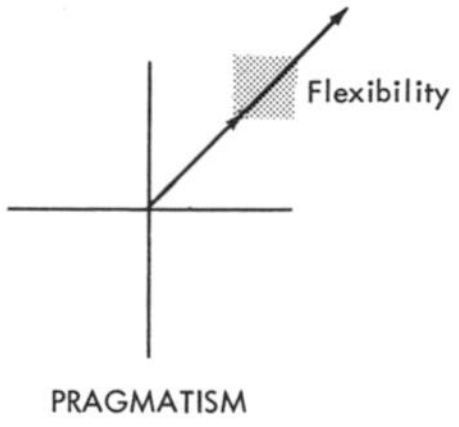

PRAGMATISM

FIGURE 4.

Pathological Style, III.

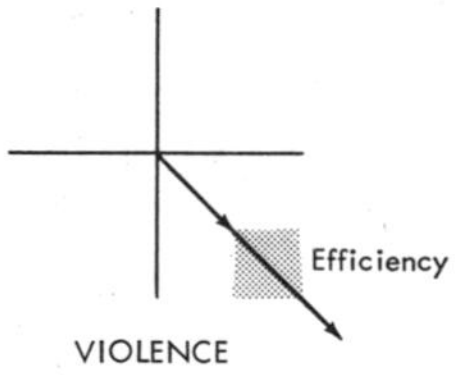

VIOLENCE

FIGURE 5.

Pathological Style, IV.

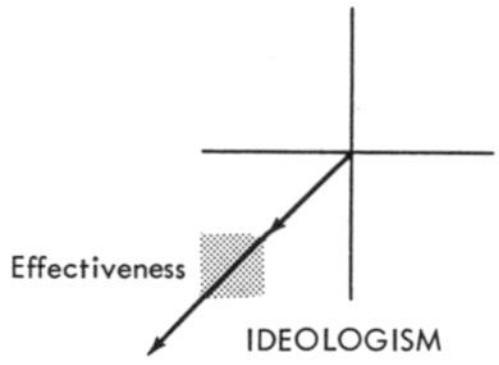

IDEOLOGISM

Exclusive concern with flexibility is the temporal antithesis of legalism. Here the desire is to keep opportunities for change permanently open. In international politics, illustrations can be taken from the unwillingness of some nonaligned states to fix long-run goals for themselves; or from the practice of the superpowers of repeatedly changing the procedures by which they pursue their apparently fixed goals, e.g., "psychological warfare," threats of nuclear warfare, use of conventional forces, insurgency and "counterinsurgency," spying, bribery of foreign officials, subsidies to "private" armies, formal diplomacy either bilateral or multilateral under United Nations auspices; "hot-line" communications, and a variety of other methods. As a result, constancy of goals actually becomes impossible and policies fail because of inability to sustain them long enough to solve the problems to which they were initially addressed. As the order of priority among problems is changed, procedures are altered as well. Opportunism, cynicism, and corruption are extreme manifestations of excessive concern with flexibility. Anarchy would be the logical end result. Members of one political system overly interested in flexibility will raise a disproportionate number of issues under (II). Their style is *pragmatic* (Figure 3).

Exclusive concern with efficiency results from the desire to achieve nothing but the immediate solution of current problems. It is revealed by technocratic focusing on the substance of problems, as these happen to be perceived at the moment, in order to bring available power and other resources to bear upon them at once. What participants desire is quick solutions—regardless of the means used, of alternative policies that may have been suggested, or of the effectiveness of these solutions in terms of goals other than pure short-term efficiency. The end result of imposition of its rule by an efficiency-minded group would be a kind of military technocracy. Such persons will raise a disproportionate number of issues under (III). In international politics, the professional military and, nowadays, the so-called "strategic intellectuals," often play such a role.[18] When they are concerned only with the application of available power to the solution of problems, regardless of the purposes for which this power is to be used, their political style in its extreme form is *violent* (Figure 4).

Exclusive concern with effectiveness is the temporal opposite of violence. It would seek to imprison the whole community in the rubrics of one ruling ideology. Ideological motivation would shape the recognition of problems and the formulation of issues, regardless of "objective" needs as these might be seen by an outside observer. All policy is put in the service of the long run substantive goals to which the ideology is committed, like world mastery by the master race or by the "workers of the world." Nothing that deviates from this ideology can remain stable, nor can adjustments be made to changes within, or in the environment of, the system, unless the ideology itself dictates such changes. Theocracy or "hierocracy," in which a fanatical intelligentsia, secular or spiritual, rules, would be the result of victory by a group committed to the exclusive pursuit of effectiveness. In international politics, fanatical fascists and Leninists-Stalinists seem to fit this model, since they interpreted every event in world politics from the viewpoint of their ideologies. Members of a more or less bal-

---

[18]See Anatol Rapoport, *Strategy and Conscience* (New York: Harper & Row, 1964).

anced political system who have this kind of commitment will raise an inordinate number of issues under (IV). Their style is *ideological* (Figure 5).

FIGURE 6.

Dynamic equilibrium or the politics of purposive compromise.

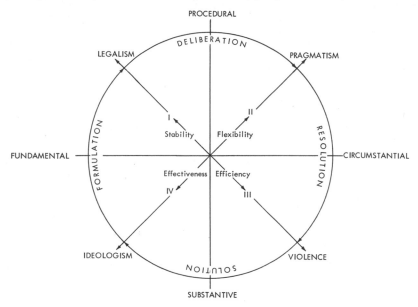

The style of a successful political system, in which the "natural" or "existential" tensions due to the simultaneous pursuit of the four basic goals maintain a dynamic equilibrium, could be described by Figure 6. This figure also relates the political process, i.e., the four phases of the flow of policy, to basic goals and to types of issues. A system is most successful when issues tend to cluster around the intersection of the procedural-substantive and the fundamental-circumstantial axes. This central clustering will happen, not because of the content of the problems dealt with, but because of the equilibrium described above. This in turn is related to the particular sequence in which each of the four phases of the political process proceeds from one to another of the four basic goals.

A problem is recognized for issue formulation, when fundamental substantive goals, i.e., the effectiveness of the system and its policies, call for its solution. Cultural values, in the broad sense, lead to recognition of discrepancies between goals and current conditions. But the particular formulation that the issue receives is shaped by the fundamental procedures in use. If there is disagreement on recognition of the problem and/or on its proper solution, this is due to differences in the fundamental substantive goals of members. But the form in which the resultant issue is stated—two or three alternative solutions, clear or vague differentiation, etc.—is shaped by the "constitution" (in the broad meaning of the word), and the fact that it is so shaped gives, and is usually designed to give, stability to the system, regardless of the content of all the various issues that have to be dealt with over long stretches of time.

Deliberation consists of the consideration of alternative solutions to a problem. The alternatives, having already been formulated, are now examined in the light of the need to adjust to changes inside the system and in its environment. Without realistic consideration of these changes, deliberation would be meaningless, and the solution would be unsatisfactory.

Deliberation normally leads to resolution, that is, the narrowing down of alternatives and the final selection of one policy. Resolution might be called "the big decision," since the word *decide* means "to cut off"—in this case, to cut off deliberation. But one should not identify only resolution with decision, because the whole political process consists of an uninterrupted sequence of decisions: what problems to recognize, how to formulate the issues, how to deliberate and resolve, what resources to use in solution, and many more decisions. While the formulation of the issue involves fundamentals, its resolution involves short-term considerations. Resolution is always addressed to the problem as it appears at the moment that deliberation is cut off. It need therefore not be final, because changes can always be made during the phase of solution. In fact, resolution rarely is final, and only rigid adherents of the mechanical doctrine of the separation of power (on the model of the Constitution of the United States) believe that the legislature deliberates and resolves, and then the executive puts this resolution into effect. Actually, the "executive," in world politics on a few occasions the Secretary General of the United Nations and whoever else participates in the final phase of the political process, often introduces new, or reintroduces old, alternative solutions to the problem. In any case, the resolution of the deliberated issue directs flexibility toward efficiency. While constitutional and economic considerations normally play important roles in the course of deliberation, economic and power considerations do so during resolution. And while an excess of constitutional regulation may prevent the optimal weighing of alternatives, a lack of available power and other resources may lead to inability to arrive at resolution of the issue.

The phase of solution deals with the substance of the problem, bringing to bear short-run power for the achievement of the community's long-run goals. Solution of a problem normally removes the goal on the road toward which the problem was an obstacle. For example, once an area of the globe suffering from extreme backwardness has achieved economic development and integration with the international economy, achievement of this goal ceases to be a goal, though the maintenance of a steady rate of economic development and of intercourse with the rest of the world may continue as a goal of lesser importance than previously. In a successful system, solution links efficiency to effectiveness and thereby clears the channels of politics for the recognition and processing of new problems that are obstacles on the road to new goals that may be newly "invented."

Formulation, deliberation, resolution, and solution are called *phases* rather than stages or departments of the political process or, preferably, of the "flow of policy," in order to emphasize that they usually overlap and do not always proceed in the same "1–2–3–4" sequence. In an emergency, for example, all four may be compressed into a matter of moments. In a nuclear missile crisis, radar devices linked to complicated electronic data processing equipment recognize the threat of missiles launched by an enemy, formulate the alternative courses open to one's own weapons systems, resolve the issues of alternative responses so raised, and attempt to solve the problem, perhaps by setting off retaliatory weapons systems. All of this may be accomplished in a matter of minutes.

Political systems differ with respect to the relative importance of the four phases, and with respect to the basic goals that are given strongest consideration in each phase of the flow of policy. For example, a system with a very legalistic style, like the League of Nations, might devote most of its politics to the concoction of "artificial" constitutional issues and their rather abstract deliberation, without ever arriving at their resolution or at the solution of its "real" problems. Or a system of very violent style, like some Latin American national and international subsystems, might concentrate its politics on the quick resolution of conflicts between various armed organizations and the attempted efficient solution of these problems, to the complete neglect of considering alternative solutions and formulating other issues arising out of different problems. The politics of the League of Nations was preoccupied with formulation and deliberation, to the neglect of resolution and solution. Politics among the participants in the various Indochinese crises (or, e.g., in World War II) emphasized resolution and solution, to the neglect of formulation and deliberation.

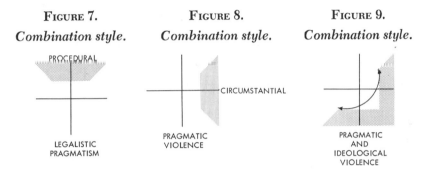

FIGURE 7.	FIGURE 8.	FIGURE 9.
Combination style.	*Combination style.*	*Combination style.*

The style of a political system is rarely as one-sided as in the preceding examples of legalism and violence. Combinations with a double or triple emphasis are more common: for example, legalistic pragmatism, as often displayed in American constitutional litigation or in the case over Southwest Africa before the International Court of Justice (Figure 7), pragmatic violence, as in criminal gang warfare and its international equivalents (Figure 8); ideological legalism, as in Calvin's Geneva or as sometimes advocated by certain juristically inclined Latin American diplomats in international politics; or alternating pragmatic and ideological violence, as in Soviet domestic politics or in Hitler's foreign policies (Figure 9).

A triple emphasis of this kind—on violence, pragmatism *and* ideologism—usually does not describe the style of a well-balanced system at one moment, because ideologism and pragmatism are true opposites, as are legalism and violence. Triple emphasis is therefore more likely to describe style over time, when radical oscillations occur, e.g., from ideologically to pragmatically motivated violence. It also sometimes happens that one subsystem behaves very violently (the military in some Latin American countries), while another behaves very legalistically (intellectuals in the same countries); a third subsystem is extremely ideological (supporters of the Roman Catholic Church), while a fourth (foreign business companies) is cynically pragmatic. The style of each of these subsystems is so pathological, that the tensions created by their coexistence within the same larger political system, instead of resulting in a dynamic equilibrium, lead either to the substantive stagnation of stalemate or to the breakup of the system.

On the other hand, simultaneous concern with effectiveness and flexibility, with stability and efficiency is possible (and desirable), when the issues of politics cluster around the intersection of the two coordinates. This would be true, for example, when the problem is jay-walking, and the issue is the means of enforcement of an ordinance. Then arguments about legality (not legalistic arguments) and about the availability of traffic police can be adduced simultaneously, without calling for a description of style as violently legalistic. Or when the issue arises out of the problem of dowries or bride price in a modernizing community, arguments about cultural values and about the distribution of income may be raised in the course of pushing the problem closer toward solution, without making the style ideologically pragmatic. The developments that led up to the founding of the European Economic Community, in the course of which economic and cultural arguments, and considerations of resources and constitutional structure were put forward, need therefore not be described as pragmatically ideological, or violently legalistic, because few of these considerations were ever advanced in isolation from other, related ones.

The greater the incidence of issues away from the central intersection, the weaker is consensus on those basic goals near which the issues cluster, and the more pathological is the style in that particular direction. For example, when the most important issues revolve around the constitutional document itself—constant proposals for its amendment or replacement, discussions of its internal consistency, of its effectiveness, of its adequacy in solving the problems different members of the system consider most pressing; if indeed this preoccupation with the constitution leads to the formulation of artificial issues, then consensus is obviously weakest on the content of the basic goal of stability, and the style is legalistic. This situation has been approached, for example, in some periods of the life of the United Nations, as over the issue of the nonpayment of special assessments by the Soviet Union, France, and certain other members. Here the problem was less one of the fiscal viability of the organization, than of the constitutionality of the operations for which the special assessments were supposed to be paid and, therefore, of the stability—or, as some pessimists put it at the time—the survivability—of the United Nations.

For most *sub*systems, preoccupation with only one or two of the four basic goals is quite normal. The judiciary, for example, and parts of the bureaucracy, are subsystems more concerned with stability than with anything else. Both the internal style of these subsystems and their contributions to the style of the system of which they are parts will tend more toward legalism than toward the other three pathological styles (Figure 10). A detail of the square shows, however, that

Figure 10.

Subsystems.

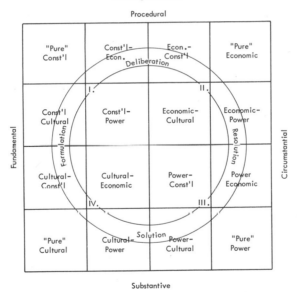

their concern with stability also has aspects of flexibility, efficiency, and effectiveness; and that, while the two phases of the central policy flow to which judiciary or certain sections of a bureaucracy mainly contribute—formulation and deliberation—deal typically with the constitutional aspects of problems, these constitutional aspects have to be looked at from the "purely" constitutional, the constitutional-economic, the constitutional-power, and the constitutional-cultural points of view.

For example, the International Court of Justice at The Hague, in preparing its various judgments on the case of South West Africa, brought before it by Liberia and Ethiopia against the Republic of South Africa, naturally conducted itself more nearly legalistically than did the General Assembly or the Security Council of the United Nations in considering the same problem. This was so because the World Court is specifically responsible for maintenance of the stability of the procedures of world politics through interpretation and application of international law. But the Court did not confine itself to considerations of "pure" law, disembodied from all contextual considerations of economics, power, and culture.

Similar details for the other three squares would show major preoccupation with flexibility on the part of, say, an international development bank during a period of economic growth (II); with efficiency on the part of the professional military in most wars (III); and with effectiveness on the part of ideologues or propagandists, like the United States Information Service in its concern with the American prestige rating abroad (IV).

Useful comparisons can be made by examining the internal political style of similar subsystems, or groups of political personnel in different systems; e.g., the governments of New York and Paris, the general staff corps of France and Germany, or of Weimar, and Bonn, Germany, different firms in the American electrical industry when confronted with the same problem of violations of antitrust legislation, top newspapers in several countries, the judges of international courts before and after World War II, the General Assemblies of the League of Nations and the United Nations, international commissioners for various functional purposes, like health or refugees, in these two periods of history, etc.

This kind of comparison would show, among other things, that the sources of authority of the personnel of these subsystems vary from one system to the next and may vary even more within a single political system. If *authority* is considered a kind of "additive" to central decisions, which leads those who are exposed to the consequences of these decisions to accept them, then the sources of authority can be classified in the same way as issues and consensus. For instance, military heroes have authority among the military as a result of substantive circumstantial achievements, like a general's victories. Some saints have authority among communicants of their religion as a result of more fundamental substantive claims, such as visions of the deity, stigmata, or the performance of miracles. The Supreme Court of the United States enjoys authority among the legal profession and other Americans, because it is identified with the fundamental procedures of the legal profession and of the Constitution. Medical researchers like Dr. Jonas Salk enjoy authority among the public, because they have addressed their innovating methods to the successful solution of current medical problems. I am willing to take the prescriptions my general practitioner issues to me and I regard him as an authority on my ills, because he has solved my medical problems before and because I know him to have been certified by meeting a combination of procedural and substantive requirements. In international politics, too, the occupants of certain offices and even some private individuals command authority because of a combination of procedural and substantive criteria, like the procedure for electing the Secretary General of the United Nations or the reputation, earned in a variety of ways and for a variety of accomplishments, of persons like Eleanor Roosevelt, Albert Einstein, Albert Schweitzer, Bertrand Russell, Jawaharlal Nehru, Pablo Cassals, Lester Pearson, Pope John XXIII, or Martin Luther King.

The Phasing of the Flow of Policy

These are examples of authority drawn mainly from subsystems. Of greater interest are the sources of authority of contributors to the central flow of policy. In a successful system, these sources vary with the phase of the political process in which particular contributors are chiefly involved. To illustrate this, we can take the American problem of the costs of medical care. In Figure 11, each of the four phases of the flow of policy is further broken down into two subphases, one on either side of the axis passing through it. The recognized problem is brought to public attention and (1) formulated as a substantive issue by leaders of affected interest groups, that is, subcommunities whose members are aware (or are being made aware) of having special goals and problems in common. Among these are leaders of underprivileged minority groups like the aged, of labor unions, of the medical profession. The issue is then (2) formulated in such a form that it can be deliberated upon, given the constitution of the system, in this case the fundamental procedures of politics in the United

FIGURE 11.

Subphases of the flow of policy.

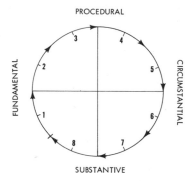

States. In this phase, legal advisers to the groups involved make their contributions, and other lawyers and the courts may also participate (e.g., if constitutional test cases are initiated). Some of the issues arising out of the general problem are formulated by the political parties (e.g., through inclusion of planks in their platforms), and by other national politicians through introduction of legislation (e.g., to change existing social security laws). These issues are (3) deliberated upon in the Congress and, occasionally, by Congressional politicians, the President, and others, outside the Congress (e.g., in public debates and on television interviews). Next, (4) deliberation begins to be carried on increasingly by less "constitutional," more interest-oriented figures, like negotiating agents for the various groups involved, perhaps with the advice of economists and business consultants. The issue will come closer to (5) resolution, perhaps after further litigation, as a result of successful negotiation between the antagonists, or through Congressional action. In Switzerland, a referendum might bring resolution at this particular point. (6) Substantive resolution can also be accomplished through threats or the use of force, as in strikes, sit-in's, or violent clashes between doctors' and patients' organizations and the police. Here men whose authority comes largely from substantive and circumstantial sources would be in charge. After resolution of the issue, (7) solution begins with participation of government and private administrators, like the Surgeon General, hospital and Blue Cross administrators, Social Security Administration civil servants. Finally, (8) the original problem is solved and thereby removed close to the "low" or "grassroots" levels at which it was first recognized through the actions of doctors and patients and subordinate bureaucrats, who operate the new medicare system that has now been set up more or less in keeping with the resolution of the issue. The authority of these people is derived from their identification (which may be a new product of the earlier phases of the process) with the substantive fundamentals of the community.

In an unbalanced system, on the other hand, sources of authority will be out of keeping with the particular phase of the policy flow to which participants contribute. For example, in subphase 3 of deliberation, which calls for authority coming from fundamental procedures, practicing physicians and organizers of the aged may be the main actors. Or in subphase 7 of solution, which calls for authority based on experience with administrative and medical organization, the bargaining agents of medical associations or labor unions may play the most important role. In either case, the success of the system in its handling of this problem would suffer. The mishap in subphase 3 might be an indication of ideological style (and the American Medical Association displayed leanings in that direction during the controversy under discussion). The malfunction in subphase 7 would suggest pragmatic style. If mob leaders or the police had to get involved in subphase 2 of formulation, this would be a manifestation of violent style. If constitutional lawyers opened new issues in the course of subphase 7 of solution, the system would be suffering from undue legalism.

The problem of race relations in the United States was treated in an unbalanced and discontinuous way. Politically conscious members of the colored community and their white supporters first recognized the problem and (1) formulated it as a substantive issue, mainly of racial discrimination reinforced by law. Next (2), procedural formulation in terms of the available "constitutional" channels was performed, among others by lawyers working for the National Association for the Advancement of Colored People (NAACP) and the national political parties. This formulation was designed to facilitate the processing of the problem as it was *then* recognized. Litigation was initiated in lower courts, through adversary proceedings, because that is the best way in which to get any problem "moving" under the legal systems of the Common Law. (3) Fundamental deliberation began mainly in the courts, congruent with the frequently pragmatic-legalistic style of United States domestic politics and sustained by the law-abiding hopefulness of the Negro community. At the same time, especially in Southern states, ideological opponents of desegregation, who had formulated the issue in their own way, refused to participate in deliberation. More circumstantial deliberation (4) involved participation by economic interest groups, e.g., experts on marketing who argued about the economic impact of integration, by psychologists and other social scientists who, among other things, offered testimony during litigation before the Supreme Court. Procedural resolution (5) was apparently given to the issue of school segregation by the Supreme Court in its decisions of 1954, and this resolution approached the more substantive subphase (6), when school districts were instructed by lower federal courts and the Supreme Court about the details of integrating their schools. At this point, the courts' resolution was not accepted, that is, it proved ineffective in some states, and (7) circumstantial solution was attempted with the participation of federal and state troops and police. In a few areas, the original problem was (8) solved fundamentally. In most, however, and for the nation as a whole, the underlying problem was (1) *re*formulated in what was frequently called a "moral issue," which was also perceived in connection with the "image" of the United States in the colored continents of the earth. (2) Procedural reformulation followed in the form of a series of Civil Rights and Voting Bills, which were (3) deliberated in the Congress, between the parties, and in other public forums. (4) More circumstantial deliberation accompanied (3), and it included demonstrations, marches on various capital cities, Washington, D.C. among them, riots in Northern cities, violence from opponents of the projected legislation. (5) Procedural resolution came with the successive passage by the Congress of the relevant bills. This was followed by (6) "executive" action against some remaining hold-outs against the "resolution" of 1954 and its successors, as well as such measures as denials of appropriated funds to school districts judged not to be complying with the new Acts by the United States Commissioner of Education. (7) Substantive solution began, e.g., when federal voting registrars registered Negro voters in selected Southern states and counties. Meanwhile, simultaneously, constant attempts were being made from all sides to reformulate the issue, and deliberation of various issues was being carried on violently (by the Ku Klux Klan), ideologically (by a few fanatic white and black supremacists), legalistically and pragmatically by most of the remainder of the public participants. The style of someone like Dr. Martin Luther King, Jr., came close to purposive compromise. He was willing to use his and his followers' power, nonviolently, in the pursuit of realistically defined goals, within the law of the land, whose adaptation to changed circumstances and changed values he was advocating with "firm flexibility." He was awarded the Nobel Prize for Peace, which helped to "lift" an initially American problem into world politics. Dr. King himself later directed some of the attention of his movement to United States policies in Vietnam, which raised new moral-political problems for American politics in his interpretation.

The processing of problems in the global political system can be analyzed in the same fashion. For example, Great Britain's declaration of its intention to give independence to the colonies of Sarawak, North Borneo (Sabah), and Brunei—all of them located on the island of Borneo, the remainder of which is an integral part of the Republic of Indonesia—created problems for several participants in international politics, both in the Southeast Asian region immediately affected and in the world at large. In the three territories concerned, the indigenous administrations, which had been created only recently, faced the problem of the institutions with which they would operate after independence. The governments and the political parties of two neighboring former British colonies, Malaya and Singapore, contributed to the formulation of this problem as the issue of a federation between themselves and the three territories on Borneo. The Sultan of Brunei resolved that issue for his territory, at least temporarily, by deciding not to join the proposed Federation of Malaysia.

The government of the Philippines used the emergence of this problem in order to assert an old claim of sovereignty over one of the territories, Sabah. President Sukarno of Indonesia used the problem in order to denounce the planned Federation of Malaysia as a neo-colonialist plot of the British. Already by formulating the issues in these different ways, each participant indicated the particular style in which it was going to contribute to the phase of international deliberation. The British and other protagonists of Malaysian federation suggested a United Nations survey of the populations of the affected territories on Borneo, to be conducted on very short notice before the "founding" date. Their position implied a kind of "United Nations legalism." The Philippines, in asserting sovereignty over Sabah, on the basis of the position of the Sultan with whom Great Britain concluded a treaty of protection in the nineteenth century, displayed a more old-fashioned type of legalism derived from conventional international law. At the same time, the Philippine government, and the governments of Japan and the United States (which dispatched the then Attorney General, Robert Kennedy, to attempt mediation with President Sukarno), by trying to effect a reconciliation between the Indonesian and Malaysian governments, either in the context of Asian solidarity, or as third parties friendly to the two principal protagonists, put both legalistic and pragmatic arguments in the service of achieving a genuine purposive compromise. These efforts failed for the time being, partly because of President Sukarno's single-minded focus upon the substantive danger which he recognized in formation of the Federation of Malaysia—which he threatened to destroy by January 1, 1965, and other later deadlines. In alternately violent and ideological style, Sukarno used troop concentrations on the Borneo frontiers, dispatched guerillas into Malaysian territory, cited the massing of some 50,000 British and Commonwealth troops in federal territory as proof of the neocolonialist character of the Federation, and withdrew his country from the United Nations under whose auspices it had gained independence from the Netherlands in the first place, and with whose help it had only recently acquired control of the remaining Dutch colony of West New Guinea.

This concourse of events illustrates how the style of deliberation may be pre-shaped by the motives that lead to original recognition of a problem, and how the same problem may, from various points of view, be formulated in different issues. The phases of the flow of policy may be compressed or extended, and they usually overlap one another. In the course of deliberation, new issues may be formulated, leading to the retroactive recognition of problems different from those that seemed initially to be chronologically prior. Thus, the 50,000 British troops were cited by Sukarno as retroactive corroboration of his claim, made two years earlier, that establishment of the Federation of Malaysia was a neocolonialist plot. Similarly, the resolutions that the process of international politics provided for this series of crises—and the meaning of *crisis* is "time for decision"—may in fact have resolved issues that differed in content from those with which deliberation was originally concerned. Again, as some of the initial problems are solved, to the greater or lesser satisfaction of their recognizers, new problems replace them. For instance, establishment of the Federation solved, for the time being, Great Britain's problem of disposing of its colonial territories on Borneo, but immediately created the new problems of supporting the defense of a threatened new member of the everchanging Commonwealth, and, after expulsion of Singapore from the Federation, of maintaining the British naval base on the island state. For those actors in world politics who were pursuing the goal of decolonization, its apparent achievement with respect to Sarawak and Sabah raised new problems, either of neo-colonialism, or of threats of violence in the region, and of the impaired effectiveness and stability of a major instrument of decolonization, the United Nations.

The Malaysian problem was (1) formulated as a substantive issue for international politics by President Sukarno's opposition to Federation, born in part of his commitment to the ideology of antineocolonialism. It was then formulated in such a form, that it could be deliberated upon, given the "constitution" of the global political system, which includes the United Nations and regional subsystems. In this phase as in others, different participants often formulate different issues and, as a result, they may "talk past one another." For Sukarno the issue was abortion and, later, destruction of the Federation. For the Philippine government, the issue was gaining some acceptance of its legal claim to Sabah. For the Japanese government, the issue was prevention of further violent conflict in Southeast Asia and a return, through its mediation initiative, to active political participation in that area. For the United States, the issue was the maintenance of stability in the area, in the face of Communist Chinese activities of infiltration, subversion, and general extension of influence. For the Chinese government, the issue was wider acceptance of its own peculiar perception of the problems of the region, in terms of American imperialism and neocolonialism, and damage to anti-Chinese and anti-Communist elements in both Indonesia and Malaysia. For most other member states and for the Secretariat of the United Nations, the issue became the continued success of that organization in the face of Indonesia's withdrawal and the continuing problem of the exclusion of Communist China from representation. Just as this was the issue "for most other members" of the United Nations, so the issues as defined above were formulated not necessarily in the same way by *all* members of a government in question, and generally only by most of the participants in the internal policy process of the particular country. There were reports, for example, that some Indonesian politicians opposed Indonesia's withdrawal from the United Nations. This and the anti-Communist violence in Indonesia in 1965 suggested that not everyone agreed with President Sukarno's definition of the primary issue.

These issues, once formulated, were (3) deliberated upon, both bilaterally between the parties most immediately concerned, i.e., Indonesia and Malaysia, and with wider participation in regional conferences, at the United Nations, and elsewhere. At the same time, (4) deliberation was also carried on by less "constitutional," more interest-oriented groups, like the mob that destroyed the British Embassy in Djakarta, or groups in the United States that advocated the termination of American aid to Indonesia. The issues might have been brought closer to (5) resolution as a result of further direct negotiations between the main antagonists, or of litigation before the World Court (as proposed by the Philippines for its claim to Sabah), or of "resolutions" passed by the General Assembly or the Security Council. (6) Substantive resolution was also attempted through threats and the use of force by both Indonesia and Malaysia and its allies in the Commonwealth. After resolution of the issues (which had not yet been achieved at the time of writing), (7) solution could have begun with the participation of civil and military officials of the two main parties to the dispute, of other states, or of the United Nations, conceivably by (among other means) conducting plebiscites or founding a new association of territories linking Malaysia with Indonesia, and possibly the Philippines, in some larger political entity. Solution could also be achieved through the destruction of the Federation or, on the contrary, through replacement of President Sukarno's government by one committed to a policy of "peaceful coexistence" with the Federation. In either case, remnants of the defeated government, whose policy failed, may fail to accept this "solution." As a result of this ineffectiveness of the policy, or as a result of persistent failure to push the problem closer toward any solution, the issue could be kept alive indefinitely, which would probably give international politics in the Southeast Asian subsystem an increasingly ideological style. However, if the circumstantial subphase of solution does succeed, then (8) the original problem and its derivatives may be solved fundamentally and thereby removed in a manner acceptable to the governments of the three excolonial territories on Borneo and the larger political systems involved.

Dynamic Equilibrium

Perfect equilibrium among the four basic goals is hard if not impossible to achieve, and it would not be desirable for purposes of success except under very rare conditions. Members of any nonstagnant political system change their ranking of the priority of goals and of the importance in which problems are recognized. If they start, for example, by considering solution of the problem of independence from outside rule most important, as colonial independence movements have, the initial style of their system may be more or less violently ideological. Once independence is achieved, leaders identified with solution of the problem of colonialism will be regarded as most authoritative in all phases of the political process. If the independence movement develops successfully into a new political system, its style will add elements of pragmatism and legalism, as concern shifts to the basic goals of flexibility and stability, the original problem having been solved (more or less) efficiently and effectively, i.e., in an acceptable fashion. In this kind of development, the phase and the procedures of deliberation would be the last to receive the backing of

FIGURE 12.
Political system moving toward independence.

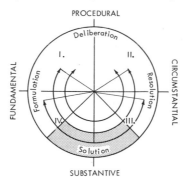

firm consensus (Figure 12). Consensus would initially be strongest on solution of the poorly formulated, undeliberated, and therefore technically "nonresolved" independence problem. But this would be true only within the movement, since between it and the ruling colonial power this would be precisely the area of greatest disagreement, leading to ideologism and violence in the larger system and, eventually, to its breaking apart into two separate political systems, the European "mother country" and the excolony.

The "Third World," as the excolonial, extra-European, generally nonwhite and noncommitted countries have been called, has as a whole passed through an analogous development of its international political style. For the fifteen years after the end of World War II, these countries, whether already states or still colonies, were preoccupied with the substantive goal of independence, on which they were in strong agreement—as shown at the Bandung Conference of 1955—and in the pursuit of which many of them were willing to use any means, including military or mob violence. After the last large group of excolonies achieved independence and membership in the United Nation in 1960, the Third World began to become more pragmatic in its dealings with both West and East, i.e., the parties of the Cold War, and at the same time showed greater concern than previously for the stability of the United Nations system and the elaboration of stable procedures for the internal politics of the Third World as an international subsystem. As evidence for this development, one could cite the Conference of Non-Aligned States held in Belgrade in September 1961, and its successors; the conferences that resulted in the founding of the Organization of African Unity in 1963, and their successors; the United Nations Conference on Trade and Development (UNCTAD) of 1964; and the postponed Algiers Conference of 1965.

By contrast, a subsystem that starts off with an exclusive pursuit of stability, perhaps out of opposition to a dictatorship which, like Adolf Hitler's, was engaged in "permanent revolution," will (1) have an initially legalistic style; (2) slowly pay greater attention to the twin needs of flexibility and popular effectiveness; and (3) finally perhaps reach a point where it is ready to use violence against the oppressive, deliberately unstable regime in order to solve its own crucial problem. The German resistance to Hitler seems to have followed this pattern (Figure 13). Its members began by discussing the legality of resistance to the tyrant (and drafting a new constitution for the *Reich*), then constructed an ideology of resistance on this foundation of constitutionality, considered how to adjust their tactical plans to Hitler's operating procedures and, finally, after several unsuccessful attempts on his life, set off the bomb in his headquarters on July 20, 1944.

FIGURE 13.   FIGURE 14.

Anti-Nazi resistance movement.   *Nazi suppression of resistance.*

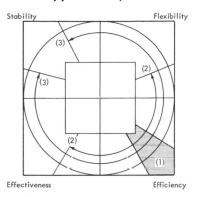

After failure of this plot, the Nazi regime's reactions followed the reverse order, though this development occurred much more quickly. The first reaction (1) was brutally violent in executing the conspirators. It then became somewhat more pragmatic, in the sense that temporary concessions were made where this seemed expedient, e.g., concerning executions. At the same time, (2) the existing antiresistance ideology was quickly elaborated. Finally, (3) the surviving major conspirators were tried by a special "people's court," so that their execution could be presented as "legal" to the public. A diagrammatic description would look like Figure 13, except that the movement starts in (III) not (I), and that final arrows from (III) to (I) would be much farther away from the central intersection of the politics of purposive compromise (Figure 14).

Attempts to regularize and stabilize international politics, like those that culminated in the founding of the League of Nations and the United Nations, have followed a pattern similar to that of Figure 13. First, world peace movements display tendencies toward legalism, e.g., by drafting elaborately detailed world constitutions, which is sometimes combined with an ideology that opposes both militarism and the doctrine of sovereignty. Eventually, members of the movement show greater flexibility, for instance by making concessions to the existence of sovereign states that do control large military establishments and

by a willingness to participate in the founding of international organizations that in fact consist of sovereign states as their primary
members and building blocks. Finally, the peace movement for world
government may even espouse the use by an international organization like the United Nations of military forces supplied by its sovereign
member states and still under their control.

The Value of Responsibility

The comparison of the resistance to Hitler and its subsequent re-
pression by the Nazi government might suggest that the development
patterns of these two or any political (sub) systems are considered of
equal value or, indeed, that this method of comparison pretended to
be *wertfrei*. It does not, for two related reasons. In the first place, the
purpose of comparison is to *evaluate* the relative success of political
systems, success having been defined as a dynamic equilibrium among
the four basic goals. Success was not defined with reference to the
achievement of the always necessarily transient substantive goals of
political systems. However, this criterion of success may be considered
unsatisfactory because, for example, we might at least conceive of an
ideologically violent repressive regime that manages to indoctrinate
its population so thoroughly in its ideology, that it retains sufficient
stability and flexibility to remain effective. No regime like this, not
even those of Hitler or Stalin, has in fact so far "succeeded" in this
sense. On the contrary, the more successful repressive regimes are precisely those that moved away from an exclusively substantive to an
increasingly procedural emphasis in both consensus and sources of
authority.

This objection is, nevertheless, well taken, and the normative assumptions underlying this approach can now be made more explicit. In
the first instance, or in the last instance, or in both, it is individual
human beings who recognize the problems that make up the raw
material of politics, because these human beings are working toward
goals: in the first instance, when individuals deliberately come together, as in modern interest organizations (including peace movements); in the last, when collectivism is at least alleged to serve the
end goal of greater individualism, as according to Karl Marx ("the
free development of *each*. . . ."). Human beings are distinguished
from the rest of creation (or "existence") by their presumed capac-

ity to work deliberately toward perceived goals. What distinguishes them even more is their capacity to invent new goals, e.g., when old ones have been reached. In this respect, human beings, or our understanding of ourselves, resemble political systems (more than our understanding of political systems resembles our understanding of human beings, since the differentiated functioning of political systems is much more accessible to analysis than is the differentiated functioning of individual persons).[19] The individual, as a personality system, also pursues the basic goals of stability, flexibility, efficiency, and effectiveness (in terms of his own built-in or acquired substantive and procedural goals). He or she also has to maintain a dynamic balance in the pursuit of these basic goals. The development of the "behavioral style" of infants or older persons could be described in the categories used here to describe political systems. Infants first are interested only in solution of the problem of hunger. As they grow older, they slowly build up considerable resolution with which to support these solutions, and almost simultaneously they become aware of the alternative, to reach or not to reach for the bottle. Finally they round out the circle of the flow of decisions by becoming capable of deliberating, i.e., "reasoning" about such issues.

Because there seems to be general agreement that human beings are capable of forging new goals for themselves and of working toward their goals, broad consensus might also be reached on the desirability of providing individuals with optimum opportunities for "realizing themselves" in this sense. The norm of individual responsibility could serve as the highest common normative denominator for the two antagonistic camps of the Cold War, and for others, at least philosophically.[20] This norm demands that individuals should be given opportunities to contribute to those central decisions whose consequences will affect themselves; and that their capacity to make such contribu-

---

[19]Plato projected his class analysis of the *polis* unto the individual, in whom he saw as many "elements of the soul" as he recognized classes. Perhaps Freud and other modern psychologists have made somewhat analogous projections from the political systems with which they were familiar to the individual and his psyche, rather than (or, at least, as much as) the other way around. When electronic computers are described as "models of decision-making systems," individual or collective, students of the human brain tell us they do not know enough about the brain to comment on that part of the analogy. One might ask whether inventors of computers got any of their ideas from their perception of the political system.

[20]See Herbert J. Spiro, "Responsibility and the Goal of Survival," *Responsibility: Nomos III* (New York: Liberal Arts Press, 1960), pp. 290–303.

tions should be proportionate to the extent of their exposure to the consequences of these decisions. The balance between opportunity to contribute and exposure to consequences describes the individual's *situation of responsibility*. To be in a sound situation of responsibility, the individual should be provided by the political system with four ingredients:

1. *Foreknowledge* of the probable consequences of his decisions.
2. *Choice* among alternative courses of action.
3. *Resources* with which to realize the choice.
4. *Purpose* or commitment on the part of the system to the norm of responsibility itself.

Without foreknowledge, one's situation in the political system would lack stability; without choice, it would lack flexibility. Without resources, the problems arising out of one's membership could not be dealt with efficiently; and without the system's commitment to the goal of responsibility, its pursuit by the individual would be thwarted even if the other three ingredients were provided. Knowledge and choice are matters of procedure; resources and purpose are matters of substance. Foreknowledge and purpose relate to fundamental goals, choice and resources to circumstantial problems (Figure 15). The pathological systems described by Figures 2 to 5 and 7 to 9 would, each in a different way, unbalance their members' capacity to pursue self-realization, that is, to achieve sound situations of responsibility, by putting one or more of its four ingredients beyond their reach. For this reason, disequilibrium and pathological style can also be criticized systematically from a normative standpoint.

If we compared the international politics of 1935 and 1965, in terms of the situations of responsibility of variously located individuals, what would we find? A Jewish citizen of Germany had better foreknowledge of the probable consequences of his internationally relevant decisions, if he took Nazi policy statements at face value, than an Israeli citizen has today, but his choices were less meaningful, his resources lower, and the Nazi system was openly committed to the antithesis of the norm of responsibility. For ordinary American citizens, the situation in both national and international politics has probably improved with respect to all four ingredients, as it has also for citizens of many of the areas that were colonial dependencies in 1935. A specific policy, like the Treaty of Moscow of 1963 on the partial ban of nuclear explosions, can also be judged by these criteria, as can the "constitution" (again in the broad sense of the word) of the international political system that facilitated the conclusion of that agreement.

FIGURE 15.
The situation of responsibility.

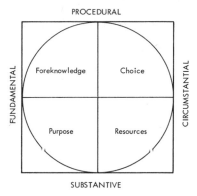

The same "four-dimensional" approach can, incidentally, be applied also to the comparison of such purely military matters as weapons systems, and the great contemporary military establishments use "weapons systems evaluation methods" which, with the use of their own categories, engage in very similar activity. For example, in deciding which of several competing nuclear missile systems to produce, defense planners are concerned not only with the destructive power of the warheads the missiles can carry, i.e., not solely with the power or resources dimension. They are concerned also with the range of launching sites and targets that will be available to the system, i.e., in terms used here, with alternatives. They will take into consideration the comparative capabilities of the guidance systems of competing weapons systems, i.e., the dimension of foreknowledge. And the weapons evaluators will weigh the comparative thrust of the engines of the missiles they are evaluating, i.e., in a sense, the resolution or purpose that can be built into the weapons system. Old-fashioned military analysis like the old-fashioned study of international relations was one-dimensional (power) or, at best, two-dimensional (power and law). Sophisticated contemporary military analysis like political analysis tries to take into account the ideological and economic dimensions as well and, through efforts toward more systematic methods, other dimensions that fit systematically into their "compass."

The Dimensions of the Method

Table 1 shows relations between various dimensions of this approach, which makes possible systematic comparison by allowing the same aspect of any two or more political systems, empirical or normative, to be "plotted" in systematic comparison to one another. Issues are taken as the basic data of politics. Their incidence can be plotted comparatively with reference to the two coordinates, Substantive-Procedural and Fundamental-Circumstantial. These in turn are related to

TABLE 1

Relationships among System Dimensions

Policy Flow						Situation of
Subphase	Phase	Coordinates	Basic Goal	Problem	Style	Responsibility
8		Subst-Fdtl 8	Effectiveness	Cultural	Ideological	Purpose
1	Formulation	Fdtl-Subst 1				
2		Fdtl-Proc 2	Stability	Constitutional	Legalistic	Foreknowledge
3	Deliberation	Proc-Fdtl 3				
4		Proc-Circ 4	Flexibility	Economic	Pragmatic	Choice
5	Resolution	Circ-Proc 5				
6		Circ-Subst 6	Efficiency	Power	Violent	Resources
7	Solution	Subst-Circ 7				
8		Subst-Fdtl 8	Effectiveness	Cultural	Ideological	Purpose
1		Fdtl-Subst 1				

the basic goals of any system, balance between which serves as a criterion of success and, at the level of the individual, of normative judgment. Political style and sources of authority can each be described systematically and in relation to one another. Style and authority can also be related systematically to the political process and to the personnel of politics. The approach also offers a tool for the comparative study of political development of systems and subsystems, in relation to their goals, problems, issues, consensus, sources of authority, types of political personnel, and the phasing of the political process. It also provides a descriptive pathology of politics. As presented so far, systematic description is the main use of this approach. Without systematic description, comparison is difficult. Without sound comparisons, explanations are impossible.

While systematic comparison is its main advantage, the method may also have other merits. Among these is avoidance of any artificial compartmentalization of one and the same system into "polity," "society," "economy," "culture," and so forth. To be sure, any system, including the global one, that is studied by political scientists has all these *aspects,* and sociologists, economists, anthropologists, psychologists, and other "social" scientists have developed their own methods for studying these aspects. The approach outlined here would rely heavily upon information gathered through application of these methods. For example, when we want to compare the efficiency of two systems, we might turn to economics, which seems better qualified than any other "policy science" to relate output to input. Sociologists might be best qualified to study consensus, especially cultural. The several component disciplines of political science similarly have their specialized contributions to make. For example, historians of political philosophy seem best qualified to study the evolution of consensus on fundamentals for periods about which few primary sociological data are available. Jurisprudence is the discipline best suited for the study of procedural fundamentals which, for international politics, are to be found partly in international law. Various "schools" of public and business administration are well qualified to compare systems with regard to their efficiency *and* their stability. Psychologists, in addition to providing insights into the decision process, may be helpful in comparing the flexibility of systems. Students of communications are well qualified to study the flow of policy as it affects consensus, and so forth. But compartmentalization among these several disciplines should be avoided, especially in the study of world politics, because it tempts scholars to think of the objects of their study as separate entities having an existence apart from each other. Any system studied by political science has all these aspects, but what makes it a political system is the processing, by means of certain procedures, of issues arising out of common problems that are obstacles on the road toward evolving goals. The procedures are applied to the whole range of problems faced: economic, power, cultural, constitutional, and others. Each of these problem areas provides the data for the several specialized disciplines. As soon as the problems are converted into issues and introduced into the flow of policy, they are, as it were, raised from the rock-bottom level of givenness, and the community that so raises them is a political system. If no problems are raised in this sense by an otherwise apparently somehow coherent aggregate of human beings, these people do not constitute a political system, except perhaps in the case of a very primitive and therefore prepolitical community, unaware of its problems, its capacity to do something about them, and the feasibility of inventing new goals.

Just as this approach avoids system compartmentalization, so it also avoids mechanical compartmentalization of functions, like legislation, execution, and adjudication, or policy making and policy implementation. Another advantage is the more systematic and more symmetrical relation in this method between functions and the other dimensions of comparison.

Moreover, this approach broadens the conventional identification of politics with power, mainly by returning to (the method, not the substance of) Thomas Hobbes's conception of power, which is wider than most contemporary usage of the term. Two advantages result. First, this method can be applied to *any* political system, regardless of size or scope or historical era, instead of being confined, as most current methods still are, to the state as Max Weber conceived of it. This is particularly useful for the study of international politics, for reasons that should have become clear by now. Secondly, this approach facilitates the systematic inclusion of more factors, and more relevant factors, than are usually considered.

By seeking to conceive of the political in genuinely universal terms, the method facilitates valid analogies while it discourages false ones. This is especially important for the study of international politics, for reasons that have already been pointed out. It should, therefore, make possible the closing of the methodological gap that has been created between the study of international politics and other types of politics (viewed comparatively). Through closing this gap, in turn, some of the relevant findings by comparative students of politics can be brought to bear upon the problems with which students of international politics have been grappling. This should be particularly helpful, because our method is as applicable to "developing" as to developed (or overdeveloped) political systems, and the system of world politics can appropriately be viewed as one that is very much engaged in the process of development.

In the past decade, great energy and some imagination has been devoted to the study of political development. Most of the approaches worked out for that purpose suffer from one or the other of two errors. Either they assume that politics in the developing areas is somehow unique and, therefore, not comparable with politics in the mature Western areas with which we are most familiar. This error leads to the opening of a methodological gap similar to the one between comparative and international politics discussed in Chapter 1. Or they assume that the developing countries will necessarily follow the same pattern of growth, through the same stages and in the same sequence to the same end result, that have been described retrospectively in the historical development of countries like Great Britain. This error leads to false forecasts and, incidentally, harmful policies, because it mistakes apparent parallels for true analogies by universalizing that which happens to be familiar, which is also quite parochial.[21] Our method avoids, among other things, this kind of ethnocentricity and especially one of its most common manifestations, which might be called the "Anglophile fallacy." This fallacy makes universally valid criteria out of "the two-party system," regular alternation in office, a neutral civil service on the current British model, or "stable democracy." It therefore judges the degree of political development of systems by the extent to which they are approaching these "achievements."

A double error is involved in this particular approach. It consists of identifying successful development with a single model, the British, and of confusing the *success* of politics with the *development* of politics. Even among the Western constitutional democracies that are generally considered successful, many different patterns of historical development can be discerned—for example, the British, the American, or the French. However—and this is a more damaging criticism of the Anglophile fallacy—politics may develop without being successful (as judged by different conceptions of success). And politics may be successful (in the same sense), without developing. For instance, when we compare colonial with independent Indonesia, we find the steady development of politics after independence, because an increasing proportion of the population is becoming politically aware and participant, more issues are being generated, and new goals are being in-

---

[21]See Spiro, *Africa: The Primacy of Politics, op. cit.,* chap. 6.

vented. However, according to most students of Indonesian politics and judged by the criteria of success that they use, Indonesian politics has been comparatively unsuccessful in handling the substantive problems which it has been processing. On the other hand, politics on Taiwan has been successful in this last-mentioned sense, but it has not been permitted to develop by the Kuomintang government.

Our method clearly distinguishes between the *development* and the *success* of politics. This distinction is particularly needed for the study of world politics, whose development is so obvious it cannot be denied, but whose success is quite another matter. To illustrate briefly a path of analysis that we will travel in greater leisure in a later chapter: The Anglophile fallacy leads one to welcome patterns of politics that resemble the so-called "British two-party system," a simplifying and therefore distorting concept. The Cold War has introduced this kind of pattern into world politics, at the United Nations and elsewhere. This can be taken as an indication that world politics has indeed "developed," in the sense that participation, the incidence of issues, and the invention of goals has grown in it. However, as judged by most criteria of political success, not only the criterion put forward here, this particular development has not necessarily improved the performance of world politics. Our approach can explain this divergence between development and success:

The two-alternative pattern is unfortunate, mainly for the same reasons that led us to criticize the model of the two-party system: It tends to exaggerate disagreements, which makes deliberation much more difficult than it might otherwise be. This suggests that the two-alternative pattern of politics has merits only in connection with the resolution of issues, not in connection with deliberation. Effective nonviolent resolution is still extremely rare in international politics. And since violent resolution of major contemporary issues could lead to the "extermination of practically everybody"—as the humor of the gallows has called it—the postponement of resolution seems much to be preferred. For this, constant and efficient deliberation, with participation of all interested parties, is required, and the road should be kept open to the introduction of new alternatives. This kind of deliberation is not likely to benefit from the two-camp alignment.[22]

Some Objections

Some objections to the approach of this book can be anticipated at this point. The first of these is likely to be directed at the definition of

---

[22]Spiro, *Government by Constitution, op. cit.,* pp. 458 f.

community that has been used, because it fails to make "the absence or presence of violence as a means to settle disputes" the main criterion.[23] For Ernst Haas, "The ideal type of political community . . . assumes, therefore, that the condition toward which the process of integration is to lead is one in which a sufficient body of general consensus imposes limitations upon the violence of group conflict."[24]

Our notion of community, on the other hand, requires as a minimum (not an "ideal type") only awareness of the pursuit of common goals, and of members' inability to solve alone the problems arising out of these goals. In this sense, there is a community between the parties to a civil or international war, as indeed between the contestants in the current Cold War, e.g., with regard to the goal of the survival of mankind. Nonviolence and loyalty to institutions, other components of Professor Haas's definition, were deliberately left out of ours, even as trends, as part of the effort to shift attention away from the sovereign state and related units. The old focus too easily leads to a preoccupation with questions of "obedience" that seems increasingly anachronistic. Community in our sense of the word is worth studying because there exists within it at least some consensus.

A second objection is likely to be raised against failure to make nonviolence in the settlement of disputes a criterion of the *political system*. All we require of a community to consider it a political system is that it process its issues—regardless of its style, including the incidence of violence, regardless even of failure to solve its problems. The motive was the same as before; for example, there is a global political system and various international subsystems within it. Most of these may not have been very successful, but they do process issues and sometimes solve some of their problems. They have politics and they are certainly worthy of study. Violence is one of several pathological means of conducting politics and should not be excluded from our purview merely because its use fortunately has been reduced and regularized within many, and between some, modern states—but more in some than in others, which again shows the need for including the incidence of violence in comparisons.

A third objection may be made to apparent neglect of *institutions*, like legislatures, executives, judiciaries, and the like. This omission

---

[23]Karl W. Deutsch *et al., Political Community and the North Atlantic Area,* cited by Ernst B. Haas, *The Uniting of Europe* (Stanford: Stanford University Press, 1957), p. xv.

[24]*Ibid.,* p. 6.

was intentional, in order to avoid fallacious comparisons based upon misleading analogies, e.g., between the United States Congress and the Swiss Parliament, or the United States Supreme Court and the International Court of Justice, or the Secretaries General of the Organization of American States and the Organization of African Unity. What matters is not the formal function, like legislation, assigned to an institution, but the phases of the flow of policy to which the institution and its personnel contribute. For example, comparison might show that the Swiss Parliament contributes less to the resolution of major issues than the Congress, because in Switzerland resolution is often provided by the referendum. Availability of the World Court may shape the formulation of issues in world politics less than the Supreme Court shaped the formulation of issues in the early politics of the United States, because there is less consensus now on the procedures of international law than there was then on the procedures of the English Common Law. An African regional executive secretary may have greater opportunities for initiatives in recognizing problems and formulating issues than a Latin American regional executive secretary in his older, stiffer, more formal organization of "less equal" member states. In the global system, formulation has been quite decentralized, except with regard to issues dealt with by some of the older specialized international agencies, like the International Labor Organization. So is resolution, while at least public deliberation is becoming increasingly centralized upon the United Nations. If we looked first for institutions and then asked what functions they performed, we would get a less comprehensive and less comparable picture than we do by first identifying the political process and then asking which subsystems and subcommunities contribute to its various phases.

A fourth objection might be raised against our apparent neglect of the role of *groups*, including international ones, in politics. This would, however, be based upon a misreading of the method. Communities whose members are aware of sharing special problems in common were discussed and are usually described as interest groups. The same is true of some of the subsystems discussed above. Again, use of conventional terms, including "political parties," was avoided on purpose, because it easily leads to universalization of the familiar, e.g., by projecting the American relation between interest organizations and parties onto, say, French or Ghanaian politics, or by assuming that interest groups everywhere are most active in bringing problems to the attention of politicians (subphase 1), i.e., in what Almond calls the articulation of interests, when they may actually contribute more to deliberation or resolution or solution in other political systems.

A fifth objection might be made to the relation between *"society" and the political system* that we have been assuming: which is "prior"? Society and its institutions are chronologically prior in the sense that all deliberately created contemporary political systems, including international ones, were superimposed upon pre-existing social systems. But these political systems often were superimposed precisely in order to bring about changes in the society or, frequently, the several societies comprising them, and changes in their social institutions and values. After this kind of change, and to the extent that it brings intended or unintended results, habits and characteristics conventionally called "social" or "national" become effects rather than causes of political style.

A sixth but certainly not final objection might raise the question of *agreement among investigators*. Even if two students accepted this approach, would they not come up with quite different descriptions of the same phenomena, e.g., the attitudes of participants in the Cuban missile crisis of 1962? Could not one scholar call President Kennedy's style pragmatically legalistic and Chairman Khrushchev's ideologically violent, while another reverses these descriptions? This kind of disagreement should not be possible after further refinement of the method, especially when making comparisons. But even if it were unavoidable, the method would still have the merit of asking sets of questions that are both comprehensive and systematically interrelated.

A Brief Application

Some of the more imaginative recent writings on world politics use as a major focus of comparison of international systems the *number* of major "actors" in a system and the relations prevailing between or among these actors. Morton A. Kaplan, for example, examines "six distinct international systems": "(1) the balance of power system, (2) the loose bipolar system, (3) the tight bipolar system, (4) the universal system, (5) the hierarchical system in its directive and non-directive forms, and (6) the unit veto system."[25] Richard N. Rosecrance dis-

---

[25]Kaplan, *op. cit.*, p. 21.

tinguishes nine different historical systems, among other criteria by their multipolarity, tripolarity, or unipolarity.[26]

The number of important participants in any political system is obviously a significant factor for analysis, and we, too, emphasized the changes that have occurred in this respect in the present century. However, this focus on the number of actors, even when it is balanced by concern for the total context within which their relations with one another are being carried on, sometimes still leads to excessive preoccupation with the "character" of the principal actors to the neglect of their international environment.[27] The following brief discussion of "summit diplomacy" at the time of the abortive summit conference of 1960 should indicate how our method seeks to avoid this particular pitfall.

The most important phases of international diplomacy are being conducted increasingly by the leaders of states and of blocs of states, instead of professional diplomats and military officers as formerly. The leaders' sources of authority and the style of their political systems are therefore of considerable interest. Despite poorer communications, international relations until World War I had a more unified style than they have today. Diplomats and military who, respectively, performed most of the deliberation and resolution, operated within a fairly strong consensus on the rules of diplomacy and warfare. Today, though improved communications have tended to centralize deliberation and sometimes even the formulation of issues upon the United Nations system, such consensus is lacking in the global political system. The sources of authority, for example, of the participants in the summit meeting of 1960 varied widely. That conference, had it not been broken up by Chairman Krushchev because of the overflight of Soviet territory by an American "spy plane," once it had reached agreement on its agenda (formulation of issues), would presumably have conducted deliberation in hopes of reaching resolution or, at least, agreement on the postponement of resolution for issues that, for the time being, could be settled only violently. But of the four participants, only Prime Minister Harold Macmillan had primarily procedural sources of authority, and only Macmillan and President Eisenhower had had much experience with deliberation conducted according to clearly

[26]Richard N. Rosecrance, *Action and Reaction in World Politics: International Systems in Perspective* (Boston: Little, Brown & Co., 1963), chap. 11.
[27]This criticism does not apply to the two books just cited.

understood rules. General De Gaulle's military career and his achievements as leader of the Free French and founder of the Fifth Republic endowed him with quite a different type of authority, somewhat closer to that held by President Eisenhower at the time of his first summit conference, when he was still regarded as the successful leader of the wartime alliance and the first Supreme Commander of NATO, Krushchev's sources of authority, as those of most Soviet leaders of the revolutionary generation, were mainly substantive.

FIGURE 16.

Deliberation of world political issues under such conditions has the disadvantages of an unbalanced system, discussed above. It also changes the types of issues that are generated for world politics. Under traditional diplomacy, typical issues related to legal and power problems. Flexibility was the most persistent goal (Figure 16). Today, cultural-ideological and economic problems, or the cultural and economic aspects of legal and power problems, are more often introduced into the international flow of policy. Stability is the most persistent and most elusive goal. This has a feedback effect by increasing the proportion of ideologically or pragmatically inclined personnel in world politics, e.g., in the case of the United States, the U.S. Information Agency and the Central Intelligence Agency. Ideologism and pragmatism have been described as true opposites, as have legalism and violence. This means that they cannot "co-exist" in a system at any one moment. This fits the international system, in which one political style is usually succeeded by its opposite. While von Clausewitz's dictum was still valid, war *was* the continuation of diplomacy by other means. Today, subversion and guerrilla warfare are the parallels to, and the continuation of, ideological propaganda by other means. Perhaps this is the crucial difference between old-fashioned international relations and world politics in the era of the Cold War.

The importance of propaganda and the possibilities presented by world-wide communications suggest another use to which this approach might be put. An understanding of the style of a political system and its subsystems in terms of the categories suggested here can be of help in deciding how to "pitch" one's appeal or what sort of "image" to present. Specialists in public relations have, of course, been doing that for decades, in terms of their own categories, and the great propoganda agencies are doing it today. Skillful politicians of all ages have accomplished the same thing more or less intuitively. Most opinion polls or attitude surveys concentrate upon the substance of their subjects' feelings, and this substance has been known to change even more rapidly and more radically than the content of the issues themselves. By getting an accurate and systematic picture of the style of politics along lines suggested here, on the other hand, one should be able to get at the more enduring patterns of attitudes and behavior, because this approach focuses on the manner in which people are likely to process whatever problems come their way, rather than on specific reactions to the substance of particular problems. This should be of some use in world politics, too, because of the quick succession of vast changes in the problems that make up its raw material.

This instability and the fluctuating, overlapping, intermeshing, clashing, simultaneously centralizing and fragmenting, expanding and contracting character of world politics points to one final advantage of our method, which has already been discussed. Whether the function of boundary maintenance was transferred to political science from biology or physics, in conventional sovereign nation states internal boundary maintenance is an academic fiction or an ideological jargon, and external boundary maintenance is taken care of by the military together with customs and immigration police. But students of politics are no longer primarily concerned with this unit of politics. Political science is concerned with politics at all levels, in all kinds of communities. Today, and in the immediate future, its attention will be drawn especially to the politics of the global community of mankind, in and for which a political system is being built up. And the boundaries of that political system do not have to be "maintained," they only have to be grown into.

Chapter 4

The Evolution of Political Style

International Relations: 1898–1918

To get a proper historical perspective on the environment of contemporary world politics, this chapter will draw comparative sketches of three periods: that of the League of Nations, i.e., roughly the years between the ends of World War I and World War II (1918–45); the two decades before this quarter century (1898–1918); and the two decades since (1945–65).

The system of European international relations between 1894 and 1914 came closer than its successors, which grew out of it, toward achieving a dynamic equilibrium, in which issues cluster around the central intersection of the Procedural-Substantive and the Fundamental-Circumstantial axes. It was characterized by considerable procedural stability due to agreement on the rules of diplomacy. There was little challenge on the substantive fundamentals of "bourgeois capitalist" European culture. Despite occasional outcroppings of legalism, e.g. in proposals for creation of a world court or in conclusion of treaty networks much less complex than those of the present, comparison with the later periods shows no excessive preoccupation with the goal of stability before World War I. Whenever diplomacy conducted for limited goals was relieved by wars conducted for limited goals, there seemed to be almost as much consensus on the rules of warfare as on the rules of peaceful negotiation between the powers. This consensus was somewhat weaker on the geographical periphery of the European state system: for example, in the Boer War between the British and the Boer Republics in South Africa, the British were accused of introducing the institution then for the first time referred to as the concentration camp; and the Russo-Japanese war of 1905 was not fought entirely according to the rules, either. But these were not wars between members of the European system, because they fought no wars directly among themselves during this period until the outbreak of the Great War in 1914. And that war, at least in its outbreak and for the most part during its duration of four years, observed the rules of diplomacy and warfare to a remarkable degree, considering the tremendous technological innovation that had taken place immediately preceding it. Military action commenced only after war had been properly declared, diplomatic immunity was respected; with few exceptions, prisoners of war were treated in accordance with the treaties governing their treatment; and the distinctions between combatant and civilian individuals, between belligerent and neutral states, were maintained. In other words, both substantive goals and procedural framework of the international system of this period were sufficiently effective to keep ineffective any open challenges to the system itself. Issues and even wars were kept contained within the system—until it began to fall apart as a result and in the aftermath of World War I.

Consensus on matters of substance and procedure was maintained, however, without such excessive concern, that important issues were handled in an ideological style, although at least two of the major governments were occasionally influenced by highly ideological internal movements with international goals, like Pan-Slavism and Pan-Germanism. Most of the governments, however, during most of this time, were at least as much concerned with the flexibility as with the effectiveness and the stability of the European system. Both the vague, long-run substantive goals of the system and its procedures were gradually adapted to the great substantive changes that were transforming Europe and, largely under Europe's influence, the rest of the world. A population explosion, mass production, the affiliation of colonially or imperially acquired or dominated territories with European economies as suppliers of raw materials and consumers of mass produced goods, and improvements in communications and transportation were among the more important of these substantive changes. The procedures of both diplomacy and warfare proved sufficiently flexible, on the whole, to contain them within the established system. Until World War I, governments and their diplomats, in their dealings with other states, were generally protected against publicity, the press, and similarly "democratic" influences. Diplomacy was conducted in secret, and the etymology of the title of a *Secret*ary of State still made practical sense. World War I was fought by mass armies of unprecedented size, using weapons of unprecedented destructive efficiency, some of which were quite new, like poison gas and armored tanks. Still, the older consensus of the professional military on the rules of warfare, with its prenational chivalric origins, was strong enough to survive World War I. Submarine warfare, introduced by Germany, constituted a partial exception, in that the U-boats indiscriminately attacked naval vessels and commercial and passenger ships, irrespective of their status as belligerents or neutrals, and on several occasions machine-gunned lifeboats with survivors. This practice was, however, officially condemned by both Germany and the Allies, and a German court tried and convicted a number of German naval officers and enlisted men for having committed such crimes. While warfare under the sea thus tested procedural consensus to the breaking point, warfare above the earth, i.e., aerial combat appeared to be simultaneously the most chivalrous and the most novel form of armed contest.

A comparison of the style of international politics at the midpoint of this period, 1904, with the midpoints of the second and third periods, 1932 and 1955, would show a more central clustering of issues at the first than the second or third midpoints, and an increase in the incidence of issues during the interwar and post-World War II periods. Some analyst might even offer the judgment that international relations was performing better at the height of World War I, despite the enormous numbers of casualties, than at any time since, because the European system itself retained greater stability than later and, therefore, the great costs of the Great War could be debited to the commitment of the various participants to the fundamental values—as each of them interpreted these—of the old European state system. One could counter this interpretation by asking whether any political system that is transformed as much as this one was between, roughly, 1917 and 1920, can be accorded this high a comparative evaluation. The trouble with both the interpretation and its critique is due to excessive periodization and the fallacy of arguing *post hoc, ergo propter hoc*. The human mind creates historical periods in retrospect, but these intellectually convenient categories should not delude one to assume that a specific point in time concretely marked the end of one and the beginning of another temporal compartment. To the human actors at that "point," no interruption or qualitative difference "before and after" appears. And simply because the deterioration of the postwar period followed upon World War I, does not mean that it was wholly or necessarily caused by the war, anymore than the sounder prewar period *had* to degenerate into the great military conflict.

International Politics: 1918–45

In the course of World War I and the years following it, the European system of international relations was transformed: Its membership was changed, as were its substantive goals and its procedural "constitution."

The change in membership was the most evident of these major alterations. One of the traditional great powers of the Concert of Europe, Austria-Hungary—host to the Congress of Vienna which had established the constitution for the era now concluded—ceased to exist. It was succeeded by many small and relatively powerless, mostly "national" states, including culturally German rump Austria, culturally Magyar Hungary, binational Yugoslavia, and trinational Czechoslovakia. One of the other traditional great powers of the Concert of Europe was transformed less in its territorial scope than in its inner substance. As a result of the Bolshevik Revolution of 1917, Russia, once the most zealous member of the Holy Alliance, was renamed the Union of Soviet Socialist Republics. Its leaders proclaimed their country to be the vanguard of revolutions in other European and non-European countries by the "workers of the world," that is, members of the proletariat, an internationally defined class. Already during the war, and to the dismay of Russia's Western allies—France, Great Britain, and eventually the United States—the Bolshevik leadership in effect denounced the existing system of international relations, opted out of the Alliance by concluding the Peace Treaty of Brest-Litovsk with the Central Powers, and began its attempts to promote workers' and soldiers' uprisings against the war in other European countries. The Russian class that had previously furnished diplomats and military officials was "liquidated," and professional revolutionaries now began to perform its functions.

One great power was eliminated and another was transformed.

Equally important was the addition of a third, the United States of America, which, during World War I became, for the first time, unequivocally a member of the international political system. Under President Woodrow Wilson, the United States in a sense took so seriously the tacit assumptions upon which the European system had been based, that it made these assumptions explicit and carried them to their logical conclusions. This was true particularly of the nationality ingredient of the concept of sovereign statehood: "As Woodrow Wilson put it, the Central Empires had been forced into political bankruptcy because they dominated 'alien peoples over whom they had no natural right to rule.' With the aid of a little sleight of hand the original claim that individuals must consent to or contractually establish the governments ruling them is thus transmuted into the natural right of nations to determine their own statehood."[1] President Wilson expanded this nationality ingredient into the universal right of national self-determination.

Wilson's advocacy of "Open covenants of peace, openly arrived at," in the first of his Fourteen Points, was related, perhaps in a specifically American way, to national self-determination. If statehood is legitimized (or made effective, in our sense) by common cultural nationality, then one could argue that secret treaties, arrived at in the closed chanceries of the Old World, lacked the authority needed to make them effective for those who would be affected by their consequences. The connection was specifically American, because American politics had been conducted democratically for much longer than the politics of the oldest of the major European democracies, France, and democratic politics demands and thrives on publicity, the opposite of secrecy. American politics had also been successfully constitutionalized-by-design for longer than politics anywhere else in the world. (British politics were constitutionalized long before the founding of the United States—not "by design" but by slow, unplanned accretion.) What, therefore, was more natural than the "grand design" of the American President, who had previously been an excellent professor of political science, for the simultaneous constitutionalization *and* democratization of international politics? The principle of national self-determination provided democratization and contributed

[1]Rupert Emerson, *From Empire to Nation: The Rise to Self-Assertion of Asian and African Peoples* (Cambridge: Harvard University Press, 1960), p. 297.

toward the removal of those barriers which had previously shielded governments and diplomats against the allegedly "fickle" ebbs and tides of a public opinion, which had at any rate played a much less important role in Europe than in the United States. Now self-determination was to be brought into the game of international relations in the extreme form of plebiscites of self-determination, in which whole populations were asked to determine by majority vote which state they wanted their territory to join.

Constitutionalization of international relations was to be provided by the League of Nations, of which Woodrow Wilson was a principal architect, though his own country, the United States, failed to become a member—ironically as a direct result of the open operations of a somewhat nationalistic constitutional democracy. The democratically elected United States Senate, which must under the Constitution ratify all treaties negotiated by the President before they become effective as "the law of the land," turned down the treaty of accession to membership in the League of Nations after a great public national debate. The United States was not the only major power that stayed out or was kept out of the League of Nations. The Soviet Union did not become a member until 1934, only to be excluded once more in 1939 as a result of her war against Finland. Japan was included as a founding member, a fact that formalized the extension of the scope of the system of international politics to East Asia. But Japan resigned in 1932 as a result of its war against China. Germany was admitted only in 1926, but withdrew contemptuously soon after Hitler's accession to power in 1933. Italy, as the least powerful or least victorious of the Allied Powers of World War I, was a founding member, but was ineffectively censured over her aggression against Ethiopia (which, with Liberia, was one of only two sub-Saharan African members of the League). Many other smaller states, especially Latin American ones, acquired and dropped, and in some cases reacquired, their membership. This incompleteness and irregularity of membership, shown on Table 2 (page 122), was, however, not the main cause of the failure of this attempt to constitutionalize—to provide a more stable procedural framework for—the international relations which were, during the interwar period, being substantively transformed into international politics. A more important reason for this failure was the open opposition on the part of European statesmen and diplomats to Woodrow Wilson's goals, and their will to carry on with the conventional procedures of international relations among sovereign national states—within the framework of the Covenant of the League, where that was convenient, outside it, where that was more convenient.

This will to perpetuate the old procedures—despite or because of the fact, that the old consensus on them had been disrupted by the changed membership of the state system—this will was written into the Covenant, which served as the League's constitution. The opening words of the Covenant demonstrate this: "The High Contracting Parties," that is, sovereign states, proclaimed themselves as the founders. (By contrast, in the opening words of the Charter of the United Nations, "We, the Peoples of the United Nations", speak.) It would have made very little sense for a book on international politics of this period to begin its central part with a chapter on the League, because it was not central and it did not manage to centripetalize international relations upon itself. Instead, it contributed to the continuing centrifugalization of international processes, in the dual sense of geography and political style.

Compared with the period before World War I, the style of international politics between the wars became increasingly ideological and violent, legalistic and pragmatic. Its "ideologization" was largely a function of world-wide irregular trends toward the democratization of national politics and, with them, of foreign policies. It was therefore brought about also by the revolutionary forces at work within states both old and new. In the Russian Revolution, action based on the Marxist ideology, as emended and amended by Lenin, first won power, and then motivated the government in its single-minded pursuit of communism at home and the world over. But ideologism was not unique to Russia, it only appeared there in its most extreme form, which soon evoked ideological reactions and echoes in other countries, in both their domestic politics and their foreign policies. France, Britain, and the United States sent troops to Russian territory in order to interfere on the anti-Communist side in the Civil War that followed the Revolution and the general Armistice of 1918. In Hungary and some German states, Communist movements inspired by and linked to the Bolshevik Revolution won control of governments.

These events generated reactions from the extreme right of the political spectrum, internal violence on a large scale and with it a spiraling ideologism. Even in countries with more successful political records, like the United States and the United Kingdom, external anti-

Bolshevism flowed over into internal anticommunist persecution, even in the absence of significant domestic Communist parties. This in turn had a feedback effect on the style of foreign policies and of international politics. During this period not only Marxism-Leninism, but also Mussolini's fascist and Hitler's national socialist doctrines received their full elaboration, which toward the end of the era predictably and logically led Hitler to launch World War II. His overwhelmingly substantive war goals included above all the establishment of his "One Thousand Year Reich," in which the Aryan master race would dominate Europe and through Europe the "inferior races" of the rest of the earth.

The great ideologies which motivated much foreign policy during this period leaned toward violence, to be exercised in both national and international politics. According to Marxism, the majority dictatorship of the proletariat overcomes the exploiting minority dictatorship of the capitalist bourgeoisie only through the "violent birth-pangs" of revolution (with the possible exception of a few advanced countries, like Holland or the United States). The virtue of this revolutionary violence was easily transferred from the realm of domestic politics to that of international politics, especially after the Bolshevik Revolution had failed everywhere but in Russia, thereby leaving the Soviet Union as the only "socialist state" and spokesman for the universal working class, encircled by the capitalist powers, which were alleged to have organized the League of Nations as an "anti-Soviet bloc." In Communist ideology, therefore, it was as easy to justify international violence against states ruled by the exploiting capitalists, whether in the form of declared, open war or undeclared covert subversion, as it was to justify internal class warfare against remnants of the old exploiting classes of Russia.

The Fascist ideologies glorified violence for its own sake and because it was the ultimate expression of human power. A highly vulgarized form of social Darwinism led them to assert the "survival of the fittest," which for Hitler meant the racially fittest and purest. Only the racially purest national community would be victorious in the international struggle for survival, and the violent purging from the national organism of threats to its purity, like the German Jews, was justified as easily as the violent liquidation of large masses of "racially inferior" foreigners, like Poles and Ukrainians. Similarly, though on a smaller scale and with less success, Mussolini used technologically superior military means against Ethiopia in a vainglorious effort to restore the grandeur of the Roman Empire and thereby fulfill the mission which the "sacred egoism" of his brand of Fascism had assigned to the Italian nation.

It seems in retrospect that the style of this period would have been more violent than that of the preceding one even without this specific inclination of its predominant ideologies, for even international politicians of the old school, who tried to maintain their traditional desire for diplomatic flexibility, were readier than before World War I to resort to international violence on extremely pragmatic grounds. This was true, for example, in relations between victors and vanquished in the postwar period with respect to the reparations payments imposed by France and her Allies upon Germany. France during her occupation of the German Rhineland, and Germans in their resistance, were quite free with threats and the actual use of violence against each other. Pragmatically motivated violence also showed up in certain other geographic regions. In Central America, the United States imposed its will to political and fiscal order upon a number of countries by military means. In South America, the immensely bloody Gran Chaco War between Paraguay and Bolivia literally decimated the population of some areas for entirely unideological, pragmatic reasons. In the Balkans, pragmatically motivated international conflict was customary. Japan's expansion in the Far East, mainly at the expense of China, though it was later inspired by a type of nationalistic militarism that bore all the earmarks of an ideological system, was initially closer to the kind of pragmatism that it well expressed by the motto, "might makes right." Thucydides put this pragmatism in the mouth of the Athenians, in their famous dialogue with the defeated Melians: "You know as well as we do that right, as the world goes, is only in question between equals in power, while the strong do what they can and the weak suffer what they must."[2] Japan and China, both members of the League, whose Covenant made them proclaim their "acceptance of obligations not to resort to war," were not equals in power, so that Japan could take over Manchuria, while China suffered this depradation and similar ones from Japan and other more powerful states.

Not only violence, but also legalism could be pragmatically or

---

[2]Thucydides, *The Peloponnesian War,* chap. xvii (Modern Library edition), p. 331.

ideologically justified during this period and showed up in more extreme form than before World War I. The founding of the League itself was evidence of an almost ideological commitment to international constitutionalism by its sincerest protagonists, including Woodrow Wilson. Those, on the other hand, who exploited the new procedures which the League made available to the pursuit of their several national interests, displayed a style best described as legalistically pragmatic. The former hoped that international relations could be stabilized through constitutionalization to such an extent, that the need for violence would be eliminated. The latter were willing to use legal pretexts which the Covenant offered them to enhance their over-all maneuverability, including the maneuverability of their means of violence. The former liked to believe that the Covenant of the League and such later treaties as the Kellogg-Briand Pact—through which the United States became a legal participant in the attempted outlawry of war—would make national armaments increasingly unnecessary and that the time for legal disarmament had, therefore, come. A series of disarmament conferences were held during this period that was to culminate in the greatest arms race and the greatest war of history up to that time. Even these conferences manifested the fixation with stability of these years. Each conference tried to fix the existing ratio of armaments among the major powers by calling for the proportional reduction of naval or military troops and equipment—as though the substance of the world were still so stable, that *relative* "power" ratios, even if they could have been ascertained, could have been kept absolutely fixed forever. The legal facade of the League was also used by those who lacked the resolution to resist ideologically inspired international violence, in order to justify the low level of their resistance or their complete noninterference. This was true, for instance, of the antisubmarine action by means of which, according to Anthony Eden, Mussolini's "pirate submarines" were sent scurrying back to their ports; of the "neutrality" of Britain and France in the ideologically motivated Spanish Civil War despite Italy's and Germany's open military support of General Franco's rebellion; of nonintervention against Italy's attack on and conquest of Ethiopia; and of failure to apply meaningful sanctions to the Soviet Union during the Soviet-Finnish War. All of these "appeasements" were justified by reference to the letter of the Covenant, so that pragmatic legalism lost out to ideological violence.

The main contrasts that this "snapshot" comparison of the two periods should bring out are these: The incidence of issues between the two World Wars tended more toward the extremes of style, while it gravitated toward the center of the politics of purposive compromise before World War I. Before the war, the powers were generally ready to use limited violence on behalf of deeply cherished and limited, reasonably realistic, balanced goals. After the war, some nationalistic movements advocated the use of international violence for its own sake or on behalf of unlimited, unrealistic, and unbalanced goals. In the well-ordered European system of the earlier period, statesmen and diplomats wanted above all to preserve their flexibility. In the apparent anarchy of the later period, international politicians attempted in vain and by a variety of mutually contradictory means to impose permanent stability upon an expanded and expanding international system. Ideologism shows up most strongly in the pathology of interwar political style. The governments of the previous period were so consciously convinced of the rightness of their own goals, so protected against domestic democratic interference with their foreign policies, and so unconsciously committed to the goals of the European system, that they did not need ideological justification. Their successors between the wars were deficient in all three respects, with the result that ideological rhetoric and action mounted as they drew nearer to World War II.

One further important contrast emerges from this comparison: There was more genuinely international activity after than before World War I. The international system had to carry a heavier load of issues and this contributed toward its deterioration, because it seems doubtful whether the postwar system could have processed successfully even the lighter load of politics which the prewar system had managed to handle. If an organization like the League of Nations had existed before World War I, chances are that it would have had much less to do than the League. This is a hypothetical comparison of international activity in the two periods. A more realistic one can be made between the Great Depression that began in 1929, triggered by the bankruptcy of an Austrian bank, and any previous economic disaster of international scope in the preceding century. No economic event before 1929 had had effects as widespread or as massive as the Depression. None engendered as much awareness all over the world of the mutual interdependence of national economies within the international economy. The causes of this interdependence were variously interpreted. Communists pointed to the final stages of international monopoly capitalism, Socialists to the irrationality of unplanned national economies, Liberals to the restrictions imposed by national tariffs upon the automatically optimal mechanisms of the international market, and the Nazis to a conspiracy by international Jewry. But all of these explanations contained internationalist elements, and all sought to make the economic catastrophe popularly understandable, which affected the masses of populations in all the industrial countries. This again contributed toward increasing ideologism in national and international politics.

In World War II itself, the tendencies toward extreme ideologism and violence came to the fore most dramatically and most disastrously. Hitler launched the war for ideological reasons and with ideologically defined goals. On the other side of the globe, the Japanese militarists, who did not share the European ethic of their profession, began to elaborate a religiously ramified and racially oriented ideology in support of their war goals. The Western Allies, especially the United States and Great Britain, responded to the challenges of ideology and violence by demanding unconditional surrender and by subjecting German and Japanese cities to strategic bombing and two Japanese cities to atomic bombings. The Soviet Union, after the German invasion of Russia, mobilized the ideologies of Soviet Communism and Russian nationalism in its costly and successful defense and was able, at the end of the war, to install in the liberated Balkan countries regimes tightly tied to it by bonds of common ideology and controls of Soviet armed might.

World Politics: 1945–65

The dropping of atomic bombs on Hiroshima and Nagasaki makes it much easier to draw a dividing line between the middle and the last of our three periods, than between the first and the second. The availability of nuclear weapons, within a few years of each other, to both the United States and the Soviet Union, introduced an unprecedented and qualitative difference. The equally novel difficulty of producing a nuclear arsenal, which delayed "operational" proliferation for more than twenty years after 1945, led to the creation of two initially rather rigid blocs as the main actors in world politics and thereby introduced a relational difference between the second and third periods much greater than that between the first and second.

During both the first and second periods, there was still a large enough number of relatively independent major actors to make it possible for one of these, usually Great Britain, to play the role of balancer in the balance of power and of powers. This is no longer possible on a global scale, and efforts by some uncommitted states to play the role of balancers have generally failed. It seems impossible even within each of the two great blocs, e.g., small communist states have so far failed in trying to work out a balance of power or of ideology between the Soviet Union and China. Similarly, members of the Western alliance, despite the overwhelming power of the United States, have been unable to work out a balance of power or of strategy between the United States and France under President De Gaulle.

After World War II, the previously noticeable trend toward ever more extreme ideologism continued in world politics. Except for Cuba, the most dangerous clashes between the two great blocs occurred in countries divided, and/or liberated from colonial rule, as a result of the war or of its aftermath: Germany, Korea, China, Lebanon, Indochina, the Congo. There the two great power blocs confronted each other, directly or indirectly, in open military posture. One could, therefore, place the interpretation of unidimensional *Realpolitik* upon these conflicts and upon the whole period, and say that only military power mattered during these years and that the ideologism of public propaganda provided only camouflage for the contemporary act of the old drama of power. However, a number of facts contradict this interpretation. One of these is the very sparing actual use that was made of the vast power available to the blocs. Nuclear weapons were never used, but equally remarkable was the fact that the conventional armies of members of the two blocs did not exchange blows across the boundaries of the blocs, except within countries divided between the blocs, as in Korea, where United States and other troops of its "Western" bloc, under United Nations auspices, fought directly against Chinese troops.

The low level of violence used in the period since 1945 is directly related to the heightening of ideological fervor as an operative motive in world politics. Soviet ideology had interpreted World War II from a Marxist-Leninist point of view, and the emergence of the Soviet Union from the war, intact and immensely strengthened in its relative position, seemed to confirm this interpretation. The Western Allies under leadership of the United States, in turn, reacted to the threat of communist expansion, which they recognized initially in Europe, from the Red Army, by constructing a counterideology which, in its more extreme forms, attributed all evil anywhere in the world to the "international communist conspiracy." Attempts were made, not always under government auspices, to construct the ultimate in self-contradiction, an "ideology of freedom." On a more profound, more subtle, less self-conscious, and, therefore, probably more effective level, a whole new conceptual vocabulary was forged which may have become the functional equivalent of an ideology. The key to this vocabulary is the term *totalitarianism*, which is meant to describe *and* to explain such diverse political systems as Nazi Germany and the Soviet Union, all of which are said to develop and function according to inherent laws or an inner logic, which of necessity drives them to pursue an expansionist foreign policy. To resist this, the "Free World," another term of ideological coinage, was exhorted to use various ingredients of its power, according to various "strategic doctrines," first for purposes of "containment," then in a policy of "massive retaliation," and thereafter alternately in the strategies of "counterinsurgency" and "graduated responses."

This ideological panoply was hammered out by Western ideologues in defense against the communist threat, and also in order to cement the Western alliance. Possession of nuclear weapons inhibits the use of power not only against the enemy, but also against one's allies. Apart from reducing or removing economic and technical assistance, what can the Soviet Union do against China's ideological recalcitrance? What can the United States do about De Gaulle's "sabotaging" NATO, the European Economic Community, and American policy in formerly French Indochina? The less can be done through the threat or the exercise of military power, the greater the need to construct ideological substitutes for military power, and the greater the hope that ideological or legal ties can provide the defensive stability that power itself no longer provides.

The high fear of nuclear violence and the low incidence of any violence are reflected, therefore, in comparatively increased ideologism and legalism in world politics. Legalism probably would have increased in any case after World War II, since all the major powers of

1945 joined the United Nations which, like the League, encourages legalism but, unlike its predecessor, came much closer toward having a universal membership. Legalism was further encouraged by the peculiar political style of the United States, the most important member of the UN, because, among other things, it pays a much heavier proportion of the organization's expenses than any other single member and because it is the host to Secretariat, Security Council, and General Assembly. Its constitutional history and structure give the domestic politics of the United States a peculiar style of pragmatic legalism, in which most important problems are subjected to constitutional litigation in the course of their processing. Legally trained personnel predominate in American politics. Frequently the leaders of the United States delegation to the UN have been lawyers with a special penchant for constitutional controversy, like Ambassador Adlai Stevenson and the former Associate Justice of the Supreme Court, Ambassador Arthur J. Goldberg. Moreover, from the time of the founding of the United Nations, in San Francisco, many Americans have viewed its prospects by analogy to those of the thirteen North American states that combined into the United States under their federal Constitution. This analogy is so obviously false that its refutation here is superfluous. It suffices to say that this analogy can help to explain the frequent legalism of United States conduct—e.g., Ambassador Stevenson's "arraignment" of Soviet Ambassador Zorin in the Security Council during the Cuban missile crisis of 1962,[3] or U. S. policy on nonpayment of special assessments by the Soviet Union, France, and others, during the session of the 19th General Assembly in 1964–65.

The pragmatism of world politics has also been more extreme after World War II than before, but unlike the pragmatism of conventional international relations, it results not from any stable desire to maintain flexibility on behalf of effectiveness and efficiency, but rather from the need of the major participants to extricate themselves from the particular *cul de sac* into which ideologism or rigid legalism has driven them, and to do so without recourse to the use of nuclear weapons and without destruction of whatever consensus on new international procedures may have been built up since the founding of the United Nations.

The issue of the nonpayment of special assessments, just men-

---

[3]United Nations Security Council, *Official Records,* 17th Year, 1962, S/1025, pp. 10–12.

tioned, can illustrate this point. The Soviet Union refused to pay its share of the peace-keeping operations in the Middle East and the Congo, on grounds that these operations had been improperly authorized by the General Assembly instead of the Security Council (where the Big Five can exercise their veto). An advisory opinion of the International Court of Justice held that Article 19 of the Charter applied as much to special assessments as to regular dues, that is, that a member could be denied his vote in the General Assembly for failure to pay the equivalent of two years' dues. The American Department of State got the United States Congress to pass a joint resolution which, in effect, "took the brakes out" of the drive of the U.S. delegation to get the Soviet Union to pay, or to deprive it of its vote. But when both sides to this controversy and the majority of members not directly affected by it realized that this legalistic rigidity (by both Americans and Soviets) might destroy the UN, a compromise was reached (to be broken only at the end of the session of the General Assembly by Albania, evidently speaking for communist China), under which the whole session was conducted without taking any roll-call votes at all. Pragmatism here could be described as having become mere opportunism. Before the beginning of the twentieth General Assembly, the United States finally announced that it would drop its demands under Article 19, for the sake of enabling the Assembly to function once more.

In many instances, the opportunism has been even more erratic, and more or less cynical. Rigidities on both sides on the unclear legal situations in the major crises over Berlin could be prevented from having more serious and widespread consequences only through very pragmatic adjustments, under which both parties deviated substantially from the fundamental legal and ideological goals to which they were avowedly committed. Something similar happened before conclusion of the Korean armistice in 1953, and during the simultaneous crises over Hungary and Suez in 1956. A more extreme form of pragmatism has been practiced by the two superpowers when they have deviated completely from the fundamental goals and international operating procedures to which they were, and continue to be, most deeply committed. The best illustrations for this have to be taken from United States intelligence operations, because Soviet intelligence operations of this type are not publicized and because Soviet ideology countenances "progressive" subversion of the kind that occurs in "national liberation wars." But certain operations of the U.S. Central Intelligence Agency were in clear contradiction to the clear substantive and procedural commitments of the United States. Among these operations are the overthrow of the government of President Arbenz of Guatemala in 1954, the support of rebels against President Sukarno, and organization of the abortive refugee invasion of Cuba by opponents of Premier Castro in 1961.

An interesting case arose in 1960, when President Eisenhower admitted that regular overflights of the Soviet Union by U–2 "spy planes" of the CIA had taken place with his knowledge and approval and thereby gave Premier Khrushchev an opportunity to prevent the summit conference then about to start in Paris. In the earlier two periods, certainly before World War I, no head of state or chief of government ever made such an admission. Certainly no President of the United States would or could have—in view of the restricted espionage activities of the American government. Though espionage was generally considered necessary and though the major European powers regularly engaged in it, diplomats and military officers of the old school did not look upon spies as colleagues or comrades, or upon espionage as a normal instrument of diplomacy. Many would have agreed with Henry L. Stimson, when he said, "Gentlemen do not read each other's mail."[4]

President Eisenhower, however, went to the other extreme by not only admitting that the U–2 plane which had been shot down over the Soviet Union had flown its mission with his permission but asserting that these spy flights were consistent with the "Open Skies" proposal he had made earlier to the United Nations. "Open Skies" would have enabled each of the two major nuclear powers to inspect the other's territory *in lieu* of on-the-ground nuclear inspections. Since the Soviet Union had rejected this proposal as a violation of sovereignty and a cover for espionage; and because it was a "closed society" un-

---

[4]". . . Stimson adopted as his guide in foreign policy a principle he always tried to follow in personal relations—the principle that the way to make men trustworthy is to trust them. In this spirit he made one decision for which he was later severely criticized: he closed down the so-called Black Chamber—the State Department's code cracking office. . . . In 1929 the world was striving with good will for lasting peace and in this effort all the nations were parties. Stimson, as Secretary of State, was dealing as a gentleman with gentlemen sent as ambassadors and ministers from friendly nations, and, as he later said, 'Gentlemen do not read each other's mail.' " Henry L. Stimson and McGeorge Bundy, *On Active Service in Peace and War* (New York: Harper & Bros., 1947–48), p. 188.

like the "open society" of the United States, where one does not need spies to detect significant nuclear installations or activities, President Eisenhower argued that the United States was forced to photograph Soviet territory from the air, in its own national interest and in the interest of preserving peace in the world. In other words, an action which would previously have been denied by its perpetrators and shrugged off by its victims, in a moderately pragmatic fashion, can no longer be treated in this way, when it involves nuclear powers in a direct confrontation. It is translated from the realm of pragmatism into that of ideology and was, in this case, left to die there as an issue, when both sides developed the so-called "eye in the sky," i.e., spy satellites, which no longer raise the old question of violation of the air space of a sovereign state.

The Cuban missile crisis of 1962, to be discussed in greater detail later, can serve as our final illustration that the style of contemporary world politics oscillates from extreme ideologism through legalism to extreme pragmatism especially on those occasions when only great immediate flexibility is capable of preventing nuclear violence. By October, 1963, the United States and the Soviet Union viewed the problems presented to each by the Cuban policy of the other through a "recognition mechanism" that had become increasingly ideological. The Soviets expected another invasion attempt, this one perhaps to be mounted by United States troops after the failure of the anti-Castro Cubans at the Bay of Pigs. According to their ideology, America's "ruling capitalist circles" could not tolerate the threat to their exploitative domination of all Latin America presented by the success of Fidel Castro's revolution. The Soviet Union dispatched intermediate-range ballistic missiles to Cuba for a variety of reasons, about which one can only make informed guesses: to prevent the feared invasion, to tie Dr. Castro's regime closer to the Soviet Union, and perhaps also to see whether they could "get away with it." The United States, on the other hand, tended to emphasize the role of force in Soviet foreign policy and was preoccupied with its own prestige and credibility, especially after the earlier Cuban invasion fiasco. The Kennedy Administration in effect asked itself: "Will our commitment to defend West Berlin or South Vietnam still be credible, if we permit the stationing of IRBM'S on Cuba?" The Administration had also worked out certain distinctions between the characteristics of "defensive" and "offensive" weapons systems. These distinctions can be viewed as integral components of "strategic doctrine" which, in its own way—and along with such concepts as "totalitarianism"—is a part of what we might call the American anticommunist counterideology. President Kennedy described the weapons system about to be installed on Cuba as offensive. He addressed his warning about the consequences which the United States would draw from their completed installation directly to Premier Khrushchev, and for a few days it seemed as though the two superpowers were headed for a nuclear clash. At least, it seemed so on the basis of the ideologically motivated and couched statements made by the two governments at each other, for the rest of the world, and to their own peoples. The clash seemed even more likely on the basis of statements made by American politicians and publicists outside the Administration, for whom there are no strict counterparts in the Soviet Union. Senator Kenneth Keating of New York, among others, had warned for some weeks that Soviet missiles were about to be emplaced on Cuba. On September 20 and 26, 1962, the Congress passed a Joint Resolution, which "resolved"

That the United States is determined
(*a*) to prevent by whatever means may be necessary, including the use of arms, the Marxist-Leninist regime in Cuba from extending, by force or threat of force, its aggressive or subversive activities to any part of this hemisphere;
(*b*) to prevent in Cuba the creation or use of an externally supported military capability endangering the security of the United States; and
(*c*) to work with the Organization of American States and with freedom-loving Cubans to support the aspirations of the Cuban people for self-determination.[5]

This resolution makes the ideological motivation and direction of the "democratic" pressures upon American foreign policy quite clear. Official Soviet statements (all Soviet statements on this issue were, of course, official) moved in exactly the opposite direction, so that a nuclear clash appeared to be imminent.

But it was avoided, only because both sides decided to act inconsistently with the ideological substance of their previous statements and because both sides, as well as other participants, devised new pro-

---

[5]U.S. Congress, *Congressional Record*, 87th Cong., 2nd sess., Vol. 108, No. 170 (September 20, 1962), pp. 18892–951; and No. 174 (September 26, 1962), pp. 19702–53. As quoted by David L. Larson (ed.), *The "Cuban Crisis" of 1962: Selected Documents and Chronology* (Boston: Houghton Mifflin Co., 1963), p. 19.

cedures of negotiation and attempted pragmatically to create new concepts of international law, in order to avert the clash of their "present means to produce apparent future good." On the way from ideology to expediency, many legalistic arguments were used by both sides, and introduced by others at the United Nations and elsewhere, but expediency won out. This happened apparently without the creation of "new" international law, but it did lead to the creation of new procedures for international politics, and the creation of consensus on these new procedures, of which the "hot-line" between the White House and the Kremlin, and the private correspondence between President Kennedy and Premier Khrushchev are representative.

In this way, extreme pragmatism offers a safety valve for a world politics in which the risks of nuclear war inhibit the use even of conventional means of organized violence, in which unlimited ideologies of global scope increasingly motivate the foreign policies—or, better, the "world policies"—of the major units, and in which legalistically constructed international organizations unsuccessfully seek to impose permanent stability upon what is in fact a fermenting process of the development of politics. But no matter whether the style at any moment is ideological or pragmatic, violent or legalistic, the incidence of issues is usually more extreme than in either of the preceding periods. Consensus on procedures is as low as during the interwar years, or lower, because professional diplomats and military play a less important role today. Only one of the members, General Maxwell Taylor, of the National Security Council's executive committee of about fifteen that advised President Kennedy during the Cuban Missile Crisis, was a professional military officer, and only two were professional diplomats. As recently as World War II, even Adolf Hitler, by contrast, drew mainly professionals into his war council. Hitler rarely negotiated directly and personally with his top adversaries and—most important—he never controlled power of the scope, destructiveness, or unprecedented modes of application that contemporary weapons systems provide. Greater consensus on procedures of both diplomacy and warfare was therefore possible even during World War II than today in "peacetime."

The downgrading of professionals, which is paralleled by the changes in professional students of international politics discussed above, is reflected not only in the personnel of such groups as President Kennedy's executive committee for conducting the Cuban missile crisis, but also in the influx into the conduct of world politics of politicians from the scores of "new states" established since the end of World War II. Since these states are new and, usually, "underdeveloped" both politically and administratively, their foreign relations often have to be conducted by men and women without experience in conventional diplomacy and without commitment to the old procedures of the earlier periods. Many of them first rose to political prominence as more or less revolutionary leaders of anticolonialist independence movements, which occasionally makes them strongly opposed to Western or white concepts of "law and order" and authority. Some have tried to replace these concepts with their own "anti-imperialist" ones or, in a less negative vein, with concepts of authority and substantive and procedural goals for the community of mankind which they consider more genuinely global, universal, or cosmopolitan. The importance of this new segment of the personnel of world politics is illustrated by the personality and background of the third Secretary General of the United Nations, U Thant of Burma.

All of these factors combine to make the over-all incidence of issues in the third and last of the periods of international politics that we have been comparing still more extreme than in the second. The style of world politics has been becoming more pathological. At the same time, the trend continues toward the increase in the load of issues that the global political system has to carry. The trend arises from the growth in the volume of problems about which there is the belief that they *can* be solved through world politics.

Chapter 5

The United Nations as a
Political System

The Centrality of the United Nations

MOST CONTEMPORARY TEXTBOOKS on international politics relegate discussion of the United Nations to one of the final chapters. Why? And why do we begin the central section of this book with an analysis and evaluation of the contribution made by the United Nations to world politics?

The answer to the first question was suggested by our earlier critique of the conventional methods. If you search for the locus of power in the world, your focus will not come to rest upon the international organization whose headquarters is located in New York. Rather, it will alternate between Washington and Moscow or concentrate upon those points, like Berlin or Havana, where power wielded by Moscow meets head-on with power wielded by Washington. Discussions carried on at the United Nations in Manhattan and work done by agencies of the UN around the world, even the few occasionally successful efforts to settle disputes between the United States and the Soviet Union at the United Nations—all of this is peripheral to international politics conceived of as power processes among the superpowers. On the other hand, or in the second of the only two dimensions in which international relations was formerly studied, there are textbooks that concern themselves solely with questions of international organization, sometimes in a rather abstract way that admittedly disregards the "facts of power," but looks forward with hope to the day when—somehow—the leap will have been made from the quadrant of violence to that of legalism.

There is one main meeting ground for these two schools of international politics in their treatment of the United Nations, and that is the role of the UN as an instrument of the foreign policies of the participants in the global "struggle for power," and especially the most powerful actors: the United States, the Soviet Union, the United Kingdom, France, and China. These are the states that possess nuclear weapons and that have also been permanent members of the Security Council of the United Nations, under its Charter from the beginning of its existence (though nuclear "Red" China did not occupy China's UN seat for at least seventeen years after the Kuomintang's expulsion from the mainland to the island of Formosa). Because the permanent membership of the Security Council was designed to reflect the facts of international power at the end of World War II, *inter alia* through the Charter's grant of the veto to the Big Five, both *Realpolitiker* and institutionalists could converge in their studies of the Security Council. The former used it as proof positive of their thesis of the primacy of force: The Big Five or, at any rate, the Super Big Two, would not have permitted establishment of an international organization capable of important action deemed inimical to their "national interest" and, through the veto, they can prevent such action. On the other hand, the emergence of the United States and the Soviet Union as the two superpowers demonstrates the derivative thesis of *Realpolitik,* namely, that even the most cleverly designed constitutional structures cannot stay ahead of changing realities of power. Great Britain, France, and Nationalist China, though they were created as constitutional equals of the United States and the Soviet Union by the Charter of the United Nations, have in fact declined even in their constitutional roles within the UN, because of the over-all decline in their absolute and relative power. Great Britain and France lost their colonial empires and, though they now possess greater force than ever before in the form of nuclear weapons, these are insignificant when compared with the overkill capacity of the two superpowers, so that membership in the Security Council and possession of the veto there does not in fact make the role of these two old powers of European international relations any more significant, even within the UN, than that of, say, Japan or India. And the government of Nationalist China has receded into utter insignificance, because it lost with the exception of the island of

Formosa, all of its territory, all of its population, and a good portion of its claim to cultural nationality, since the indigenous majority of the population of Formosa is not culturally Chinese.

Conventional students of international organization can, if they are so inclined, agree with conventional students of power politics that the United Nations can function as a partial framework for certain limited aspects of international relations, to the extent that it offers member states an additional instrument for the implementation (but presumably not the formulation) of their foreign policies. Since there are obvious methodological parallels between compartmentalization of the study of world politics into the water-tight or "politics-tight" compartments labeled "power" and "organization," and the compartmentalization of the study of national politics under the headings of the mechanical separation of powers, it is quite easy and natural for a student of international organization to look upon the United Nations purely as a tool of those who "execute" the foreign policies of sovereign national states "in the national interest." The conduct in the UN of the Soviet Union and the United States, of France and the United Kingdom, offers much to justify such an interpretation and it is possible, therefore, to read a whole series of books, written mainly by students of international organization, and to conclude that the UN functions mainly as a tool, and a rather unwieldy one at that, for the major powers, used against each other—hence its unwieldiness—or, on the rare occasions when *they* are in agreement against the minor states, used against the rest of the UN's membership. When studied in this perspective, the United Nations is seen mainly as a playing field for a somewhat up-dated game of multilateral diplomacy, in which the interests of the major players are bound to prevail against the minor participants or to cancel each other out. The United Nations is not seen as an entity in its own right, as a political system that makes its own distinctive contribution to the style of world politics.

If these are the main reasons why most writers on international politics relegate the United Nations to a relatively insignificant position toward the end of their textbooks, then why do we place our discussion of the UN at the beginning of the central section of this book? We are *not* doing this because of any "soft-headed, wooly-brained, starry-eyed" illusions that the United Nations *it*self (to the extent that one can speak of *it* in the singular) is the single most important actor in world politics. It clearly isn't. Nor are we doing it because of the leap-frogging kind of hopefulness that characterizes some of the books on international organization, mentioned above. We are doing it rather, because the existence of the United Nations makes a central difference for the style of world politics; because the UN itself is the single most obvious and accessible evidence of the transformation that has occurred, and the changes that are taking place in global political style; and because an increasing proportion of the issues of world politics—virtually all the more important ones, nowadays—eventually find their way to the United Nations during one or more of the phases of their processing if, indeed, they are not originally formulated in the United Nations.

"White settlers" in those parts of Africa that have been under pressure to convert from minority to majority (i.e., black African) government often tell Americans who sympathize with the majority political movements that the United States is in an historical glass house to be throwing stones at the white minorities of Africa: When the original "white settlers" in North America, and their descendants of the nineteenth century, proceeded to push back or in some instances to liquidate the Indians, and to import millions of slaves from Africa, they were in no way impeded by anything like the United Nations. Nowadays, by contrast, although the white settlers of Southern Rhodesia or the white minority of South Africa are engaged in neither liquidation nor slavery, their every move and policy is commented upon, criticized, or condemned at the United Nations—by representatives of other African states, of governments whose populations are nonwhite, and even of white states, including those which, like the United States, have historical and contemporary racial minority problems of their own. The Americans are told that their forefathers were simply lucky in that they did not have to worry about "world public opinion" as expressed in the institutionalized forum of the United Nations. (To this "argument," an American might reply that at the very birth of the United States, in the Declaration of Independence, Thomas Jefferson referred to the requirements of "a decent respect to the opinions of mankind," though —to be sure—these still plural opinions were not to be provided with an institutionalized forum for another 140 years.)

This is one illustration, and not the most significant, of how the mere existence of the United Nations makes a difference. Even if we made the false assumption that the African colonies that achieved their independence would have done so without the UN as speedily and smoothly as they did, in the 1950's and '60's, then the manner and style of applying pressure to the remaining colonies and other minority-dominated territories would still be quite different without the UN. To simplify greatly, without the UN, these pressures would have to be applied directly to, say, South Africa, or indirectly to, say, the United States, in efforts to get it, in turn, to apply various direct pressures to South Africa. With the UN, these direct and indirect efforts are being made by the African states, but in addition they and others are also engaged in a variety of maneuvers within the United Nations system, which includes, *inter alia,* the Security Council and General Assembly, the International Court of Justice, and such specialized agencies as the International Labor Organization and the World Health Organization. The availability of these forums and South Africa's membership in them has had the result that the issues arising out of the South African problem are being formulated differently than they would be without availability of the UN system. The style of treatment for these issues in world politics is therefore different, though the substance of the problem *may be* very similar to what it would have been in any case. Actually, the substance of South African problems *recognized* for the flow of world politics has been quite different in the United Nations and its predecessor, the League of Nations, as a result of differences between their constitutions, membership, and historical "timing." These organizational differences may be mere effects of changes in the global power situation, rather than causes of the changes in the treatment given the South African problem. The point here is that, even if the United Nations were only epiphenomenal and symptomatic of more profound "primary" transformations elsewhere in international politics, the United Nations is still the one place where evidence for all these transformations appears in its most concentrated form and where it is most readily accessible to study.

Constitution Building in the United Nations

The question about the contribution made by the United Nations to world politics can be answered from different points of view. Here we shall deal with this question in the light of the intentions of the founders of the UN, including the authors of the Charter; from the standpoint of those who hope to establish in the United Nations a "parliament of man;" and on the basis of criteria for the success of political systems established in Chapter 3.

What were the purposes of the founders of the United Nations, and have these purposes been achieved? "The founders" did not, of course, make up a monolithic group of single mind and purpose. They were pursuing different goals which were often contradictory or even incompatible with one another. These contradictions were revealed in the course of the drafting of the Charter and the negotiations that preceded its signature and ratification by the "charter members." There was, however, as there must always be at a founding, sufficient consensus among the original member-states to make the founding possible. In order to answer the question about accomplishment of the founders' purposes, we have to identify the goals that commanded consensus in 1945.

The goals that commanded the widest agreement arose out of World War II, which had not yet been concluded by the "nations united" in their common opposition to the Axis powers. These substantive goals were partly positive, circumstantial, and indeed very immediate—the final defeat of the enemies—and partly negative, fundamental, looking as far ahead into the future as it had taken the League of Nations in the past to fail in the prevention of world war.

The United Nations was made up by the alliance of states that had been fighting against the Axis. This origin of the organization is reflected in various articles of the Charter, including Article 107: "Nothing in the present Charter shall invalidate or preclude action, in relation to any state which during the Second World War has been an enemy of any signatory to the present Charter, taken or authorized as a result of that war by the Governments having responsibility for such action." This article later facilitated legalistic arguments by means of which the United Nations could be denied jurisdiction over disputes, primarily among the victors, arising in divided Germany. It has also contributed to keeping both the Federal Republic of Germany and the German Democratic Republic, i.e., the Western and Soviet parts of the country, from membership in the absence of a German peace treaty.

Since defeat of the Axis was expected at the time that the drafting labors on the Charter were begun, and Germany had already surrendered unconditionally when the Charter was signed in San Francisco on June 26, 1945, this positive circumstantial substantive goal played a less important role than the negative fundamental goal of preventing recurrence of world war. That there was strongest consensus on this objective is shown by the very first phrase in the Preamble to the Charter: "We the peoples of the United Nation determined to save succeeding generations from the scourge of war, which twice in our lifetime has brought untold sorrow to mankind. . . ."

To establish an international organization capable of achieving this goal, which commanded the broadest consensus among states then feasible, procedures were needed for both the preratification negotiations and the operation of the United Nations itself. Negotiating procedures were drawn from established diplomatic practice, supplemented by "summitry" among various combinations of the leaders of the Big Five—Roosevelt, Churchill, Stalin, Chiang Kai-shek, and De Gaulle. Even these summit meetings, however, could draw upon the experience of the Big Four—Wilson, Lloyd George, Clemenceau, and Orlando—who had met in Paris in order to negotiate the peace treaties with the Central Powers and the Covenant of the League. Operating procedures could be borrowed from the League of Nations of which most founding members of the UN, with the notable exception of the United States, had been members at one time or another, and with whose procedures their diplomats were, therefore, familiar.

The founders started out with this strong negative substantive agreement on the desirability of preventing recurrence of world war. It was mainly for this purpose that the constitution of the United Nations was designed. The quality of the design produced by the constitutional architects of the UN could, therefore, be judged by the fact that World War III has not yet occurred. Since, however, other causes seem to have made more important contributions to this fortunate circumstance, we should apply other criteria to the design of the Charter, criteria generally applicable to the building of constitutions.

These standards look for the achievement of a dynamic equilibrium among the basic goals of stability and flexibility, effectiveness and efficiency. They represent the normative dimension of a theory of constitution building, which also has its analytical dimension, in that it seeks to explain the conditions of the success and failure of constitutions.[1] The founding of the United Nations, like the founding of the League of Nations, of the United States, any of the five French Republics to date, or of any other constitutional system, at whatever level or of whatever scope, can be examined comparatively by means of this theory, which is in turn "enriched" by the results of additional comparisons.

This theory suggests that conditions at the time of its founding were unfavorable to the success of the United Nations, and that the drafters of the Charter did not even make optimal use of those circumstances that seemed to favor the success of the organization. The prevalence of substantive agreement, in the absence of strong procedural consensus, among founders of a new political system usually works to its disadvantage. The reason is that achievement of the substantive goals can take away the *raison d'être* of the system. Moreover, the euphoria often produced by strong substantive consensus leads members of the political system not to anticipate the disagreements that are bound to occur later on and, therefore, to neglect the development of experience with and of commitment to procedures capable of resolving these future issues. The Fourth French Republic can illustrate this point, because the euphoria generated by the resistance against Germany during World War II gave its constitution a substantive bias that contributed to its failure and early replacement by the less substantively biased constitution of the Fifth Republic. This is not to imply that strength of substantive in the absence of procedural consensus dooms a new constitution to failure, as is suggested, among other cases, by that of the German Federal Republic. At the time of its founding, in 1949, serious substantive disagreement among the German founders was virtually *verboten* by the Allied military governments in the Western zones of occupation, and a strong "natural" consensus on the desirability of economic reconstruction existed in any case. The drafters of the "Basic Law" of the Federal Republic, however, refused to let themselves be tempted by this situation and restricted the content of the constitution, by and large, to the highest common denominator of agreement on matters of substance, embedded within a framework of procedures that have so far demonstrated their capacity for processing all the substantive

---

[1] See Herbert J. Spiro, "The Conditions of Constitutional Success," *Government by Constitution: The Political Systems of Democracy* (New York: Random House, 1959), Part Six and *passim*.

problems, anticipated and unanticipated, and disagreements generated by them, that have arisen since 1949. At least this is the conclusion at which one arrives after comparing two German cases of constitution building, that of Bonn in 1949 and that of Weimar in 1919.

An analogous comparison of international constitutional engineering, in Paris in 1919 and in San Francisco in 1945, suggests that the draftsmen of the Charter, though building upon less substantive agreement than their forerunners with the Covenant, produced a much more substantive document, which runs to about three times the length of the Covenant of the League. This partial comparison might have led to pessimistic forecasts of the future of the United Nations, based on reasoning along the following lines: The Paris Conference, though rarely unanimous, faced no cleavage like the incipient one, in San Francisco, between the Soviet Union and the Western Allies. The Covenant was nevertheless kept largely procedural and relatively short. The Charter turned out much longer and more heavily substantive, with the result that some mutually contradictory substantive goals had to be included in it. Since mutually incompatible goals cannot be fulfilled and their simultaneous pursuit is likely to have frustrating effects, the Charter in its other provisions is likely to be regarded as a "mere scrap of paper" even sooner in the life of the UN, than was the Covenant in the life of the League.

Another pessimistic line of argument could have been added to the above during the first few years of the United Nations, this one based on the retrospective reasoning, by false analogy to the League, which strongly affected the design of its successor. The League had been founded to prevent recurrence of World War I, but was unable to prevent World War II. The UN was to be established to prevent recurrence of the "scourge of war, which twice in our lifetime has brought untold sorrow to mankind." It was therefore natural for the drafters of the Charter to ask which constitutional and other shortcomings of the League contributed to its failure and to the outbreak of World War II—just as the founders of the Bonn Republic asked which constitutional errors of design contributed to the collapse of the Weimar Republic and to the rise of Hitler. The founders of the United Nations produced two major answers to this question, one concerning membership, the other relating to "collective security" in the face of aggression. The League failed in part, so they reasoned, because the United States was never a member, the Soviet Union belonged for only five years in the 1930's, and among other members there was a great deal of "coming and going." (See Table 2, pages 122f.) This reduced the effectiveness of its policies, which were less likely to be found acceptable by nonmembers than by members, especially in view of the legal and power "fact" that these policies were not considered binding on even the members. Therefore, so this argument concluded, membership in the United Nations should aim at universality.

The UN has certainly come much closer toward this goal than its predecessor. No member has been expelled from it and only Indonesia withdrew in the twentieth year of the life of the organization. Of the countries defeated by the original united nations, only Germany has not become a member, but that mainly because no peace treaty was concluded with Germany as a result of its division by the Cold War into two parts. Of other independent states, only the divided countries of Korea, Laos, and Vietnam, are not members. (For China, the issue is not one of membership, but of representation—by the government on Formosa or the government in Peking.) There is, however, one weakness in this analogy between the League and the UN, which might lead to a reversal of the initial judgment in favor of the UN after comparing its membership with that of the League. A more shifting and less stable membership could be considered more appropriate and less harmful to the system of international relations which, in the 1920's and 30's, had not yet become nearly as interdependent and integrated as in the 1950's and 60's. Conversely, the "underrepresentation"—at worst, "misrepresentation" —of China by the government on Formosa by itself may be more dangerous, and has already generated more controversy inside and outside the UN than most of the membership disputes of the League put together. A simple, mechanical comparison of the membership performance of the two international organizations is, therefore, inadequate.

Even more inadequate and misleading would be a simple comparison of the constitutional provisions and the performance of League and UN in the field of collective security against aggression. Here the retrospective orientation of the drafters of the Charter becomes even more evident than with respect to membership. It has been said that generals are often trying to win the last war in preparing for the next one. Similarly, the founders of the United Nations

TABLE 2

*List of Members of the League of Nations**

Member	Date of Entry†	Withdrawal Notice
Afghanistan...............	September, 1934	
Union of South Africa......		
Albania...................	December, 1920	Annexed by Italy, April, 1939
Argentina.................		
Australia.................		
Austria..................	December, 1920	Annexed by Germany, March, 1938
Belgium..................		
Bolivia...................		
Brazil....................		June, 1926
United Kingdom..........		
Bulgaria.................	December, 1920	
Canada..................		
Chile....................		June, 1938
China...................		
Columbia................		
Costa Rica..............	December, 1920	January, 1925
Cuba....................		
Czechoslovakia...........		
Denmark.................		
Dominican Republic........	September, 1924	
Ecuador.................	September, 1934	
Egypt...................	May, 1937	
Estonia.................	September, 1921	
Ethiopia................	September, 1923	
Finland.................	December, 1920	
France..................		
Germany................	September, 1926	October, 1933
Greece..................		
Guatemala..............		May, 1936
Haiti...................		April, 1942
Honduras...............		July, 1936
Hungary................	September, 1922	April, 1939
India...................		
Iraq....................	October, 1932	
Ireland.................	September, 1923	
Italy....................		December, 1937
Japan...................		March, 1933
Latvia..................	September, 1921	
Liberia.................		
Lithuania...............	September, 1921	
Luxemburg..............	December, 1920	
Mexico.................	September, 1931	
Netherlands.............		
New Zealand............		
Nicaragua..............		June, 1936
Norway.................		
Panama.................		
Paraguay...............		February, 1935
Persia..................		

Table 2—*Continued*

Member	Date of Entry†	Withdrawal Notice
Peru......................		April, 1939
Poland..		
Portugal..................		
Roumania.................		July, 1940
Salvador.................		August, 1937
Siam.....................		
Spain.....................		May, 1939
Sweden..................		
Switzerland...............		
Turkey....................	July, 1932	
Union of Soviet Socialist Republics...............	September, 1934	December 14, 1939‡
Uruguay..................		
Venezuela.................		July, 1938
Yugoslavia...............		

*Adapted from F. P. Walters, *A History of the League of Nations* (London: Oxford University Press, 1952), vol. I, pp. 64–65.
†The date of entry is not given for original members.
‡Declared to be no longer a Member of the League, by Council Resolution.

were trying to prevent the failure of the League of Nations through improving on its Covenant. The main failure of the League had been its failure to prevent or punish aggression: by Japan against China, by Italy against Ethiopia, by Germany against Austria, Czechoslovakia, and Poland, by the Soviet Union against Finland. In each of these cases, overt military action was conducted or threatened by one sovereign state against another and, subsequently, some or all of the territory of the victim state was annexed by or put under the administration of the aggressor state. Each of these actions was territorially definable. Characteristically, Hitler stated after each of his successes in this field that "Germany has no further territorial demands in Europe." Even the Spanish Civil War need be considered no exception to this rule, since territorial battle lines were visible throughout and the involvement of the Soviet Union on the side of the Loyalists, and of Italy and Germany on the side of the Rebels was sufficiently overt to have made the application of sanctions under auspices of the League of Nations at least feasible. Yet the League never successfully applied sanctions, military or economic, against any of the "aggressors."

The founders of the United Nations were keenly aware of this failure. They were, moreover, members of a belated military alliance, about to be finally victorious, who could think of themselves as acting on behalf of the collective security of mankind against the "fascist aggressors." They therefore wrote into the Charter provisions for collective security which, had they been included in the Covenant, might well have enabled the League to prevent some of the worse cases of aggression in the 1930's. Chapter VII of the Charter concerns "Action with Respect to Threats to the Peace, Breaches of the Peace, and Acts of Aggression," and was obviously designed to correct short-comings in this area under Articles 15 and 16 of the Covenant. For example, under Article 45 of the Charter, which had not been implemented by 1965, "Members shall hold immediately available national air-force contingents for combined international enforcement action." According to Article 47, a Military Staff Committee accountable to the Security Council "shall be reponsible under the Security Council for the strategic direction of any armed forces placed at the disposal of the Security Council." While the Covenant of the League required unanimity among the members of its Council to make its decisions binding upon all members of the League, the Charter requires unanimity only among the permanent members of the Security Council. And even this requirement, the so-called "veto" of the Big Five, has been circumvented through the Uniting for Peace Resolution of 1950, discussed below. In other words, the whole tenor of Chapter VII is of collective security through a pooling of organized force of sovereign member-states, to be controlled jointly by these states. Except in cases of direct self-defense against overt military aggression against the territory of a state, this would be the only type of force whose use would be considered legitimate by the United Nations and its nearly universal membership.

However, this "Axis type" of overt military aggression by sovereign states against sovereign states, aiming at the acquisition of territory and, often, the acquisition of a culturally related "national" population, has been quite insignificant in the years since 1945. The main actors have not been sovereign national states but the two great blocs, or proxies—often quasi-sovereign parts of divided countries—acting on behalf of the blocs. The main form of "aggressive" action has not been by foreign armies invading across territorial boundaries, but by indigenous guerilla and counterguerilla personnel within a country, supported from the outside by the blocs with material, technical, and propaganda assistance; or by the two superpowers directly against each other, without crossing each other's frontiers, as in the Soviet Union's Cuban "base stealing" "missile sneak" and the United States' response to it.

The differences between the Spanish Civil War and the Korean War can illustrate this change in international politics, which the founders of the UN failed to anticipate, partly because they designed the Charter by retrospective analogy of the future with the past of the League. While the Korean War was still going on, comparisons were occasionally made between it and the Spanish Civil War as "rehearsals" for the next world war. In both "civil wars," it was said, the real contenders were not the Spanish Republicans and Rebels, or the South and North Koreans, but major parties to the next world war. In Spain, the real contest was between Italy and Germany on the one hand and the Soviet Union on the other. In Korea, the real conflict was between the United States on the one hand and communist China and the Soviet Union on the other. Both wars provided opportunities for the testing of weapons systems to be used in the greater conflicts for which they were expected to prepare the way. Proponents of the thesis of the resemblance between these two conflicts then sometimes note a major difference between them: In the Spanish Civil War, attempts at collective security (outside the League) failed. In the Korean War, collective security action by the United Nations succeeded. The Spanish Civil War, therefore, ended in the victory of the fascist rebels under Generalissimo Franco, while the Korean War was settled by an uneasy armistice which restored the territorial boundary between North and South Korea to approximately the same line where it had been before the outbreak of hostilities.

Off-hand, this comparison suggests that the United Nations has been more successful than the League because of its direct constitutional corrections of the League. But this conclusion is superficial and false, for several reasons. Although there has been some controversy whether the war was started by North or South Korea,[2] neither side, in accusing the other of initiating the conflict, denies that in resisting it acted on behalf of, and in concert with, its "Big Brother" in the communist or the Western bloc. In the Spanish Civil War, by contrast, there was apparently little or no foreign involvement at the beginning, and the later participation, e.g., of Germany and Italy, had

---

[2] Isidor F. Stone, *The Hidden History of the Korean War* (New York: Monthly Review Press, 1952).

no bloc and few "Axis" characteristics. More important, the apparent "success" of collective security against North Korean aggression was the result not of constitutional differences between League and UN, but of the impact of bloc politics on a UN that actually resembled the League in important constitutional respects.

When the United States brought the issue of North Korean aggression before the Security Council, it happened that the Soviet delegate was absent from its meetings for that whole month, because the Soviet Union was boycotting the Council on account of the "misrepresentation" of China by the "Kuomintang clique" from Formosa. But for this "accident," the Soviet Union could have vetoed the collective security measures which the Council then voted to take in support of South Korea. These measures, which set up a United Nations Command, headed by a United States general, were supported by a large number of UN members, the overwhelming majority of them identical with the Western bloc. Subsequently, when the Soviet delegate returned, the Security Council's control over the Korean action was deliberately transferred to the General Assembly, by means of the "Uniting for Peace Resolution" introduced by the American Secretary of State, Mr. Dean Acheson. This resolution circumvented the veto, because the Assembly, under the Charter, can make "important decisions . . . by a two-thirds majority of the members present and voting." The United States, as leader of the Western bloc, could use this procedural device, which really amounted to a constitutional amendment, because the Soviet Union was then in a pitifully small minority in the General Assembly—again a consequence of bloc politics. (It should be added, however, that this kind of maneuver would have been useless and therefore not attempted under the League, whose Covenant required, with certain exceptions, "the agreement of all the Members of the League represented at the meeting" for decisions of its Assembly.)

There are other important differences between the Spanish Civil War and the Korean War. Foreign participation in the latter was much heavier than in the former. Communist China, which is contiguous to North Korea, poured hundreds of thousands of troops into the country, as did the United States and its allies within the United Nations. However, the most advanced weapons systems involving atomic warheads, although at the disposition of both the United States and the Soviet Union by this time, were not used. In the Spanish Civil

War, the most advanced weapons systems of that time, like dive bombers, were tested out. Within a few years after the Spanish Civil War, the Soviet Union and Germany, joined by Italy, were at war with each other. Twelve years after the conclusion of the Korean War, no direct conventional or nuclear war between the United States and communist China or the Soviet Union had yet broken out, though the Cold War persisted.

Collective security, we may therefore conclude, has not been more successful under the UN than under the League, because there have been no important occasions to invoke it. Collective security was intended to be, as the term implies, action collectively by and on behalf of the collectivity of individual sovereign member-states against one or, at most, a few who refused to comply with decisions of the Security Council, taken by "an affirmative vote of seven members, including the concurring votes of the permanent members," i.e., the Big Five. In world politics after World War II, no important situations have arisen to which these constitutional provisions of the Charter of the United Nations are applicable. Important threats to the peace and acts of aggression have come from members of blocs, which have always included one or the other of the two superpowers, and later China, which control both a veto in the Security Council and nuclear weapons. And if the UN were to act now as some critics of the League say that organization should have acted against aggressors, unhampered by the veto, e.g., by utilizing the General Assembly in accordance with the Uniting for Peace Resolution, then nuclear force might be used between the Soviet Union and the United States, and a policy intended to promote collective security would bring about collective incineration in a nuclear holocaust of world-wide scope.

The retrospective outlook of the architects of the Charter has not brought about the intended results of constitutional provisions with respect to either membership or collective security, because the problems faced by the UN in its life have not been analogous to the problems faced by the League in its life. The constitution builders "failed" not only in this respect, but also in that they did not make optimum use of those circumstances that obtained at the founding of the UN which favored their success, including relatively low substantive consensus. They have "succeeded" in their intention of preventing recurrence of World War II only in the sense that the conditions prevailing after World War II could not generate *that* kind of world war. The problems recognized by these two international political systems have been quite different. Procedures that might have prevented the failure of the League have been of little use to the United Nations. The fact that World War III has not (yet) occurred cannot be ascribed to the Charter of the United Nations. *Realpolitiker* easily jump from this judgment to the conclusion that the UN has been an utter failure or, at best, peripheral to world politics, and that this conclusion corroborates their thesis of the primacy of power. For purposes of the study of world politics, they therefore relegate the United Nations to a position of insignificance, to the backs of their books. Is this conclusion warranted?

A *"Parliament of Man"?*

Even if the intentions of various founders of the United Nations have not been realized and the expectations of its protagonists have not been fulfilled, it is still possible that the UN presents a case of beneficial though "unintended consequences of purposive social [or political] action."[3] We suggested earlier that world politics would be different without the United Nations. How it would differ we cannot tell with accuracy, because of the irreversibility of history. The closest we can come toward getting an idea of differences between world politics with and without the UN is by comparing contemporary world politics with international politics in other periods, *mutatis mutandis*, i.e., allowing for those factors that are nonanalogous. Such a comparison indicates that the United Nations has centered upon its institutions, and is "sieving" through its processes, a greater proportion of the total transactions of a steadily rising volume of world politics than any previous system of international organization. Most of the important issues of world politics either start at the UN, end at the UN, or pass through the UN during one or more phases of their processing.

Adherents of the school of *Realpolitik* might reply to this proposition that the great powers take issues to the UN only for purposes of window dressing—to put a better face upon their manipulations of power—or because powerless states and other groups, who think that a UN airing of their grievances would embarrass a great power,

---

[3]See Robert K. Merton, "The Unintended Consequences of Purposive Social Action," *American Sociological Review*, Vol. 1 (December, 1936), pp. 894–904.

drag the latter into the UN forum. Some near-great powers, especially France under President De Gaulle, do not even bother to use the United Nations as a facade for their politics of national interest, but rather treat it with the same contempt that General De Gaulle used to show for the parliamentary politics of the Fourth Republic. The Republic of South Africa exposes itself to the vociferous and bitter criticism of Asian and African members over its *apartheid* policy, uses the UN in turn in order to lecture these states and the white rest of mankind on their own shortcomings and the superiority of *apartheid,* but meanwhile continues unerringly on the path toward the full, rigorous implementation of *apartheid,* not only in its own territory, but also in the mandated territory of Southwest Africa. In other words, politics in the world is not really affected by the existence and functioning of the United Nations. To make an analogy between world politics and an electric circuit, the UN is like exposed sections of wiring that include two terminals and are spliced unto the circuit after it had been operating for some time before. You can see sparks flying from one terminal to another in this exposed section, but no significant amount of energy is lost, and the over-all functioning of the circuit remains quite unaffected.

One reply to this "realistic" critique of the thesis of the centrality of the United Nations asserts that, over the long run, the regular observance of certain procedures, methods, ways of doing things, no matter how mechanical, merely formal, and reluctant it may be, affects the behavior of those who practice this observance. It may even affect their motivation. It may build up in them, sometimes subconsciously, a commitment to these procedures, though they were originally opposed to using them, or even though they used them only in order to exploit them entirely for their own purposes. There are, for example, contemporary parliaments whose major present upholders and defenders are the very groups who refused to participate in their work only two or three decades ago, because they considered parliament an instrument of colonialist oppression; the Indian Congress Party is a case in point. There are older European parliaments whose functions have been transformed by socialist democratic majorities against the strong and sometimes violent opposition of conservative parties representing more traditional sections of the population, like peasantry, nobility, church, and army. Nevertheless, these conservative parties are now sometimes the staunchest upholders of the pro-

cedures and institutions of the very parliament which produces substantive policies to which they are deeply opposed. Similarly, so this
argument continues, even those states which are unhappy with the
policies of the United Nations may be developing, more or less subconsciously, a certain commitment to "the UN-way of doing things."

The argument is evidently based upon an analogy between the
United Nations and national as well as prenational parliaments. Is
this a valid analogy? The answer depends upon the type of parliament to which the United Nations is compared. Ever since the beginnings of the "Mother of Parliaments" at Westminster, there has
been a variety of types, and the English Parliament itself has passed
through many stages in its evolution from the King's Council into
the contemporary Parliament of the United Kingdom of Great Britain
—which continues to change its membership and components, the relations among these and between itself and the rest of the British
political system, and its functions. In view of this variety of parliamentary types, we need not reject the analogy between the United
Nations with a parliament simply because one of the most frequently
made objections against it: In contemporary parliaments, individual
voters are represented; in the United Nations, sovereign states are
represented. (This particular objection to treating the UN as a parliament is obviously related to the conventional arguments for segregat-
ing the study of international relations from the comparative study of
national politics.) We need not reject the parliamentary analogy on
these grounds, because there have been parliaments consisting of representatives of sovereign states or their historical forerunners. This was
true, for example, of the Diet of the Holy Roman Empire, which consisted of the Emperor, the Princes Elector, other Princes, and representatives of the Free Imperial Cities.

Even the English Parliament has not for long included, as its most
active component in the House of Commons, Members of Parliament
who are elected directly by voters qualified under a broad franchise.
In the beginning of its growth, it consisted of the King and the great
nobles and bishops in his Council. To these, knights from the shires
and burgesses from towns were gradually added. These "commoners"
were sometimes elected on a very narrow franchise, sometimes selected by the same great territorial magnates who predominated in
the House of Lords. Even the Congress of the United States, until
ratification of the XVII Amendment to the Constitution in 1913, contained one house, the Senate, in which the States—some of which *still*

like to be referred to as "sovereign" states—were represented, not by directly and popularly elected Senators, but by men elected by the state legislatures. Similarly, but with still greater emphasis upon direct representation of member-states, the *Bundesrat* or upper house of the Parliament of the Federal Republic of Germany consists of members of the governments of these member-states of the federal system, who can cast the votes of their state only as a unit.

The fact that the ambassadors who participate in the deliberations of the General Assembly and the Security Council, and cast votes there, are delegates, bound by instructions, of entities known to international law as sovereign states does not, therefore, invalidate the parliamentary analogy. In this context, we should mention that the judges on the International Court of Justice, an organ of the United Nations, though also nominated by sovereign states, are not allowed to be bound by instructions or other influences from their governments. These international judges are, of course, not members of the General Assembly or the Security Council, but the highest British judges are and always have been members of the House of Lords, though they have not always been as independent as in recent centuries of those who appoint them, especially in the days when the King could also remove them. The point here is that the method of getting into a parliamentary and/or judicial organ, and the degree of independence after one gets there, vary widely among institutions and within one set of institutions over its lifetime.

Awareness of this variety and of the evolutionary pattern in many historical parliaments has prompted certain proposals for reform of the parliamentary organs of the United Nations. One of the most imaginative and, because of its systematic comprehensiveness, potentially most influential of these proposals was made by Grenville Clark and Louis B. Sohn in their comprehensive and constructive critique of the Charter, *World Peace through World Law*.[4] They would have the Charter amended, so that the composition of the General Assembly would be based upon the following provisions:

ARTICLE 9

1. The General Assembly shall consist of Representatives from all the member Nations and from the non-self-governing and trust territories under their administration.

---

[4]Grenville Clark and Louis B. Sohn, *World Peace through World Law* (2nd ed.; Cambridge: Harvard University Press, 1960).

2. For the purpose of determining the number of Representatives in the General Assembly from the respective member Nations, the member Nations shall be divided into six categories as follows:

a. From each of the four member Nations having the largest populations there shall be thirty Representatives.

b. From each of the eight member Nations having the next largest populations there shall be fifteen Representatives.

c. From each of the twenty member Nations having the next largest populations there shall be six Representatives.

d. From each of the thirty member Nations having the next largest populations there shall be four Representatives.

e. From each of the remaining member Nations there shall be two Representatives, provided that any such nation has a population of over 1,000,000.

f. From each member Nation having a population of not over 1,000,000 there shall be one Representative.

3. The apportionment of Representatives pursuant to the foregoing formula shall be made by the General Assembly upon the basis of world censuses. . . .

6. Representatives shall be chosen for terms of four years. . . .

7. For the first three terms after the coming into force of this Revised Charter, the Representatives from each member Nation shall be chosen by its national legislature, except to the extent that such legislature may prescribe the election of the Representatives by popular vote. For the next three terms, not less than half of the Representatives from each member Nation shall be elected by popular vote and the remainder shall be chosen by its national legislature, unless such legislature shall prescribe that all or part of such remainder shall also be elected by popular vote; . . . Beginning with the seventh term, all the Representatives of each member Nation shall be elected by popular vote. The General Assembly may, however, by a two-thirds vote of all the Representatives in the Assembly, whether or not present or voting, postpone for not more than eight years the coming into effect of the requirement that not less than half of the Representatives shall be elected by popular vote; and the Assembly may also by a like majority postpone for not more than eight years the requirement that all the Representatives shall be elected by popular vote. In all elections by popular vote held under this paragraph, all persons shall be entitled to vote who are qualified to vote for the members of the most numerous branch of the national legislature of the respective nations.

. . . .

9. The Representatives shall receive reasonable compensation, to be fixed by the General Assembly and to be paid out of the funds of the United Nations.[5]

---

[5]*Ibid.,* pp. 20–25. Reprinted by permission of the publishers from Grenville Clark and Louis B. Sohn, *World Peace Through World Law* (Cambridge, Mass.: Harvard University Press, Copyright 1958, 1960, by the President and Fellows of Harvard College).

Under Article 18 of Clark and Sohn's revised Charter, the "Representatives shall vote as individuals, and each Representative shall have one vote."

These proposals can be fully understood as integral parts of the comprehensive Charter revision advocated, and explicated paragraph by paragraph, in *World Peace through World Law*. For example, the reformed General Assembly consisting eventually of popularly elected Representatives would have the equivalent of the "legislative powers" of a national parliament and would, in addition, elect a new Executive Council, consisting of seventeen Representatives. This Executive Council, whose elected members, like those of the Assembly, "shall vote as individuals," would perform some of the functions now taken care of by the Security Council, which it would replace.

The main point to note here is one obvious purpose of these proposals, so far as they would affect discussion in the General Assembly. That purpose is to make the Assembly more nearly deliberative. In the first twenty years of its existence, the General Assembly has carried on very little real deliberation in its plenary sessions. Discussion there has, on the whole, been restricted to the formulation and resolution of issues. Delegates of member-states have spent most of their time explaining how their governments saw a problem, usually in ideological and legalistic terms, but very little time in the weighing of alternatives or in efforts to persuade other delegations. In roll call votes, in which each member-state, regardless of size or "power," casts one vote, normally on instructions from its government, members simply declared their "will" on the issue under discussion. But this was not the kind of resolution that follows upon true deliberation or precedes the solution of problems. On the contrary, partly because of the skipping or foreshortening of the deliberative phase, the quasi-resolution achieved by votes on contentious issues was usually not accompanied by or backed up with any "decisive" consensus of determination or purpose among the membership sufficient to push the problem toward its solution in accordance with the resolution of its issue. Many debates in the General Assembly might as well have ended with the first statements made by delegates, i.e., with their formulations of the issue. In a sense, even this first phase sometimes seemed superfluous, because any experienced observer could predict how various members of the United Nations would formulate the issues arising out of specific problems, on the basis of their affiliation with one of the two great blocs and various of the subsidiary caucuses, whose patterns of voting usually show less cohesion than those of the blocs them-selves.[6] Direct election of members of the Assembly and their conse-quent "liberation" from instructions issued by their governments would be designed to change the nondeliberative, declaratory character of debates in which speakers simply register the wills of their states.

At this point the challenge to the parliamentary analogy may well be raised again: Since reforms along the lines proposed by Clark and Sohn are not likely to be put into effect for a long time if ever, and since this *is* the current character of debates in the General Assembly, is it not in fact too dissimilar from a parliament to allow the analogy? This particular challenge can easily be disposed of, because there are many contemporary national parliaments, including some compara-tively successful ones, where debates have been similarly nondeliber-ative and declaratory as a result of parliamentary party discipline, roughly the functional equivalent of the UN combination of instructed delegates and bloc voting. In the British House of Commons, for ex-ample, the votes of Members of Parliament can also be predicted with a high degree of accuracy, as can the stand which the Conservative, the Labour, and the Liberal Parties will take on any issue. The two main parliamentary parties do not try to persuade each other through parliamentary debates, and significant changes in bills introduced by the Government are made only very rarely as a result of parliamentary debate. In the French Parliament, under the Third and Fourth Repub-lics, genuine deliberation intended to culminate in the resolution of issues was quite uncommon. The rules of procedure of the National Assembly, in at least one respect, even encouraged declaratory, "will registering" debates, by making it possible for the secretaries of the various parliamentary party groups to cast proxy ballots for their en-tire delegation. In other words, deputies did not have to be present during "deliberation," did not have to participate in the weighing of alternatives, in order to let their wills be registered *en bloc* by their party Secretary. The following two sets of relationships seem more or less analogous:

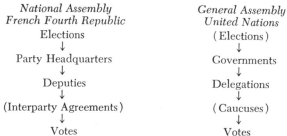

National Assembly French Fourth Republic	General Assembly United Nations
Elections	(Elections)
↓	↓
Party Headquarters	Governments
↓	↓
Deputies	Delegations
↓	↓
(Interparty Agreements)	(Caucuses)
↓	↓
Votes	Votes

[6] See Thomas Hovet, Jr., *Bloc Politics in the United Nations* (Cambridge: vard University Press, 1960).

We could list "Elections" in the sequences of actions at the United Nations for some but not all "Governments." "Caucuses" and "Interparty Agreements" are placed in parentheses because they do not always intervene between the receipt of instructions by deputies or delegations and their voting in the assembly.

There is a second answer to the challenge of the realists: The declaratory, nondeliberative character of debates in the General Assembly is no more important than the declaratory, nondeliberative character of debates in many national parliaments, because deliberation, which involves persuasion including self-persuasion of the deliberators, takes place not mainly in the plenary meetings of parliamentary assemblies, whether national or international, nor even in the meetings of their committees, but outside the main chamber and the committee rooms, in much more informal situations. This is where the real "talking" goes on—and "parliament" is related to the French word *parler*, to talk. It makes little sense to set up some sort of "definitional" requirement under which only those institutions will be considered parliamentary which can pass the test of formal public deliberation. On the contrary, it could be said that the withdrawal of deliberation from formal forums to the cloakrooms, lobbies, antechambers, and "smoke-filled" caucus rooms in both national and international institutions was in part caused by the "excessive" demands for publicity made by advocates of the American type of democracy *and* diplomacy. Great public interest in the substantive outcome of a national or international controversy, if it exposes the negotiations to the glare of publicity, forces the negotiators to conduct themselves so formally and rigidly—out of a variety of considerations, including respect for their constituents—that they may make no progress at all, unless they can escape to greater privacy and even secrecy for the actual bargaining and all the give-and-take which may also include the reformulation of issues. The first of Woodrow Wilson's Fourteen Points was this: "Open covenants of peace, openly arrived at, after which there shall be no private international understandings of any kind but diplomacy shall proceed always frankly and in the public view."[7] Since international diplomacy had remained protected by secrecy even after the national political processes of a few democracies like the United States had been deprived of much of their secrecy, Wilson's Point about "open covenants openly arrived at" could have been pre-

---

[7] See Henry Steele Commager (ed.), *Documents of American History* (New York: F. S. Crofts & Co., Inc., 1934), p. 318.

dicted to have some of the same, partly self-defeating results that excessive publicity brought about in American domestic politics. Genuine deliberation by and among parliamentarians or their equivalents was taken out of the public forum, to be conducted according to less formal procedures.

However, for both national parliaments and the United Nations these developments have been accompanied or followed by others enhancing their role as deliberative organs in the flow of policy of the political system *as a whole*. While efficient intraparliamentary deliberation may have been withdrawn to the cloak rooms, members of both national parliaments and the General Assembly have sought support outside these bodies, for their own policies and sometimes for these parliamentary institutions.

For example, when the suffrage was extended in Great Britain during the nineteenth century, usually on the initiative of the "governing class;" or when the American party system was built up and extended after the Constitution had established the Congress, but before any party system existed; processes occurred which were analogous to the search for support by the founding members of the United Nations among other members including the new states of Asia, Africa, the Middle East, and the Caribbean. Elaborate efforts to appeal to various publics in the world, by the propaganda machineries of the two great blocs, and less costly or well-organized attempts by the United Nations Secretariat and organizations like the UN Associations, bear analogy to the propaganda activities of parties that gained prominence in the national politics of various countries through parliamentary representation and only thereafter tried to find a firm backing among a more or less popular electorate, both for themselves and for the parliament through whose existence they were able to gain some political responsibility.

There is in all of this analogy, however, one basic weakness because one component is lacking that is needed to make the analogy between the United Nations and parliaments complete. This component is the equivalent of a government. In the history of most prenational and national parliaments, government existed before (the increasingly democratic) representation of interests came into being. In the evolution of most (but not all) political systems, organs of resolution developed before organs of deliberation—just as, in the development of the individual human being, the capacity of resolution is developed before the capacity of ratiocination. In England, for example, the Crown's capacity to govern was established before various interests of the realm gained representation vis-á-vis the Crown-in-Parliament. Again, however, we should guard against excessive periodization, because these developments overlapped and the Crown's capacity to govern was enhanced by the accession to parliamentary representation of groups aware of their common special problems. This overlapping and interdependence of the principal organs of resolution and of deliberation is particularly visible in English constitutional history, because there Parliament has always been conceived of as consisting not of the House of Lords and the House of Commons alone, but of "the King-in-Parliament," as the ancient constitutional phrase has it. Even today—perhaps especially today—the enacting formula of Acts of Parliament reveals this fact: "Be it therefore enacted by the Queen's most excellent Majesty, by and with the advice and consent of the Lords Spiritual and Temporal, and Commons, in this present Parliament assembled, and by the authority of the same, as follows."

On the other hand, in the United Nations and in other international organizations (except those clearly dominated by one member, as NATO by the United States or the Warsaw Pact by the Soviet Union), a principal resolving organ usually comes into being and becomes effective only some time *after* the organs of deliberation are created and have established some sort of effectiveness for themselves. This means that the deliberative organs themselves have to produce resolution, not only on major issues like "war and peace"—this, after all, is constitutionally true also in the United States political system, where the Congress declares war—but also on less important, day-to-day issues, like, in the same military field, the dispatch of troop contingents and the composition of United Nations peace-keeping forces. In the UN, both the Security Council and, as a result of the Uniting for Peace Resolution, the General Assembly have had to provide resolution, because the Secretary-General's position was not constitutionally endowed with capacity for resolution, though it has acquired more of this capacity informally through the work of its Secretaries-General than the Charter intended.

When institutions that were constitutionally designed to perform mainly deliberative functions have to address themselves to the tasks of resolution, they usually perform that function very unsatisfactorily.

This has happened in the case of the Security Council and the General Assembly. It again shows, incidentally, that there are analogous stages of evolution in some national parliaments. For example, the French Parliament under the Third and Fourth Republics was also designed as a mainly deliberatively institution, to deliberate, on the basis of the interests represented in it, upon issues resolved by the government, i.e., the Cabinet and the President—as the British Parliament deliberates upon "resolutions" put forward by the Cabinet acting for the Crown. In France, however, Parliament also had to create out of its own midst the resolving organs. It often proved incapable of performing this task, when it could not form a cabinet coalition or when it took weeks to elect a new President of the Republic. Even when a cabinet was governing, in between the frequent cabinet crises, the cabinet, for political and constitutional reasons, could provide so little day-today resolution, that this task also fell to Parliament, and it gave about as little resolution to France as the General Assembly and Security Council have given to the United Nations.

These partial parallels suggest a possible fault in the proposals for reform of the Charter advanced by Clark and Sohn. In their apparent effort to improve the deliberative capacity of the Assembly, they assign to the Assembly also some of the resolving functions now poorly performed by the Security Council and, in addition, the election of the seventeen Representatives who are to make up the new Executive Council. Moreover, they do not propose any important changes in the constitutional position of the Secretary-General. In one respect, this weakness in the proposals advanced in *World Peace through World Law* should come as a surprise, because its American authors were otherwise evidently much influenced by the experience of the American federal system.

Many advocates of strengthened international organization, including proponents of "world government," have based their schemes upon analogies to federal systems on lower levels, as is indicated, e.g., by the title of the organization known as World Federalists. In the history of some nonhegemonial federal systems, the chronological priority of resolution to deliberation is not nearly as clear as in the history of a unitary parliamentary system like the English. For example, the United States under the Articles of Confederation were constitutionally endowed with good deliberative and poor resolving capacity. During the War of Independence, when they recognized the primacy of the problem of resolution against Great Britain, the Continental Congress made it possible for General George Washington to provide much of that resolution. And when the inadequacy of the Articles of Confederation was recognized, the Constitutional Convention, which was presided over by Washington, provided optimum resolution for the future in the office of the President, with the clear expectation that Washington would be the first occupant of the office. If we date the history of the United States from the adoption of the Constitution, then we would have to say that the organs of deliberation and resolution were created simultaneously. If the United States has rarely lacked resolution since then, this must be attributed to the imaginative foresight of the constitutional founding fathers, who assured the President (short of impeachment or death) of at least one term's tenure of four years and provided, in the Electoral College, a procedure capable of filling the Presidency but separated from the mainly deliberative Congress. The later development of what has become for all practical purposes the direct popular election of the President is one of those happy consequences of purposive political action which the Founding Fathers had not intended, but for which their Constitution left the way wide open, through its brevity, its procedural bias, its low substantive content, and its flexible stability.

The Authority of the United Nations

The constitutional founding fathers of the United Nations endowed both General Assembly and Security Council with both deliberate and resolving functions, though they evidently intended the Assembly to be more an organ of deliberation and the Council to be more an organ of resolution. They seem to have had no intention whatever of making the position of Secretary-General an organ of resolution, based on the model of other constitutional "executives" like the President of the United States. In fact, however, the Secretary-Generalship has occasionally provided resolution when the other organs failed to do so. This, too, is a case of unintended consequences which are, moreover, regarded as highly undesirable by some of the charter members of the organization.

The authors of the Charter did give the Secretary-General greater opportunities for initiative in his relations with Council and Assembly than the authors of the Covenant of the League. The Covenant simply stated: "The Secretary-General shall act in that capacity at all meetings of the Assembly and of the Council." It dealt with his position and the entire Secretariat in one article consisting of five paragraphs. The Charter, on the other hand, is somewhat more detailed in five Articles (97 to 101), comprising eight paragraphs, and scattered other references elsewhere. For example, Article 20, on procedure of the General Assembly, provides that "Special sessions shall be convoked by the Secretary-General at the request of the Security Council or of a majority of the Members of the United Nations." Much more important, however, is Article 99: "The Secretary-General may bring to the attention of the Security Council any matter which in his opinion may threaten the maintenance of international peace and security." The opinions of the person who is Secretary-General may be, as a result of this provision, of considerable importance. This fact has influenced the members of the Security Council, upon whose "recommendation" the General Assembly appoints the Secretary-General, in their selection of the men who have held the job. By contrast, Sir Hugh Drummond, the former British foreign service officer who served as Secretary-General of the League during most of its life, was not viewed as particularly crucial to the functioning of that organization. In fact, he conducted himself in a much more neutral, anonymous, self-effacing, civil-servant-like way than any of the three first Secretaries-General of the United Nations, Trygve Lie, Dag Hammarskjöld, and U Thant.

Each of these men has brought to the attention of the Security Council and thereby of politically aware men and women everywhere matters which in his opinion threatened international peace and security. As a result of such constitutionally permitted initiatives, the Secretary-General has taken actions understood and criticized as inimical to the interests of one or another of the great blocs and individual member states both major and minor. Trygve Lie so offended the Soviet Union, that it refused to communicate with him personally in his position as Secretary-General. Dag Hammarskjöld offended both the Soviet Union and the United States, as well as Belgium, competing governments of the Congo, and uncommitted states of Africa and Asia, during various stages of the United Nations operations in the Congo.

Early in the Congo operation he had made clear to the Council the necessity of moving ahead in the absence of specific guidance:
"I have a right to expect guidance. That guidance can be given in many

forms. But it should be obvious if the Security Council says nothing I have no other choice than to follow my conviction. . . . *Implementation obviously means interpretation.*" (U.N. Security Council, Fifteenth Year, *Official Records*, 888th Meeting, Doc. S/PV. 888 [August 21, 1960], p. 21.)

Exercising initiative and guided by his understanding of the Charter and the Council resolutions, Hammarskjöld utilized fully the powers of his office, recognizing at all times that his capacity to act effectively was ultimately derived from the diplomatic and material support of the coalition of states committed to the operation.[8]

Like Lie before him Hammarskjöld antagonized the Soviet Union more than the United States. Alexander Dallin has suggested that

Soviet discomfort may have been compounded by comparisons with the Spanish Civil War of 1936–39. The sequence, on the Soviet side, had not been so dissimilar then: involvement, surprise, conflict with the League of Nations' policy; failure to defy the League completely, but also failure to follow through with troops of its own; and unwillingness to risk involving itself in war. Both conflicts took place in remote areas during periods of general "coexistence."[9]

Even if Soviet diplomats did indeed have this comparison on their minds, the consequences for Soviet action in the League and in the United Nations were quite different, as were the policies of the two organizations. The Soviet Union basically ignored the League's minor involvement in the Spanish Civil War and certainly did not seek to bring about any constitutional changes in the structure of the League in order to affect the current or similar future international conflicts.

Only three months after the outbreak of the international crisis over the Congo, the Soviet Premier himself spoke before the General Assembly in New York City. He advocated precisely constitutional reform of the Charter: "It is necessary that the executive agency of the United Nations reflect the actual situation now obtaining in the world. . . . We deem it wise and fair that the United Nations executive agency consist not of one person, the Secretary-General, but of three persons enjoying the confidence of the United Nations."[10]

---

[8]Ernest W. Lefever, *Crisis in the Congo: A U.N. Force in Action* (Washington, D.C.: Brookings Institution, 1965), pp. 57–58. Italics supplied to underline Hammarskjöld's awareness of the inseparability of implementation and interpretation or, in our terms, of solution and (re)deliberation.

[9]Alexander Dallin, *The Soviet Union at the United Nations: An Inquiry into Soviet Motives and Objectives*, (New York: Frederick A. Praeger, 1962), p. 150 (footnote). Quoted by permission of Frederick A. Praeger, Publishers.

[10]Cited from Khrushchev's speech of September 23, 1960, *ibid.*, p. 153.

This was Premier Krushchev's famous "troika" proposal, to replace the single Secretary-General with a committee of three, "each representing a definite group of states," the communist and Western blocs and the uncommitted members of the UN. The troika proposal was interesting, not only because it was an instance of Soviet *Realpolitik*—the "real power" situation in the world consists of three blocs, which should be realistically reflected in the "executive agency" of the UN—or because of the unideological pragmatism with which the Soviet Union gave up the troika concept, at least temporarily, when it agreed to let U Thant replace the dead Hammarskjöld, first as Acting Secretary-General, then for his own full term of office. Even more significant was the fact that the Soviet Union chose to bring all of its opposition to the policies of the United Nations and of the "imperialist bloc" in the Congo and elsewhere to a focus in this constitutional issue affecting the UN itself. This is a prime example of the conversion of a problem that was originally recognized in substantive terms into a primarily procedural issue, by Soviet politicians whose style in both domestic and international politics has generally had a comparatively substantive bias.

This case can be taken as an instance of the ways in which new layers of consensus on certain procedures of the United Nations slowly accrete. All three incumbents of the office of Secretary-General to-date have been able to draw upon a capital of international authority for policies advanced by them, even when the policies went against the interests of powerful members or blocs within the United Nations. This authority has been steadily growing, that is, U Thant enjoys greater authority than his two predecessors. This growth in the international authority of the Secretariat and its head, the Secretary-General, is in part an intended consequence of Article 100 of the Charter:

1. In the performance of their duties the Secretary-General and the staff shall not seek or receive instructions from any government or from any other authority external to the Organization. They shall refrain from any action which might reflect on their position as international officials responsible only to the Organization.

2. Each Member of the United Nations undertakes to respect the exclusively international character of the responsibilities of the Secretary-General and the staff and not to seek to influence them in the discharge of their responsibilities.

These provisions, especially Paragraph 2 to the extent that it has been respected by members, have enabled the Secretariat to build up an authority of its own in world politics, because people affected by its actions could believe that these were not disproportionately shaped by interests and groups inimical to their own interests. The Soviet Union, to be sure, as part of its "realism" when it put forward the troika proposal, denied that individuals could be neutral, though states might be. To this charge, the man against whom it was leveled, Secretary-General Hammarskjöld, made a partial reply: "It is not the Soviet Union, or indeed any other 'big powers' who need the UN for their protection; it is all the others. In this sense the Organization is first of all *their* Organization." And he added that he would not resign so long as these smaller members retained their confidence in him—which they then expressed by an overwhelming vote of the General Assembly in favor of his Congo policy.

Hammarskjöld's appeal was directed to the "neutralism" of small size and little power rather than the "neutrality" of individual international civil servants or of European states like his own Sweden in conventional international relations. But the fact of his success in this crisis—success in the sense of the survival of his Office, which was tragically followed by his own death on the way to negotiate with Mr. Tshombe—served to augment further the authority of the Office in the particular direction intended by him.

His successor, U Thant, echoed this belief when he said, at Uppsala on 6 May 1962: "I am in complete agreement with my distinguished predecessor, Mr. Dag Hammarskjöld, when he said that it is the small nations, rather than the great powers, which need the protection the United Nations can give."[11] U Thant was enabled to take this position with special authority, because he himself was a citizen of one of the neutralist states which now make up a majority of the United Nations, whereas his two predecessors had been citizens of Scandinavian countries, one of which, Sweden, has been neutral in the old-fashioned sense, while the other, Norway, became a member of NATO. The fact, in turn, that a Burmese should have been agreed upon by the members of the Security Council as the third Secretary-General may be taken as a measure of the confidence that even the two superpowers had by then developed in the independent authority of the office. U Thant has also had his difficulties with the two blocs,

---

[11]Andrew Boyd, *United Nations: Piety Myth Truth* (Baltimore: Penguin Books, 1962), p. 178.

but more with the Western states than the communist members. For a while, e.g., the United States seemed to be snubbing his efforts to mediate in various crises of the Cold War, including Cuba, Vietnam, and the Dominican Republic. In the summer of 1965, however, the United States appeared to be altering its policy in this respect, when it tried for a while to "dump in his lap" the Vietnamese problem and appointed as its Ambassador to the United Nations former Associate Justice of the Supreme Court Arthur J. Goldberg, who was expected to act as a vigorous advocate of the "UN way" within the American President's Cabinet.

The increasing recourse to and focus upon the United Nations has enhanced its authority so much, that the domestic political careers of men and women who have been prominent in the UN, either as ambassadors for their states or as officials of the organization, can benefit from a kind of "derivative UN authority" that adheres to them after their departure from its institutions. Examples of whom this has been true to varying degrees include Henry Cabot Lodge, who became the Republican vice-presidential candidate after his service as President Eisenhower's Ambassador to the UN; Andrei A. Gromyko, who served as Soviet representative on the Security Council before he became Foreign Minister; Abba Eban, who represented Israel at the UN for many years before he became foreign minister of Israel; and Ambassador Alex Quaison-Sackey of Ghana, who was President of the General Assembly when President Nkrumah appointed him Foreign Minister. This derivative authority seems to be more useful in the politics of small states than great powers, for reasons which are related to the statements by Hammarskjöld and U Thant cited above.

At the same time substantive consensus has also been building up on various goals proclaimed by the United Nations, from those contained in the Charter itself, through the content of documents like the Universal Declaration of Human Rights and the Genocide Convention, to matters on which the great antagonists of the Cold War find themselves in voting agreement at the United Nations. While the Charter was being drafted, substantive consensus was most evident on the urgency of defeating the Axis and the desirability of preventing recurrence of a world war caused by the Axis type of aggression. As already mentioned, this consensus was written into the constitution of the United Nations. However, a great many other substantive matters were included in—the temptation is to say "slipped into"—that document, which was subsequently ratified by all members of the United Nations, though many of them must have had a very weak, if any, commitment to these principles, goals, and implied time tables. Some probably subscribed in the expectation that pious declarations would remain only that, so that their own policies could continue as unaffected by the United Nations as by the League of Nations before, if their national interest should require this.

One can begin the textual analysis of the Charter in this light: Did the South African government, whose Prime Minister, Jan C. Smuts, had been a principal contributor to both Covenant and Charter, really want "to reaffirm faith in fundamental human rights, in the dignity and worth of the human person"? Did the rulers of certain Islamic kingdoms want to reaffirm faith "in equal rights of men and women"? Did the Soviet Union want to reaffirm faith in the equal rights "of nations large and small"? Were the great European colonial powers, just about to regain control of their colonies from Japan, determined "to promote social progress and better standards of life in larger freedom"?

This last question can be repeated for the "Declaration Regarding Non-Self-Governing Territories" of Chapter XI of the Charter. The whole tenor of this Chapter differs markedly from Article 22 of the Covenant:

1. To those colonies and territories which as a consequence of the late war have ceased to be under the sovereignty of the States which formerly governed them and which are inhabited by peoples not yet able to stand by themselves under the strenuous conditions of the modern world, there should be applied the principle that the well-being and development of such peoples form a sacred trust of civilisation and that securities for the performance of this trust should be embodied in this Covenant.

2. The best method of giving practical effect to this principle is that the tutelage of such peoples should be entrusted to advanced nations who, by reason of their resources, their experience or their geographical position, can best undertake this responsibility, and who are willing to accept it, and that this tutelage should be exercised by them as Mandatories on behalf of the League.

This article, which applied only to mandated former colonies of the Central Powers, not to the "possessions" of other colonial powers, contrasts sharply in its paternalism with the Declaration of the Charter regarding all non-self-governing territories:

Members of the United Nations which have or assume responsibilities for the administration of territories whose peoples have not yet attained a full measure of self-government recognize the principle that the interests of the inhabitants of these territories are paramount, and accept as a sacred trust the obligation to promote to the utmost, within the system of international peace and security established by the present Charter, the well-being of the inhabitants of these territories, and, to this end:

a. to ensure, with due respect for the culture of the people concerned, their political, economic, social, and educational advancement, their just treatment, and their protection against abuses;

b. to develop self-government, to take due account of the political aspirations of the peoples, and to assist them in the progressive development of their free political institutions, according to the particular circumstances of each territory and its peoples and their varying stages of advancement. . . .

One wonders whether British, French, Dutch, and Belgian diplomats realized that genuine acceptance of this Declaration would have signed the death warrants of their colonial empires. And since, with the possible partial exception of the British, it is unlikely that they were then willing to contemplate liquidation of these empires, the conclusion arises that they did not expect this Declaration of the Charter and many of its other "idealistic" but "unrealistic" substantive goals to be taken seriously or to be implemented. The same conclusion would emerge from the provisions of Chapters XII and XIII, "International Trusteeship Systems" and "The Trusteeship Council," which are even more explicit with respect to the goal of "their progressive development towards self-government or independence" and at the same time set up institutions and procedures within the United Nations to supervise implementation.

Whatever may have been the motives and intentions of various contributors for including these substantive goals and principles in the Charter, in 1945, the remarkable fact of 1965 is that virtually all the trust territories have achieved independence, normally accompanied by membership in the United Nations. And, with the exception of South Africa's Mandate over Southwest Africa and the Portuguese colonies in Africa, virtually all the colonies have gained their independence. In the General Assembly of the United Nations, these "new states," together with other "developing countries" that have been states for longer periods, can command a voting majority on issues on which they are in agreement. Their contribution to world politics is of sufficient importance for us to devote Chapter 8 of this book to it.

At this point, "realists" might argue that decolonization would have happened in any case, regardless of the existence of the United Nations or the provisions of its Charter, because decolonization was necessitated, was made inevitable, by the realities of power obtaining in the world after the end of World War II. Among these realities, they would cite the loss of prestige of the white powers flowing from their interracial power struggle and from the occupation of large parts of Asia by the nonwhite Japanese, their loss of power and economic resources resulting from the ravages of war, the extension of Soviet power and its support of "colonial liberation movements" against capitalist imperialism (in another "final" stage of development), and corresponding growth in the power of "nationalist" movements all over the colonial world.

We can safely admit that each of the "causes" contributed to decolonization, as part of a complex concourse of causes. However, to dump all of them under the heading of "loss of power" hardly facilitates a comprehensive or systematic understanding of the processes at work. For instance, soon after the end of the war, the colonial powers had regained their monopoly of the means of organized force in their overseas possessions. Nevertheless, the colonies gained independence by forceful or less violent means. Sometimes the colonialists lost their "will to govern," their "nerve," or, in our terms, their capacity for resolution. Why? The independence movements, on the other hand, marshaled great resolution behind their drives though they usually suffered from a poverty of power. Why? Their contributions to formulation of the issue of colonialism was often highly legalistic, couched in the phraseology of the Charter. This is understandable, but why did the colonial powers let themselves be drawn into the argument on these terms that were so unfavorable to their cause? The independence movements participated in deliberation of the independence issue, both directly vis-à-vis their white rulers and in world politics, in an often ideological manner. Sometimes they constructed a whole system of knowledge out of their opposition to colonialism, and some have carried this ideology over into the period of their independence as opposition to neocolonialism. The colonial states, again partly as a result of their ratification of the Charter, by accepting this framework for the debate, allowed themselves to be put on the defensive.

All of this suggests that the substantive goals written into the Charter had taken on an authority of their own, which gave to the process of decolonization a form *and* a content different from those it would have taken without the United Nations or with a different Charter. Without the UN, it seems likely, for example, that a "pure struggle for power" along lines envisaged by some adherents of the school of *Realpolitik* would have occurred over the colonies and between them and their outside rulers. This suggestion might prompt some "realists" to take their argument back to the time of the signing of the Charter by "explaining" its contents as reflecting the power relations obtaining in the world in 1945, but we have already, we trust, demonstrated the unidimensional inadequacy of such explanations.

The accretion of consensus on the authority of the substantive goals enunciated by the Charter can be shown also, though less definitely, for matters not directly related to decolonization, like equal human rights. Here the founders were evidently motivated by their common revulsion against the Nazi principles and policies of discrimination on the basis of race, religion, sex, language, and nationality, which had been carried to the point of the attempted liquidation of entire population groups. This opposition was written into the Charter, and later elaborated in a number of conventions and declarations, among them The Convention on the Prevention of the Crime of Genocide, the Universal Declaration of Human Rights, and other conventions concerning the rights of women, children, and other special classes of persons. The drafting of these conventions has generally entailed greater difficulties than did the drafting of the briefer statements in the Charter itself because, in the course of their elaboration, it was discovered that phrases like "fundamental human rights," promotion of "social progress" and of "higher standards of living, full employment, and conditions of economic and social progress and development" meant different, even diametrically opposite, things to different members of the United Nations.

For the United States, the goals contained in the phrase cited last could be approached best through a system of private ownership in a mixed economy; for the Soviet Union, through its system of socialism; for a country like Mexico through state ownership of mineral resources. Nevertheless, opposing interpreters of these goals and of the best means for realizing them usually found a common denominator of agreement, which was then written into the conventions. Many of these conventions have not, however, been ratified by a sufficient number of states to put them into formal effect. The United States, for example, has ratified neither the Genocide Convention, nor the Universal Declaration of Human Rights, nor the conventions on slavery, forced labor, and the political rights of women. The three last mentioned, though drafted by the UN in the 1950's, were submitted to the US Senate for ratification only in 1963, by President Kennedy. Still, the very fact that commissions of the United Nations could reach agreement on these documents not only demonstrates the existence of some consensus on their contents, but adds new consensus on the more general aims and operating procedures of the UN. This happens, among other ways, through the use made of UN conventions, regardless of the status of their ratification, in international controversies. When politicians who can act with some authority in world politics accuse others of planning or committing genocide, or of violating fundamental human rights as anchored in the Universal Declaration, even though they may be doing this for entirely pragmatic or even cynical reasons of expediency, these arguments usually add something to the over-all authority of the United Nations. Moreover, the availability of such arguments also contributes toward the increasing centralization of global political processes upon the focus of the UN.

The authority of the United Nations gains most when the leaders of the two great blocs are found to be in voting agreement on issues within the organization, and the more controversial an issue was before agreement could be reached, the greater the gain that accrues to the UN. It benefits, of course, from agreements reached under its auspices on such technical and scientific matters as the International Geophysical Year or world health policies. It benefits also from occasions when the Soviet Union and the United States vote on the same side of an issue before the Security Council, though for different reasons, as for example during the invasion of Egypt by Israel, France, and the United Kingdom in the Suez Crisis of 1956, and during the war over Kashmir between Pakistan and India in 1965. The authority of the UN benefits from agreement reached after prolonged hard bargaining between the two superpowers, as preceded establishment of the International Atomic Energy Commission, or their concurrence with a

General Assembly Resolution against placing nuclear weapons on satellites in outer space. The partial Test Ban Treaty, whose signatories agreed to conduct no nuclear tests in the atmosphere, in outer space, or under water, also added to the authority of the United Nations, though it was not negotiated in its final phases within the United Nations framework. The authority of the UN grows as a result even of prolonged but *un*successful conferences, like the one held under UN auspices and with participation of uncommitted states in Geneva, to make the partial test ban complete by extending it to underground tests and to move on from there to nuclear and general disarmament.

In fact, according to this interpretation, virtually any problem that leads to the generation of issues within the United Nations system is likely to add to the authority of the UN, *regardless* of the success of the organization in resolving the issue or solving the underlying problem. This statement will seem paradoxical, but it is consistent with our conception of the development of politics. The more the members of a political system avail themselves of its procedures, the more experience with and commitment to these procedures are they likely to develop, even though use of the procedures does not bring them the intended results (up to a point of diminishing returns). This proposition applies with unique forcefulness to the global political system of today, because all smaller political systems are components of it and have no alternatives to this condition.

The ideologically violent Nazis in the Weimar Republic exploited the procedures of parliamentary constitutionalism in order to destroy them, though even the Nazis retained some of the legalism they acquired in the course of their subversion of the constitution. Even if one made the mistake of describing the style in world politics of the Soviet or Chinese Communists as more ideologically violent than the Nazis' style in German national politics, they are restrained from using their equivalent of the full violence eventually used by the Nazis against the Republic by the unlimited destructiveness of contemporary weapons systems. In the Weimar Republic, both Nazis and Communists subverted parliamentary procedures through violently obstructionist tactics in and outside the Reichstag. To Western observers it has sometimes seemed as though the Soviet Union and other members of the communist bloc in the United Nations had been trying to accomplish the same end there, e.g., through "excessive" use of the veto in the Security Council or through Premier Khrushchev's famous desk-pounding and shoe-thumping demonstration in the General Assembly. In fact, however, both types of practices again redounded to the benefit of the authority of the United Nations, basically because there has turned out to be no alternative to the United Nations so far.

The veto of the Big Five was written into the Charter by their agreement at the time of the founding, and while the Soviet Union has interpreted these provisions more legalistically than the other Big Four (who vary among themselves on this score), every discussion of differing interpretations of this constitutional procedure has added consensus *at least* to the procedures by means of which these discussions are carried on. Attendance by the head of the government of one of the two most powerful states in the world as the leader of his delegation at a meeting of the General Assembly—as it happened, along with many other heads of governments—also adds to the authority of the United Nations, no matter how deplorable his "unparliamentary" conduct may be regarded by parliamentarians and diplomats of the old school, so long as the Soviet Union neither withdrew from the organization, nor was desirous or capable of pushing other members out of it.

We can, in fact, turn against its authors the thesis (discussed in Chapter 1) that serves as the foundation for the divorce between the study of national politics and international politics, according to which these two are qualitatively different and nonanalogous, because the legitimate monopoly of force that exists in sovereign states is lacking in international relations. To the extent that internal sovereignty is a reality, it can make an internal power struggle a battle whose outcome must be everything or nothing at all. To the extent that sovereignty in international relations is a reality, it can make international power struggles battles for absolute ends, like absorption of all or parts of the territory of one state by another. In contemporary world politics, on the other hand, in the absence and present unattainability of world sovereignty, the all-or-nothing-at-all alternative does not exist and battles for absolute ends against other formally "equal" systems will be impossible at least until our global system engages in politics with other worlds. The boundaries of our global political system, as we said at the conclusion of Chapter 3, do not have to be maintained, they only have to be grown into. As a result, virtually anything that is done at, in, through, or with the United Nations, regardless of motives or outcome, adds to the authority of the United Nations. Even those states which, "objectively" seen, are least committed to the goals of the UN and most worried by its detrimental effects on their own national interest have demonstrated, in their policies, with occasional lapses, their continuing awareness of this fact.

The Contribution of the United Nations to World Politics

What has the United Nations contributed to world politics? We shall now try to answer this question by trying to gauge the effects of the functioning of the UN upon pursuit by the global system of the four basic goals of stability, flexibility, efficiency, and effectiveness.

The *stability* of world politics has been helped by the United Nations, in the sense that, without the UN or some similarly almost universal organization, the channels through which world politics flows would probably have been more shifting and the long-run goals toward which its flow is supposed to be directed would probably have commanded less consensus. The United Nations has provided a structural and procedural framework for a doubling of the number of independent states in the world and for great growth in the number of regional and functional international organizations. It seems doubtful that the excolonies could have been absorbed by the international system in as orderly a fashion, as has in fact been the case, without the UN. What little international business these countries formerly had to conduct was taken care of for them by their "mother countries"; in any case, most of the international business of any colony was with its metropole in Europe or the United States. Now each of the excolonies also has to engage in international intercourse "laterally" with its neighbors in its own "developing area," with other excolonies, and with the older states of the international system. The United Nations has helped to stabilize this welter of new relations in a variety of ways, including provision of its own institutions as central points of contact, and encouragement for the creation, within its own general framework, of new regional international organizations, like the Organization of African unity and the UN Economic Commissions for various continental areas.

Because of the difficulty of the formal amending process of the

Charter, this was used successfully only once in the first two decades of the United Nations, in order to expand the Security Council and the Economic and Social Council. The constitutional rigidity of the UN has also contributed to the legalism of world politics, during this period. However, the very fact that this constitutional rigidity forced all members to work with the same basic institutions, throughout the whole time of their membership until 1965, has endowed fundamental procedures with greater authority than would have been the case if amending majorities could frequently have been mustered for important alterations of the Charter. Moreover, in a situation where unlimited nuclear violence is the diametrical alternative to extreme legalism, the latter is obviously to be preferred for the sake of the simple survival of the system and of the three billion human beings who are its most important components.

The *flexibility* of world politics has been helped by the United Nations, because it has offered—often through improvisation—some procedures for dealing with a wide range of novel, sometimes unanticipated or even unanticipatable problems, including the attainment of statehood by scores of colonies, the general growth in the awareness of the existence of a community of mankind, the development of nuclear and space technology, and the Cold War itself. The UN has managed to keep itself fairly flexible despite the rigidity of the Charter just mentioned, by circumvention, as in the case of the Uniting for Peace Resolution, and by less formal devices, like those used to keep the Nineteenth General Assembly operating without roll-call votes during the dispute over the payment of special assessments under Article 19. Through the creation of new and the adaptation of old specialized international agencies, the UN contributed to the capacity of the global system to make adjustments to the many great substantive changes that have been taking place in the past two decades. And by keeping all of these specialized substantive agencies in relation with each other, by encouraging them to adopt regularized operating procedures, by facilitating near universal membership for them, the UN helped to avoid overemphasis on flexibility at the expense of stability and effectiveness. In other words, its contribution to flexibility has not degenerated into the promotion of pragmatism.

The *efficiency* of world politics has been helped by the United Nations through its contributions to solving technical problems, to ending "brushfire" conflicts, and to postponing the violent resolution of major issues of the Cold War between the nuclear blocs. The specialized agencies just mentioned have facilitated approaches to the solution of a vast range of technical problems, through a systematic, procedurally regularized pooling of resources. The resources have included scientific and cultural, legal, economic, technological, and military personnel, and everything from money to medicine and from bullets to law books. Without the availability of the United Nations or an organization very much like it, solution of the problem—for world politics, not just for Middle Eastern politics—of relations between Israel and its Arab neighbors would presumably be farther away than it is today and would have generated greater violence than has so far been the case largely because of the presence of the United Nations Emergency Force that was first organized during the Suez Crisis of 1956 and in the beginning consisted of almost 6,000 troops furnished by members of the UN who were genuinely neutral in that particular controversy. The United Nations appears to have contributed to the general tendency of nonnuclear states to deliberate about controversies among themselves more often in legalistic than in violent style, and to postpone for years resolution of issues, like that over Kashmir between India and Pakistan, where quick resolution could be obtained only through violence. After the actual outbreak of military violence, they seemed prepared to let the UN provide the "legal excuse" for its termination.

One can argue whether the United Nations contributed to the efficient solution of the international problems raised by the Congo's achievement of independence from Belgian rule, or rather magnified and aggravated these problems for the global political system. Those who take the latter position maintain that United Nations intervention made a Cold War problem out of what could have been kept contained within the Congo and between it and the NATO states, especially Belgium and the United States. They insist also that the United Nations Force in the Congo itself was inefficiently operated, was usually unable to get various Congolese factions to accept its policies, and often violated the mandate it had received from the United Nations. These arguments overlook the likelihood that, without UN intervention, the Soviet Union might have intervened directly in the Congo, thereby producing a direct confrontation in Central Africa between the two superpowers and their respective allies in the two blocs. Ernest W. Lefever, in his study of this "U.N. Force in Action," concludes:

The Congo peacekeeping effort was a novel, controversial, and a less-than-efficient enterprise. It sometimes fumbled. It made many small mistakes. It was assailed on all sides. It precipitated a financial crisis for the United Nations. But in the final analysis, the U.N. Force must be judged by its contribution to international stability, regardless of what other interests it might have served. So judged, the mission succeeded. It contributed to peace and security in Central Africa and in the wider world.

As the largest and most complex internationally authorized and administered operation in history, the Congo peacekeeping effort is rich in lessons and warnings for the future.[12]

In the Congo, as also for problems arising out of direct face-to-face clashes—or, as journalists put it during the Cuban Missile Crisis, "eyeball-to-eyeball" confrontations—between the United States and the Soviet Union, we must bear in mind, in judging the United Nations' contributions to the efficiency of world politics, the order of priority assigned by members of the global political system to its problems. Here again, as on page 151 above, we can turn against its authors the thesis about the qualitative difference between national and international politics. "Realists" ultimately judge the performance of states by their capacity to survive in the allegedly inevitable and continuous struggle for power among states. For national states, this criterion is false, or at least historically limited in its applicability, and those who commit this error do so, because they assume the universality of the function of external "boundary maintenance." National and other states can in fact be highly successful without surviving, e.g., by merging with other states in order to form more comprehensive and, therefore, more efficient and more effective, more stable and more flexible political systems. This has frequently happened as a result of changes in the order of priority in which the members of the smaller system recognize their problems. The reverse is also possible, i.e., a large political system can "succeed" by failing to survive, as did Sweden and Norway when they agreed to split one kingdom into two, or the British Empire when it gradually converted itself into the multisystem of the Commonwealth. However, neither of these options, which can become available for states as a result of changes in problem priorities, exists for the contemporary system of world politics. It can neither merge with a more encompassing system, because none exists; nor can it split into two or more smaller systems, because the facts of global interdepen-

---

[12]Ernest W. Lefever, *Crisis in the Congo*, p. 181.

dence make this impossible in the nuclear age. Hence we must conclude that ability to survive, which is not a proper criterion applied to national states, is the ultimate standard by which we must judge the performance of the political system of mankind. Survival of mankind is the first problem for world politics. The United Nations' contributions to efficiency must first of all be evaluated with respect to solution of this problem.

Any "minor" problem, like that of the Congo, so long as it threatened to escalate into nuclear world war, can be judged as having been solved relatively efficiently, so long as it prevents this escalation. And the survival—indeed, the constant growth and expansion of its capacity to process issues—of the global political system speaks well of UN contributions to efficiency, especially in view of the number of direct confrontations between the two big nuclear powers which the United Nations has helped to "defuse." This is not meant to assert that we can assume in each such case that the crisis would not have been allayed without intervention or participation of the UN. In some cases, like that of the Congo, it has even been argued that the United Nations brought about a direct clash between the two nuclear giants by forcing them to keep in daily touch with each other on *all* the problems handled by the UN, many of which are otherwise peripheral to the national interests of the United States and the Soviet Union. This line of argument takes the general position that UN politics serves to raise an otherwise calmer and cooler international relations to fever heat and to keep its temperature permanently high. This position is opposed in principle to ours, in that it denies the primacy of politics and the independently high value we place upon politics as the highest form of *human* activity.

The *effectiveness* of world politics has been helped by the United Nations mainly for issues where a UN majority capable of action did not go counter to the interests of the states affected by the action. For example, UN policies toward the solution of technical problems, including those coming under the purview of the specialized agencies, have been widely accepted by both givers and receivers of assistance. But even policies that were in the first instance vigorously opposed by relatively powerful states have been effective on those occasions, when they had the backing of both the United States and the Soviet Union, as for example the intervention by the UN in the Suez Crisis of 1956, and in the Kashmir conflict of 1965, (both of which excluded direct intervention by the two superpowers). Sometimes the reverse has happened, as when a majority of the General Assembly persuaded the publicly reluctant United States and the secretly perhaps equally reluctant Soviet Union to support a resolution banning the stationing of nuclear weapons in outer space. However, efforts by similar majorities of the General Assembly to get the nuclear powers to cease all nuclear testing, reduce their nuclear stockpiles, and conclude a disarmament treaty, had not been effective by 1965. On the contrary, two nuclear states, one of them, France, a member of the UN, the other, China, not yet represented in it, refused to accede to the partial Test Ban Treaty of 1963, and both China and France failed for a number of years to participate in the Geneva Disarmament Conference. When majorities in the United Nations have attempted to act against the Soviet Union, as during the Hungarian uprising of 1956, these policies of the UN have not been effective, at least not over the shortrun. But here the point should again be made, that Soviet and Hungarian diplomats at the UN, though they refused to accept its jurisdiction or the content of the resolutions based upon the assumption of UN jurisdiction, never expanded this opposition to the existence of the United Nations itself or to their own membership in it. On the contrary and as usual, they refused to accept these resolutions on legalistic grounds of their own strict interpretation of the Charter, especially Paragraph 7 of Article 2, as applied to Hungary:

> Nothing contained in the present Charter shall authorize the United Nations to intervene in matters which are essentially within the domestic jurisdiction of any state or shall require the Members to submit such matters to settlement under the present Charter; but this principle shall not prejudice the application of enforcement measures under Chapter VII [Action with Respect to Threats to the Peace, Breaches of the Peace, and Acts of Aggression].

Over the long-run, this controversy like many others may actually have contributed toward building up a little more procedural consensus within the United Nations.

Contributions toward the effectiveness of world politics have been greatest in the area of decolonization, ever since this was incorporated as a legitimate and early goal for the UN in its Charter. This policy, as already mentioned, was eventually accepted by all the colonial powers, with the exception of Portugal. However, even Portugal tried to make a legalistic adjustment to the relevant provisions of the Charter by converting its overseas colonies to the constitutional status of provinces. Because Portugal had long ago adopted the policy of racial "assimilation," it also claimed not to be in violation of the Charter's Purposes, which include, in Article 1, Paragraph 3, the following: "To achieve international cooperation in solving international problems of an economic, social, cultural, or humanitarian character, and in promoting and encouraging respect for human rights and for fundamental freedoms for all without distinction as to race, sex, language, or religion. . . ." Critics of Portuguese colonial policy in the UN insisted that the inhabitants of Portugal's overseas territories in Africa and, before her expulsion by Indian troops, in Goa, were in fact being discriminated against on the basis of race, language, and religion, but the point is again that the controversy was being kept within the framework of the Charter.

Unlike Portugal, the Republic of South Africa, whose policy of *apartheid* serves as the very foundation of its being, could not disclaim to be making distinctions based upon race. It therefore asserted that *apartheid* was best designed to promote economic and social and other human rights for its population, and it denied the jurisdiction of the United Nations on the same legalistic grounds of Article 2 (7) that have been used by other states for a variety of purposes. South Africa's position in defending its refusal to convert its Mandate over the former German colony of Southwest Africa into a United Nations Trust was different again, but it also moved within the framework of the Charter and the Covenant and involved prolonged litigation before the International Court of Justice, in which the South African government participated with what can best be described as immense legalistic enthusiasm. Although African and Asian members of various specialized agencies of the UN succeeded in excluding South Africa from these organizations, South Africa had not withdrawn from the United Nations by 1966, as she had withdrawn from the Commonwealth in 1961.

One could compare various legalistic controversies about the meaning of the Charter with the argument about the meaning of the British constitution between the settlers in the thirteen North American colonies and the British Parliament—with the crucial difference, that the settlers won their separation from the Empire, while the Soviets, the Hungarians, the Portuguese, and the South Africans have stayed in the UN, as have the Congolese even while governed by Premier

Tshombe, whose forces were for a time in military conflict with forces of the United Nations.

The best index of the contribution the United Nations has made to the effectiveness of the "constitution" of world politics is the fact that all governments, including those of communist China and of Indonesia after it withdrew from the organization, have claimed to be acting in conformity with the Charter, its procedures and principles. A favorite means of attacking other states is to denounce *their* violation of the Charter. This, as well as professions of adherence to its goals and institutions, often amounts to little more than an exercise in hypocrisy. However, over the long run even the most transparent hypocrisy redounds to the benefit of the global authority of the United Nations and of the political system to which the UN was intended to give some constitutional coherence. To put it a little differently, the United Nations has demonstrated to leaders of less comprehensive subsystems within the global system and to other people everywhere, that it makes less and less sense nowadays to express the political wish: "Stop the world, I want to get off."

If the style of world politics has been getting increasingly ideological and legalistic since the end of World War II, this has been despite the UN's contribution to it, which has been more than canceled out by other factors. *Its* main contribution has consisted of the "centripetalization" of world politics, upon itself and its own procedures. Especially the formulation of the issues arising out of problems "fed into" the global system by various recognition mechanism has been increasingly centralized upon the UN. These issues are increasingly being formulated in ways suited to the procedures of the United Nations. Fewer issues are being formulated in ways not suited to UN procedures. Deliberation is also often attempted within the framework of the UN, but most deliberation of world political issues is also being carried on simultaneously, and much of it still exclusively, outside the UN, through conventional diplomacy and through what might be described as "multilateral propaganda." The resolution of the most important issues usually either still takes place outside the institutions of the UN through bilateral diplomacy between the two superpowers or their proxies, or it is postponed for the sake of avoiding the "solution" of the underlying problems through nuclear violence. The solution of international problems, where it is deemed possible, is still largely performed by states, the great blocs, or their agents, except when specialized international agencies, operating under the aegis of the United Nations, solve specialized problems on a regularized basis. This method does not at the same time "depoliticize" these problems, since the governing boards of the specialized agencies are made up of the delegates of states or representatives of special groups within states (like workers and employers in the International Labor Organization).[13] The United Nations Emergency Force in the Middle East and the UN Force in the Congo are the most important exceptions, because these arms of the UN actually did solve, at least for the short run, the problems of threats to international peace and security that great and small powers and the Security Council and General Assembly had recognized in those two areas.

The most important contribution of the United Nations to world politics consists of its demonstration of the inescapability or the irrepressibility of world politics. The United Nations has demonstrated that no lesser political system can stay out of world politics, that events in world politics have their repercussions on lower systems, and that the more important policies in national and other less comprehensive systems have their ramifications for world politics. The UN has demonstrated these facts of political life to widening circles of politically aware people all over the world and has simultaneously expanded the capacity of global politics to handle the growing volume of problems which it has to deal with as a result of this widening of human awareness of the possibilities of world politics.

---

[13]Specialized international organizations sometimes serve to *re*politicize dormant political issues within member states. For example, in June 1966, United States worker representatives at the International Labor Organization, on instructions from Mr. George Meany, President of the AFL-CIO, and against the wishes of the U.S. Government delegation to the ILO, boycotted ILO meetings in protest against the election of a communist Pole as presiding officer. The Vice President of the AFL-CIO, Mr. Walter Reuther, thereupon publicly accused Mr. Meany of sabotaging President Johnson's policy of normalizing relations with Poland and other selected communist states.

Chapter 6

Law and Politics

Law VERSUS *Power*

INTERNATIONAL LAW, like the United Nations, is often treated in an all-or-nothing-at-all fashion. *Either* students of international politics put all of the delicate, fragile eggs of peace and security into the basket of international law, *or* they assert that the paramountcy of power reduces the significance of international law in world politics to negligible proportions. The majority of textbooks on international relations leans toward the latter, "realist" view. Some of the works do not deal with international law at all, while many of them discuss it as performing a peripheral role in regulating relations among states. On the other hand, the "realists" dub as "idealists" those who urge substitution of the rule of law for the rule of force in world politics. For a time in the 1950's, this division between realists and "idealistic legalists" was particularly acute in the United States because of what was briefly called "The Great Debate on the National Interest."

The debate was initiated by students and practitioners of United States foreign relations, including Hans J. Morgenthau, the political scientist, and George Kennan, a career diplomat, who criticized the emphasis upon universalized democratic ideals and international law which, in their view, had been introduced into American foreign policy by Woodrow Wilson. They urged that the United States use its "*national* interest" as the lode star of its foreign policy, instead of trying to make the *world* safe for democracy and from communism through observance of international law or through the attempted imposition of international law upon relations among states. At the time, each side to this argument was generally identified with fairly specific substantive foreign policies. Protagonists of the concept of national interest took a relatively "hard" line, defenders of Wilsonian idealism and legalism a relatively "soft" line on United States-Soviet relations. A decade later, however, these substantive positions had become blurred, especially on the side of the realists, where George Kennan and Hans J. Morgenthau favored more relaxed American postures vis-à-vis the communists. Kennan, the author of the policy of containment, could claim consistency in view of the loosening process that was taking place within what was no longer a monolithic communist "bloc." Morgenthau, in his opposition to what he termed the overextension of American power in Southeast Asia, could claim consistency because of the redistribution of world power that followed the communist revolution in China. Neither of them favored any heavier reliance upon international law or the United Nations in 1965 than in 1955. On the other side of the fence, advocates of "world peace through world law" thought that their claim to intellectual consistency was stronger than that of the realists, because they continued to couch their criticism of the foreign policies of their own or other governments in the same international-legal terms in the 1960's as in the 1950's. For instance, they charged the United States with multiple violations of international law in Vietnam and Cuba, and the Soviet Union in Hungary or in the UN, over nonpayment of special assessments.

Because protagonists of international law and their critics in the Great Debate were identified with definite substantive foreign policies, the gulf between these two major schools of international relations was widened and the inadequacies of both approaches were made clearer. Both suffer from an excessively narrow and static conception of the origins, the functions, and the scope of law in political systems, and from false analogies of the role of law, so misconceived, in national states and international relations.

The "realists" return to what they consider the basic, crucial, and irreducible difference between these two levels of politics: presence and absence of a "sovereign," i.e., of some institution that can say the last word—by force, if necessary. Only if "law" is regularly observed, partly because of the possibility of enforcement, is it truly law. Within sovereign states, law *is* habitually observed, because it can be enforced and because most law is known to have been "made" by the sovereign. Since international law deals mainly with relations between sovereigns, which still as in Thomas Hobbes' day recognize no superior upon earth, no one has the last word in quarrels among sovereigns each of which, if prudent, will pursue its own national interest. National interest may go counter to observance of international law and when this happens, then, according to the realist argument, the interests of power should and usually do win out over the observance of law. It follows that little understanding of the realities of international politics is to be gained from the study of international law.

Protagonists of "world law" accept the basic premise of the realists, that law requires enforcement by some ultimate institution. This is made evident, for example, by Grenville Clark:

The fundamental premise of the book is identical with the pronounce-ment of the President of the United States on October 31, 1956: "There can be no peace without law." In this context, the word "law" necessarily implies the law of a world authority, i.e., law which would be uniformly applicable to all nations and all individuals in the world and which would definitely forbid violence or the threat of it as a means for dealing with any international dispute. This world law must also be law in the sense of law which is capable of enforcement, as distinguished from a mere set of exhortations or injunctions which it is desirable to observe but for the enforcement of which there is no effective machinery. . . .

The following are the basic principles by which Professor Sohn and I have been governed.

First: It is futile to expect genuine peace until there is put into effect an effective system of *enforceable* world law in the limited field of war prevention. This implies: (*a*) the complete disarmament, under effective controls, of each and every nation, and (*b*) the simultaneous adoption on a world-wide basis of the measures and institutions which the experience of centuries has shown to be essential for the maintenance of law and order, namely, clearly stated law against violence, courts to interpret and apply that law and police to enforce it. All else, we conceive, depends upon the acceptance of this approach.

Second: The world law against international violence must be explicitly stated in constitutional and statutory form. It must, under appropriate penalties, forbid the use of force by any nation against any other for any cause whatever, save only in self-defense; and must be applicable to all individuals as well as to all nations.

Third: World judicial tribunals to interpret and apply the world law against international violence must be established and maintained, and also organs of mediation and conciliation—so as to substitute peaceful means of adjudication and adjustment in place of violence, or the threat of it, as the means for dealing with all international disputes.

Fourth: A permanent world police force must be created and maintained which, while safeguarded with utmost care against misuse, would be fully adequate to forestall or suppress any violation of the world law against international violence.[1]

The reference to "the experience of centuries" reveals the analogy upon which Mr. Clark bases his plan for the maintenance of world law and order. It is the analogy to the historical evolution of the sovereign national state into that institution which has a monopoly of the legitimate use of physical violence and is, therefore, capable of making "clearly stated law against violence," of establishing "courts to interpret and apply that law," and of marshaling "police to enforce it." On the other hand, "realists" who are skeptical about the "world peace through world law" approach, though they agree with the historical portion of Mr. Clark's analogy, deny the possibility of centralizing power internationally in the current duocentric or bipolar world, since neither great nuclear power would be willing to surrender its nuclear capabilities to the other or to a world government. For the same reason, Mr. Clark advances the key point of his plan:

Fifth: The complete disarmament of all the nations (rather than the mere "reduction" or "limitation" of armaments) is essential for any solid and lasting peace, this disarmament to be accomplished in a simultaneous and proportionate manner by carefully verified stages and subject to a well-organized system of inspection. It is now generally accepted that disarmament must be universal and enforceable. That it must also be complete is no less necessary, since: (*a*) in the nuclear age no mere reduction in the new means of mass destruction could be effective to remove fear and tension; and (*b*) if any substantial national armaments were to remain, even if only ten per cent of the armaments of 1960, it would be impractical to maintain a sufficiently strong world police force to deal with any possible aggression or revolt against the authority of the world organization. We should face the fact that until there is *complete* disarmament of every nation without exception there can be no assurance of genuine peace.[2]

International and National Law

One flaw in the analogy to the "experience of centuries" is that sovereign (and later national) states were created, and power was cen-

---

[1]Grenville Clark and Louis B. Sohn. *World Peace Through World Law* (Cambridge: Harvard University Press, 1960), pp. xv and xvi. (Quoted by permission of the Harvard University Press, Copyright, 1958, 1960, by the President and Fellows of Harvard College.)

[2]*Loc. cit.* The final point follows. *Sixth:* Effective world machinery must be created to mitigate the vast disparities in the economic conditions of various regions of the world, the continuance of which tends to instability and conflict.

tralized within them, not in order to reduce or eliminate the use of force, but to enlarge the means of violence and to make it possible to bring them to a clearer focus, against *both* external and internal enemies of the state. The successful unifiers of states and centralizers of force generally achieved these "positive power objectives." They did not pursue the unification of countries like France, the United Kingdom, or Germany as a result of any fear of the "overkill" capacity of one or more of the components out of which these states were put together, but out of a desire to harness the power of dynastically, territorially, and culturally related groups against others. The Kings of France were not afraid that the other princes of France would bring about the genocide of the population of France unless the Kings completed their work of nation building. Prussia achieved hegemony over the other German states, because its rulers were willing to use military force against them and because they were able to persuade the other rulers to commit their pooled armies against Austria, Denmark, and France—each of which responded in turn to the challenge with its own military force to be defeated on the field of battle. Even the federal unification of the thirteen United States of America, which is often regarded as more nearly analogous to the goals of contemporary world federalism, were not seriously motivated in the unification movement by fears of wars among them, but by the twin desires, in the words of the Preamble to the Constitution, "to provide for the common defense," that is to pool their military power *externally* for use against outsiders; *and* to be able to use their pooled military power *internally*, in the words of Article I, Section VIII (15), which gives the Congress the power "To provide for calling forth the militia to *execute the laws of the Union, suppress insurrections*, and repel invasions." (Italics supplied.)

The fault in the analogy lies not only in the differences between national and global unifiers and their respective attitudes toward force; but also in the discrepancy between the expectations of the protagonists of world law and the actual historical consequences of the firm establishment of enforceable national law. The greater efficiency in the use of power which resulted from national unification has by no means always been accompanied by corresponding gains in the effectiveness of government in the unified territories or in a consequent reduction in the over-all incidence of violence. One notorious and tragic proof of this contention is provided by the American Civil War. However, in

Europe, too, the establishment of central legislative, executive, and judicial authorities has often been followed by an increase in the total use of organized force, partly because the centralization of power increased the volume of violence at the disposition of governments and of those who wanted to overthrow them. This happened regardless of the position of the cleavage between a government and its challengers, which might be vertical, as in a geographically defined civil war between sections of a country, or horizontal, as in an economically and socially defined revolutionary struggle between opposing classes. The provision of centrally enforceable law raised the stakes for which politics was being conducted; it could, therefore, lead to an increase in internal tensions, with the result that periods of the "maintenance of law and order" were replaced by periods of "internal war," or, in our terms, political style oscillated more or less radically from legalism to violence.

These facts have lead "realist" critics of the various advocates of establishment of a central world authority—from world federalists to the "world peace through world law" movement and the protagonists of world government—to insist that the goal of centrally enforceable world law could be achieved only on an exact or "realistic" analogy to national unification, namely, by *one* hegemonial imperial power that succeeds in its pursuit of the goal of world domination. Western *Realpolitiker* usually—though not always—identify the Soviet Union or China as such imperialist powers with unlimited goals, while they deny that the description could be applied to the United States. Communist *Realpolitiker* always identify the United States as such an imperialist power with unlimited goals, while they deny that the description could be applied to the Soviet Union or China. The parties whose agreement is at present a prerequisite for establishing enforceable world law are, as a result, opposed in principle to the very idea. Moreover, on each side vocal groups claim that the United Nations—i.e., the eventual enforcement agency—is becoming a tool of the other side in its pursuit of world dominion, every time a small step seems to be taken in the direction of world law.

The qualitative transformation of power, and the related unique peculiarity of the global political system as one that does not perform the function of "boundary maintenance," thus combine to prove false both the "realist" analogy between hegemonial national unification and global imperialism, and the "idealist-legalist" analogy between nonhegemonial national unification for purposes of establishing the rule of law and the movement toward "world peace through world law." Ironically, even if the latter analogy were valid, policies based upon it would still stand very little chance of acceptance by the governments of the United States and the Soviet Union, because these governments generally base their policies upon expectations of their adversary that are congruent with the former analogy.

Both of these approaches to international law conceive of law as an emanation of the state as defined by Max Weber, or of an institution very much like that state; i.e., law is produced by that institution in a community (national or international) which has the monopoly of legitimate physical violence. Conversely, both schools consider it to be the main or only function of the state, or the political system, to make, interpret and apply, and enforce laws. Chief purpose of this law-producing activity of the political system is the reduction and, if possible, the elimination, of violence within it. We noticed the prevalence of this identification of the political system with the reduction of violence through enforceable law before: in Almond's focus on "legitimate physical compulsion," which refers back to Weber's point that, "specifically, at the present time, the right to use physical force is ascribed to other institutions or to individuals only to the extent to which the state permits it";[3] and in the definitions of *community* advanced by Deutsch, which makes "the absence or presence of violence as a means to settle disputes" the main criterion, and by Haas, whose "ideal type of political community ... imposes limitations upon the violence of group conflict."[4] Even the otherwise very imaginative work on *The Political Foundations of International Law*, by Kaplan and Katzenbach, to which we shall return below, takes the view that only enforceable law *is* law:

> The presence or absence of institutional means of enforcement of legal principles determines whether a system of law exists or not. Municipal

---

[3]Gabriel A. Almond and James S. Coleman (eds.), *The Politics of Developing Areas* (Princeton: Princeton University Press, 1960), pp. 6 and 5. See also p. 7 above. In Max Weber's essay, "Politics as a Vocation," this passage continues: "The state is accepted as the sole source of the 'right' to use physical force [or violence]. 'Politics' therefore means for us: striving to share in power or to influence the distribution of power, be it among states, or within one state among groups of men which it comprises." *Max Weber: Schriften zur theoretischen Soziologie zur Soziologie der Politik und Verfassung,* Max Graf zu Solms (ed.) (Frankfurt am Main: Georg Kurt Schauer, 1947), p. 147.

[4]See p. 85 above.

[i.e., national] courts are able to call upon the assistance of sheriffs, or, if necessary, the total armed force of the state, to aid in the execution of sentence. The political arm of government is obligated to sustain legal process. And a municipal system of law that is not sustained by the cooperation of the body politic will not persist. The assertion that the Covenant and the Pact of Paris [Kellogg-Briand Pact of 1928, which provided for the renunciation of war as an instrument of national policy] outlawed wars of aggression seems excessive when measured against the realities of the international society of the time. These were statements of wishful thinking, not law. The norms of the nineteenth century with respect to the limitations of aims in war or the restoration of defeated major states were not enforced by formal international government. But they were enforced by an international society, which was organized in a manner that permitted it to respond in an appropriate manner. The times were out of joint for the League, and its announced principles represented ideals rather than rules; no alliances existed to enforce them.[5]

Kaplan and Katzenbach do not go as far as the others cited in insisting upon law enforcement for the purpose of eliminating violence, since they do accept enforcement of *limitations of aims in war* as demonstration of the existence of a system of law in the nineteenth century. But the "enforcement test" proposed in the first sentence of the paragraph just quoted makes their position similar to those previously mentioned, to the extent that all of these authors tend to focus upon the capacity of the national or international political system to make and enforce *substantive* law.

Before discussing the distortions that can result from this substantive preoccupation, we should try to explain it. Students of international relations who are dismayed, for whatever reasons, realist or idealist, by the large role of force, the potential violence, and the lack of regularities in international politics, often wish they could replace these aspects of "politics" with a comprehensive and detailed system of international law. Students of comparative politics and some "statesmen" of less successful political systems frequently display the same aversion or, at best, ambivalence toward politics. Politics is open to choice and, for this and other reasons, irregular, unpredictable, disorderly, and potentially violent. To overcome all these "negative" characteristics of politics, one needs a comprehensive code designed, if possible, to eliminate these aspects by eliminating the need for future

---

[5]Morton A. Kaplan and Nicholas deB. Katzenbach, *The Political Foundations of International Law* (New York: John Wiley & Sons, 1961), pp. 291 f. *Quoted by permission* of John Wiley & Sons, Inc.

choices. Of course, flexibility is also foreclosed by this full option for stability. And in order to make such a comprehensive legal code effective, it must be assured the preferably "permanent" support of efficient enforcement agencies. Although the true "experience of centuries" teaches that those legal systems and constitutions last the longest, which have the lowest substantive content (because of constant and considerable substantive changes that occur in the world around us), the desire for enforcement of stability detracts from the procedural emphasis that longevity requires in a changing environment. Both in legislation and in analysis, the result is that the following questions are raised very seldom: *How* does law grow and function, *how* do its procedures operate, *how* is it used? But these are asked all the time: *What* does law do, for *whom*, backed up by *what* sanctions?

An extreme result of this substantive bias that flows from a strong aversion to force and irregularity consists of denial of the *political* foundations of international law and, indeed, of all law (i.e., a denial which is the opposite of the aim and achievement of Kaplan and Katzenbach's work.) This denial can either take the realist form that denies the existence of international law because of the primacy of power politics (which provides no foundations for enforceable law); or the legalist form which sets up elaborate charters, conventions, and codes that define the substantive international rights of everyone on earth without paying the slightest attention to the fact that all law emanates from politics.

The Scope of International Law

A more moderate and more common result of the substantive bias in the study of international law consists of taking a rather narrow view of its scope and content. The table of contents of a standard American case book on international law of the 1930's gives an outline of conventional notions about the scope and content of *The Law of Nations*. The eighteen chapters were entitled: The Law of Nations: Nature, Sources, Subjects; Recognition; Succession in the Law of Nations; Nationality; Territory in the Law of Nations; Jurisdictional Rights and Immunities of Foreign States in the Courts of Other States; Jurisdiction over Persons, Extraterritoriality, Extradition; Jurisdiction over Vessels; Status and Immunities of Diplomats and Consuls; The Law of Treaties; Aliens; The Law of State Responsibility and International

Claims; Pacific Settlement of International Disputes; Hostile Measures Short of War; War; Legal Effect of War on Private Rights; Rights and Duties of Neutral States; Neutral Rights and Maritime Law.[6]

International law was basically conceived of as applicable, in varying degrees depending largely on their own discretion, to states only, and not to individuals or to organizations other than states, including international organizations. It could be used primarily for the processing of issues like the following: Does a state exist? Is a government in control of a State? What territory belongs to the state? What persons come under the control of the state? What can ships do in international waters? What can states do with or against one another, in peace and in war? What distinguishes peace from war? What can belligerents and neutrals do in their relations with one another? It could also be used for dealing with the following issues: How, that is, by means of which procedures, can the substantive questions raised above be answered? The procedures most prominently considered were adjudication by national or international courts, arbitration, mediation, or negotiation.

In 1958, C. Wilfred Jenks, an English barrister and international jurist, proposed a radical rearrangement of *The Common Law of Mankind*, based upon the transformation of international relations into world politics:

The "law of nations . . . , profoundly transformed by modern developments, is rapidly evolving from a law between sovereign States, concerned primarily with the delimitation of their jurisdiction, towards a common law of mankind. The thesis which has been elaborated can be briefly summarised, at the price of apparent dogmatism which brevity implies, as follows :

1. International law can no longer be adequately or reasonably defined or described as the law governing the mutual relations of States, even if such a basic definition is accompanied by qualifications or exceptions designed to allow for modern developments; it represents the common law of mankind in an early stage of development, of which the law governing the relations between States is one, but only one, major division.

2. By the common law of mankind is meant the law of an organised world community, constituted on the basis of States but discharging its community functions increasingly through a complex of international and regional institutions, guaranteeing rights to, and placing obligations upon,

---

[6]Herbert W. Briggs, *The Law of Nations: Cases, Documents, and Notes* (New York: Appleton-Century-Crofts, Inc., 1938). pp. ix–xx.

the individual citizen, and confronted with a wide range of economic, social and technological problems calling for uniform regulation on an international basis which represent a growing proportion of the subject-matter of the law. The imperfect development and precarious nature of the organised world community is reflected in the early stage of development of law, but does not invalidate the basic conception.

3. Such a conception implies a complete recasting of the traditional arrangement and presentation of the law; the newer developments can no longer be satisfactorily presented within the framework of pre-existing structure of the law.

4. The following may be regarded as a convenient presentation of the contemporary public international law of peace:

(a) the law governing the structure and law-making processes of the international community, including:

(i) the law governing the existence, recognition, and succession of States as elements in the structure of the international community,

(ii) the law of international institutions, including the constitutional, parliamentary, and administrative law of international organisations and the law governing the mutual relations of international organisations,

(iii) the law governing the law-making processes of the international community, including the status of established custom in an international community with a changed and changing composition and distribution of influence, the extent to which the collective practice of States expressed through international organisations is a significant element in the growth of custom, the effect of the regulative and quasi-judicial powers of international organisations, the relationship of the law-making treaty to the general body of international law, the role of judicial and arbitral decisions, national and international, in the contemporary development of the law, and the prospects for the codification of international law,

(iv) the relation of international to municipal law (on a comparative and positive basis, with due regard to any modifications of existing national law or practice necessary to secure a fuller integration of the structure of the international community and to the implications of the merger of the substantive content of international and national law which is taking place in a wide range of fields);

(b) the law governing peaceful relations between States, including:

(i) the traditional core of the law of peace, comprising such questions as territory, the freedom of the seas and sovereignty of the air, jurisdiction, the responsibility of States, intercourse between states, immunities, and similar subjects, and including nationality, the treatment of aliens, extradition, and co-operation in restraint of crime as matters between States,

(ii)   rules governing economic relations between States, including obligations in respect of monetary and general economic policy, the liability of one State to another in respect of loss or damage of an economic character, and financial transactions between States,

(iii)   the rights of States in respect of the application and enforcement of the parts of the law which relate primarily to individuals;

(c) human rights protected by international guarantees, including civil liberties and political, economic, and social rights;

(d) property rights of a distinctively international character, including copyright and patent;

(e) common rules established by international agreement which apply to public services, corporations and individuals rather than to States, a division which comprises a large part of the content of modern law-making treaties, including aviation, much of maritime law, postal matters, sanitary regulations and telecommunications, and those parts of the International Labour Code which are not more conveniently dealt with under human rights;

(f) international rules governing the conflict of laws;

(g) the law of treaties and other international instruments including the conclusion, validity, effect, interpretation, termination and modification of such instruments; and

(h) the law governing international arbitration and judicial settlement, including jurisdiction, procedure, interim measures of protection, evidence, damages, and the execution of decisions and awards;

(i) the law governing the use of force in international relations.

(5) In outlining this method of presentation of the law, special emphasis has been placed on matters which are liable to be overlooked or in respect of which a radical departure from the traditional arrangement is proposed; this is necessary for the purpose of presenting the thesis but is not intended to imply any belittlement of the relative importance of well-settled parts of the law the arrangement of the details of which does not present comparable new problems or to express any judgment concerning the degree of attention which should be given to the older and newer topics in a balanced survey of the law as a whole at any particular stage of its development. Any such presentation is necessarily experimental. It must be tested by experience and adapted from time to time to further developments in the substantive content of the law. It may, for instance, at some stage become desirable to include as further recognised subdivisions of international law the general principles of law recognised by civilised nations to be applicable to certain types of international commercial transaction, including in particular foreign investment transactions or the

principles applicable to inter-State contracts of a commercial character. In the nature of things it does not eliminate the problem inherent in any arrangement or classification of the law that certain questions can be, and in some cases must be, dealt with in more than one context. Subject to these reservations, it is submitted that it affords a more convenient framework for the presentation of the contemporary law than the less radical modifications of the traditional framework currently in vogue. The adoption of some such arrangement would, it is believed, contribute powerfully to a clearer and wider understanding of the scope and content of international law and in this manner facilitate its further development towards a generally accepted common law of mankind.[7]

The titles of the ten chapters of Jenks's book, when compared with those of Briggs's case book, give an indication of the changed and changing subject matter of international law: The Scope of International Law; The Universality of International Law; The Impact of International Organisations on International Law; World Organisation and European Integration; International Law and Colonial Policy; Employment Policy and International Law; Atoms for Peace in International Law; An International Regime for Anartica?; International Law and Activities in Space; Craftsmanship in International Law.

Roman Law and Common Law

It comes as no surprise that this imaginative rearrangement and broadening of the scope and content of international law should have been made by a practitioner and student of English Common Law and not by a jurist coming from a background of codified Roman Civil Law. These are the two great European legal systems, from which all other Western systems of law were derived, and which have also influenced many non-Western systems. They differ in many respects,[8] one of which is relevant at this point. The Roman Law, codified on orders of the Emperor Justinian in the sixth century A.D., was "received," i.e., rediscovered, on the Continent of Europe, in one body at the end of the Middle Ages. It served as the model for

---

[7]C. Wilfred Jenks, LL.D. Cantab. of Gray's Inn, Barrister-at-Law, Associate of the Institute of International Law, *The Common Law of Mankind* (New York: Frederick A. Praeger, 1958). Published under the auspices of The London Institute of World Affairs. Copyright Stevens and Sons Limited, London, 1958. Pages 58–61. Quoted by permission of Stevens and Sons, Limited.

[8]See Herbert J. Spiro, "Legalism," *Government by Constitution: The Political Systems of Democracy* (New York: Random House, 1959), chap. 15.

continental legal reform, especially during the codification movement that culminated in the Code Napoleon of 1805. On the Continent, legal reform has usually been undertaken on a comprehensive scale, as a result of legislation, and on the initiative of the
"sovereign," that is, either an individual like Napoleon or a national
parliament. In England, by contrast, comprehensive legal reform has
never been undertaken, the Roman Code was never received, and the
English Common Law "just grew" from precedent to precedent,
largely on the initiative of judges who enjoyed a greater measure of
independence from the "sovereign" than their continental brethren.

As a consequence of these differences in the development of law
on the Continent and in England (and in other areas affected by
either of these legal systems), the continental or Civil Law view of
international law has tended to be more formal, to expect greater
comprehensiveness, and to favor heavier substantive content than the
British or Common Law view. The American view of international law
has been closer to the British than the Continental view in its procedural bias, because of the Common Law tradition which the United
States inherited from England and firmly incorporated in its Constitution at the time of the founding. However, in its tendency to emphasize legislative origins, at least of constitutional law, the American
view has been closer to the Continental conception. This is due to
the deliberate design, to the "made" origin of the Constitution of the
United States and to the great success of that charter in achieving
the intentions of its authors, by contrast with the wholly unplanned
evolution of the British "constitution," which, of course, does not consist of any single document, but of an ill-defined series of documents
and naturally grown parliamentary and other political procedures.
Both British and American students of international law usually accord a more important role than do continental jurists in shaping its
development to international courts and other tribunals, because of
the crucial role played by judges in the development of the Common
Law and by the Supreme Court of the United States in the development of the Constitution.

Familiarity with the history of their own Supreme Court makes
Americans somewhat less skeptical than Europeans about the long-run
effectiveness and efficiency of international tribunals whose decisions
are not accepted by states because acceptance would violate their
understanding of their national interests. There were cases in the

early history of the United States in which Supreme Court decisions were not accepted. Perhaps the most famous of these involved two American missionaries to the Cherokees in the State of Georgia, who were arrested, tried, and convicted for inciting the Indians to resist their expulsion from Georgia. Chief Justice John Marshall and a majority of the United States Supreme Court decided that the missionaries had been convicted in violation of treaties between the United States and the Cherokees which, constitutionally, were part of "the supreme law of the land," binding upon "judges in every State," according to Article VI, Paragraph 2 of the Constitution.

The attorneys for the missionaries sought to have this judgment enforced, but could not. General Jackson was President, and would do nothing of the sort. "Well: John Marshall has made his decision: *now let him enforce it!*" was his commentary on the matter. So the missionaries languished years in prison, and the Cherokees were finally (1838) driven into exile, in defiance of the mandate of our highest judicial tribunal.[9]

Such set-backs for the authority of the Court, which have happened also in more recent times, usually through slowing down enforcement rather than flagrant rejection of decisions, have not detracted from its important contribution to the flow of American policy and to American political style.

The sympathy which American students and advocates of international law have for international courts does contain two dangers. One of these is overemphasis of the role likely to be played by the International Court of Justice and other tribunals in the development of the law. In its extreme form, this overemphasis considers the scope of international law to be identical and coterminous with those matters which have been handled by international courts. It therefore ignores the other "sources" of international law, which include treaties, custom, general principles of law "recognized by civilized nations," the writings of scholars, and "reason." The other danger implied by the American sympathy for international courts consists of a transfer to international politics of the same simplistic and mechanistic functionalism derived from the constitutional separation of powers, which often distorts studies of American politics and which we criticized in Chapter 3. Those who commit this error view national and international law as being "made" in one compartment or stage, "executed"

---

[9]Horace Greeley, *The American Conflict* (Hartford: O. D. Case & Co., 1864), Vol. I, p. 106. See also *Worcester* v. *The State of Georgia,* 6 Peters 515 (1832).

in another separate compartment or stage, and "interpreted" and "adjudicated" in a third separate compartment or stage. Kaplan and Katzenbach specifically warn against this compartmentalization, because it also leads to an unrealistically nonpolitical and "segregated" conception of the role of courts and the "judicial function."

> The mythology of impartial adjudication overlooks the political role of judges as well as the impact of existing legal norms upon the legislative process, and seeks an unrealistic dichotomy between judicial and legislative processes. Our purpose here in stressing this interaction is not to obliterate valid analytical distinctions between the adjudicating and policy making roles of officials, considered conceptually, but merely to stress the relationship and interdependence of the legal and political processes—to give emphasis to the political context in which doctrine is operative in helping to shape effective decision.
>
> It is not necessary to reach far into the political past of England to find functions of policy prescription and adjudication unsegregated. . . .[10]

In other words, and to use our terminology, the flow of policy, in national as in international politics, is a contitnuous flow, whose (for analytical purposes distinguishable) phases overlap with one another. In successful political systems, the courts contribute to achievement of all four basic goals, to maintaining a dynamic equilibrium among them, and especially to providing the stability of the system by emphasizing fundamental procedures. They also play a part in adjusting fundamental procedures to circumstantial changes (flexibility), as when they devise new formulas in order to achieve change, e.g., the "all deliberate speed" phrase in the school desegration decision; in resolving the circumstantial substance of issues (efficiency), as when they decide a case involving material conflicts of interest; and in solving the fundamental substance of problems (effectiveness), as when their participation in the processing of a problem makes policy and the constitution generally more acceptable to specially affected groups and to the population as a whole. Their major contribution, however, is to stability. Their very existence as guardians of the law and, occasionally, of the constitution, shapes the way in which issues will be formulated and therefore contributes heavily toward keeping politics flowing in the same procedural channels, regardless of its varying content. This means that for young, "developing," or for other reasons unstable systems, the role of the courts can easily

---

[10]Kaplan and Katzenbach, *op, cit.,* p. 11. Quoted by permission of John Wiley & Sons, Inc.

be exaggerated, as it often is for the contemporary system of world politics. The exaggeration is made both by some scholars, on the basis of analogies between stages of development of the international and national systems that are not comparable, and by some politicians as a result of their haste to overcome the ever-shifting pragmatism of international relations with a solidly stable framework of enforceable international law.

The World Court

At the present stage of the development of world politics, the substantive content of decisions of the International Court of Justice and other international tribunals is less significant than the procedural direction which their existence and availability can impart to world politics.

The "sources" of international law have become stereotyped; they are treaties, custom, general principles of law, judicial precedents, textbook writers, and reason. What is not made clear by the writers who describe these "sources" is that the concern here is with method and technique. How does a decision maker support or refute a claim that a given act is or is not consistent with international law? Where does he look for argumentation, support, and reasoning?[11]

In all political systems, formal authority must be legitimized in some way. The rules formally prescribed and enforced constitute the law for all those subject to them. The authors have defined law simply as formal authority coupled with authoritative doctrine. We have sought to distinguish it from pure force by requiring that the exercise of force be subjected to the test of authority, to rules of law known and adhered to.

The authors take no position regarding the substantive contents of the rules other than that these contents exist, can be discovered by observers, and, within unspecified limits of tolerance, are operative as standards governing official action.[12]

These two citations from *The Political Foundations of International Law,* while applicable to contemporary international law in general, are valid in particular for the role of international courts.

For example, those who took the Corfu Channel Case, South Africa's administration of the Mandate of Southwest Africa, and the question of the applicability of Article 19 of the Charter to special

---

[11]*Ibid.*, p. 231.
[12]*Ibid.*, p. 17.

assessments, to the International Court of Justice, as well as those who argued before the Court—even if they argued against its jurisdiction—all of these parties let their perception of the problems out of which these cases arose be shaped by the litigation and their participation in it, irrespective of the substantive content of the decisions or their acceptance or rejection of them. It is also conceivable that over the long run more substantive consensus may come into being among states whose governments, or international judges appointed by whom, have found themselves in agreement on an increasing proportion of international court decisions. But this kind of substantive consensus will benefit the successful growth of world politics much less than the kind of procedural consensus that results from repeated recourse to institutions of "structured impartiality" within a framework of ever-strengthened procedural stability.

In order to achieve this kind of strengthening, the World Court and others, like the European Court of Human Rights, need more business, just as the Supreme Court of the United States in the early years of its life needed more business. Courts, like other political systems including those of which courts are subsystems, before they can develop successful politics, must develop politics, that is, must increase their capacity to process problems and issues. This development of business for constitutional courts is often hindered by the thesis that they are unqualified to handle "political" as distinguished from "legal" issues. This thesis is obviously based upon the false segregeation between politics and legislation on the one hand, and adjudication and interpretation of the law on the other. Those who present it often add that, by forcing "political" issues upon the World Court, one contributes to making it ineffective, because it is ill equipped to dispose of political issues in a manner acceptable to the parties, whose flouting of its verdict will detract from its prestige.

This thesis has been brilliantly refuted by another scholar and practitioner of the Common Law of the English-speaking world, Thomas M. Franck:

> Judicial abdication there must be; not every case posed to a court need be decided by a court. But the test must *not* be whether the issue is too "hot" to handle, too difficult or too "important." *It should be whether some better alternative method of settlement can be found in the instant case, that is, whether the judicial remedy is inappropriate as judged solely by the standards of good order, creation and problem solving.* The test ought not to be whether the issue is too big, or the defendant too stubborn, but

whether the question posed is one which a court is properly equipped to *answer*. The word merits stressing: to "answer," not to "enforce." In deciding whether to decide, a court must look to the *issues* and not to the *clients*. It must not by swayed by the power, sensitivity or bellicosity of the parties; otherwise it is not a court worthy of the name.

To evolve such a test requires re-examination of the *third-party lawmaking* function. . . .What are courts all about? What are judges, lawyers, witnesses, plaintiffs and defendants all doing in their assigned roles and even their assigned positions in the courtroom? Third-party lawmaking, its particular genius, encourages both parties to a dispute to construct rival cathedrals of contention supported by massive flying buttresses of evidence and thrusting aloft towering spires of logic, thus presenting a neutral third party with the most dramatically clear and evident choice possible: "yes" or "no"; "right" or "wrong"; "win" or "lose." The onus is on the parties to construct the choice, to be the principal mover in the process. The court must watch and, at the end, choose. . . .[13]

The adversary process of a court of law is best suited to disputes in which there are a limited number of questions that are dispositive of the dispute, each of which can be posed in terms of two clear alternatives. The process is least amenable to an issue which by virtue of its complexity is better regarded as a matter of degree or synthesis, or in which the number of questions to be answered is not limited.[14]

This refutation of the distinction between "political" and "legal" issues is based upon a peculiarity of the Common Law. The peculiarity is the adversary method of pleading, whose influence upon the political style of the Common Law countries has been of great importance. Under the adversary method, clear definition of the issue in dispute between them is the task of the parties. It is not a task of the court. Since Common Law Courts do not have to spend their energies on this task, as Civil Law courts often do, they can devote greater attention to applying and developing procedures. Their lesser substantive involvement in disputes leads to the greater effectiveness of their judgments. The narrowing down of the conflicts by the parties makes the courts' performance more efficient and as a result draws an increasing volume of disputes into the courts. In these and other ways, the adversary method of pleading has contributed to enabling the courts and judges of the Common Law countries to make much greater and more beneficial contributions to the success of their

---

[13]Thomas M. Franck, "Structuring Impartiality in International Third-Party Lawmaking," *Indiana Law Journal*, Vol. 39, No. 3 (Spring, 1964), p. 454. Quoted by permission of the Editors of the *Indiana Law Journal*.
[14]*Ibid.*, p. 458.

political systems than has been made by their counterparts on the Continent to theirs. Professor Franck clearly recognizes this advantage:

> These efforts to limit the adjudiciability are praiseworthy in that they represent attempts to devise a more meaningful formula for judicial abstention than is apparent in the bold phrase "political dispute." Yet, they are unsatisfactory in that they employ special pleading to explain a readily observed phenomenon: not the "political" quality of the dispute but the nature of the disputant who will not litigate, especially the powerful state. To neutralize that familiar but frustrating obstacle, the international lawyer summons his tape measure and saw to cut a hole in the court's jurisdiction that will allow the obstacle to pass, no matter how offensive this may be to the symmetry of logic. He might better summon historical perspective. The Supreme Court of the United States had to wait fully fifty years after its birth before the average annual number of cases submitted to it rose from 10 to 70. Some forty years later, its annual docket bulged with 1,500 applications to litigate. The International Court, too, needs patience and time. More, it needs reform that will attract customers. Instead, it is offered theories which would simply classify as "political" and "non-justiciable" the sorts of things the consumers have been refusing to buy: "important" issues, issues where they know the law to be against them, and so on. To elevate the patterns of national resistance against law *to* law is to avoid rape by consenting to be ravished.[15]

In other words, the growth of international law requires, among other things, an increase in the number of issues taken to international courts. Courts are most likely to contribute to the growth of international law, and especially to strengthening procedural consensus in international politics, if they are handling questions that they can answer, issues that they can process because these issues are suited for their procedures. Whether they can enforce the verdicts, or solve the problems that gave rise to the issues, is much less important for their contribution than the volume of suitable issues brought into the courts for litigation.

Law, Will, and Jurisdiction

The low incidence of overt, formal recourse to a prominent institution of international law like the World Court has causes that can be traced back to the multiple sources of international law and es-

---

[15]*Ibid.*, p. 453.

pecially to the two great mainstreams whose confluence in the seventeenth century signaled the beginnings of modern international law. These mainstreams were the ancient tradition of natural law, whose original spring was in the garden of Greek rationalism, whence it flowed to be enriched by the cosmopolitanism of Rome and to be strengthened by the religious authority of medieval Christendom; and the newer concept of the sovereign and its capacity to make law through the exercise of its will. Kaplan and Katzenbach describe the coming together of these two currents of international law:

> The basic tenet of the Spanish School of the sixteenth century—Vittoria, Vasques de Menchada, Ayala, and Suarez—was simply that relations among nations were governed by principles of Justice, and that such principles, according to Suarez, for example, were perpetual, immutable, universal principles of natural law. Gentili, the great Italian who taught civil law at Oxford, had the same idea when he envisioned the Law of Nations as that "which is in use among all the nations of men, which native reason has established among all human beings, and which is equally observed by all mankind. Such a law is natural law." With Grotius, perhaps the greatest and certainly the most systematic and comprehensive of the early writers, there is a slight shift of emphasis toward modern positivism when he sees the law of nations as deriving its obligatory character "from the will of all nations or many nations." (We can see as early as 1625 the emergence of the great European nations and the deference Grotius pays their power.)[16]

Hugo Grotius was an original contributor not only to the theory of international law, but also to the theory of sovereignty, which means that we should understand the cited phrase as referring to the will of sovereign states. This emphasis on will as a basis and source of law is much more marked among writers coming from a Roman Law background than among Common Lawyers. Since the most important "founders" of modern international law were all continentals, they endowed it with a comparatively strong voluntarist bias. Just as, within the state, law is what the sovereign wills it to be, so, among states, law is what sovereigns in their relations with one another will it to be—and, because sovereigns are each other's equals and recognize no other superior under God, much less can function as international law than as national law. This view, which prevailed in the formative period of modern international law, persists to the present. It is a major reason for the intellectual division between the

---

[16]Kaplan and Katzenbach, *op. cit.*, p. 58. Quoted by permission of John Wiley & Sons, Inc.

comparative study of politics and the study of international politics. It serves also as the basis for the refusal of many states, especially great powers including the United States and the Soviet Union, to accept unlimited compulsory jurisdiction of the World Court.

In the United States, the issue of the jurisdiction of the Court was discussed by the Senate Foreign Relations Committee in 1946, in connection with the Senate's consent to the U.S. Declaration accepting the Court's compulsory jurisdiction. This consent was given, but only after the so-called Connally Amendment was added to the resolution: ". . . Provided, that such declaration shall not apply to— . . . b. disputes with regard to matters which are essentially within the domestic jurisdiction of the United States *as determined by the United States.*" (Italics added. The italicized words constitute the "Connally Amendment.")[17] This means, in effect, that it is up to the good or ill will of the government of the United States to decide whether to accept or reject the jurisdiction of the World Court and its interpretation and application of international law to issues raised by other states against the United States by claiming that these fall essentially within its domestic jurisdiction.

There are, of course, some issues that have been taken to the Court, over which it cannot be denied jurisdiction, either on legalistic grounds like the one just discussed, which is intimately related to the peculiarities of the United States Constitution, or on the basis of other types of reasoning. An example is provided by the General Assembly's request for an advisory opinion on the question whether special assessments voted by it to pay for the United Nations Emergency Force in the Middle East and the United Nations Force in the Congo were "expenses of the Organization" within the meaning of Article 17 (2). The Court, by vote of nine to five, held that they were expenses in this sense, thereby indirectly opening the way for the abortive attempt by the United States to get the Soviet Union either to pay, or to be deprived of its vote in the General Assembly. Neither the Soviet Union nor France accepted the opinion of the Court. Neither paid its share of these peace-keeping expenses, because the operations were voted by the General Assembly, not the Security Council (where they could have vetoed them). But the processing of

---

[17]Ernest A. Gross, *The United Nations: Structure for Peace* (New York: Harper & Row, 1962), p. 120, note 6.

this issue by the World Court, and participation in the suit by states that refused to accept the judgment, may still have added a little procedural consensus which may become useful later, for the processing of other issues that arise out of substantively quite different problems.

Consensus on Law

Among both "believers" and skeptics about international law, many tend to place an excessive emphasis upon the contribution of international courts to the growth of observance of law. The skeptics do this by pointing to any flouting of an opinion or decision of the World Court by an affected state as proof of the inefficacy of international law. The believers exaggerate the contribution of such courts when they sound as though expansion of the role of international courts were the only cause and symptom of the growth of international law. This attitude is implied by some of the literature on the European Court of Human Rights.

The European Court of Human Rights was established by the Council of Europe, consisting of the following member states: Austria, Belgium, Cyprus, Denmark, Federal Republic of Germany, France, Greece, Iceland, Ireland, Italy, Luxembourg, The Netherlands, Norway, Sweden, Turkey, and the United Kingdom. Of these states, all except France ratified the Convention for the Protection of Human Rights and Fundamental Freedoms, which was designed to make possible realization of the goals contained in the United Nations Universal Declaration of Human Rights. The Convention also set up the European Commission of Human Rights, which can refer cases to the Court on application by states. In exceptional cases, when a state has declared its acceptance of this form of procedure beforehand, individuals may petition the Commission directly, and the Commission can then decide to take the case before the Court. This was done in the case of a Mr. G. R. Lawless, a citizen of Ireland, who claimed that the Government of Ireland had violated his rights under the Convention for the Protection of Human Rights and Fundamental Freedoms. The Commission took the case to the Court, which decided that the Irish Government had not denied Lawless these rights and freedoms. Since this so-called *Lawless* case was the first case decided by the European Court of Human Rights, some advocates of international law attributed great importance to it.[18] It seems unlikely, however, that such courts and their limited activities will in fact make a major contribution to the growth of consensus on old and new international law.

The overemphasis on the role of courts is connected with the mistaken notion that only enforceable law is true law. It is related also to a rather narrow and substantive conception of law. According to this view—to simplify it somewhat—laws are made, in order to forbid specific actions, by creating sanctions, i.e., punishment, to be applied to those who are found to have committed these prohibited actions. Since the "accused" usually denies his guilt, and because some body must decide this issue, the extent of his responsibility, and the severity of the sanction to be applied to him, the scope of effective law is assumed to be identical and coterminous with the activities of courts. Consensus on law is said to exist only to the extent that the decisions of courts are accepted by all those who come under their jurisdiction.

There is, however, a great deal more than this to law. Law, and consensus on law, grows in ways which may not involve "enforcing" courts at all or which, if it does involve courts, lets these play a role, in a sequence, quite different from that suggested by the three functions of the American separation of powers. In international as in national political systems, after they have reached an advanced stage of development, laws are often deliberately "made," after deliberation, in order to solve specific substantive problems like the incidence of murder or genocide, the difficulties arising out of commerce within one state or between citizens of several states. In such cases of deliberate law making, the "law maker" often, but not always, assigns specific functions to courts. Sometimes, of course, courts themselves are among the law makers in this sense of the term. Most substantive international law that is made in this sense results from international treaties, and treaties frequently provide that specific national or international courts will resolve conflicts arising under the treaty or about its interpretation. This is also true of some deliberately made procedural international law, like the conventions formulated at the

---

[18]See, e.g., "European Court of Human Rights: The Lawless Case," *Duke Law Journal,* Vol. 1962 (Spring, 1962), pp. 249–58. See also The European Commission and European Court of Human Rights, *Yearbook of the European Convention on Human Rights* (The Hague: Martinus Nijhoff, 1959–).

"Second Congress of Vienna" in 1961, which sought to bring up-to-date the forms of diplomatic protocol and to regulate the size and activities of diplomatic representation.

This United Nations Conference on Diplomatic Intercourse and Immunities, which met in Vienna from March 2, to April 14, 1961, was attended by representatives of 81 states. A draft prepared by the International Law Commission of the United Nations served as basis for their discussions. Some issues turned out to be quite controversial, and the dividing lines were not always those of the Cold War. For example, the Big Four—United States, Soviet Union, United Kingdom, France—fought against a majority of smaller states in their insistence upon the right to unlimited wireless communications out of embassies in host countries. The smaller countries apparently objected to this, because they could not afford to maintain world-wide telecommunications networks in any case. The Vienna Convention on Diplomatic Relations was to come into effect after it had been ratified by 22 states.[19]

However, whenever new international law of this type is indeed "made," the makers follow certain agreed procedures in the course of their law-creating activity. These procedures are also a part of the law. In our view such procedures are a much more important, because they constitute a much more fundamental component of international law than the content of treaties, including such basic multilateral treaties as the Charter of the United Nations itself. Generally, the most fundamental "laws" in any political system deal with procedural rather than substantive matter. Moreover, these most fundamental laws are so deeply "engraved on the hearts of the citizens"—to use a phrase from Jean Jacques Rousseau's *Social Contract*—that people are only dimly if at all aware of their acceptance of these rules. When the American Founding Fathers assembled in Congress to declare the independence of the American colonies and, later, in convention to establish the Constitution of the United States, there already existed among them a deep and less than conscious consensus upon procedures by means of which to conduct their debates. When the founders of the United Nations met for the deliberations that eventu-

---

[19]Ernest L. Kerley, "Some Aspects of the Vienna Convention on Diplomatic Intercourse and Immunities," *American Journal of International Law*, Vol. 56 (1962), pp. 88–129. For the text of the Convention, see *op. cit.*, Vol. 55 (1961), pp. 1062–94.

ally produced the Charter, they were more conscious of the shallower and more substantive consensus that prevailed among them. In neither case could most of the objects of this consensus have been deduced from extant documents of national or international law.

Similarly, even courts of law themselves, though they are brought into being as a result of formal legislation, as were both the United States Supreme Court and the International Court of Justice, operate on the basis of a procedural consensus which is deeper and more fundamental than their enabling statutes or formally published rules of procedure. The difficulties involved in "capturing" and describing the scope and content of this consensus are great, but at bottom it must minimally include agreement on methods by which to communicate. These methods, in turn, must include the languages in which this communication is to take place. On the other hand, there need be no agreement on the ultimate substantive purposes or goals which a court is meant to achieve. In most cases, such agreement would be impossible to state, except in the vaguest of terms, because the various parties that come together in order to found it are usually pursuing different and even antagonistic goals.

The scope and content of the consensus that went into establishment of the World Court—of the agreement that made possible its founding—is adumbrated in the provision for its composition: fifteen Justices, who should represent "the main forms of civilization and the principal legal systems of the world." The major systems of law include the Roman Law and the Common Law, Communist legal systems, Islamic Law, and legal systems based in part upon such Oriental forms of civilization as those represented by Japan and India. According to the Statute, the Justices must also have "recognized competence in international law." Because of the Western origins of modern international law, this means that World Court Judges, whatever their competence in non-Western legal systems, are learned above all in European law and are likely to have received their basic training in the Roman Law, the Common Law, or a legal system derived directly from one or the other of these two.

This basically European character of international law has raised two types of obstacles to full participation in and acceptance of international law by non-Western states. The first is of a substantive nature and was expressed, among others, by the Indian government at the time of India's military take-over of the Portuguese colony of Goa.

Portugal and some others in the West asserted that India was violating international law, including the Charter of the United Nations, by taking the Portuguese enclave over by means of force. The Indian representative at the United Nations, on the other hand, claimed that any international law which could be twisted to such conclusions was unacceptable to India and other anticolonialist states, because it was created in the course and service of the imperialist and colonialist expansion of Europe. The obstacle which self-styled anticolonialist states recognize here is similar to that seen by Soviet students and practitioners of international law. Since Marxism understands law as an emanation of the state and a reflection of the interests of the ruling class within a state, capitalist and socialist states should have diametrically opposed legal systems. This opposition should presumably manifest itself also in their interpretations of the content of international law. However, in the post-Stalin period,

> the view came to prevail . . . that international law was the totality of elements common to both capitalist and socialist superstructures, just as criminal law under socialism and capitalism shared certain features. This is the approach that has led Moscow at times to describe the agreed covenants and *procedure* of international organizations as the common denominator of the two systems, and that, more recently, led Khrushchev to declare that "only such decisions should be taken in the United Nations which everyone would vote for."[20]

More serious and more subtle than the first, substantive obstacle to full acceptance of international law by non-Western states is the second, procedural obstacle. Westerners, including Soviet Russians, whatever the finer differences between their two major systems of law may be, generally conceive of laws as having highly specific objects and objectives that can be spelled out in considerable detail and that can be used by individuals in their daily lives and by participants in litigation as practical guidelines for action and as weapons in forensic situations. The Oriental and Black African conceptions of law tend to differ from the Occidental, in that law for them generally lacks a high degree of specificity, and litigation makes less use of sophisticated "oppositional" legal argumentation. Among the reasons for these differences—to which we will return in Chapter 7—are the

---

[20]Alexander Dallin, *The Soviet Union at the United Nations* (New York: Frederick A. Praeger, 1962), p. 7. Italics supplied. Quoted by permission of Frederick A. Praeger, Publishers.

effects of the heritage of Aristotelian logic, with its rule of the excluded middle, which is not always operationally recognized in non-Western, non-Aristotelian systems of logic, so that different laws within one and the same system occasionally seem to Western analysts to contradict one another and some laws impress them as generalized "pearls of wisdom." Another reason may be found in the consensual character of many non-Western communities, especially before their modernization, industrialization, or general "Westernization." Western communities, by contrast, have not been consensual at least since the Industrial Revolution. By comparison with non-Western communities not heirs to Greek dialectical logic, Western ones were comparatively nonconsensual even before the Industrial Revolution. They developed ideologies, including the medieval and modern Christian international legal doctrines of the *bellum iustum* or just war, which Pope John XXIII and the Vatican Council "up-dated" by rejecting any nuclear war as unjust. Western communities tend to take a theoretic and analytical view of the world. Oriental communities are shaped by philosophies based upon what F. S. C. Northrop has called the "undifferentiated aesthetic continuum."[21] There, facts and values, and views of different types, instead of being posited as mutually exclusive opposites, blend over one into the other. Indigenous equivalents of specific legal doctrines like the just war are lacking. (For purposes of this discussion, Islam must be classified as Western because of its exposure to Aristotelian logic; this helps explain the concept of the "holy war.") While the purpose of litigation in the West is usually thought to be the definitive ascertainment of who is right and who is wrong, without much of an opportunity to "split the difference" and compromise, the purpose of litigation in the non-West traditionally seemed to lie closer to restoration or confirmation of old consensus and careful construction of new agreement in the community. At the conclusion of litigation, neither party (if there were two) is necessarily told that it was right or wrong, but instead that they should get back together and behave themselves in keeping with the prescriptions of legal-philosophical wisdom.

The substantive needs of the modernization to which all countries are being subjected today with varying intensity and at varying rates of speed, is gradually changing non-Western concepts of law. Populous

---

[21]F. S. C. Northrop, *The Meeting of East and West* (New York, Macmillan Co., 1946), pp. 335 ff.

modern industrial systems require detailed and specific legal regulation and, among other things, methods for the speedy and clear settlement of disputes between individuals and organizations. Consensus of the traditional type, which was founded also upon lack of awareness of the possibilities of change, disappears in the face of efforts by the modernizing leadership to create a less "natural," more self-conscious consensus behind the official ideology that invariably is of European origin. These changes will eventually help to reduce this procedural obstacle to full participation in and acceptance of international law by peoples of non-European background.

Individual Responsibility under International Law

Another distinctive feature of modern Western philosophies and legal systems is their individualism. Individualism is historically and logically related to the specificity of law and the highly "oppositional" nature of litigation. In consensual communities, on the other hand—whether their consensualism be that of relatively "primitive" or of relatively "developed" but non-Western systems—consciousness of individuality is rarely as far advanced. In primitive societies individuals are more aware of their belonging to their group—family, village, clan, or tribe—than they are aware of their separate existence as single human beings who can recognize their own problems and deliberate about them in order to solve them. This early stage in the growth of human self-consciousness is usually found within a "system" of law—perhaps it would be better to say, "notions of justice"—that includes collective or communal concepts of responsibility and liability. A whole family, village, or tribe is punished collectively, because the whole group is believed to have been responsible for a particular event.

From the viewpoint of the unself-conscious members of such communities, collective accountability in this sense corresponds to their notion of justice or, to use our terminology, collective accountability does not deny them a sound situation of responsibility. However, as they develop a greater sense of individuality and, along with it, a more highly differentiated understanding of causation, they will also expect that "retribution" should primarily affect those smaller groups and, ultimately, those individuals, who can be isolated as having been specifically responsible for, in the sense of having "caused," the event in question. A legal system thus provides its members with a sound situation of responsibility, in their own view, so long as it appiles sanctions to collectivities *or* individuals that correspond in their degree of differentiation or "specification" to those collectivities or individuals believed to be capable of having committed the delicts for which the law provides sanctions.

A close parallelism exists between political philosophies that advocate individual responsibility and legal philosophies, or schools of jurisprudence, that advocate individual legal liability or accountability, although political philosophies usually look forward in time, while legal philosophies generally have a more retrospective outlook. In other words, jurists tend to be concerned with the proper placement of accountability for events that lie in the past or that will lie in the past when a court or other agency of the law resolves an issue brought before it. Political theorists tend to be more interested in structuring the flow of policy in such a way that individuals and groups can become responsible for—can make causal contributions to—central decisions, the consequences of which will affect them in the future.[22]

This parallelism with a difference in temporal outlook is reflected in writings on international law by legal and political philosophers. Hans Kelsen, one of the most influential contemporary philosophers of law, has stated that collective forms of accountability are characteristic of primitive societies. Professor Kelsen consequently considers the international legal order a relatively primitive one.[23] These scholars view as signs of progress those efforts that have been made to apply international law to individuals accused of having violated its provisions. An famous early but ineffective such effort was made in the provisions of Articles 227 and 228 of the Treaty of Versailles, under which Kaiser Wilhelm II was to be tried "for a supreme offence against international morality and the sanctity of treaties." The Kaiser was never tried. But during World War II, the Allies agreed by treaty on the Charter of the International Military Tribunal which, after the War, sat in judgment at Nuremberg on the men accused of having committed major "war crimes" on behalf of Adolf Hitler's Nazi state.

---

[22]See also Chapter 8.

[23]Hans Kelsen, *Law and Peace in International Relations* (Cambridge: Harvard University Press, 1942), p. 25 see also his "Collective and Individual Responsibility for Acts of State in International Law," *Jewish Yearbook of International Law*, 1948, p. 226; and his *Peace Through Law* (Chapel Hill: University of North Carolina Press, 1944).

There is still considerable controversy about the justice of the particular verdicts handed down by the Nuremberg and other war crimes trials, and about the general question of what constitutes "precedent" under international law.

Regardless of how these controversies will be resolved—if they ever will be—we should here remark upon a peculiar phenomenon that accompanied the first large-scale international trial of individual politicians for crimes committed in international politics. This phenomenon was the simultaneous widespread popular condemnation of the German people as a collectivity for having become responsible for the same crimes in less specifiable ways. There had been talk of German "war guilt" during and after World War I, when no international tribunal tried war criminals, though a German court did try some German naval personnel for acts committed on the high seas after their submarine had sunk Allied shipping.[24] One might have expected that the international and the American war crimes trials conducted in Germany after World War II would have deflected such feelings from the German nation as a collectivity upon specific individuals who were convicted of having committed specific acts. But this was not to be so, as least not for the five postwar years before the Federal Republic of Germany became a staunch ally of the United States in its global struggle against the same Solviet Union which had been its partner in setting up the International Military Tribunal.

By this time, i.e., by 1950, the West German Government itself seemed to be admitting a degree of collective German responsibility for war crimes in the course, ironically, of trying deliberately to deny any collective guilt. It made this denial by, among other things, paying restitution to victims of war crimes committed by Germans. For example, the Federal Republic paid nearly one billion dollars worth of restitution to the State of Israel as a sort of residuary legatee of the six million European Jews killed by the Nazis. It also paid restitution to individuals who could show that they or their killed relatives had been victimized by the Nazis. In 1966, the West German Government continues to bring to trial individual Germans charged with having committed war crimes and "crimes against humanity" under the Nazi regime, thereby seeking to localize and specify the responsibility of

---

[24]See Claud Mullins, *The Leipzig Trials* (London: H. F. and G. Witherby, 1921).

individuals for these events. However, by assuming the burdens of restitution as a government—which claims, incidentally, to be acting also on behalf of the Soviet-occupied Zone of Hitler's former *Reich*— the West German government also seemed to be saying, in effect: We speak, and in a sense, we seek to atone, for all those Germans who, as citizens of one political system, permitted conditions to arise in which it was possible for individuals to commit these crimes. At the same time, by taking certain constitutional and legal steps in reconstructing our political system, we are seeking to create better situations of responsibility for our citizens now than existed under the Weimar Constitution, so that a genuine replacement of collective by individual responsibility will take place.

At this point, the retrospective concerns of jurisprudence converge with the prospective concerns of political philsophy. The jurist prefers situations in which clear individual responsibility (in the sense of causal responsibility) can be ascertained for events lying in the past. The political philosopher, if he is committed to the norm of individual responsibility, prefers to create situations which enable individuals to contribute to central decisions to the extent to which they are likely to be exposed to the consequences of these decisions. Among the components of the sound situation of responsibility is foreknowledge of the probable consequences of one's actions. This foreknowledge can be provided in large measure by law, including international law

Within national legal systems, the procedural aspects of law, especially "constitutional" law in both the formal and the informal sense, help in the maintenance and improvement of sound situations of responsibility. Unless procedural law provides foreknowledge through contributing to pursuit of the basic goal of stability, individuals cannot participate responsibly in the central flow of policy *even though* they enjoy a plenitude of resources and a multiplicity of choice. Within national legal systems, individuals do not always participate in, and are not always exposed to, the flow of policy *as individuals*. National legal systems assign more or less clearly defined roles to collectivities of various types, like corporations, voluntary and compulsory organizations, administrative districts, and age and sex groups. In the United States, for example, farmers may participate in special polls on agricultural policy and benefit or suffer as an occupational group from government farm policies. Under the Anti-Poverty Program, citizens qualifying as "poor" elect members of local boards administering the program, which is meant to improve the living conditions and, in a very real sense, the situation of responsibility of poor people both as individuals and as members of a subsystem with special problems differing from the general problems faced by the national political system. These examples—and they could be multiplied many times—of legally ramified "pluralism" in the highly developed legal system of the United States suggest, incidentally, that Professor Kelsen may be wrong if he was asserting that the trend from collective to individual forms of liability is a unilinear and continuous trend that exactly parallels the development of a community from primitiveness to highly differentiated maturity. It seems possible that such a trend did, in certain Western countries, prevail until they reached the highly individualistic stage of the capitalism of the mid-nineteenth century. Roughly since then, however, more collective types of accountability have been "creeping back," partly perhaps because of a widespread realization that unorganized individuals were incapable of shaping the fate of their communities and, therefore, of themselves as individuals. Trade unions and employers associations, ever more active political parties, and a host of other functionally and/or geographically defined organizations have, as a result, been recognized by the legal systems of advanced industrial countries. The legislators or policy makers of these countries act upon these organizations and their members as special classes of persons, i.e., they expose them as collectivities to policy. The political systems have, therefore, been structured so as to facilitate direct contributions to policy from these organizations.

Analogously, under international law and in international politics, collectivities contribute directly to the flow of world policy and are exposed as collectivities to the consequences of the global political process. It used to be contended, in opposition to this analogy, that *only* states are subjects of international law. For example, in 1928, the fourth edition of L. F. L. Oppenheim's authoritative treatise, edited by Arnold D. McNair, stated: "Since the Law of Nations is a law between States only, and since States are the sole exclusive subjects of International Law, individuals are mere objects of International Law, and the latter is unable to confer directly rights and duties upon them."[25] Twenty years later, however, this position had already been

---

[25]L. F. L. Oppenheim, *International Law*, Section 149, Arnold D. McNair (ed.) (4th ed.; New York: Longmans, Green & Co., 1928).

revised by H. Lauterpacht, editor of the seventh edition of the same work:

> As States are the *normal* subjects of International Law, they—and only they—are, *as a rule,* subjects of international delinquencies. On the other hand, to the extent to which individuals are made subjects of international duties—and, consequently, of International Law—they are also subjects of international delinquencies. This is the case *not only* with regard to piracy and similar topics of limited compass. . . . The increasing complexities of international relations . . . may call for far-reaching extensions of individual responsibility expressly declared by International Law.[26]

We have already seen, in the citations above from Clark and Sohn's *World Peace through World Law* and from Jenks's *The Common Law of Mankind,* that the scope of individual responsibility under international law has been growing further since 1948, and that its wider extension is being advocated by some influential students and practitioners of international politics. This fact and the hopes attached to it by protagonists of the principle of individual responsibility should not, however, lead us to overlook the possibility of having international law which is effective though it is in the main collective at the same time.

Indeed, it seems quite possible that advocates of the expansion of the role of international law in world politics may have been "barking up the wrong tree" with their insistence upon the indispensability of individual responsibility, for two reasons. The first is the professed anti-individualism, at least for their and others' present stage of development, of the Soviet Union and other "socialist states," including China. Soviet and other communist theories of international politics are based upon an analysis of conflict between *classes.* For instance, the Soviet Union claims to act on behalf of "workers and peasants" everywhere on earth, and the United States is asserted to be the spokesman for international capitalist imperialism. The class war, once it was won by the proletariat within countries like the Soviet Union and China, is transferred to the global sphere, where the great blocs in effect act as representatives of the great classes. The role of individuals in this process—even of great historical figures—is minimized by the Communists, e.g., in denunciations of the "cult of personality." It therefore seems unlikely that the Communist consent that would be required in order to broaden and deepen consensus upon international

---

[26]*Ibid.,* Section 153(a) H. Lauterpacht (ed.) (7th ed.; New York: Longmans, Green & Co., 1948).

law could be obtained by any deliberate further individualization of international law, at least at the present stage of the development of world politics. This last qualification has to be made, because Communists like other Marxists always insist that collectivization is necessary only in order to prepare the road for the establishment of full communism, in which true individualism—as distinguished from the oppressively antiproletarian individualism of bourgeois capitalism—will flourish under the motto: "From *each* according to his ability, to *each* according to his needs," in a society in which "The freedom of each will be the condition of the freedom of all."

The second reason why insistence upon further individualization of international law may have results the opposite of those intended is related to the consensualism of most non-Western countries, mentioned above. This consensualism takes on a variety of forms and has different causes in different contexts. In some very "civilized" regions of Asia, where Buddhism, Taoism, Confucianism, and related religions-philosophies are dominant, consensus and harmony are valued highly and almost for their own sake. In some relatively "primitive" areas of Africa, consensus has hitherto been indispensable to the very existence of communities living on the margin of subsistence. In other slightly more advanced areas, consensus helped win independence from colonial rule and disagreement can, therefore, be condemned as playing into the hands of the neocolonialists. In both densely populated urbanized systems and sparsely populated rural communities, where notions of privacy of the kind with which most people in the West grow up from infancy are inconceivable for practical reasons, the individual's understanding of his self and place in the community is bound to differ from that of a citizen of, say, the Federal Republic of Germany, whose right to privacy, including the secrecy of his postal and telecommunications, are guaranteed in the constitution and a whole body of legislation. As a result, it seems possible that any marked further individualization of international law would tend to alienate rather than to attract countries in the "developing areas" of the world. Their socialism, which often differs sharply from Soviet socialism, but which objects at least to individual private property on conventional European lines, could constitute a further reason for this possible alienation.

All of this suggests that the promotion of world peace through world law requires least the formation of some substantive consensus

among states and peoples, beyond agreement on common opposition to
the extermination of mankind through global nuclear war or some
similar catastrophe. In any case, except for this vague negative substantive consensus, it seems virtually impossible to enlarge areas of
agreement on matters of substance among those states whose dissent
can effectively "veto" any proposed statement of consensus. As usual,
the best hope for the future, as the best performance in the past, of
international law seems to lie in the accretion of consensus on matters
of procedure. Any disagreement, any issue, even if it barely gets beyond the phase of formulation, and regardless of whether it is ever
resolved or not, requires use of common procedures by all those who
act upon recognition of their interest in the issue. No matter what
the substance of a problem, and no matter what positions one takes on
such substantive issues as those between individualism and collectivism, or between the stimulus of dissent and the harmony of consensus,
or between the benefits of colonialism and the fruits of independence,
or between constitutional democracy and socialist people's democracy
—all these controversies, whether they arise within one country or
among states, can be processed by the same sets of fundamental procedures. The greater the volume of substantively varied issues that are
fed into the world political system, the better are chances for the
growth of consensus upon one common procedural law of mankind.
The respect accorded international politicians who are chiefly specialists of procedure, like U Thant, even by states who substantively disagree with their stand on a particular issue, points in the same direction.

The Contribution of International Law

The range of matters potentially "covered" by international law has
been increasing tremendously in the past two decades. Jenks's proposal
for the rearrangement of the subject matter of international law gives
one indication of this expansion of coverage. The work of the International Law Commission of the United Nations provides another.[27]
The establishment, at American universities, of a number of institutes,
usually located within or affiliated with schools of law, for the special-

---

[27]See Herbert W. Briggs, *The International Law Commission* (Ithaca: Cornell
University Press, 1965).

ized study of international-and-comparative law, is virtually without precedent in the period before 1945. The volume of treaty-making activity continues to increase, partly because of the network of international organizations that make up the "United Nations family," partly because of the network of regional treaty organizations that has been spun in the course of the Cold War.[28]

If the content of these treaties and other new international law could be systematically compared with the content of newly made international law of the period between 1925 and 1945, or of the twenty years before World War I, the results would probably show steady increases in the proportion of substantive over procedural content. The reasons for this are related to both the Cold War, which revolves around issues of substance, and the technological revolution which demands the specific regulation of an ever-expanding spectrum of relations, involving such substantive matters as trade, health, land, sea, air, and space travel, telecommunications, science, and armaments. The "birth" of new (misnamed) "nations," all of whom have to enter into relations with each other, with old states, with the United Nations and other international organizations, has added to this general trend. Each of these factors—Cold War, technological revolution, decolonisation—has had destabilizing effects upon world politics. More important, phenomena arising out of these factors *were expected* to cause further disorder in an already unstable international environment. In reaction to these expectations of instability, states and other organizations, and individuals, including scholars (some of them cited in this chapter), made generally unsuccessful efforts to maintain or reestablish older forms of stability through the creation of various forms of international law. Hence the legalism of the present, third period of international politics. In a condition of continuous flux, that is, in the absence of stability, stability is sought so earnestly and almost feverishly, that one tries permanently to freeze relations among states as they exist at a moment in time favorable to one's own state or bloc. This is one aspect of the legalism of contemporary world politics.

These efforts to stabilize global politics of the Cold War within the

---

[28]Between 1920 and 1929, 4,600 treaties were registered with the League of Nations (League of Nations, *Treaty Series,* Vol. CXCVI). Between 1946 and 1963, 10,423 treaties and agreements were registered or filed and recorded with the United Nations; *Yearbook of the United Nations 1963* (New York: Office of Public Information of the United Nations, 1965), p. 524.

rigid rubrics of treaties of regional organization have usually failed, often in rather ironic ways. For example, the United States persuaded Pakistan to join both the Bagdhad Treaty Organization (later renamed the Central Treaty Organization or CENTO, when Iraq, of which Bagdhad is the capital, left after its pro-Western King was killed in the revolution of 1958) and the Southeast Asia Treaty Organization or SEATO. Both treaties, which made new substantive international law, were designed as defensive measures against the Soviet communist threat and as integral components of the nexus of alliances completed by Secretary of State John Foster Dulles. Successive American administrations were critical of India because of its general neutralism and its particular refusal to join the anticommunist alliance. The United States itself was indifferent on the issue of Kashmir, between India and Pakistan. It became even more critical of India over its "conquest," by force of arms, of the four-centuries-old Portuguese colony of Goa, because India was alleged to have violated international law, including the Charter of the United Nations, with this unilateral and forcible action. Then, when the Chinese-Indian border conflict broke out in 1962, the United States began to give some military aid to India, under the condition, previously also attached to military equipment supplied massively to Pakistan, that it not be used against the adversary in the Kashmir dispute. About this time, the Soviet Union began to sell armaments to India. Pakistan meanwhile improved its relations with China, partly on the principle that one's enemy's enemy must be one's friend. Formally, however, Pakistan remained a member of CENTO and SEATO. When the war over Kashmir erupted between India and Pakistan in 1965, the United States and the Soviet Union found themselves eagerly supporting mediation efforts within the United Nations Security Council and through the Secretary-General, a citizen of neutralist Burma, while communist China, the erstwhile ally of the Soviet Union, was apparently trying to intensify and expand the war by reviving its border dispute with India, this time over the Indian Protectorate of Sikkim. During all this time, both India and Pakistan continued as members of an older, more flexible, less deliberately created international organization, the British Commonwealth. And the United States and other "treaty partners" of Pakistan's were involved in a bitter struggle over Vietnam with North Vietnam and, at least indirectly, communist China. In other words, even the firmest of treaty commitments—and circa two billion dollars worth of aid from the United States to Pakistan—did not suffice to maintain alignments that may have appeared as "natural" to the international lawmakers of the 1950's. However, the existence of so much recently created international law encouraged politicians, in all of these conflicts, to refer constantly to each other's legal obligations and to accuse one another of having violated these. Respect for this kind of international law could hardly grow as a result of this increasing legalism of world politics.

The yearning for permanent stability, of which the treaty organizations are a symptom, is caused also by the disappearance of the deep and partly less-than-conscious consensus that used to prevail on fundamental procedures among diplomats and military of the old school, especially before World War. I. In those days, the most important features of international law were also the least discussed ones. In part they had been "laid down" by the Congress of Vienna; for the most part, however, they were the conventionally grown procedures of diplomatic intercourse. Certain things were done, certain other things were not done, and professional diplomats knew which were which. They did not usually need "experts" on international law to tell them what they could, and what they could not do, legally. Nowadays, to exaggerate the contrast somewhat, the equivalent of diplomacy is often not being carried on by professional diplomats at all, but by an ill-assorted bunch of professional revolutionaries, popular politicians, successful businessmen, engineers, and even scholars of various types. And the foreign offices of the major states (and of international organizations and private business firms with important international activities) are assisted by large staffs of professional international lawyers. Usually these legal staffs act in a mainly advisory and expert capacity. They do what Harold Laski said economic and other substantive experts should generally do: Stay on tap, but not on top. In such a capacity, their functioning bears witness to the evaporation of the older, more natural procedural consensus among professional diplomats themselves. Sometimes, however, an international lawyer himself becomes an important international politician, as did John Foster Dulles as United States Secretary of State. Then the legalism of the profession can inform the foreign policy of a whole bloc of states, and the lack of genuine procedural consensus becomes even more evident.

The contribution of international law to *stability*, that is, to the basic goal where its contribution could be most noticeable, has consequently been of only limited value. This is especially true of much of the deliberately made new international law which was brought into being precisely for stabilizing purposes. It is less true of new international law that has grown up around institutions like the World Health Organization or the older International Labor Organization. Availability of the International Court of Justice does not seem to have helped international political stability to any marked degree. In general, the tendency of those seeking stability through law has been to lapse instead into a more or less pathological legalism.

The contribution of international law to the *flexibility* of world politics may, ironically, have been greater than its contribution to stability during the two first postwar decades. This would be ironic, because stability is generally regarded as the primary function of law. It appears nevertheless to be true, because of the transitory character of many of the treaties that were designed to freeze the regional *status quo* prevailing at a particular time in the Cold War. These treaties, in effect, provided *temporarily* effective frameworks for change. They enabled the signatory states to "signal" to the rest of the world, especially the other camp in the Cold War, what their own intentions were, at least for the time being, and how far the other side could go before violence might erupt.

One could, for example, evaluate the North Atlantic Treaty Organization from this point of view. NATO gave notice to the Soviet Union, at a time when the United States and western European states feared the numerical superiority of its land forces, that it could expect the members of NATO to come to each other's military assistance in case any one of them were to be overtly attacked. Under Soviet leadership, the Warsaw Pact was organized in response to NATO. While these two treaty organizations functioned along the lines originally intended by their founders, a great deal of change occured within each of them and in relations between them and their several members. For example, West Germany became the most powerful country in western Europe, and East Germany the most highly industrialized country in eastern Europe exclusive of Russia. West Germany and the Soviet Union established diplomatic relations. The United States improved its diplomatic, and initiated substantial commercial and aid, relations with eastern European members of the Warsaw Pact. Soviet-American relations "thawed." Greece and Turkey tried to find some sort of accommodation with each other and with

Cyprus, which gained independence outside NATO but inside the Commonwealth. Many other adjustments were made on both sides and between them. However, by the time that President De Gaulle began his efforts to disentangle France from NATO, a maximum of utility for flexibility had probably already been "squeezed out" of NATO and its counterpart. France had been able to solve its colonial problems, in Indochina and Algeria, while enjoying some external protection and less internal support from NATO. The Common Market had reached a stage of development where it would either have to survive on its own merits or fail, because arguments of anticommunism no longer sufficed to induce countries like France to let themselves be integrated into a more or less federal Europe. President De Gaulle, therefore, announced that France would try to renegotiate the Treaty upon its twentieth anniversary, in 1969, as the Treaty itself provides, or withdraw from NATO. In this sense, by setting such a relatively short renegotation date, the authors of the Treaty themselves may have recognized that their contribution to world politics was oriented more toward the basic goal of flexibility than toward that of stability.

The results of conferences like those, held at Vienna, on diplomatic intercourse and immunities made greater contributions to flexibility than the more substantively biased defense and technical agreements. The same is true of conferences, both official and unofficial, which tried to look ahead to the era, over whose threshold we have already stepped, when international law would have to be extended into outer space. Fascinating problems were raised in anticipation of space travel. For example, should questions of jurisdiction in outer space be answered by analogy to the law of the open seas or by analogy to international aviation law? The more nearly analogous situation was that of the high seas, where no particular sovereignty exercises jurisdiction, rather than air space, over which the subjacent state exercises jurisdiction, at least up to a certain height, on which there is no universal agreement. These efforts to anticipate the legal problems of space exploration constitute a very rare case of imaginative foresight meant to help the political system to adapt to radical but predictable substantive change. However, thinking ahead is not the same as acting ahead, and the states most likely to succeed in outer space have not yet agreed to any far-reaching set of rules of the game for their competitive or cooperative enterprises of exploration, except for the joint votes of the United States and the Soviet Union in favor of the resolutions of the General Assembly against claiming planetary territory for states and against the placing of nuclear weapons on board of space satellites. The flexibility of actual or potential new international law here stands in tension with its effectiveness.

The contribution of international law to the *effectiveness* of world politics for our third period cannot be evaluated very highly. Perhaps it would be useful at this point to introduce a convenient but not in any way rigid distinction between the specific content of new international law, e.g., treaties, and the institutions which may take on a life of their own as a result of these treaties. Thus, the Charter of the United Nations is an important document of international law, which accounts for much of the legalism of contemporary world politics. The United Nations as an institution, first created by the Charter, has grown far beyond the provisions of the Charter in some respects, while in others it has not yet entered the openings for action which the document offers. The United Nations, as we judged at the conclusion of the last chapter, has made valuable contributions to the effectiveness of world politics, but in ways that frequently go counter to the intentions of at least some of the drafters and original ratifiers of the Charter. In this sense, more generally, one could assign a lower value to the contribution of international law to the effectiveness of world politics. This applies with particular vigor to those sectors of the law which are in contention between the two great blocs, or between the Western and the non-Western parts of the world. Nor would the very few cases in which international arbitration or judicial settlement of disputes was actually accepted really contradict this basic judgment. For example, Thailand and Cambodia submitted to the World Court their dispute over a sacred temple located near their common boundary. Though both are, of course, Oriental states, both Cambodia, the winner, and Thailand, the loser, accepted the verdict of the World Court which operates on the basis of essentially Western law. The case was ideally suited for impartial third-party adjudication, according to Professor Franck's criteria. But such cases, where international law judgments turned out to be effective over the intermediate run, are few and far between. If international law is making a major contribution to the effectiveness of world politics—to the acceptability of the policies turned out by the global system and of its "constitution"—then this may be happening at the more fundamental, more subtle, less easily discernible level of new procedures. These new procedures for international intercourse—not only intercourse among states—are being developed by a tortuously groping process, simply because the old procedures, on which there was such a strong professional consensus, are no longer suited for handling the radically novel problems of international politics. The new procedures, which are undeliberately being made a component of new international law, may for that very reason turn out to be more effective. Conversely, those new procedures that have been designed deliberately, precisely because of the high degree of self-consciousness involved in their design and suspicions of self-interest which consequently fall upon their designers, usually turn out to be less acceptable to those who did not participate in their design. We will return to some of these new procedures in our discussion of problems raised by strategy in world politics.

The contribution of international law to the *efficiency* of world politics, i.e., to the capacity of the global system to maintain an efficient ratio between the input of problems and the output of policies, seems least impressive, at least with respect to those problems which have widely been considered of highest priority. On the contrary, whenever legal arguments have been resorted to in the course of dealing with such important international problems, their solution, and the resolution of the issues arising out of them, has often been delayed, made more complicated and less acceptable to various parties. The increasing role of experts on international law in foreign offices has not necessarily made a positive contribution, as noted above. The lead given by prominent jurists from Western and neutralist countries, but not from the Soviet Union or communist China, to movements like the one for world peace through world law has not necessarily improved the prospects in this regard. Napoleon is reported to have said that war was too important to be left to generals. During the presidential campaign of 1964, Senator Barry Goldwater paraphrased this, with reference to the United States Supreme Court, to say that constitutional law was too important to be left to constitutional lawyers. Both war and constitutional law, in the opinion of Napoleon, Goldwater, and others of differing political persuasions, are above all the business of the people exposed to the consequences of military devastation or of judicial decisions and the business, therefore, of those who speak for them, that is, of politicians. The same could be said of

world peace, even if it could be achieved primarily through the establishment of an enforceable system of world law: It is too important to
be left to international lawyers, except in a capacity as experts who
are on tap to, but not on top of, international politicians.

This negative evaluation of the contribution of international law
to the efficiency of the world political system in handling its most
important problems is not meant to denigrate the useful contributions made by international law and lawyers to efficiency in the
processing of less crucial but sometimes equally persistent problems,
especially technical ones. The various agreements on matters of health,
telecommunications, scientific research including the International
Geophysical Year, on the related treaty demilitarizing Antarctia, were
helped by the careful draftsmanship of legal craftsmen. However, the
more fundamental contribution of international law is likely to come
from the unplanned growth of political procedures commanding wide
and deep consensus in areas of the world whose legal systems and
ideologies otherwise differ greatly. If this forecast is at all accurate,
then it may at some later date be appropriate to paraphrase Jeremy
Bentham's panegyric on the rules of the House of Commons, in order
to apply it to basic procedural rules of international law:

> In this bye-corner, an observing eye may trace the original seed-plot
> of [world-wide] liberty: it is in this hitherto neglected spot that the seeds
> of that invaluable production have germinated and grown up to their
> present maturity, scarce noticed by the husbandman, and unsuspected by
> the destroyer.[29]

This conclusion about the contribution of international law to
world politics is consistent with our criticism, at the outset of this
chapter, of the inadequacies of both the "realist" and the "idealist" interpretations of the role of international law and, as for that matter,
of law in other, less comprehensive political systems. The most fundamental contribution that law can make to any kind of politics is to
shape and give flexible stability to the forms of procedure, within
which substantive political actions are cast. These procedures not only
provide the channels or circuits through which political action will
flow, but they also have a crucial effect upon the "prepolitical" phase
of the flow of policy, that is, upon the problems that will be recognized for political processing. Participants in world politics, espe-

---

[29]Quoted in Spiro, *op. cit.*, p. 247.

cially if they are single-mindedly dedicated to the exclusive pursuit of their own "national interest," are bound to "pick up" *those* problems, and introduce them into the global flow of policy, which they expect to be dealt with most advantageously for themselves by the procedures of that process. In their own national interest, they will not formulate issues as they would formulate issues in their own domestic politics, but so as to suit the procedures of international politics and international organizations, i.e., the procedures of international law. The arguments that they present in the course of deliberation will be designed to exploit the procedures of the particular forum of deliberation used, from bilateral secret diplomacy, to multilateral public propaganda at the United Nations and to prolonged litigation before the World Court. They will see to it that the resolution of issues in which they have an interest is couched in terms—is cast in forms—best designed to harmonize solution of the problem with their interests, and their participation in the phase of solution will similarly make optimum use of these procedures.

In this sense, international law has always been "used" by states, because, among other things, it was in their self-interest to develop a reputation for procedural honesty (a point to which we will return in our discussion of strategy). But before the age of nuclear weapons, that interest was weaker and less widespread than it is today, because there was always the possibility that a particular state might "get away" with "cheating." Even if it was caught, and even in the unlikely event that it should be destroyed as a result, that was *its* business or, more specifically, its rulers' business. Today, procedural dishonesty by one state—not necessarily one of the superpowers—could lead to the substantive annihilation of mankind. This fact has given all participants in world politics a greater stake than ever before in those "layers" of international law which provide the fundamental procedures for world politics. The content of these layers, and the strength of politicians' commitment to them, are only rarely if ever articulated clearly. They are never stated as clearly as the content of—and the weaker commitment to—the more circumstantial layers of international law. In order to obtain a clearer view of the more fundamental procedures of the new world politics—procedures which are still being laboriously shaped—we have to leave the literature on international law and turn to the field of strategy.

Chapter 7

Strategy, Power, and Knowledge

The Limits to Strategy

STRATEGY USED to mean simply "generalship," since the word is derived from *strategos*, Greek for "general." *The American College Dictionary* (1957) speaks of strategy as "the science or art of combining and employing the means of war in planning and directing large military movements and operations." In the years since 1945, however, the scope of strategy has been expanded, perhaps because of the expansion in the volume, and the consequent change in the quality, of military power. With the illimitability of power came its removal from control by generals in war since, in any case, the old clear-cut distinction between peace and war could no longer be made. Conventional power whose effects could be controlled, power which could reasonably be used as "present means to some apparent future good," such power could safely be turned over to generals and admirals and air marshals, to let them combine it in planning and directing large military operations. Principles of strategy, generalizations based upon observations of generalship of the past, had been accumulated and more or less systematized in a body of knowledge called "military science."

Beginning in the 1950's, however, when both the United States and the Soviet Union had developed hydrogen bombs and were about to perfect weapons systems that would facilitate almost instant delivery of H-bombs by means of intercontinental ballistic missiles, it became apparent, on both sides of the easily breachable, merely *Iron* Curtain, that this new unconventional power was of a kind that did not operate according to the established principles of conventional military science.

As part of the over-all breakdown of professional specialization in international politics, the field of strategy was invaded and eventually taken over by people other than generals, and a much wider scope than ever before was assigned to strategy. Some thought that the new power was so vast, that *its* potential should determine the goals of policy rather than the other way around. They almost seemed to be saying that policy and politics should become the handmaidens of strategy:

> Strategic doctrine transcends the problem of selecting weapons systems. It is the mode of survival of a society, relating seemingly disparate experiences into a meaningful pattern. By explaining the significance of events *in advance* of their occurrence it enables society to deal with most problems as a matter of routine and reserves creative thought for unusual or unexpected situations.[1]

Such statements suggest that strategy and not politics should be regarded as the master science. Before the invention of nuclear weapons systems, it was the function of politics and political philosophy to relate "seemingly disparate experiences into a meaningful pattern" for a society. When its survival was threatened, or when it wanted to threaten the survival of another society, its politicians would turn to their generals to let them apply strategy in the service of policy. Nowadays, the reasoning seems to be that the "brooding omnipresence" of unconventional power has eliminated the former distinction between strategy and politics, and the functional differentiation between political and strategic theorists. Because of the priority of nuclear power, however, the strategic-political theorist should take as his starting point the "realities of power," as understood by the particular school of strategic doctrine, rather than the universals and the particulars of politics, as interpreted by various political philosophies.

This (not entirely academic) "imperialism of strategists" is a more sophisticated extension of the one-dimensionalism of *Realpolitik* and the counterpart of the advocacy of institutional legalism. As these other schools of thought, it claims too much for itself. Most of its protagonists suffer, moreover, from a defect not frequently found among the schools we have already examined, and that is their narrowness of perspective. They usually propose "strategic doctrine" for only one side—their side—in the Cold War and, therefore, fail to perceive the

---

[1]Henry A. Kissinger, *Nuclear Weapons and Foreign Policy* (Garden City, N. Y.: Doubleday Anchor Books, 1958), p. 224.

emergence of the single global political system—perhaps because this emergence has exactly paralleled their own emergence as strategists with an insistent claim to attention from international politicians and publics.

The Sociology of Knowledge

Most of what we know about the specialized aspects of a subject like international politics, and especially about some of its subdivisions like strategic doctrine, comes from scholars and other publicists who specialize in the field. The background of these specialists is therefore of considerable interest. There are several competing approaches to the study of the factors that shape the attitudes and outlook of purveyors of knowledge. Some approaches take as their starting point the primacy of power and assert that "intellectuals," in the broad sense of that term, gravitate toward the sources of power in a society and will generally "produce" the kind of "knowledge" tending to support the incumbent power holders. Karl Marx's concept of ideology is based upon the assumption of the primary importance of the control of the means of production in a society. Dominant forms of knowledge in a society will reflect the interest of the ruling class, i.e., of the class that controls the means of production. But this is not "true knowledge"—it is *mere* ideology, not part of the substructure, but part of the superstructure, not capable of influencing the course of history by itself, but a mere tertiary reflection of fundamental reality. According to this approach, a correct critique of knowledge requires the examination of the class interest of the intellectuals who maintain, elaborate, and guard knowledge.

Marxists have generally asserted that the ideas and the doctrine advanced by Karl Marx himself was exempt from this class-bound character of other systems of knowledge, because his critique of bourgeois capitalism of the nineteenth century was already based upon a brilliant insight into the irreconcilable contradictions between the mode of production and the mode of distribution. Marx therefore generated "proletarian knowledge," and since the proletariat was that class which would ultimately win the class struggle and thereby lead to the abolition of classes in society and to establishment of the classless and stateless society, his knowledge transcended class interest and was, therefore, "true" knowledge. For this reason, Marxist

knowledge of the "natural laws" of society and history was also believed by its possessors to give them a strong element of power—and,
we might add, of resolute purpose—in their engagement in the class
struggle.

The Marxist conception of the origins and function of knowledge
still informs intellectual work, including strategy, in communist countries. It tends to give this kind of work a strong substantive bias. For
our purposes, the influence of Marx's notion of ideology upon conceptions of knowledge and upon the understanding of the role of intellectuals in *non*communist parts of the world is of equal importance.
There, neo-Marxian and non-Marxian analysts of the political function
of knowledge have also become much more skeptical about the possibility of achieving "the truth," and the general tendency is to begin
a critique of any system of knowledge with the examination of the
power interests of its upholders. Such examinations can, of course,
come to a variety of conclusions. For example, the European sociol-
ogist Karl Mannheim thought that, in modern societies, with their
division into classes, only the "free-floating intelligentsia" might be
able to arrive at a "total orientation and synthesis," that is, to see
things the way they really are.[2] Mannheim seemed to be saying that,
because intellectuals are committed to the truth *per se* rather than the
power interests of any of the competing classes in a society, the internal procedural standards of their professions provided more adequate standards for the critique of particular systems of knowledge
than the answer to the question, *cui bono?* This position overlooked
the likelihood that the members of a national intelligentsia look upon
themselves as members of a class—the intelligentsia—whose property
consists of knowledge of certain techniques without which no modern
system could operate. Their class interest lies in enhancing the value
of this property. This they can do by making themselves and their
knowledge indispensable, by persuading the rest of society that complete "true" knowledge exists, that intellectuals have access to it, and
that they should therefore run things (thereby incidentally contributing to ideological style).[3]

Despite this serious shortcoming of Mannheim's sociology of knowl-

---

[2]Karl Mannheim, *Ideology and Utopia: An Introduction to the Sociology of Knowledge* (New York: Harvest Books, 1936), p. 161.

[3]See Herbert J. Spiro, *Government by Constitution: The Political Systems of Democracy* (New York: Random House, 1959), p. 279.

edge, however, it can direct us toward a less one-sided approach to the study of those factors that shape the attitudes and outlook of specialists on international politics. Instead of inquiring only into their substantive interests and position, we can inquire also into the procedural or methodological standards and perspectives of their profession. Since both aspects are of course related, this kind of balance is needed in any case, and it is made particularly necessary for this study, at this time, by the transformation of power in world politics; by the slow coming into being of what Mannheim might have described as an international intelligentsia—which, to be sure, is no more free-floating than its national counterparts; and by the evaporation of the earlier procedural *consensus opinionis doctorum* on the methods of their disciplines among scholars of international relations.

Today the study of international politics is characterized by methodological chaos. This situation is unfortunate, not merely—not even mainly—for academic reasons. This is one meaning of the call for improved legal craftsmanship, made by Jenks and many other international jurists.[4] Without fundamental agreement on standards of legal craftsmanship among expert legal advisers to governments and international organizations, it is very difficult to reach agreements on issues of substance. Even if such agreement is reached "in principle" by the politicians, a lack of methodological consensus among their lawyers might make it impossible to articulate and to capture on paper the content of this agreement. Such a state of affairs is analogous to people who do not understand one another's languages and, therefore, have a hard time even in defining the things that they disagree about. In this respect, as we have noted, there has been significant consensus among international lawyers from substantively divergent traditions, at least at the level of procedural fundamentals.

Parallel methodological agreement is sometimes even easier to achieve among natural scientists, both when they get together at international scientific or political conferences simply as scientists, and when they act as expert advisers to governments engaged in international negotiations. For example, the annual Pugwash Conferences, initiated by the American industrialist Cyrus Eaton, bring together scientists, especially from fields having some relevance to weapons

---

[4]See Jenks, p. 173 above, and Arthur Larson, *When Nations Disagree: A Handbook on Peace Through Law* (Louisiana State University Press, 1961).

technology, who occasionally assert that, if problems of arms control and disarmament were left to them without "political" interference from their governments, they could have solved them long ago. Similarly, negotiations among scientific expert advisers to Soviet and United States delegations to official conferences on issues like a nuclear test ban have usually had less trouble arriving at "technical" understandings and agreements than their political superiors. The reasons are obvious. Physicists, chemists, geologists, as scientists, are by definition in procedural agreement on the fundamental methods of their respective disciplines.

Until about 1945, one could have said that military scientists similarly agreed on the method of their discipline, regardless of their interpretations of particular military events and their stands on individual issues. Military science was recognized as a legitimate field of study, a discipline with its classics, including the works of von Clausewitz, Mahan, and De Gaulle. Military scientists generally agreed on the meaning of such concepts as power, maneuverability, offense and defense, strategy and tactics, and on the fundamental and permanent significance of ancient and modern battles, like those fought at Cannae, Trafalgar, Verdun, or Stalingrad. By 1965, however, methodological agreement had been seriously weakened, if it had not disappeared altogether. The once clearly defined membership of the profession of military science has been replaced by a heterogeneous conglomeration of men and, for the first time in history, women, of very diverse professional backgrounds. Military scientists, who used to wield a virtual monopoly of disciplined discussion of the use of military power, and who usually were themselves members of the military professions, have lost their monopoly. Why?

An answer must begin with the vast changes that have taken place in the technology of organized violence as a result of the discovery and development of new sources of energy and the enormous improvements in communications and transportation, which contributed also to the dawn of genuine world politics. The older, conventional type of military scientist was not prepared, in terms of his technical schooling, his actual experience, or his methodological equipment for adapting to radical changes in his environment, to cope with these changes. In the United States, for example, virtually all military scientists received their education in military academies which imbued them with what might be described as a certain methodological conservatism. They tended toward inflexibility in both their conception of the scope of military science, including the intellectual boundaries between it and political science, and in their understanding of the intellectual tools with which they could attack their own subject matter.

As one illustration of this attitude, admittedly not in an academic but in a political situation, one can cite words uttered by a former Commandant of the United States Military Academy at West Point, General Douglas MacArthur, while he was Supreme Commander of United States and United Nations forces during the Korean War: "In war there is no substitute for victory." Previously, he had written that his "views are well known and clearly understood, as they follow the *conventional* pattern of meeting force with maximum counter-force as we have never failed to do in the past."[5] General MacArthur was not willing to recognize that the Korean War was unlike previous conventional wars, including World War II which he himself had prosecuted in Asia until Japan surrendered unconditionally to him in 1945. He was unaware that under the conditions of the Cold War such words as "victory" and "defeat" had lost their former meaning, even though he later adopted the vocabulary of the Cold War and implied the common analogy to Munich, when he wrote: "As subsequent events so clearly demonstrated, the only substitute for victory lies in appeasement."[6]

Conventional military science more or less sticks to the "eternal verities," derived from the experience of history and assumed to be as valid in the age of nuclear weapons as in the days of Hannibal or Caesar, of Napoleon or Ludendorff. (In this context, we should note that the American service academies have vigorously expanded their curricula in political and other social sciences since the war, and that the war colleges and staff schools of the services are now quite as advanced as certain university-connected institutes, discussed below, in their offerings and "outputs" in the area formerly covered by military science.)

The Possessors of Knowledge

As a result, when it became apparent that the old approach was incapable of grasping the qualitatively new realities, something of an

---

[5]Douglas MacArthur, *Reminiscences* (New York: McGraw-Hill Book Co., Inc., 1964) p. 385. Italics supplied.

[6]*Loc. cit.* See also General MacArthur's speech to a joint session of Congress, *Congressional Record*, Vol. 97, Part 3, pp. 4123–25; and Richard E. Neustadt, *Presidential Power* (New York: John Wiley & Sons, 1960), p. 25.

intellectual vacuum arose in the area previously virtually monopolized by military science. This vacuum was filled by professions and individuals to whom the thought of interesting themselves in problems of strategy and the like would not have occurred before World War II. By the 1960's, the material that was previously the preserve of military scientists was dominated by natural scientists, engineers, mathematicians, psychologists, economists, a few lawyers, a variety of other so-called "strategic intellectuals," including political scientists and some "retooled" military scientists who accepted at least the vocabulary introduced by their new colleagues.

Natural scientists probably make up the largest single contingent among the new breed of experts in this area. Many of them were initially involved in problems of defense and armaments during World War II, especially in connection with the Manhattan Project, which produced the first atomic bombs. This involvement by itself, however, was not without precedent, because scientists had served governments in similar capacities in previous wars, e.g., by designing tanks or inventing mustard gas during World War I. The difference in their behavior after World War II resulted directly from their immediate insight into the qualitative transformation in the nature of power which had been brought about by the production of the A-bomb. Albert Einstein had brought the possibility of the atomic weapon to the attention of President Franklin D. Roosevelt. Subsequently many of the best physicists, chemists, mathematicians, geologists, and other pure and applied natural scientists participated in the creation of the A-bomb. Some of them made their first attempt to influence strategy when they urged that the first atomic bombs not be dropped upon Japanese cities and that the war against Japan instead be won by other, more conventional means, which according to some suggestions might have included a "demonstration explosion" of an A-bomb in the ocean off Japan.

Launched shortly after the end of World War II, the *Bulletin of Atomic Scientists* has been the principal forum of discussion in the Western world for the strategic views of natural scientists of this type.[7] In many cases, their novel concern was touched off by an awe for what they and their colleagues had wrought, frequently accompanied by a bad conscience due to their contribution to production of the bomb. However, chances are that scientists would have become en-

---

[7] See Morton Grodzins and Eugene Rabinowitch (eds.), *The Atomic Age* (New York: Basic Books, Inc., 1963).

gaged in discussions of strategic doctrine in any case, because the government needed and sought their participation for not only the technical production of the weapons, but also strategic advice on their use. Many top scientists were appointed to full-time managerial or part-time advisory positions by the government of the United States, where this innovation was more noticeable than in the Soviet Union, whose scientists—in the absence of private industry or institutions—had always worked for the government. They became members of the newly created Atomic Energy Commission, supervised increasingly important research and development activities in the Department of Defense, served on newly established scientific advisory committees to the President, manned the many new research institutes concerned with strategic questions, some of them fully or partly governmental, others attached to universities or private corporations. Questions about the feasibility of constructing a hydrogen bomb or of the advantages of competing proposals of new weapons systems could no longer be answered by members of the conventional military establishment alone. Even if this had not been so, the potential effects of the use of the super-weapons, e.g., the effects of radioactive fall-out, would have drawn biologists, biochemists, geologists, medical scientists, and others into these controversies, even if the government had tried to prevent their participation, for political reasons.

One interesting aspect about the involvement of natural scientists in discussions of strategy is that their participation, whether it was initiated by themselves or invited by the government, frequently had no strictly speaking political content or intent at the beginning; or that, where national political interest did exist at the outset, this was soon expanded into a concern with world politics. This happened regardless of the substantive position of the individual scientist involved; e.g., it has been as true of a J. Robert Oppenheimer as of an Edward Teller, or of a Herman Kahn as of a Linus Pauling. It occurred partly because partisans of conflicting policies on issues of strategy and foreign policy would seek the support of these "scientific experts." The significant thing about this politicization of scientists, however, was the growing inadequacy of the advice and support of the more or less "pure" military scientists and strategists of the older, conventional type. To illustrate this, one might compare the role of expert advice and support in any controversy about weapons systems in the period since 1945, with the controversy generated by Colonel Billy Mitchell's advocacy of air power in the 1920's. The court martial (of which General Douglas MacArthur was a member) tried and in December, 1925, convicted Colonel Mitchell on formal grounds not involving the relative merits of competing weapons systems. About the same time, however, President Calvin Coolidge appointed a board to inquire into the substantive merits of the controversy. Its chairman was the financier Dwight Morrow, who was interested in aviation (and later became Charles Lindbergh's father-in-law). The other members included a United States Circuit Judge, a United States Senator and a United States representative, a retired general and a retired admiral, Dr. Durand of Stanford University, and one person from the aviation industry. The board, in turn, was assisted by an unofficial technical advisory committee of three members, including a Dr. Edward Warner of the Massachusetts Institute of Technology.[8] All this suggests that Billy Mitchell's case, in 1925, involved no significant participation from the community of natural scientists. However, those nonmilitary people who were involved were probably better prepared by previous training and experience for an understanding of the political implications of the strategic issues of that time than many of the natural scientists who have been drawn into more recent strategic controversies.

The inadequacy of training and experience is not the responsibility of the individuals involved or of the institutions that may have educated them, but is due to the unprecedented nature of the problems out of which contemporary strategic issues arise. These problems were not and probably could not have been anticipated, and neither military scientists nor mathematical physicists could therefore have been trained to solve them. In this sense, the natural scientist may have an advantage over the military scientist precisely because of his ignorance of the substance of no longer valid "eternal truths" and his innocence of the now irrelevant controversies of the past. At the same time, however, the application of methods taken from mathematics, physics, chemistry, and the like, to problems of strategy also makes more difficult achievement of consensus on method in an area where consensus on substance is even more remote.

To give some idea of the freshness and diversity of the scientists

---

[8]Major Alfred F. Hurley, USAF, *Billy Mitchell: Crusader for Air Power* (New York: Franklin Watts, Inc., 1964), Watts Aerospace Library. See also Roger Burlingame, *General Billy Mitchell: Champion of Air Defense* (New York: McGraw-Hill Book Co., Inc., 1952).

who are involved in discussions of strategy, we can look at the names on the roster of participants and visitors at the Summer Study on Arms Control of the American Academy of Arts and Sciences, held in 1960, characteristically in a building owned by the Massachusetts Institute of Technology. Of about 60 participants, at least 12 are identified as physicists, another 10, more or less, are identified as "systems analysts" of one kind or another, a discipline that did not even exist until World War II. There are about three engineers, two members of institutes of mental health, a psychologist, a chemist, a biologist, a specialist on industrial management, four economists, four lawyers, no more than five political scientists, but not a single person who would at any time have been identified as a military scientist. The only "admitted" politician on the list is Philip Noel-Baker, the Labour Party Member of Parliament and Nobel Peace Laureate. Another Nobel Laureate who participated, Victor F. Weisskopf of M.I.T., won his prize in physics. This Summer Study resulted in the book on *Strategy and Arms Control* by Thomas C. Schelling and Morton H. Halperin, of the Center for International Affairs of Harvard University, to which we will refer again later in this chapter.

At this point, we should realize that even the physicists, chemist, electronic engineer, psychologists, lawyers, and political scientists, when they participate in such study groups, do not make only the kind of contributions that one would "conventionally" expect of members of their disciplines. Psychologists, and also mathematicians, for instance, bring to bear their knowledge of and experiments in game theory, a field pioneered by the late John von Neumann, a mathematician at the Institute for Advanced Studies in Princeton, of which Einstein was a member, and which Oppenheimer was later to head. When lawyers, even international lawyers like Louis Sohn, co-author of *World Peace Through World Law* and a participant in this Summer Study, take part in discussions of this type, their contributions, too, may not conform to conventional expectations. Professor Sohn is credited, for example, with the proposal according to which the Soviet Union and the United States could select at random areas to inspect in each other's territory to insure themselves of compliance with underground test-ban or nuclear disarmament treaties. One can picture a situation in which conversations between international lawyers, game theorists, and physicists could generate such imaginative proposals, designed to break deadlocks in international political negotiations, which none of them could have thought up by himself. In this particular instance, attendance by various members of this Summer Study at Pugwash and other international conferences may also have stimulated the imagination.

The comparatively small proportion of professional political scientists who participate in conferences of this type and who play a significant role in the larger debates on strategic issues also constitutes something of a "new breed." Those with the most impressive reputations are frequently the younger political scientists who, because they do not carry a heavy burden of deep historical knowledge which might lead them to false analogies, may "benefit from the the blessings of ignorance." Their older or, at any rate, more experienced colleagues, on the other hand, may commit just such errors, e.g., by arguing from the role of power at the Congress of Vienna and in the Concert of Europe to its role in the 1960's, without adequate regard to the transformation of power and of the context within which it may be employed.

Whether they are political scientists, economists, experts on mental health, or natural scientists, most of the "strategic intellectuals," who have replaced both conventional military scientists and conventional students of international relations, are affiliated with research institutes belonging to universities or working directly or indirectly for the government. Centers for international affairs, foreign policy research, war and peace studies, and the like, have mushroomed at universities all over the United States, though they have very few counterparts in western Europe, where such subjects continue the prerogative of government bureaucracies, including the professional military. Most of these centers are supported in part by the great private foundations, like Ford, Rockefeller, Carnegie, and in part by government grants and research contracts. Some of the research institutes are, like the RAND Corporation, creatures of the government (the U.S. Air Force in the case of RAND), or in large part or *in toto* dependent upon government contracts. Some of the professional students of strategic problems are direct employees of the government, in military or civil servant status.

Some private critics of specific substantive positions taken by individual writers on problems of strategy emphasize the difference between the "free" and the "captive" theorists of strategy. Soviet critics of such American literature naturally condemn all that disagrees with Soviet views as the product of intellectual lackeys of American imperialism. The source of this uniform condemnation should not lead us, however, to make too much of the distinction between "government servants" and "free professionals." For one thing, perhaps because they are in great demand, strategic thinkers are highly mobile and circulate rather freely from universities to government research institutes, from foundations to government service. For example, Jerome B. Wiesner, an electrical engineer, who is listed on the roster of the Summer Study as Director, Research Laboratory of Electronics, M.I.T., subsequently became Special Assistant to President Kennedy and Chairman of the President's Science Advisory Committee, and later returned to M.I.T. as Dean of Science. Arthur W. Barber, who is listed as an official of the Sperry Rand Corporation, had previously been chief of the Systems Analysis Office at the Air Force Cambridge Research Center. Educated as a physicist, he subsequently became Deputy Assistant Secretary of Defense for International Security Affairs, with primary responsibility for disarmament. Dean Rusk, (not on this list), a conventional political scientist with previous experience as Assistant Secretary of State for Far Eastern Affairs, left the presidency of the Rockefeller Foundation to become Secretary of State.

The foundations play a crucial role in the allocation of resources, both human and financial, for research in this whole area. Scientists who are dependent upon either government or foundation support for their work often expect the foundations to "take up the slack" in years when, as a result of Congressional displeasure, government allocations are reduced, as happened after the so-called "Camelot affair" in 1965. The Defense Department was financing a study of the causes of social revolution, and means of channeling or suppressing it, in Latin America, which was being conducted in a number of Latin American countries without the knowledge of their governments or, according to the State Department, of the American ambassadors. As a result, Congressional appropriations for this type of research were severely reduced for the next fiscal year. This incident could illustrate, if the story is ever fully told, the complex interdependence of scholarly research, government operations, intragovernmental rivalries, and the roles of university institutes, independent research establishments like the Brookings Institution, and the foundations.

Adumbration of these interrelations is not meant to suggest that the "sociology" of this particular "knowledge" about world politics should necessarily have "debunking" effects. The objectivity of experts becomes questionable no more when they are on the direct or indirect payroll of a government than when they are "free professional" critics on the outside, who would like to replace the inside experts because they consider their own advice superior to that being currently accepted and paid for by the government. Rather, the background of the new students of strategy is of importance for several other reasons. First, it illustrates the surrender by default of their monopoly over this area by conventional military scientists. Second, it highlights the difficulties of finding a consensus on method in a field in which consensus on substance—in this case, on foreign policies to be adopted—is elusive at present if not always. And third, it points to the absence of a normative consensus among the strategic specialists, whose forerunners in the classic tradition of military science would generally have agreed on some vaguely defined basic values, like the national state and its interest, and on a minimum of norms relating to human life, derived more or less from the "Graeco-Roman" and "Judaeo-Christian" traditions. This normative consensus seems to be absent today, not so much between strategic thinkers from different sides of the Iron Curtain (or the "Bamboo Curtain"), as among strategic thinkers within the Western camp and especially in the United States, where there are more of them—at least more who publish their thoughts—than in all other countries combined.

Even Prussian military scientists and other publicists who glorified war for its own sake, in the nineteenth century, did not and could not have engaged in "thinking about the unthinkable," the title of a book by Herman Kahn, one of the most prominent of the strategic theorists who, incidentally, also took part in the Summer Study at M.I.T.[9] They could not have thought about such alternatives as the liquidation of anywhere from nine tenths to one quarter of the population of their own country, not to speak of the populations of enemy states and the earth, because they did not have available to them the means of destruction required for "achieving" any such goals. Some of the contemporary strategic intellectuals, on the contrary, because their previous education and experience has been uninfluenced by the humanities and mainly or only in the more nearly "value free" natural sciences, are capable of compartmentalizing their own thought to such an

---

[9]Herman Kahn, *Thinking about the Unthinkable* (New York: Horizon Press, Inc., 1962).

extent, that their actuarial calculations about a nuclear world war and its aftermath appear to be quite cold, *wertfrei,* and unhuman if not inhuman. Other strategic intellectuals with background in the natural sciences who, in their own view, hold more strongly humanistic values, criticize their scientific colleagues for this alleged one-sidedness.[10]

Such debates have two interesting aspects of relevance to our central theme here. One is the inability even of the strongest advocates of the "national interest" to keep themselves confined to consideration of the long-run effects of various strategies upon their own state and society alone. Those who advocate the use of nuclear weapons as qualitatively not different from the strategic saturation bombings of World War II, for example, usually speak of the role of the United States as leader of the "free world" and its protector against the international communist conspiracy. On the other hand, their forerunners who glorified the virtues of war in the nineteenth century, and the Nazis and fascists in the twentieth, did confine themselves strictly to the beneficial consequences for their own nation of the martial experience.

The other interesting aspect of these debates of strategy among intellectuals who began their careers as natural scientists is the fact that the debates are being carried on at all. Within each of the disciplines from which these scientists come, sufficient consensus on method usually exists to enable the peers of the profession to arrive at a (sometimes only temporary) consensus on the relative merits of competing sides in a substantive controversy, e.g., on molecular, nuclear, genetic, or cosmological theories. The existence of agreement on method means that competing explanations of reality can be tested by others for their internal consistency and, usually, their correspondence to reality. However, when natural scientists-turned-strategists advance competing strategic theories and policies, the policies cannot be tested against reality, because they deal with potentialities of the future. And it may be impossible even to test the theories for their internal consistency, because of the inchoate character of the contemporary "discipline" of strategy, the diverse backgrounds of the scientists who have been converging upon the field, and the consequent lack or, at best, tentativeness, of criteria of craftsmanship.

---

[10]See Anatol Rapoport, *Strategy and Conscience* (New York: Harper & Row, 1964).

All of this leads to the conclusion that scientists and other intellectuals who argue about questions of strategy do not constitute a "free-floating intelligentsia," either national or international, and that they cannot arrive at a "total orientation and synthesis." They may be able, as scientists, to arrive at agreement on "technical" problems related to political issues, but they seem incapable of converting into political consensus either this technical agreement or any dawning awareness on their part that, as members of an incipient international class, they may have a common class interest that might be expressed in the motto: "Scientists of the world, unite, you have nothing to lose but your political chains!" Rather than helping to resolve methodological chaos in discussions of strategy, they have helped to compound it. Their drive for methodological flexibility, caused by their newness to the field, combined with their professional inclination as natural scientists toward efficiency, has led most of them to concentrate upon the circumstantial here-and-now problems of strategy, to the neglect of fundamental traditions of the past and long-run values of the future.

In this situation, to whose confusion the new breed of strategic thinkers has made a considerable contribution, can one detect the beginnings of a consensus, at least on the basic questions that should be addressed to the ever fluid realities of world politics? Will it be possible for another von Clausewitz to write another classic on strategy, adequate to the present if not the future?

The Politics of Power

A search for the emergence of agreement on approaches to the study of strategy can start with an examination of critiques of conventional methods, preferably from "outside" conventional military or political science, and made by persons having no immediate substantive axe to grind, i.e., advocating no short-run solutions to specific problems of policy. These critiques are likely to focus upon the preoccupation with power, in the third quadrant of our diagrammatic representation of the political system, because this has conventionally been regarded as the proper field of strategy. Such critiques will, therefore, not be as broad as ours, "Politics and Power," in Chapter 1, because they are based upon acceptance of the basic equivalence between politics and power, but raise questions about the conceptual apparatus by means of which conventional strategists try to grasp the realities of power in world politics.

The Summer Study mentioned above resulted in a critique of this type, *Strategy and Arms Control*, by Thomas C. Schelling, an economist, and Morton H. Halperin, one of the new breed of political scientists. Both authors were associated with the Center for International Affairs at Harvard University, and the Summer Study was financed and the book published by the Twentieth Century Fund. The book accepts the ubiquity of power and the primary importance of considerations of military power in world politics. It accepts also the desirability of maintaining or establishing some sort of "strategic balance" between the two great blocs or their leaders. At this point, however, it criticizes the conventional meaning of such concepts as *balance, stability, offensive* and *defensive*, "civil defense," and the like, and tries to introduce and popularize a new, more up-to-date and, therefore, more "realistic" vocabulary into discussions of strategic questions.

Schelling and Halperin cite the widely accepted view that the "dangers of war and aggression" could best be minimized by reducing the *general level of armaments* and by keeping the *ratio* of strengths of the two blocs from becoming too disaligned, a view "implied in such phrases as 'balanced reduction,' 'phased reduction,' or 'proportionate reduction' of armaments."[11] Since they had shown earlier in their book that the "arms race" today is a *qualitative* rather than a quantitative one, as formerly,[12] they reject this approach:

> While it seems almost certain that any comprehensive and explicit arms accommodation between the two main power blocs would, as a practical matter, entail a reduction in military forces and that the relative strengths of the two blocs will be a major consideration, it is not at all certain—in fact, it is unlikely—that these two considerations should be dominant. There are many others: the vulnerability of strategic weapons to attack; the susceptibility of weapon systems to accident or false alarm; the reliability of command and communication arrangements; the susceptibility of weapon systems to sudden technological obsolescence; the confidence with which each side can estimate the capabilities of the opponent's weapons; the reaction time that weapon systems allow to decision-makers in a crisis; the susceptibility of weapon systems to control and restraint in the event of

---

[11]Schelling and Halperin, *Strategy and Arms Control* (New York, The Twentieth Century Fund, 1961), p. 49. Quoted by permission of The Twentieth Century Fund.
[12]*Ibid.*, p. 37.

war; the suitability of weapon systems for blackmail, intimidation, wars of nerves, and general mischief; and the effects of different weapons systems on the internal relations within alliances. These are important considerations and are not closely enough correlated with the general *level* of weapons on both sides or the simple arithmetical *ratio* of strength between the power blocs to permit "balanced reduction of forces" to be an adequate description of the strategic objective of arms control.[13]

Because of the qualitative transformation of the power which is the central subject of their analysis, Schelling and Halperin, in advocating replacement of the conventional distinction between "offensive" and "defensive" by the distinction between "first-strike" and "second-strike," make the following statement:

It is important to note that the old distinctions between offensive and defensive weapons are quite inapplicable in the present era, and are more nearly applicable in reverse. Weapons that are particularly effective against enemy weapons, and capable of launching a "disarming" attack, are precisely the weapons needed for the initiation of war. Weapons that are potent against populations, urban complexes, and economic assets have essentially a punitive rather than military quality. They are capable of retaliating, and of threatening retaliation, but are incapable of disarming the enemy and thus give their possessor little incentive or none at all to launch an attack. In that sense they may be reassuring to the other side. . . . *defensive* measures may be at least as characteristic of a first-strike strategic force as of a purely retaliatory force. . . .

It is worth observing in this connection that even passive defenses of the population, like fallout shelters and evacuation procedures, food stockpiles or organizational arrangements for the aftermath of war, are as natural a component of a first-strike force as they are a supplement to a purely retaliatory force. While this observation cannot do justice to the complex and important question of civil defense, it does help to illustrate that the traditional distinction among weapon systems, the traditional qualitative arms-control categories, are misleading in the present era of deterrence.[14]

Schelling and Halperin emphasize that the qualitative comparisons between the armaments of opposing blocs, upon which any estimate of the possibilities of arms control must be based, should take into account "the entire weapon *system,* not just the missiles or the aircraft: . . . the base configuration, the hardening or the mobility, the communications, the warning system, and everything else that goes to make up a strategic force."[15] Moreover, the weapons systems must always be viewed in comparison with opposing ones, on a global

---

[13]*Ibid.,* pp. 49–50.
[14]*Ibid.,* pp. 52 f.
[15]*Ibid.,* pp. 51 f. Italics supplied.

scale. They write that their distinction between "first-strike" and "second-strike" military capability "is not absolute, but relative to the enemy's own forces: a missile-carrying submarine may be a useful first-strike weapon if the enemy has fixed land-based missiles near his shores, but not if he, too, has his missiles under water."[16] This last advice has often been ignored by military commentators, politicians, and strategic theorists in the last two decades, probably on both sides of the Iron Curtain, but certainly in the United States. On many occasions, "actuaries of doom"[17] have predicted the certain doom of the United States as a result of an impending shift in the strategic balance of power in favor of the Soviet Union, unless a certain weapons system were immediately placed into production. Since these demands have not always been met by the Congress or the President (as commander-in-chief), and since the United States has not yet met its doom in the predicted manner, these prophecies have not been accurate. Even to the extent that such demands were acted upon, we do not know whether the forecasts were accurate or not, whether the balance of power, of terror, or of deterrence was operating in these cases. This is so, because construction of a new weapons system by the United States, on the basis of such forecasts, by bringing about a response of constructing the complementary, competing weapons system on the part of the Soviet Union, may have acted as a self-fulfilling prophecy. Schelling and Halperin are aware of this possibility:

Each side is guided by its *estimate* of what the other side is doing. If each greatly exaggerates what the other side is doing, the competition is exacerbated; if each underestimates the other's accomplishments the race will be damped. But in matters as uncertain as strategic warfare, neither can be certain of its estimate of the other's military potential. In the absence of reliable evidence of what the other is doing, each may feel obliged to err on the "safe" side—to impute an extreme capability and potential to the other. (If each does this, and responds accordingly, the result may actually bear out the extreme estimates!)[18]

The Publicity of Secrecy

In such situations, maxims derived from the conventional theory of the balance of power no longer apply and, if used, will prove self-defeating to the user. Moreover, this would be true regardless of

---

[16]*Loc. cit.*

[17]This phrase was coined by Professor Nicholas Wahl of Princeton University.

[18]Schelling and Halperin, *op. cit.*, p. 34.

whether one accepts or rejects the more principled critique of the theory of the balance of power made in Chapter 1 above, or by Professor Inis L. Claude in his *Power and International Relations.* A number of other maxims of military conduct, generally considered fixed and sacrosanct in the past, have to be dropped or at least amended as a result of the qualitative transformation of power in world politics. In the past, relations between potential enemies of the future were looked upon as basically relations of conflict. One's own armaments were treated as fairly absolute military secrets. The officer or politician who revealed these secrets to the enemy was treated as a traitor. Nowadays, as Schelling and Halperin recognize: ". . . our military relation with potential enemies is not one of pure conflict and opposition, but involves strong elements of mutual interest in the avoidance of a war that neither side wants, in minimizing the costs and risks of the arms competition, and in curtailing the scope and violence of war in the event it occurs."[19]

This basic common interest in the avoidance of a global war needs to be communicated to the other side, along with the means that each side chooses to promote its interest. In the conventional past, these communications were of course transmitted and received mainly by professional diplomats from and to the government for which they worked. In the novel present, when mass involvement in international politics can be instantly demonstrated by the propaganda of both constitutional and other types of government, and when everything can be instanteously communicated around the world, techniques of communicating messages between governments have become more complex and more fluid, but command less consensus than did diplomatic procedure in the past. However, the messages that make up the growing volume of communications are much more varied than previously, and they include military information that would then have been classified as secret.

The possibility exists, therefore, that the arms race might be damped if each side possessed better information about what the other is doing. . . .

It deserves to be emphasized—especially to the Soviets—that *secrecy* may be a dangerous and unreliable support for strategic security. Missiles and air forces that depend for their protection on universal secrecy—on secrecy of their fixed location—are vulnerable to improved intelligence. And it may be in the nature of an intelligence break-through that the loss of secrecy is sudden and extensive. . . . If arms control is inconsistent with such

---

[19]*Ibid.,* p. 1.

secrecy, or impairs it, the response should not be to rely less on arms control but to rely less on secrecy. The development by the Soviets of strategic forces that depend less on universal secrecy may be a proper subject of arms negotiations.[20]

Both the United States and, to a lesser extent, the Soviet Union nowadays publicize military information which would have been regarded as top secret before 1945. They engage in many bilateral cooperative ventures, including large-scale "cultural exchange" and trade, but also such specialized strategic communications as the private correspondence between President Kennedy and Premier Khrushchev and whatever messages may have passed over the "hot-line" between the Kremlin and the White House. When President Eisenhower made his "Open Skies" proposal in 1955, the Soviet Union rejected it as a pretext for espionage, a position they thought was confirmed when they shot down a U-2 airplane belonging to the United States Central Intelligence Agency in 1960. By 1965, however, both the United States and the Soviet Union were receiving regular photo intelligence from "spy satellites" that are orbiting around the globe, so that neither side could undertake certain experiments or measures of strategic significance—like test missile launchings or nonsubterranean nuclear explosions—without the other knowing about it. It has also become easy for each side to force strategic information about itself upon the other, in order to impress it with its own preparedness or resolve to let the other side not trespass beyond certain (not always territorially definable) lines. Of course, the publication of books like Schelling and Halperin's *Strategy and Arms Control* and others on the subject of strategy, whether published privately or under the auspices of foundations or the United States government, are also likely to be understood by the Soviet Union and other communist governments as honest or deceitful communications of official American intentions. Similarly, the United States government and those who work for it on problems of strategy can assume with greater certainty that anything published on strategic problems in a communist country is intended to be communicated to the United States.

The Ambiguity of Communications

Even if one or the other side sincerely wanted to make an unambiguous communication to its opponent, during a noncritical period

---

[20]*Ibid.*, pp. 34 and 36 f.

of the Cold War, i.e., not at a time like that of the Cuban Missile Crisis of 1962—this would be a very difficult and certainly more difficult than it ever was before 1945. There are two main obstacles to unambiguous communication between the superpowers. One is the difficulty of achieving clarity within a single political system about its willingness, its resolve, to use the ultimate—and ultimately self-defeating—weapons when and if a critical situation does arise. This question of resolution will occupy our attention in Chapter 9, because it is related to the role of ideologies in world politics. In the present context, we can cite the crisis over Berlin of 1961 to illustrate the obstacles to unambiguous communication of purpose. President Kennedy evidently wanted the Soviet leaders to understand that he was ready to commit American force, including nuclear force, if West Berlin were seriously threatened by the German Democratic Republic or the Soviet Union itself. But Kennedy's prior problem lay in demonstrating his own resolution to the American people in a sufficiently dramatic fashion to enable him subsequently to communicate their determination to the government of the Soviet Union. But what could be considered a serious threat to the security of West Berlin? The building of the wall that was overtly designed to cut off the only remaining route of egress out of East Germany? Apparently not. Nor was sporadic interference by communist troops with convoys of American troops at checkpoints on the *Autobahn* from West Germany through the Soviet Zone to West Berlin considered sufficiently serious for this purpose. But what could be considered sufficiently provocative to push the American President into risking the destruction of American cities and the outbreak of a nuclear war? Whatever the answer might be, repeated statements by successive Presidents and their secretaries of defense, of their willingness to use nuclear weapons in defense of West Berlin, made in noncritical periods of the Cold War, have not sufficed to communicate unambiguously to the rest of the world under just what conditions the imaginary "line" would be crossed that will trigger the nuclear deterrent of the free world. Nor have the Soviets communicated their resolve in this respect with any less ambiguity, though they have indicated that the Soviet Union would not be the first to use nuclear weapons. Such hints, incidentally, have been rejected as "phoney peace propaganda" by official Western sources, because the communist bloc's alleged superiority in ground troops was supposed to make the West's nuclear weapon systems "defensive" against the communists' conventional capabilities (under the obsolete

conventional vocabulary of strategy). In 1966, communist China offered the United States an agreement not to be first in the use of
nuclear weapons against each other. The United States replied by
making China's accession to the partial nuclear Test Ban Treaty a prior
condition which was unlikely to be accepted, in view of China's relative backwardness in testing.

The second obstacle to unambiguous communication between the
superpowers arises from the nature of the alliances each has constructed. As suggested above, the "blocs" were brought into being partly
for purposes of stabilizing the seemingly increasing anarchy of world
politics. However, despite their sometimes bloc-like appearance, the
treaty organizations were incapable of preventing considerable internal flexibility, rivalry, and hostility to the point of disruption. President De Gaulle insisted upon building France's independent nuclear
force partly because he held doubts whether the United States would
use its nuclear weapons, and incur the risk of nuclear retaliation upon
its soil, in defense of the "national interest" of France or other European states. France, where the Supreme Command of NATO was located, and China, the most important partner of the Soviet Union,
both refused to sign the Treaty of Moscow which banned all but
underground nuclear explosions. China, somewhat like France about
the United States, is doubtful about the determination of the Soviet
Union to undertake nuclear risks on behalf of its allies, including
China, North Vietnam, or Cuba. As a result of these intra-alliance
doubts, generated by problems of the use of power, disagreements
within each camp about the reliability or credibility of the purpose of
its leader become known to the leader and members of the other
camp, thereby making unambiguous communication of determination
in noncritical periods virtually impossible.

During crucial, potentially explosive crises of the Cold War, unambiguous communication of purpose seems easier to achieve. When
"the chips are down," as during the Cuban Missile Crisis, each of the
two superpowers, which then became the key actors in direct confrontation with each other, was pushed so much closer to using its
force, including nuclear force, that "bluffing" was no longer as suitable
as it might have been before, after the threshhold of the Soviet "missile sneak" had been passed. On the contrary, each side made great
efforts to display its maneuvers as publicly as possible, and it is characteristic that the now institutionalized communications procedure

of the "hot-line" between White House and Kremlin was invented during this crisis.

The Rationality of Irrationality

Though both sides may recognize the dangers of secrecy and may therefore be aware of their stake in unambiguous communications, they may also seek to exploit the unavoidability of ambiguity to their own advantage. One way of doing this is by pretending to behave irrationally, or at least in a way which appears to remove control over some of their policies out of their own hands. This type of conduct has been called the "rationality of irrationality," because it serves the ultimate purpose of communicating a resolve which, in view of the self-defeating consequences of a nuclear exchange, it may no longer be possible for a nuclear state to communicate directly. "Doomsday machines" and similar devices that will be triggered automatically by specific events, like the crossing of a boundary line or the impact of nuclear weapon's on one's territory, were mentioned in Chapter 1. Any state that would be willing to install them would presumably be pursuing the goal of stability, conceived of in terms similar to the dream of the architects of the network of treaty organizations that was being constructed in the 1950's, and it would be at the mercy of the same instability of technology and of political affinities, only at an accelerated rate. To the extent that we can expect sufficient realism on the part of politicians to make for awareness of the futility of attempts to freeze the *status quo* through such rationally irrational behavior, we may assume also that it is unlikely that the government of any nuclear power will be willing to bind itself permanently to any particular set of substantive memories stored in a doomsday machine. At least this assumption would seem valid about any moderately rational government of the type now in control in all states with nuclear weapons; though it would not be valid about a government like that of Hitler who, without any "overkill" capacity, was able to stage a magnificent *Götterdämmerung* in Germany.

The Emergence of Methodological Consensus

The main thrust of critiques like that offered by Schelling and Halperin is toward a complete reappraisal of what it is that makes up the "stuff" of strategy. While strategy still obviously involves the uses of power, it also involves much more than that. In the past, superior generalship prepared its strategic plans in peacetime—when it left the conduct of foreign relations to professional diplomats—and excelled in wartime through military efficiency: achieving optimum output against the enemy, defensively or offensively, for a given input of power from its own political system. Today, the distinction between war and peace can no longer be made. Neither professional military, nor professional diplomats retain their monopoly over the warlike or peaceful relations between states. Each is involved in the affairs that used to be the preserve of the other and, more important and on a larger scale, both are being pushed out of their realms by members of quite different professions. Schelling and Halperin, who are neither generals nor diplomats, took as the starting point of their study the proposition that arms control is an integral part of strategy. This means that strategic action is a continuous flow of policy which involves the entire political system (especially of nuclear states), all the time, instead of engaging only the military, in wartime, on the basis of plans made in peacetime. It means, too, that strategy has to consider much more than one's own potential power resources and those of potential enemies and allies. Strategy has to take into consideration also the expanding, fluid network of communication for world politics, and the determination with which any particular political system, national or international, is likely to be committed to any particular set of goals on behalf of which alternative strategies are being worked out. The goals, national and international, are of course also in a condition of constant flux, and the mistake of taking "the national interest" as some kind of fixed quantum is nowadays made mainly by adherents of obsolete conventional approaches to foreign relations and international politics. The erosion of hard-shelled territoriality of states, combined with the on-going qualitative technological revolutions, has brought about the kind of situation with respect to goals which, while it is unprecedented for international relations, has characterized the domestic politics of modern states, especially of democracies, for a long time past. Participants in politics, as they approach or reach a particular goal, or for whatever reasons become aware of other problems, change their understanding of this goal and of the priority they assign to it relative to other goals they are simultaneously pursuing. In this process, relations with other participants in politics, previously recognized as relations of conflict, may become partly or wholly cooperative. Different issues are being processed at the same time, and individuals or groups that agree on one issue, will disagree on others, so that a caleidoscopic film of ever-changing conflict and consensus emerges from the political process—in national as in international politics.

This has the effect, among many others, that strategists become aware of common interests they share with potential opponents, and also of conflicts of interests with current allies. It means that what used to be referred to as strategy has become the work of the "peace establishment," and what used to be narrowly understood as foreign policy has become the work of the "war establishment." Above all, new approaches are required for the *study* of strategic questions, and a new consensus on them may be beginning to emerge in critical works like *Strategy and Arms Control* which, before they arrive at the point of making substantive policy proposals, have to cut through the confusions resulting from the application of outdated concepts to unprecedented realities—realities of power and of much else besides. Since the confusions are directly due to the rapid and radical changes taking place all the time in the substantive technology and environment of world politics, any really searching critique is likely to make an effort to isolate and analyze those phenomena that are more stable and enduring than the current weapons technology of the superpowers or the transient composition of the alliance blocs led by them. And these more enduring features of politics are precisely those which *any* adequate approach to the comparative study of politics would focus upon and would seek to analyze in systematic relation to one another.

The center of gravity of different approaches will lie in different places. Schelling and Halperin place theirs on the procedures of bargaining, as already suggested by Professor Schelling's earlier work on *The Strategy of Conflict.* Their focus is therefore upon roughly the equivalent of the phase of deliberation, the weighing of alternatives, in the approach outlined in Chapter 3. But they relate this central focus upon the process of bargaining to the "power" and the "purpose" that are used as inducements, and to the effect upon the alternatives being bargained about of the "forms" in which world politics recognizes its problems. In this sense, *Strategy and Arms Control,* and other works like it, make unexpectedly constructive contributions to the study of world politics—unexpectedly, because they might just have superimposed on the already existing gulf between "realists" and "idealist-legalist" another gap between the old-fashioned and the avant-garde within each of these schools. Instead, however, they have—perhaps unintentionally—demonstrated the irreality of the realist-idealist conflict, by ignoring it. And, although, as students of strategy, they had to start out with concern for the military power that could be used in war, they conclude by detecting the growth of procedural consensus among the nuclear powers that may lead to the avoidance of military conflict between them.

Unconsciousness of Agreement

Deliberation, which can also be called bargaining, is a basic human activity, which goes on much of the time within individual human beings and in human communities and political systems. It begins with awareness of the possibility of choice among alternative courses of action. When deliberation goes on among people who want to follow different courses of action, it can be called bargaining, regardless of its substantive content, which may involve anything from the bed-time of children to the price of a house, or the proliferation, control or abolition of nuclear weapon systems. By recognizing this basic nature of the bargaining process, Schelling is able to make valid analogies between the bargaining that goes on, the procedural and substantive consensus it requires, and the degree of formality by which it may or may not be accompanied, in national politics and world politics.

What makes statutory law possible in democratic society, and what may make arms-control agreements possible, is that people and nations can agree on actions, restraints, laws, and programs, without necessarily agreeing in detail on their purpose or on the expected state of the world at every future point in time.[21]

An interesting question is how much consensus is likely to be reached on the spirit and intent of an agreement. One of the things that makes it possible to get laws passed in a country like the United States is that people can agree on what to do and what not to do without having to agree on the motives and purposes. Certainly the discussion of the nuclear-test ban illustrates that a variety of motives can bring an issue to the point where agreement on some act, or on abstention of some act, is a live possibility, without any agreement among the participants as to the motives, and

---

[21]*Ibid.*, p. 114.

without even any consensus within some of the individual participating countries on the relative emphasis to be given different motives.[22]

Schelling and Halperin point out that: "It is noteworthy that we already abstain from quite an array of [mutually provocative] actions without formal agreement, without direct communication about it, without even an appreciation that this in itself is a form of arms control—of military cooperation between enemies."[23] And they suggest that, as the volume of initially informal but increasingly formal cooperation of this type grows, agreement will also grow on the procedures by means of which both disagreement and agreement on a wide range of substantively diverse issues of the Cold War can be communicated and processed. Their contribution to our understanding of world politics is particularly useful at this point, because the realists would deny the possibility of this kind of military cooperation between enemies even in a straight balance of power; while the institutionalists would deny the benefits of either communication or agreement without a formal framework for the former, formal international law for the latter, and full awareness on the part of all participants for both.

These conventional approaches similarly overlook one of the most important reasons for the success of national political systems troubled by divisions on issues of substance, but nevertheless held together by consensus on "constitutional" procedures, which seems to be strengthened by each new substantive problem that is fed into the system. According to the realist understanding, any group currently in control of power—in a democracy, a temporary majority—should simply impose its "will" upon the current minority. According to the institutional legalists, the rational design of the constitution is more important than the controversies that agitate the members of the society. In fact, however, people know that they are in majority or minority positions with respect to different issues at any one time, and that today's majority on the most important issue may become tomorrow's minority. This knowledge often results in giving them a greater commitment to the procedures—the rules of the game—which protect them while and where they are in a minority and give them some support from members of a "defeated" minority when they themselves belong to the majority.

This foundation of procedural consensus, and of procedural sources

---

[22]*Ibid.*, pp. 87 f.
[23]*Ibid.*, p. 33.

of authority, has its analogue in the fact, recognized by both the Soviet Union and the United States, that the rapidity of technological innovation can change today's qualitative advantage of one over the other into its opposite: "*either* we *or* the Russians may be the victim or beneficiary of technological break-through, of moments of military weakness, or of political incentives that override the fear of general war. Each of us may well be willing to relinquish capabilities in future contingencies on condition that the other side do likewise."[24]

One might add to this that the "future contingencies" also include realignments within and between the blocs, like those caused by Yugoslavia in 1948, by Cuba after Dr. Castro came to power, and by France and China, Pakistan and India, in the mid-1960's. The importance, ubiquity, and basic similarity of the fundamental, informal, unwritten rules of the "game of strategy" in contemporary world politics become especially evident when a state leaves one bloc in order to become more or less closely affiliated with the other, *if* it conducts its business with its new partners according to procedures similar to those prevailing among its old or expartners.

The analogy between national and world politics also holds true between constitution building at the lower level and treaty making at the higher:

As with other laws and contracts, including laws and contracts in novel areas, it is not necessarily true that every effort should be made to make the agreement as detailed as possible and to anticipate as many contingencies as one can. While it is important on the one hand to incorporate as much as possible of the understanding in a written document to preclude further misunderstandings, it is also important to avoid freezing detailed answers to very simply perceived questions in a document that is supposed to guide the participants in their relations to each other through fairly uncharted territory. It may also be important to reach agreement early rather than late, and not to hold up agreement pending the exhaustive exploration of all its possible implications by the participants.[25]

This is analogous to the guidelines for constitution makers, according to which a constitution should include only the highest common denominator of agreement, or understanding, among the participants. In national as in international, in developed as in developing

---

[24]*Ibid.*, p. 13.
[25]*Ibid.*, p. 87.

political systems, this is likely to extend only to limited substantive matters: vague positive long-run goals like the general welfare, and more specific negative goals like the common defense or the prevention of nuclear world war. Otherwise, in most constitution building situations, agreement can initially be reached only on the fundamental procedures by means of which to process future substantive disagreements, as these arise, and, crucially, on that most fundamental procedure of all, the procedure by which to make formal alterations in constitutional procedures, that is, the amending procedure. The treaty on the partial nuclear test ban came close to following these general guidelines.[26]

Unconventional Conventionalities

While new theories of strategy are being forged for world politics, old strategies also continue to play their role in world politics. People adhere to them, they are still being taught in war schools, and they are apparently being used actively in some of the "minor" military conflicts, many of which nowadays carry within themselves the potential of "escalation." As in world politics generally, so in the field of strategic theory, the old and the new coexist, at different levels of action and in the minds of the practitioners. During the Cuban Missile Crisis of 1962, for example, President Kennedy justified United States reactions to the introduction of Soviet missiles to Cuba by claiming, among other things, that this would change the balance of power to the advantage of the Soviet Union, though some members of his small executive committee of the National Security Council, which participated in strategic planning with the President, wanted to ignore the "missile sneak," because the United States had been living under the threat of Soviet intercontinental ballistic missiles for some years, just as the Soviet Union had been living under the threat of American ICBM's and submarine-born Polaris missiles, and the presence of intermediate-range ballistic missiles in Cuba made no more difference, in their view, than the much earlier installation of IRBM's on the soil of Turkey, a NATO ally. This view could be taken as the more up-to-date and the President's as the more conventional one, but the latter of course prevailed.

---

[26]See Appendix.

We have already cited the dispute about the meaning of the distinction between "offensive" and "defensive" weapons systems between Kennedy and Khrushchev. To this one could add another illustration of the continued coexistence of the old and the new, and that is the distinction, formerly thoroughly meaningful, between "strategy" and "tactics." As mentioned in Chapter 1, teaching military scientists used to bear the title of "professor of military science (meaning strategy) and tactics." The line between the two types of military action was relatively easy to draw. For example, during World War II, the United States Army subjected prisoners of war first to tactical interrogation, then (if of high enough rank) to strategic interrogation. The tactical interrogator asked questions about the disposition of enemy forces, and their short-run plans, in his immediate vicinity. The strategic interrogator asked about the disposition of armies and army groups and about long-run plans including, in that "total" war, plans for war production.

This distinction between the strategic and the tactical was briefly used, in the mid-1950's, to suggest the possibility of "limited nuclear wars," in which only "tactical nuclear weapons" would be employed by the United States and the Soviet Union.[27] However, this suggestion turned out to be theoretically meaningless and practically inapplicable, for reasons already discussed. The attempt to create this distinction might usefully be studied by intellectual historians as an abortive contribution to the self-contradictory "ideology of freedom," which might have strengthened the resolution of United States strategists actually to begin dispatch of "low yield" nuclear weapons in the conviction that no escalation would ensue. Since the other side, in this instance, the Soviet Union's strategists, was unwilling from the outset to accept this redefinition of the rules of the game, no such conviction ever took a hold on either side.

This does not necessarily mean, however, that all of what was formerly understood by the term "tactics" must now be subsumed under the term "strategy." Two types of situations come to mind in which it may be possible to uphold the conventional distinction between strategy and tactics. Both are often cited as contemporary examples of "limited war." One is military conflict between nonnuclear states not firmly committed to alliances with a nuclear state; the other,

[27]See p. 38, above.

guerrilla warfare. The fighting between India and Pakistan over Kashmir, in 1965, for example, could be thought of in entirely conventional terms. Neither contestant controlled nuclear weapons. India had been unaligned since independence and partition, and Pakistan had for all practical purposes read itself out of CENTO and SEATO, without concluding a military alliance with China. Both used conventional weapons systems, including airplanes and tanks provided them largely by the United States and the United Kingdom. Military officers of both countries had been raised in the British tradition, and their highest ranking general officers—including Pakistan's President—had received their training at the British military academy of Sandhurst. Could they not have "played" their very serious war games according to basic rules learned before the development of the newer strategic theories?

The fact that they did not do so, and the rules according to which the Kashmir "war" was in fact conducted, illustrates the overlap of old and new strategic theories and points to the causes of this overlap. India's retention of control over the state of Kashmir immediately after partition, despite its overwhelmingly Muslim population, resulted in mob violence and military action between the two countries. It led also to the primary formulation of this problem as an issue suited for deliberation (if not resolution) by the United Nations. The UN remained seized of this issue continuously. The war of 1965 was triggered by guerrilla action inside Kashmir, by guerrillas representing internal Kashmiri opposition to Indian rule according to Pakistan, by troops infiltrated from Pakistan according to India. (This makes the Kashmir conflict an example of both limited war and guerrilla warfare.) When overt cross-boundary fighting actually broke out, the predominantly legalistic style of world politics asserted itself at once and the major "theater of operations" was not the Indian-Pakistani frontier area or the cities subjected to aerial bombardment, but the United Nations.

At the outset, most news analyses concentrated upon the comparative military resources of the two countries, that is, upon their "power" as conventionally understood. This turned out to be a mistaken focus. It was mistaken in at least two complementary ways: neglect of the factor of relative resolution or purpose and, more important, neglect of the illimitable, global character of virtually all international violence today. The first factor was, significantly, not overlooked by the parties to the war themselves. The leaders of both India and Pakistan made major efforts from before the outbreak of actual military violence to demonstrate, not so much to each other as to the rest of the world, the "unshakable determination" of themselves and their respective populations to "settle this thing once and for all." They recognized the need for demonstrating their firm purpose to other governments and international organizations *outside* the subcontinent, because—regardless of their power relative to each other—they would not be able (as it turned out they were in fact unable) to carry on with the war unless their determination to do so was believed to be greater than the determination of outsiders to put an end to it.

Which outsiders managed to muster resolution superior to that of Pakistan and India? How did they communicate their greater purpose? Why? Initiatives came from the United States and the Soviet Union, from senior members of the Commonwealth, including the United Kingdom and Canada, and from individual Asian and African states including the United Arab Republic. All of these made direct bilateral communications to the two "belligerents"—the term was not formally applicable, since no declarations of war were exchanged. The United States placed a moratorium upon its massive economic aid programs to both countries. The Soviet Union invited President Ayub Khan and Prime Minister Shastri to meet in Tashkent on Soviet territory and presided over successful negotiations to settle the dispute. The most effective and efficient demonstrations of purpose, however, occurred at the United Nations, in the Security Council, where representatives of the states mentioned and of others, as well as the Secretary-General— who flew out to Rawalpindi and New Delhi for direct negotiations with the two governments—registered resolution, and deliberated about alternative temporary solutions to the problem of Kashmir, which in relatively short order led India and Pakistan to agree to a truce, to be supervised by United Nations officials. During this period of international deliberation, in which demonstrations of determination were perceived as more persuasive than demonstrations of force, China was the only outsider which apparently tried for an expansion of the military conflict. China clearly had the military power to bring this about, and such a policy would have been consistent with China's opposition to the United Nations as presently constituted and operating, and with its dispute with the Soviet Union. Chinese communist strategic doctrine, especially the writings of Mao Tse-Tung, also show great awareness of the importance of commitment and determination, as we will see below in the context of our discussion of guerrilla warfare. Evidently, however, even the Chinese government did not consider the extension of the Kashmir war, which it could have achieved at relatively low cost, worth a major demonstration of resolve or an at least initially minor expenditure of force.

The reasons for this "low-keyed" approach to the Kashmir problem by virtually everyone, including the two direct parties to the war, can be found more easily in the newer than in the older theories of strategy. Just as relations between Pakistan and India had involved both conflict and cooperation from the time of the founding of both, so did the relations between other participants in this controversy, including relations between the United States and China, involve both conflict and cooperation. The "balance of power"—to the extent one could ever speak of one—between Pakistan and India was not a purely quantitative one, so that neither a reduction in the general level of armaments of both, nor a balanced reduction maintaining the ratio of strengths would have been likely to prevent the outbreak of hostilities, even at their relatively low conventional and nonnuclear levels of 1965. At that time, both sides may have been thinking that radical qualitative changes in this "balance" had occurred or were about to occur, as a result of any number of concurrent external changes, including Pakistan's closer relations with China, the Sino-Soviet dispute, the war in Vietnam, Indonesia's quarrel with the Federation of Malaysia, and the apparent rapprochement between the Soviet Union and the United States, which might bring about enhanced capabilities for the United Nations.

All of these were relational changes, bound to have qualitative effects upon the positions of India and Pakistan relative to one another. There was full awareness of the significance of these changes on both sides, though estimates of their probable consequences may have differed. However, the fact that both governments seemed to want to settle the dispute by force of arms, once and for all, suggests that these estimates in fact tallied pretty closely. The most important feature of the Kashmir war was, however, that those outsiders who had the capacity to stop it did not permit it to continue, because they were aware above all of the difficulties of keeping it confined to the subcontinent. Even military conflicts between nonnuclear and not firmly Cold War-allied states, it was thought, could not be kept either geographically or technologically limited. As a result, a war that would previously have been fought according to the well-known rules of conventional strategy and tactics, was begun and then quickly ended under the emergent procedures of the newer strategy. This made for a lower clarity and higher incidence of issues arising out of a basically simple problem, for much greater active participation than a similar problem would have elicited before World War II, and for more ambiguous communications among the participants.

Guerra *and* Guerrillas

Guerrilla warfare is the second type to which the teachings of conventional military science and tactics may still be applicable. The Spanish term *guerilla* is simply the diminutive of *guerra* or war. In the years since World War II, it has been used with decreasing frequency. The communist opponents of the Greek government, in the 1940's, whose threat led to enunciation of the Truman Doctrine and the provision of United States economic and military assistance to Greece, were generally called guerrillas, as were the Greek fighters on Cyprus in the 1950's. Fidel Castro's small band in the Sierra Maestre, fighting against Batista's large, American-equipped army, was often described by the same term, partly perhaps because of their Spanish-speaking environment. The guerrilla bands that fought on the Loyalist side in the Spanish Civil War have been immortalized in Ernest Hemingway's *For Whom the Bell Tolls*. They were clearly of a different type from the communist rebels (or whatever one wants to call them) in Malaya whom the British efficiently suppressed, from the Indonesian troops which were being infiltrated into the Federation of Malaysia in the mid 1960's, and from the Vietcong whom the South Vietnamese and United States armed forces were fighting in the same period.

The differences between conventional guerrillas and their contemporary counterparts have been recognized by a changed and changing terminology. In the United States, the Kennedy Administration introduced the term "insurgency" to describe movements of the Castro and Vietcong type, though there have been some obvious differences between the two even after Dr. Castro was accused of exporting his style of warfare to other Latin American countries. A whole theory of strategy was built up under the title of "counterinsurgency." The

United States Army established several training centers for counter-insurgency, one of which, at Fort Bragg, North Carolina, was officially named the "John F. Kennedy School of Special Warfare." The communists, on the other hand, frequently attach the term "national liberation war" to conflicts in which members of the Western bloc apply the doctrines of special warfare. Both labels, "counterinsurgency" and "war of national liberation," might suggest, despite their coinage in the ideological mints of two great opposing global movements, that the military conflicts they describe could be confined to a limited territory and could be fought according to some revised and up-dated set of essentially tactical maxims.

In fact, the opposite is true. Special warfare is the manifestation in definable, limited territories of the unlimited and global "Game of Strategy," which is a game of both conflict and cooperation. It represents pragmatic adaptations to the illimitable effects which the ideologically directed use of nuclear force would have for the community of mankind. At the same time, the theorists of special warfare and national liberation wars are the captives of their own ideologies to such an extent, that they are unable or unwilling to rationalize their pragmatism about violence in nonideological terms. However, the full impact of their actual pragmatism is revealed, for instance, by the fact that Western theories of counterinsurgency carry profuse citations from Mao Tse-Tung's writings on the subject. These have been translated as manuals for Western armies, not so much because these want to learn about the enemy's strategic doctrine, nor even because one has to "fight fire with fire," but because of the presumed intrinsic and almost "universal" validity of Mao's theory under the conditions of contemporary world politics.

"Copying from Mao" in this sense involves a misleading analogy. Assuming that, by copying from Mao, one can keep national liberation wars from escalating, involves more than one false anology and ignores the origins of both insurgency and its opposite. The Chinese communists came to power in China after a protracted conflict lasting over two decades. They alternately fought and were allied with the Kuomintang, headed then as in 1965 by Generalissimo Chiang Kai-Shek. In uneasy alliance with Chiang, the communists resisted the Japanese invasion of China. They had established a firm base in the remote provinces of the north where Mao Tse-Tung had led them in the great march. Within three years after Japan's surrender to the

United States, and despite Chiang's control of overwhelming military power, most of it supplied by the United States, the communists were able to drive the Kuomintang off the mainland. Out of this unique experience, combined with certain essentials of Marxism-Leninism which helped shape it, Mao distilled some strategic guidelines, which undoubtedly influenced the operations of the Chinese guerrillas in Malaya. That revolt, which occurred in a country not contiguous to China and before communist China had recovered sufficiently from decades of civil war to pursue independent global policies, was put down with great resolution, tactical imagination, and at considerable cost, by the British colonial administration. About the same time, in French Indochina, the Viet-minh, led by Ho-shi-minh and his General Giap, were developing their own tactics against the large French army that had been committed in the vain effort to maintain colonial rule. The Viet-minh were also influenced by the Chinese experience and Mao's writings, especially by the successful attempts to win the support of the peasants in the countryside while the Kuomintang remained in full control of the towns and cities.

After France's defeat in Indochina and the withdrawal of her troops, the United States gradually increased its involvement in the successor states of the area, with the exception of Cambodia, which managed to maintain its neutralist position at least to the extent of getting overt foreign troops off its territory. The Vietcong, a label applied by the South Vietnamese government to guerrillas it charged with being communists, increased their military activities in the rural areas of South Vietnam and their terrorism and general subversion in the towns. In a parallel development, the United States stepped up its military, counterinsurgency, and propaganda involvement in Vietnam. Partly in specific response to the challenge perceived as coming from the Vietcong, the Kennedy Administration generated the theory, and the practical schools, of counterinsurgency. Both, as already mentioned, relied, among other things, upon Mao's earlier writings, not only in order to "learn from them," but also in order to copy them. This attempt clearly overlooked crucial differences between, on the one hand, a rural revolutionary movement fighting against a rather infirm urban military organization, the Kuomintang, and, on the other, an overseas military power allied with a similarly infirm urban military organization, the South Vietnamese government, fighting against a rurally based military organization receiving varying degrees of help from outside South Vietnam. In the former case, the three postwar years were the culmination of more than three decades of armed conflict within one country. In the latter, the period starting in 1961 saw the continuation of the global conflict between communist China and the United States which had broken out overtly the first time during the Korean war a decade earlier. The Chinese Revolution, whatever else it may have been, was not a national liberation war of the type that Chinese revolutionaries, after their own success, wanted to promote in other countries and areas.

No matter how much the Vietcong may have been trying to model themselves upon Chinese guerrilla tactics, they were not in a situation that permitted them either to maintain a distinction between tactics and strategy or to fight a Chinese type of action—for the same reasons that made it impossible for the United States to model its own strategy upon retrospectively corrected versions of Kuomintang, French in Indochina, British in Malaya, *or* to base the tactics of its own and allied troops upon Mao's maxims. Sometimes American policy seemed to be based upon recognition of these "analogical impossibilities," but at times American policy was obviously based upon the false analogies themselves. Here again we observe coexistence of the old and the new, the conventional and the advanced, in world politics and in the strategies of a single state. The United States was bombing "military targets" in North Vietnam along lines of aerial bombardments of the early years of World War II, before the introduction of strategic bombing. It was forcing "loyal" South Vietnamese rural people into "strategic hamlets" on the model of a device that succeeded in Malaya. It was providing "special warfare teams" to lead Montagnard tribesmen in attempts to exploit tribal rivalries and to win over some of the more primitive and martial-minded rural population, virtually following Mao's advice to work with the people, eat with the people, sleep with the people, and fight with the people. (This had also been tried, without success, by the French in Algeria, after their Indochinese defeat.) They were encouraging the South Vietnamese government to win the support of its rural population by starting massive rural community development programs. And at the same time, they were seeking out Vietcong units of battalion strength in order to engage them with full-sized U.S. Army and Marine divisions, to fight battles reminiscent of some in the Pacific Theater of Operations in World War II. United States strategic jet bombers, based on the island

of Guam, were also bombing areas in *South* Vietnam, near its capital
of Saigon, suspected of containing large concentrations of Vietcong.
All of these policies were being followed simultaneously, and though
all were based more or less upon false analogies, no one could say
that they were either failing or succeeding, because the goals of the
United States in this conflict had never been stated clearly and were
not susceptible to unambiguous statement. The "war" was being carried on without clear internal or external boundaries. In South Vietnam, an area of land would be controlled by the government's forces
in the daytime, by the Vietcong at night. And while the border between South and North Vietnam was clearly marked and usually not
a scene of fighting, charges were constantly exchanged about the infiltration of Vietcong from North Vietnam via Laos and Cambodia into
the South, and the violation of Cambodia's frontier by United States
and South Vietnamese troops from the South. United States bombings
of North Vietnam covered an area that was expanded or contracted
unilaterally by the United States, and that would creep up to the
Chinese boundary and then appear to creep back again, while China
claimed repeated violations of its air space over the island of Hainan
and the mainland.

In the course of all of this, no one seemed to doubt that the United
States had the military power literally to wipe North Vietnam off the
map and to inflict enormous devastating damage upon China. But
those who accused the United States of wanting to do just that claimed
that it did not have the resolution—that it was a "paper tiger"—while
the United States government itself asserted that its objectives were
in truth much more limited: To get North Vietnam and its alleged
agents, the Vietcong, to "leave its neighbor alone" and to guarantee
the independence and self-determination of the people of the Republic
of South Vietnam. This Republic had been brought into being only in
1954, on the understanding, written into the Geneva Agreement, that
a plebiscite would be held on the issue of unifying South and North
Vietnam. The United States also accused China of master-minding
North Vietnamese and, therefore indirectly, Vietcong operations
against the South Vietnamese government. Everyone also assumed that
Peking was so much more powerful than North Vietnam, that it could
get Hanoi to do its bidding, just as Washington was so much more
powerful than Saigon and should be able to get its leaders to dance
to the tune of the American government piper. In fact, matters did not

work out that way and both Hanoi and Saigon displaying varying degrees of independence at different points in time.

In this armed conflict which could not be described as war, carried out by ill-defined entities against opponents fuzzily conceived of, in pursuit of objectives bearing little resemblance to either victory or peace, the plethora of power harnessed to treaty obligations brought not stability but its opposite and did not even result in the moderately efficient solution of problems recognized by the participants. In the absence of stability and of any clear definition of goals, both sides tried to bolster the determination of their domestic populations and of their warriors in the field by elaborating the relevant parts of their respective ideologies and seeking to make ideological principle congruent with changing strategies that were pragmatically responsive to the actions of the other side. This resulted in some situations whose irony, commented upon by intellectuals, was necessarily not noticed by its human victims in Vietnam.

All the while, however, even during the conscious ideological build-up, a less conscious, very tenuous and experimental procedural rapprochement was taking place as a result of the very same conflict. Except when the American and the Chinese leaders appeared victims of their own ideologies, neither side was prepared to "go it all the way," a phrase meaning employment of nuclear weapons for the United States and the unleashing of its army of millions, plus the possible use of a still comparatively negligible nuclear arsenal, by China. A language of communications, procedures for "signaling," were being worked out between these two states. It was a very imperfect set of procedures as of 1965, that permitted a multitude of misunderstandings, encouraged ambiguities, and facilitated more or less rational irrationalities. But consensus seemed to be growing on some such set of very slowly expanding procedures. This was happening not despite but because of the unlimited goals pursued by China—which included wars of national liberation in all developing countries allegedly suffering under American imperialism—and the equally unlimited ideological counterstatements with which the United States reacted— which included the promise to oppose any threats of wars of liberation or communist-tending revolutions in Latin America, contained in a resolution of the House of Representatives, and a general condemnation of wars of liberation from the Johnson administration. These exchanges of threats between Washington and Peking, during which

Moscow seemed to be enjoying the role of *tertium gaudens,* were part of the newer strategy, according to whose emergent rules the exchanges were being made.

The Convergence of Strategies

The surprising feature of the Vietnamese conflict, as earlier of the Cuban missile crisis, was the low level of violence actually used. During the missile crisis, only one military death was reported, of a United States pilot of a U–2 photographic reconnaissance plane brought down over Cuba. In Vietnam, United States combat fatalities reached the 1,000 mark only in November, 1965, i.e., after four years of constantly intensified fighting and American involvement. And Vietnamese casualties, though vastly higher on both sides, were surprisingly low relative to the destructive power available to the parties to the conflict.

Here may lie the main "contribution" of strategy—insofar as we can speak of the contribution of something as "unmade" as strategy. The problem of "overkill" is generally accorded highest priority among all problems recognized for the system of world politics. When power was scarce, states were resolutely willing and sometimes eager to use their limited power against one another. Now that power is overabundant, participants in world politics are afraid of escalation and in consequence, made irresolute in their handling of even only conventional force. The qualitative transformation of power combined with other revolutionary factors to erode and destroy the old consensus on the procedures of conventional diplomacy and warfare, that used to provide a stable and flexible, efficient and effective framework for international relations before World War I. This has made it even more difficult for the diplomats and politicians of the present period to communicate their purpose or lack thereof. The network of treaty organizations provided but an inadequate substitute for the vanished procedural consensus, since the treaties were insufficient for purposes of drawing territorial or qualitative "lines" whose crossing by the other side would set off "defensive" action. This insufficiency arose from the impermanence of the treaties, due in turn to political changes within member states and to the effects of technological change upon perceptions of "national" and other interests. These disadvantages of legalism, together with the impossibility of using nuclear weapons as *power* in the Hobbesian sense of "present means to promote some apparent fu-

'ture good," contributed to the increasing ideologism of world politics, especially in the style of the superpowers. If treaty organizations could not tie fundamental bonds between weaker allies and the superpowers, perhaps an improved ideology could do the job. Moreover, a more persuasive ideology might also endow one's own population with the commitment needed to impress foreign opponents and partners with the "credibility" of one's nuclear arsenal.

Overkill capacity—fear of nuclear violence—legalism—ideologism. This chain leads back to a heightened danger of nuclear violence. But nuclear violence has always so far been averted, by way of a radical oscillation of style to pragmatism. The possibility exists—perhaps it is only a hope—that these oscillations, whose frequency has been increasing with the mounting volume of the global flow of policy, may have a centripetal effect upon the incidence of issues. Each more or less "nuclear" crisis, when it backs out of the dead-end alley of ideological violence, results in international deliberation which occurs a little bit closer than the last to the center of the politics of purposive compromise. Each one builds up another wafer-thin layer of consensus on procedures for communicating understanding, interests, intentions, and goals, for giving the other side(s) and the world insight into one's own foreknowledge, alternatives, resources, and purpose. The tensions resulting from pursuit of the basic goals of stability and effective efficiency may be pushing toward greater flexibility and thereby diminishing the overwhelmingly substantive bias in sources of authority toward a better equilibrium between the substantive and the procedural. The continuing chain reaction of technological revolutions which knock unto the trashheap of civilization the traditions and values of centuries, may lead to the realization that, in a time of great substantive change, anchorage in the past and locking one's guidance system into the stars of the future can best be accomplished through the fundamental stabilization of procedures. Such a realization would move our concerns from the shifting sands of extreme circumstantials toward a golden mean in temporal outlook. If any of this is happening already, it is occurring at a low level of self-consciousness—and the later men become aware of this growing consensus on the rules of the great global game of strategy, the firmer is their consensus likely to be.

Just how excruciatingly slow the process and how brittle its product is, can be seen from instances when Western theorists of strategy attempt a "codification" of the strategic theories of the Soviet or the

Chinese leadership. The communists usually reject these portraits of their operating procedures out of hand as imperialist propaganda, but even in the Western world, other strategic theorists frequently warn of what might happen if the communists proceeded on the assumption that the United States expected them to behave in exact accordance with the codification—and they therefore behave in exactly the opposite way! Such speculations could, of course, be taken to an infinite regression. . . .

In the old game of European diplomacy, cheating was permitted, but there were agreed-upon rules even for cheating, and the players did not want to eliminate their fellows and in any case they usually lacked the capacity to eliminate them. In the new game of strategy, which covers the earth and even extends into outer space, some players would like to eliminate others if they could get away with it. In the absence of agreed rules for the game, their fear of cheating by the other players incites them to procedural dishonesty of their own. Game theory, a branch of higher mathematics, has been consulted to advise governments on their chances of "getting away with it." Strategy, the art and science of generalship, has been taken away from the generals in what may be the most notable but least noted defeat of their profession in history. More states and more individuals are playing at the game of strategy than ever played the game of diplomacy. Most of the players are inexperienced with the new game, because it has been played for such a short time. Many have not even had experience with the old game of diplomacy, because they had not been admitted to membership in the exclusive club of players, their states having only just been created. As a result, there coexist in world politics not only the old and the new, but also those who are innocent of any interstate experience. The new states further complicate the confusion of strategies and the politics of the Cold War. We turn to them next.

Chapter 8

The Developing Areas and the Development of World Politics

The New Majority of Mankind

MOST OF the member-states of the United Nations were not states when the United Nations was founded. Most of the population represented in the United Nations in 1965 was not directly represented in the United Nations at the first session of the General Assembly. Many of the representatives of the new states, at the United Nations and in the capital cities of other states, could not have dreamed in 1945 of performing the diplomatic tasks assigned to them in the 1960's. The tremendous growth of the volume of world politics was due in large measure to this invasion of international politics by these new states and to the development of politics in older states whose peoples had previously been politically dormant.

Throughout the period leading up to World War II, a majority of mankind had no opportunity to make even the most indirect contributions to international decisions whose consequences were bound to affect them. This majority lived in the overseas colonies of European states or of the United States, or in areas which, though not directly administered as colonies by foreign whites, fell in the spheres of influence of what was generally referred to as European or American "imperialism." These peoples, in other words, could contribute neither to the international flow of policy—less voluminous, less centralized, and less important though it was at that time than now—nor to the central flow of policy in the political system of which their own territory was an administered subsystem. They were genuinely passive "objects" of colonial, imperial, and international politics. Most of them, moreover, were not aware of this status of theirs or of the fact that various types of politics were being carried on elsewhere with important consequences for themselves. There were, to be sure, incipient independence and anti-imperialist movements in various dependent areas, but these were either diverted into the "constructive" channels of constitutional procrastination, as by the British in India, or they were simply suppressed, as by the Dutch in Indonesia. Not a single colony was granted independence between the two world wars (though the Philippines might have been given its independence by the promised date, 1944, had not the Japanese attack intervened). The most dramatic "colonial" event of the period was a retrogressive one: the subjugation in 1936 of Ethiopia, one of the only two African countries never to have been ruled from Europe, by Italy, whose first attempt on Ethiopia's independence had been repelled in a great military disaster in 1896.

Since the end of World War II, independent statehood has been acquired by almost all the colonies, the only major exceptions being the African possessions of Portugal. Equally important for world politics has been the political awakening of the previously dormant populations of not only these new states, but also some relatively old ones, especially in Latin America. The twenty Latin American republics, with the exception of Panama, a twentieth century creature of the United States, had gained independent statehood during the liberation wars of the earlier nineteenth century. They had been members of the League of Nations, though not all of them for all of the League's life. But their domestic politics were revolving in the same substantive ruts in which they had gotten stuck during the early postindependence period. Especially for countries with racially divided populations, this meant that "national politics" went on only among the small ruling class and dealt with problems internal to it and its divisions between landowners, military, church, and occasionally the intellectuals. Mexico was the major exception, because its revolution, begun in 1910, continued to elicit increasing popular participation between the world wars. Since the end of World War II, politics has been developing apace in most of the other Latin American countries as well, even those—like Paraguay and Haïti—where unpopular dictators sought to suppress politics. This development of politics in *older* states has led to a growth in the volume of international politics. This growth—if we could isolate it, which we cannot do—might be found to be as great as that caused by the addition of *new* states to the global system. More people in both old and new "developing" states have been made aware of the importance of politics to themselves. Frequently, they found out—no matter in how distorted a fashion—about the importance of world politics before they had brought home to them the importance of domestic politics, or the connections between the two.

Analogous processes have been at work in the development of the politics of the so-called "developing areas" and the development of the politics of the world. In both, a wider range of problems is being recognized for politics than ever before. In both, the proportion of those affected by politics who participate in politics is increasing. In both, the volume of the flow of policy is expanding steadily and, usually, irreversibly. These processes of political development are of course never exactly parallel, either between any two developing countries, or between developing countries and the world-wide political system. But they stimulate one another and each grows by what the other feeds on: Two neighboring developing political systems tend to have a spillover effect on each other, unless the rulers of one manage to seal it off completely from the other. The global system is "neighbor" to all lesser ones, since they are its components, and what goes on in world politics has repercussions on the politics of the developing countries (with the same proviso against isolation). Conversely, the development of politics in Cuba and Zambia, in Iraq and Nepal, has its repercussions on world politics.

These repercussions are more difficult to gauge than the contributions made to world politics by the international organizations, the international law, and the strategic theories, all of which have their origins in conventional European international relations, no matter how unconventional their contemporary expressions may be. The effects of the participation in world politics by so many new states have been variously interpreted. Some have voiced negative expectations because of the inexperience and alleged irresponsibility of the young "nations." Others assert that the avowed neutralism of most of them is bound to have calming consequences for the Cold War. Many analysts have changed their interpretation from one crisis to the next, depending upon the particular alignment or nonalignment of particular states in particular situations. Since the stand of most of the new states tends

to shift from one substantive problem to the next, the task of interpretation has been made more difficult than it is for the political behavior of more mature states. France, for example, is so "old" as a
political system with a firm integrity and identity of its own, that its
stand on "the German problem" at any particular time in history can
be predicted with fair accuracy by persons with intelligence and historical perspective—even today, when technological change has eroded
geographically defined concepts of the "national interest." But Pakistan
has been in existence only since 1947, and Tanzania since 1964, and
both have seemed to shift their international conduct and their own
definitions of national interest more than once during their lifetime
so far. Since most of the excolonies started statehood with very low
levels of force, their power potential, both absolutely and in relation
to other states, has been subject to rapid change. As a result, efforts to
fit the political role of the new states into the global picture with the
paints and brushes of *Realpolitik* have generally failed. Institutionalist
analyses have been no more fortunate, because constitutional documents and legal provisions are even more likely to be treated as "mere
scraps of paper" in non-Western than in Western states. Since neither
the facts of power nor the norms of law provide an adequate index of
the contribution of the developing political systems to world politics,
the concept of political style may be more useful for this purpose.

Ideologism of Political Thought

Most of the colonies that have achieved independence and statehood since World War II have done so under the leadership of an anticolonial independence movement. Most colonial powers naturally tried
to suppress these movements whose members were completely powerless at the time of the founding. The goal of self-government and independence was adopted from Europe or North America by all the
major anticolonial movements. Long before anyone could hope to
reach these goals, they were "received," implanted or transplanted
from the white West—regardless of the specific identity and origins of
the goals, from "liberty, equality, fraternity" of the French Revolution,
"life, liberty, property, and the pursuit of happiness" of the American
Revolution, to "socialist equality" of the Russian Revolution. Whatever
the ideas and ideals, when first adopted by the intellectuals who
usually founded incipient independence movements, they were "only"

ideas and ideals, goals dimly perceived on the far horizon. Their advocacy in the colonial context generally led to the imprisonment or worse of the advocates. Utter deprivation of power and responsibility in turn encouraged the "victims of colonialism" to attribute all the ills of their country to the evils of colonialism. In many instances, independence leaders then began to spin forth elaborate ideologies—comprehensive, closed, internally consistent systems of knowledge—in support of their single substantive goal, independence. These ideologies, as all ideologies, were unrealistic. They sought to explain too much and they promised too much. But they persuaded many people precisely for these reasons. They persuaded those who had already reached political consciousness, and they brought many others *to* political awareness precisely because of their simplifications. Their adherents were peculiarly susceptible to the more ideological, less realistic Western ideologies especially to Marxism-Leninism and Its theory of imperialism, which was designed partly with an eye to this special appeal to colonially and imperially dominated intellectuals.

Overt indications of tendencies toward ideologism, regardless of its substantive content, can be found in all independence movements, though the variations were naturally very wide. These variations depended upon both the style of precolonial indigenous politics and the style of the colonial administration, with the latter usually having more important effects, especially in systems that had been brought into existence by colonial rule and/or had been under it for a long time. For example, most independence movements in France's Asian and African colonies (and in Quebec) were strongly ideological—usually socialist or communist—because French political parties became directly active in these colonies, and because leaders from the colonies generally received their education and much political experience in the ideological politics of metropolitan France. By comparison, independence leaders in Great Britain's Asian and African (and, in the eighteenth century, North American) colonies tended to be less ideological, partly because British domestic style lies closer to the politics of purposive compromise than French, partly because Britain's political parties did not try to establish branches in India or Africa, partly because independence leaders were given no opportunities to participate in British home politics.

There are also some noticeable variations in respect of ideologism between different "developing areas." The tendency was stronger among Middle Eastern independence movements than among Black African ones, partly because of certain ideological elements of Islam contrasted with the reluctance of the more ahistorical Africans to accept any "permanent" philosophical system. In Latin America, the traditional and persistent influence of the Roman Catholic Church with its inclination, at least until recently, toward ideologism, and the equally ideologically inclined anticlerical "liberal" opposition to the Church had made for relatively ideological postindependence politics long before one could speak of Latin America as one of the "developing areas." However, once this designation did become appropriate, style in many Latin American countries became even more ideological than before World War II, often because the leadership found new objects—including United States imperialism and Cuban Communism— to which to transfer the ideological hostility of the earlier period.

In other regions, too, disappearance of colonialism, the original "first cause" of all evil against which the ideology of independence movements had been directed, did not lead to the disappearance of ideological style. In Asia and Africa, only in part on communist initiative, the concept of "neocolonialism" was coined, a less visible and therefore more dangerous monster that replaced the once visible slain dragon. Sukarno of Indonesia and Nkrumah of Ghana constructed their postindependence philosophies largely around the threat of neocolonialism. At the same time, these and other leaders sought also to construct less negative, more positive political philosophies in more or less ideological style. "Guided democracy," "African socialism" and Pan-Africanism, Pan-Arabism, and Fidelismo or Castroism are only some of the systems of political thought that have been developed in the developing areas. Each of them has had its international implications and most have contained explicitly international components. Again, the specific content of any particular system of political thought at a particular moment in time is less interesting and important, from our point of view, than the style in which it is introduced into world politics. The point of the present discussion is that it should have come as no surprise if the politicians of independence, after becoming (literally) "states-men," had persisted in the ideological style into which their background of unresponsibility and powerlessness had pushed them.

In many cases, ideologism did indeed persist in the international as in the "national" political conduct of politicians from the new states and other developing countries. Just as they were explaining internal difficulties, especially subversive violence, fissiparious tendencies, and lack of economic progress, in terms of neocolonialist machinations, so they were explaining the global problems of unequal economic development and international violence peripheral to the Cold War—like the Korean war, the Indochinese conflicts, and the Arab-Israeli quarrels— as consequences of postcolonialist schemes on the part of their formally departed rulers whom they accused of wanting to continue their exploitation by means other than direct colonialism. To paraphrase von Clausewitz: "Neocolonialism is the continuation of direct exploitation by other means." Issues arising out of problems initially quite unrelated to colonialism or to the process of decolonization were thus often "artifically" connected with this issue which was still uppermost in the minds of many politicians who had failed to realize that *that* problem had been solved, at least so far as their own territories were concerned. Of course, leaders of the new states were being encouraged in keeping their attitudes fixed in this obsolescent anticolonialist stance by both the Soviet Union and communist China, since this could be used for the attempted "integration" of the unaligned countries in the "socialist camp" of the Cold War.

However, as early as 1961, at the Belgrade Conference of unaligned states, Prime Minister Nehru of India rejected as obsolete his colleagues' preoccupation with anticolonialism, and urged them to focus on currently more important problems like disarmament.[1] It was characteristic that this antiideological tone should have been introduced into the deliberations by the leader of one of the first colonies to gain independence after World War II, by a man who had spent many years in British prisons because of his leadership, as Gandhi's principal lieutenant, of the Indian Congress Party, the independence movement upon which many others in British colonies were later to model themselves. Although both Gandhi and Nehru had the determination to risk their own lives in the cause of Indian independence—through hunger strikes, among other things—and though Nehru's wife died as a result of British imprisonment, he and his movement always retained sufficient flexibility in their understanding of the ends they were pursuing and the means by which they hoped to move toward them, to

---

[1] *The Conference of Heads of State or Government of Non-Aligned Countries held in Belgrade, September 1st to 6th, 1961* (Belgrade: Publicisticko-Izdavacki Zavod, 1961).

avoid petrification of their attitudes of the moment of most bitter struggle. Moreover, by 1960 Nehru had had almost fifteen years of responsibility for government, an experience likely to disideologize even doctrinal fanatics of a type to which he had never belonged. After 1960, both Nehru and his successors were to get even less ideological and more pragmatic, as a result of India's border conflicts with China and Pakistan. The border war with China especially demonstrated to them the errors of another belief which had almost been raised out of powerlessness into an ideology—the belief that common past exploitation by the West and common present underdevelopment would automatically provide an identity of interests on other issues. India and China had been leading spokesmen for the Third World at the Bandung Conference of 1955, and then and subsequently the "spirit of Bandung" had at times been converted into an ideology, not only by the President of Indonesia, the host country.[2]

The mouthing of ideological phrases by itself should not be taken as proof of ideological style, unless some commitment to the values of the belief system can also be demonstrated. This is a particularly important point to bear in mind in analyzing the contribution of non-Western politics to world politics. As already mentioned, the ideologies of independence movements were largely based upon Western systems of knowledge. But in the course of their transfer from the historical environment in which they were first generated to the Orient and Africa, they had to be reinterpreted. In the course of this adaptation, crucial and integral components of the original were often lost or distorted. Sometimes this happened because the very notion of an *ideology*, as a theoretically differentiated, *logically* consistent system of *ideas*, is a Western and fundamentally non-Oriental concept. As

---

[2]The "Final Communique" of the Bandung Conference, stated *inter alia:* "The Asian-African Conference deplored the policies and practices of racial segregation and discrimination which form the basis of government and human relations in large regions of Africa and in other parts of the world. Such conduct is not only a gross violation of human rights, but also a denial of the fundamental value of civilization and the dignity of man. The Conference extended its warm sympathy and support for the courageous stand taken by the victims of racial discrimination and especially by the peoples of African and Indian and Pakistani origin in South Africa. . . ." "The Asian-African Conference discussed the problems of dependent peoples and colonialism and the evils arising from subjection of peoples to alien subjugation, domination, and exploitation. The Conference agreed: First, in declaring that colonialism in all its manifestations is an evil which should speedily be brought to an end. . . ." See Carlos P. Romulo, *The Meaning of Bandung* (Chapel Hill: University of North Carolina Press, 1956), pp. 97 f.

already mentioned in Chapter 5, most Oriental philosophies do not stress the mutual exclusiveness of different views of life and do not demand of their adherents a commitment so complete, that they should be willing to risk their lives on behalf of one belief battling against another.

F. S. C. Northrop, in explaining the "un-Western" behavior of the troops of traditional Chinese war lords, who would determine through relatively harmless noise making which side had more power so that the weaker party could withdraw without bloodshed, points to the absence from Chinese history of a figure like Jesus, who is believed to have died a martyr for a clear, determinate, differentiated, theoretic cause.[3] As a result, "crusades"—of which the Occident has had many since the first, including, recently, crusades against the Nazis and the communists—were unlikely to happen in the Orient, before it was Westernized. Even then, the ideologies that may motivate crusades or their equivalent, and the crusades themselves, were likely to appear in a different light to members of communities without a centuries or millenia-old heritage of (in this case) Christian ideologism. With this perspective, the behavior of certain Chinese politicians in the last three decades, who have switched their allegiance back and forth between the Kuomintang and the communists, appears as less baffling than it has often been made out. On the other hand, there is reason to assume that even the Chinese reception of Marxism-Leninism(-Stalinism) has also resulted in some "stylistic" reinterpretation. This was suggested, for instance, by the very words with which Chairman Mao-Tse-Tung invited ideological discussion in 1957: "Let a hundred flowers blossom and a hundred schools of thought contend!" This blossom season, to be sure, was not allowed to last more than a few months, when the Communist Party returned to insistence upon the monopoly to truth of its logically consistent set of Marxist ideas. But who but a Chinese poet and calligrapher—Mao is said to be a good one—would

---

[3]"This war was not fought with too great seriousness. The soldiers on either side did not have their hearts in it, in the Western sense. They had no interest in laying down their lives in the name of a moral or religious conviction. In fact, their morality never asked this of them, but on the contrary taught them that such an attitude is immoral and irreligious. Their moral savior was never presented to them as a leader nailed to a cross. Such a giving of one's life for a determinate human thesis on any side of any dispute would, from the standpoint of their religion and morality, be evil rather than good." (F. S. C. Northrop, *The Meeting of East and West: An Inquiry Concerning World Understanding* [New York: Macmillan Co., 1946] p. 392.)

have invited ideological critique in such flowery words? The substance of the philosophy is likely to be affected by this form of expression and of thought. To say this is not to say that the Chinese communist leadership, at least, is not as committed to its version of Marxism as the Soviet leadership is committed to its, or as the American leadership it committed to its anticommunist ideology. Ideological commitment can be acquired, just as ideological habits of thinking can be learned. Nevertheless, pre-existing patterns of thoughts, behavior, and politics are bound also to affect the understanding of the role and function of an ideology by those who consider themselves fully committed to it—including the Chinese communists.

In other Asian countries, whose communists and other potential ideologues did not pass through the commitment-hardening experience of the Great March and all that happened before and after, or whose indigenous philosophies—like Hinduism—are more syncretistic than those of China, ideological commitment is likely to be considerably weaker, and the understanding of ideologies rather more diffuse. Again, however, as in our discussion of international law, we should exempt Islamic peoples from these generalizations, because Islam is heir to the Occidental tradition of Aristotelian logic and, at least through its opposition to the Crusades and its own concept of the Holy War, a part of the historical stream of religious ideologism. There are, however, variations of religious commitment and, consequently, susceptibility to ideologism, within Islam. For example, Indonesian Muslims, whose religion has been more syncretic than that of Pakistani Muslims, and whose precolonial political style seems to have been more consensual, may be less susceptible to ideologism than Pakistanis. They may subject Western ideologies to more reinterpretation than other Muslim peoples. And they may find it easier to achieve internal reconciliation between adherents of opposing ideologies whose counterparts elsewhere in the world found reconciliation or even long-term coexistence within one political system impossible. When Indonesian Muslims and others engaged in massive violence during the great anticommunist purge of 1965-66, the justifications advanced for the killing of up to 300,000 persons did not have a very ideological ring.

In Black Africa, Western ideologies are even more likely than in Asia and the Middle East to be reinterpreted and to elicit comparatively low commitment. Most of the African communities were nonliterate until recently. As a result, they had no written history, no temporally "deep" popular historical consciousness, and, therefore, little incentive to identify an ideological cause with old traditions of enmity or friendship. Moreover, because the concept and the institution of territorial frontiers was imposed upon Africa by the colonial powers, few African peoples could identify traditional territorial "national" loyalties with newly imported ideologies. The Western concept of treason, in the sense in which it has in the present century been expanded to include class treason and ideological treason, makes relatively little sense in the Black African context, where states are less than a decade old and nations nonexistent, and where several leaders have explicitly set about the adaptation of Western ideologies like socialism to specifically African problems as *they* recognize these.

In Black Africa, too, commitment seems so far to have been weaker than in the other developing areas, both to new ideologies and to older bonds. Leaders of countries who appeared bound for head-on collisions with each other turned out to be able to compromise their positions. Soldiers—sometimes, perhaps, merely "so-called soldiers"—who were expected to slaughter each other in the Congo had such low commitment to their respective causes, that the "civil war" sometimes ended in a beer party and white mercenaries were ultimately imported in order to provide the discipline which only commitment—even if commitment for mercenary motives—can provide, and without which modern war, civil or external, cannot be fought for long. And the Charter of the Organization of African Unity was subscribed to by all the new African states, and the old ones of Liberia and Ethiopia, despite their many ideological differences and antagonisms. As a result, the Charter has relatively low substantive and ideological content, except for its provisions concerning remnants of colonialism and racial discrimination on the Continent. Especially when they consider the Republic of South Africa, do the independent African states seem to be talking and acting with ideological commitment in international politics. But even on this issue, some states that had relatively close commercial relations with South Africa have been unwilling to break this commerce off immediately in the cause of Pan-African solidarity, and most of their fellow members of the OAU have been reasonably sympathetic to their problem.

In international organizations, members of the OAU have gone about their attempts to exclude South Africa and to dramatize their opposition to the policy of *apartheid* in a flexibly persistent way. In the General Assembly and the Security Council, they have introduced a series of initially strongly worded resolutions condemning *apartheid*, but have in every instance been willing to dilute the wording in order to gain wider support, especially from the major members of NATO, because the Africans were aware that without this support, chances of South African compliance would be even lower than with it. This policy of purposive compromise has gained the African states increasingly more satisfactory resolutions, from their point of view, with increasing Western support. For example, in December, 1963, the United States, United Kingdom, and France all voted for a Security Council resolution highly critical of *apartheid*, and the United States at the same time announced an embargo on the shipment of arms to the Republic of South Africa. Of course, none of this goes far enough to satisfy the goals of the Organization of African Unity, which include not only the abolition of *apartheid*, but also the introduction of the principle of "one man, one vote," i.e., majority African political participation. The fact that the OAU and its member states have so far been willing to take less than the whole hog, as long as the other members of the United Nations have been giving them a little bit more of what they want in each round of resolutions, should be taken as evidence of their comparatively low tendency toward ideologism in international politics even on this single most important substantive issue in their list of priority of international problems.

The Black African colonies, however, achieved their independence in peculiarly advantageous circumstances, at the end of the world-wide decolonization process, with a minimum use of violence, after only relatively brief independence "struggles" (usually involving a minimum of struggling), and with the assistance of a functioning United Nations (the importance of which, moreover, was frequently exaggerated by the Africans themselves). These circumstances, combined with indigenous traditions of procedural consensualism, provided a climate unfavorable to the growth of ideologism.

Other developing areas were not favored in such ways. Much of the Arab Middle East, for example, gained a kind of independence after World War I, when the Ottoman Empire, an ally of the Central Powers, broke up, and territories like Palestine and Syria became Mandates (of Great Britain and France, respectively) under the League of Nations. Syria was also a French Mandate. Egypt continued under British protection and general administrative supervision. Lybia was an Italian colony. In all of these countries except perhaps Lybia, the stirrings of nationalist and, usually, anti-European aspirations mounted during the interwar years. In none but Egypt did the European admin-istration permit the development of any genuine internal politics, and in Egypt politics was controlled by a thin and corrupt upper crust. The societies of Syria, Lebanon, and Palestine were deeply divided along cultural lines, both religious and racial. Palestine faced the additional problem of the growth of Zionism after World War I, in the course of which the British Government, in the so-called "Balfour Declaration," had appeared to promise the Jewish people a homeland in Palestine.

Immediately after World War II, Jewish immigration to Palestine mounted, the French Mandates and British Protection were termi-nated, and the Jews in Palestine carved the State of Israel out of Palestine by force of arms, with subsequent United Nations inter-vention for peace-keeping purposes. The Kingdom of Jordan came into being, consisting of the non-Israeli parts of the former Mandate of Palestine, and remaining for practical purposes a British protectorate until 1958. Israel's Arab neighbors refused to recognize its existence as a state and vowed to destroy it. The Suez Crisis of 1956, which began with an invasion of Egyptian territory on the Sinai peninsula by Israeli armed forces, further exacerbated Arab, and especially Egyptian, ideologism against Israel. Leaders of the neighboring Arab countries tended to attribute all their ills to the (juridically unrecognized) exis-tence of Israel. Repeated meetings of the Arab League, the rather loose international regional organization of these states, attempted to concert action designed to drive the Israelis into the sea. By 1965, none of these efforts had succeeded, largely because of the deep in-ternal divisions among the members of the Arab League, who range from absolute monarchs like King Faisal of Saudi Arabia to revolu-tionary military officers like President Nasser of the United Arab Re-public and French-trained politicians like President Bourguiba of Tunisia. Nevertheless, the ideology of opposition to Israel has been maintained and even strengthened, and representatives of Arab states at the United Nations tend to couch their statements there in terms of this ideology whenever possible. The voting cohesion of members of the Arab League in the General Assembly has been relatively high,[4] and this can also be understood in terms of the anti-Israeli ideology.

---

[4]Thomas Hovet, Jr., *Bloc Politics in the United Nations* (Cambridge: Har-vard University Press, 1960).

For the Arab countries, there are other causes of their tendency toward ideologism, in addition to lack of political responsibility under colonialism and the existence of Israel. Islam as a religion does not encourage the development of politics (as politics is understood in this book). Its antipolitical outlook is related to its emphasis upon the consensus (*ijmā́*) of the community (*umma*) of the faithful. The Prophet revealed *the* Law (*sharīā́*) in the Koran, and soon after Mohammed's death, the "gate" closed on its interpretation. Thereafter, "good government," from an orthodox point of view, should have consisted of the application by rulers of laws laid down in the *sharīā́*. The recognition of new problems, disagreement about ways of solving them or about the meaning of the law, factionalism, disputation, the weighing of alternatives—all of these political activities not only had low value assigned to them, but were discredited. The Koran and the *sharīā́* contained the single, complete, internally consistent truth about life in communities, and when novel problems did arise— as they inevitably do— *if* they were recognized, then usually in terms of these ideological categories which also dictated the right solution. In cases of disagreement over interpretation, because of the low capacity for deliberation, resolution could typically be achieved only by violent means. In other words, violence was the best route out of the *cul de sac* of legalistic ideologism when change simply had to be brought about. As a result, many of the Arab states which had, prior to the European interlude, been administered by the Ottoman Empire, suffered from a marked dearth of politicians—men capable of inventing and popularizing new goals and dramatizing issues, of achieving compromises of antagonistic stands on the road toward goals—when the era of development began. In Egypt and Syria the military performed these political functions when no one else seemed capable of doing so, but the military are preoccupied with the basic goal of efficiency, by both training and experience. In their political activities, including international politics, they therefore tend to search for a permanent substantive source of guidelines for "strategic doctrine" (to use Professor Kissinger's phrase), and if they are Muslim Arabs, the Islamic style of thought is there, ready-made for the purpose. Regardless of the substantive position that they may take on specific issues of world politics, however, their style will tend toward ideologism. That is the main point of the preceding discussion.

Ideologism of political thought, when accompanied by commitment, is frequently related to violence of political action. However, in gauging the contribution of the new and developing states to world politics, we should bear in mind certain obvious differences between the content of Western (including Soviet) and non-Western ideologies *and* arsenals. As of 1966, none of the non-Western states except China was a member of the nuclear club. Equally important, no leader of a developing country not contiguous with the communist "bloc" (geographically defined), except Castro, was committed to communism as one of the competing ideologies of the Cold War. In other words, even when politicians from developing countries tended toward ideologism, like President Nasser, the substance of their ideologies usually cut across the substance of communist and anticommunist ideologies, thereby introducing additional issues into world politics. As a result, even an ideological contribution from the developing countries might further the development of politics in the global system. By enhancing the value of politics, such contribution, ideological *an und für sich*, might even contribute to the reduction of ideologism in world politics. The issue of Israeli-Arab relations seems to have done exactly that, by forcing political relations upon the immediate contenders and by cutting across the hardened divisions of the Cold War and, *inter alia*, bringing the Soviet Union and the United States to engage in conflict and cooperation additional to what would be going on without their involvement in this major problem of the Middle East.

Violence of Political Action

The Latin American Republics achieved their independence from Spain and France by means of military and mob violence in the nineteenth century. (Brazil remained a monarchy until late in the century, having separated itself from Portugal without violence.) The founders of these republics were military men, "men on horseback" who, unlike General George Washington, failed when they tried to be also "first in peace." Their authority came from the substantive source of military success, and the military have ever since played important roles in the comparatively violent politics of most countries in the region. Since Latin America has become a "developing area," the role of the military has developed to even greater importance than before. Their mere existence and availability led the United States to set up special training schools for Latin American officers for the purpose of schooling them in the doctrine and the techniques of counterinsurgency and special warfare. This American policy was put together in response partly to United States experience in other parts of the world, especially Southeast Asia, but mainly in response to the "loss" of Cuba under Dr. Fidel Castro. Castro himself had overthrown the military dictator Fulgencio Batista and eventually replaced the conventional military with an ideologically indoctrinated "popular" militia. The United States, in 1961, through its Central Intelligence Agency, had sponsored a small brigade of anti-Castro Cuban refugees, trained its members in special warfare, and supported the defeated invasion at the Bay of Pigs. The United States subsequently sought and received some token military cooperation from Latin American republics during the Cuban Missile Crisis of 1962 and during the intervention in the Dominican Republic of 1965, which was put under the aegis of the Organization of American States. This crisis in Santo Domingo grew out of problems of succession to its slain military dictator Rafael Trujillo, who had left the country with a disproportionately large military "caste."

Latin America, ever since it started to have new states, and increasingly since the development of politics began in the area, has had violent style in both the internal politics of most of its twenty republics, and in the regional international politics of the area comprising the Organization of American States, which includes the "giant of the north," the United States. Both internal and regional "neighborly" violence has tended toward the pragmatic rather than the ideological. When the military held power, they used it in their own interest, and they fought about the control of power among themselves, for immediate gain, without much regard for "systems of knowledge" or the fundamental "national interest" of their country as defined from any profound historical perspective. The nonmilitary "out's" would fulminate against the military "in's" in ideological terms, but this was usually without consequence, until Fidel Castro's successful bid from powerlessness, which was followed by his "conversion" to Marxism-Leninism. Since then, ideologically motivated violence has played a role of growing importance in much of Latin America, through pro-Castro guerrillas and the reactions of established governments and the United States against them. Both the Organization of American States and the United Nations have repeatedly in the

1960's been dealing with Latin American problems of violence, presented in increasingly ideological, Cold War-related terms.

The tendency toward violence in the new states of Asia and the Middle East is also generally strong, though it has different origins. Both regions were theaters of operations of World War II. Most of the South Asian and Southeast Asian countries that achieved statehood after the war had witnessed the humiliation by Japanese armies and fleets of their European colonial masters, had been under Japanese occupation, and many of them had mounted anti-Japanese resistance movements. Often, there was direct continuity from the resistance movement against the Japanese occupation to the independence movement against restored European colonial rule. The Indonesian independence movement fought a full-scale war against the Dutch. In Indochina, where the Japanese had permitted French administration to continue during most of the war, the scope of communist-led fighting against the French steadily increased until its "victory" in 1954. In the Philippines, another communist-led guerrilla movement, the Hukbalahap, was put down by concerted action of the United States and the newly independent Philippine government. British suppression of a similar movement in Malaya has already been mentioned.

At first glance, one might want to exclude the Indian subcontinent from these generalizations about the violent style of Asian independence movements. It is true that the British, in India as elsewhere, responded more flexibly toward demands for political responsibility from indigenous groups—indeed, that the British, at least some British, encouraged the formation of independence movements. In response to demands by the Indian National Congress, Indians were admitted to elective parliamentary office, the administration became more and more accountable to these parliaments, and Indians were also admitted to the famous Indian Civil Service. Still the Congress, led by Gandhi and Nehru, demanded more, and often achieved it through "nonviolent resistance" including hunger strikes by Gandhi himself. This emphasis on "nonviolence" may explain an erroneously low estimate of the role of violence in Indian politics by many outside observers, and their subsequent disillusionment over the invasion of Goa and the Kashmir conflict. However, a hunger strike "to the death" unless one's demands are met, or the practice of lying down across the railroad tracks to force one's will upon the imperial administration, also involve threats of violence: against the threatener, who in several cases "lived up" to the threats and died. Moreover, the masses of the people in their practice rarely lived up to the preachings of the political saint who was their leader (and who himself fell victim to the bullets of ideologically violent fanatics), and this not only because of the enormous cultural diversity of the subcontinent. This diversity, too, especially the religious split between the majority of Hindus and the minority of Muslims, had bred an old tradition of political violence, which erupted into communal mass murders during the partition of the old India, along religious lines, into the new India and Pakistan. Estimates vary, but hundreds of thousands were slain, and the bitterness of these memories continues to inform relations between the two states, as shown during the several violent eruptions over Kashmir. While India, until 1966 at least, managed to retain top leaders with largely procedural sources of authority, even after the death of Prime Minister Nehru, Pakistan's "political" leadership, probably for reasons related to the professed Islamic character of their state and the antipolitical bias of Islam discussed above, was ousted by the military in 1957, and at least since then substantive sources of authority have predominated in Pakistan.

These tendencies toward violent style, which manifested themselves during the "tone-setting" period of the independence movements, have continued to be in evidence in the internal politics of the many countries of the developing areas of Asia. They were bound to lead to the frequent treatment of international Asian problems, both regional and global, as issues of violence. This has been true of Kashmir from the outset, of Indonesia's demand for Dutch West New Guinea and its attack on the Federation of Malaysia, that led to Indonesia's withdrawal from the United Nations. It was true of the Korean and the Indochinese wars, and in a number of other situations. Often the low level of armed forces with which the colonies gained independence, combined with the conventional European type of military training received previously by their officers (or officers-to-be), led leaders to view their external problems from the perspective of the traditional balance of power, in which the crucial factor was possession of greater military power than one's potential enemies.

This perspective would have been adequate for international relations within the area, if two conditions could have been met: insulation of the region from external interference, including interference from the major parties to the Cold War; and return to conventional interstate warfare, excluding unconventional guerrilla or special warfare. However, these two conditions could not be met. Virtually every instance in which violence was used between states of the region involved at least one of the major parties to the Cold War, and frequently—especially when the issues also came up at the United Nations—both major parties, or all three. Most of these conflicts also involved the use of special warfare—sometimes only a special warfare, as in Indonesia's actions against the Dutch in west New Guinea and against Malaysia. As a result, the prevailing balance of military forces between any two opponents in the area became irrelevant to the probable outbreak or outcome of any conflict. This fact, however, did not deter politicians, including military politicians, in the area, from trying to play their game of regional international relations according to their understanding or misunderstanding of the old, conventional set of rules and simultaneously to engage in "one-up-manship" against their opponents by devising new rules of unconventional guerrilla warfare. Perhaps even more dangerous were occasional efforts by leading Asian politicians to play global roles, either as mediators between the blocs or as leaders of the "Third World," on the basis of their power within the region. Before World War II, Japan succeeded in playing such a role, in her own "national interest," on the basis of her considerable means of organized violence, as the strongest non-white nation in the world. But Japan's temporary success ended, symbolically, in the incineration by the first atomic bombs of Hiroshima and Nagasaki, and Japan at least has acted, since its recovery from defeat, in awareness of the limits of power in the nuclear age, partly in congruence with the reduction of violence in its domestic political style. For many of the new states of Asia, by contrast, the violence of domestic style has shaded their behavior in world politics, thereby making for an even more variegated "mix" of the old and the new in perceptions of new realities through old-fashioned categories.

Middle Eastern tendencies toward violence in politics have already been discussed. Here we should add the ancient Arab practice of political *assassination* (a word of Arabic origin), which fits into the need for finding some way out of apolitical rigidity in the absence of "professional" politicians capable of producing compromises. Since independence came to the Arab states, their leaders have frequently accused one another of assassination plots across boundaries, and several top leaders have in fact been victims of political assassination. This suggests a certain lack of procedural consensus on the rules of diplomacy *within* the Arab world and explains in part the inability of the Arab League to arrive at effective substantive agreement even on issues arising out of their common problem of the existence of the State of Israel. When no reliable rules of negotiation can be used between substantively hostile states—even states whose leaders speak the same language, as the President of Egypt and the King of Saudi Arabia do—disagreements can easily erupt into open violence, as they did between Egypt and Saudi Arabia through the proxies of contending factions in Yemen. Further incentive for the continuation of violence in politics comes from the incompleteness of the independence movement for the area as a whole; e.g., armed attacks and other violence, including assassinations, in the terminal British Protectorate of Aden and the neighboring Trucial States of Oman. After attainment of independence, violence and the importance of the military in politics often continues, apparently as a direct function of the degree of violence used during the independence struggle. Algeria fought a bloody war of seven years against ideologically motivated resistance from the French *colons* and the French Army. In 1965, three years after President De Gaulle had solved France's Algerian problem, President Ben Bellah, the political leader of the independence movement was replaced by a military commander of the National Liberation Front. Prior to that, Algeria and Morocco, both members of the Arab League and both formerly ruled by France, fought a border war over disputed territory. This dispute was settled by the Organization of African Unity, through mediation presided over by the Emperor of Ethiopia and the President of Mali, i.e., two non-Arab politicians.

Of all the developing areas, only Black Africa escaped the massive use of organized or mob violence in the course of its independence movements, at least until the revolt against Portuguese rule in Angola, which began in 1961 and gradually changed into intermittent, brutally suppressed guerrilla warfare that also spread to Portugal's other African possessions, Mozambique and Portuguese Guinea. Great Britain, France, and Belgium permitted their colonies to gain self-government and, thereafter, membership in the United Nations as independent "sovereign" states, for a variety of motives and by a variety of methods and time tables. Sporadic violence occurred on a small scale almost everywhere; e.g., sixty Africans were killed by white security forces in Nyasaland during an "emergency" in 1959, and similar incidents occurred in French colonies and in the Belgian Congo in connection with more or less spontaneous riots. The bloody Mau Mau movement of the Kikuyu in Kenya took in the neighborhood of 10,000 lives, including thirty-six white civilians who were murdered by Mau Mau rebels. Mau Mau, however, though it was subsequently "declared" part of the independence struggle by the government of independent Kenya, has generally been interpreted as an atavistic tribal outbreak. In fact, instead of speeding up Britain's grant of independence, Mau Mau delayed it. In Kenya as in every other Black African country (except the Sudan, properly considered part of the Middle East for this purpose), the top leadership, since independence and until 1965 at least, has consisted of politicians with genuinely political careers, usually deriving their authority from sources more procedural than substantive. Before the rash of more or less military coups of 1965–66, no "technicians of violence," men who won their claim to fame as leaders of the military or of the mob, had become heads of government. In Togo, where the minutely small army assassinated President Sylvio Olympio, perhaps unintentionally, they immediately restored a civilian politician to leadership. In the former Belgian Congo, where the postindependence conflicts brought noncommissioned officers of the former *Force Publique* into positions of leadership in various factions, top leadership in each group was retained until 1965 by genuine, albeit inexperienced, politicians, and even General Mobutu, who then took over the presidency, was not a genuine "military" type. The military who took over the governments of Nigeria and Ghana in 1966 conducted themselves in a relatively "civil" manner and appeared closer to professional civil servants than to soldiers of fortune in their career patterns and goals. Except for the territorial border fights between the Somali Republic on the one hand and Ethiopia and Kenya on the other—which can be understood in terms of the Somalis' closer approximation to conventional "nationalism" and the peculiarities of Italian policy in the area—no serious violence had erupted between Black African states. The internal politics of most of these systems, at least by comparison with those in other developing areas in similar stages of independence, also showed a remarkably low incidence of political (or other) violence. Ethiopia, a developing but not a new state, seemed to be an exception to this generalization. Its Emperor suppressed a "palace revolt" with consid-

erable loss of life in 1960, and the country was spending a higher proportion of its gross national product on its military establishment than
any other in Black Africa. Nevertheless, Haile Selassie was successful
as mediator in the international quarrels of others, perhaps because
he shared with them, though for different motives based upon unique
experience, their attachment to the procedures of the United Nations.
This high regard for the UN was an important factor in facilitating
the founding of the Organization of African States in 1963, despite
the radically diverse proposals and motives with which various chiefs
of governments came to the charter-drafting conference in Addis
Ababa. Here the politicans from Black Africa and Arab Africa demonstrated that, given proper conditions, a more or less purposive pragmatism can prevail over violent and ideological style in the regional
politics of developing areas.

Pragmatism of Political Life

Among the five "standard" developing areas, which also include
South and Southeast Asia, the Middle East, and Latin America, the
countervailing inclination toward pragmatism is particularly strong
in sub-Saharan Africa. One reason for this has already been mentioned:
Africa was the last region to achieve independence, and its populations have the lowest consciousness of their historical past. This makes
them more interested in the here-and-now than the peoples of any
other area in the world, certainly more so than, e.g., Indians who are
constantly living in the visible, physical, tangible presence—in the
form of ruins and castes—of five millenia of customs, traditions, and
taboos. Despite these differences among developing areas, however,
the very concept of "development" implies a relatively high degree
of pragmatism, that is, of a desire to be flexible and efficient in the
quick solution of problems, especially problems of modernization. In
most of the developing countries, the most modern people are also
the political leaders. Even in a country exceptional in this respect,
like Ethiopia again, an absolute monarchy whose ruler claims direct
descent from the biblical Queen of Sheba, this old man is trying almost frantically to modernize his subjects. When this consuming
desire to achieve modernization conflicts with a traditional ideology, e.g., the popular religion, the political modernizers are likely to
try to sacrifice religious injunctions to the pragmatically perceived

needs of the present and future. In any case, the modernizing leaders have usually adopted, and sometimes adapted to their local needs, a modernizing ideology like socialism or "Americanism" (this may be a major ingredient in the Philippines' reasonable facsimile of an ideology), which in practice can tend toward purposive compromise and away from ideologism.

There are other, more negative causes of pragmatism in the internal and external politics of countries in the developing areas, arising out of the colonial situation. Colonial rule, on both its administrative and business sides, was often extremely pragmatic, again with wide variations among ruling white states. Portuguese and French administration probably involved more corruption than British and Dutch administration, but it is doubtful that corruption was entirely absent from any colonial situation, simply because of the immense power in the hands of the ruling minority, power on which there were usually no internal checks within the colony, and only few external checks from the mother country. Even where the colonial service itself was absolutely honest—and the British colonial service probably came closer than any other to this goal—corruption was practiced at lower levels, by native civil servants who provided the links between the population and the "guardians," as the colonial civil service has been called on the model of the rulers of Plato's *Republic*.[5] In the persons of indigenous civil servants of the colonial administration two types of rather extreme pragmatism converged: the cynicism and corruption of powerful outside rulers, and the clash between traditional non-Western political patterns and Western bureaucratic legalism. In the more consensual, less complex and less impersonal non-Western communities, the fixed price for merchandise and the fixed fee for administrative services were unknown (as they had been unknown in the West one or two centuries earlier). Chiefs and judges were often offered gifts in return for their services, a practice which the Europeans regarded as bribery. Colonial administrators, however, had to rely upon the assistance of indigenous personnel, simply because there were not enough Europeans to rule territories with millions (in India, hundreds of millions) of people. They therefore put themselves at the mercy of their native assistants, but put the native populations

---

[5] Philip Mason, *The Men Who Ruled India* (London: Jonathan Cape, Ltd., 1953–54), 2 vols.

even more at the mercy of their own fellows. As a result, even an honest colonial administration, like the Indian Civil Service, must have appeared utterly arbitrary, incomprehensible, and responsive to bribery to most ordinary people aware of its existence in a country like Burma. George Orwell describes this aspect of the colonial situation most perceptively in his novel *Burmese Days*.

In some colonies, such conditions prevailed for a century or more. Pragmatic style was evident to the local population not only in their relations with the government administration, but also in their dealings with commercial enterprises, including the great trading companies which in some colonies provided the first European administration (e.g., the British East India Company, the British South Africa Company, the Dutch East India Company). These commercial enterprises, even when they were engaged only in trade and the extraction of minerals or produce, did not apply the same standards of probity and business ethics to which they undoubtedly adhered in intra-European dealings. They could not have observed these standards and made a profit, for the simple reason that there was no procedural consensus on the rules of business bargaining between themselves and the populations of the overseas colonies. In many colonies, interaction between European companies and the natives could not even be described as bargaining, because of the conditions of utter inequality prevailing, e.g., in King Leopold's Congo of the period described in Joseph Conrad's *The Heart of Darkness*. In such situations, a commercial company that also provided administration for the colony frequently engaged in a pragmatic type of violence designed to enable it to solve most efficiently *its* problem of highest priority, i.e., the return of high profits to its owners.

Except possibly in the Portuguese colonies with their system of "contract labor"—in fact closer to forced labor—such conditions did not prevail on a large scale in any European colonies after World War II, and they had been terminated by and large in the Congo when King Leopold was forced to convert this personal possession of his into a colony of the Belgian State. Nevertheless, most independence movements "grew up" in environments of political pragmatism, when colonized and colonizers were dealing with each other according to different sets of rules and when colonial public and business administrations were generally prepared to change their own procedures for purposes of expediency. Again, this applied least to the British, most to the Portuguese, with other colonial powers scattered between these extremes of the spectrum. However, regardless of the degree of political and commercial pragmatism and of its extension into cynical corruption, the colonial situation was often pushed toward pragmatic style by the process of self-selection which brought administrators, businessmen, and "white settlers" into the colonies in the first place.

In *Prospero and Caliban: The Psychology of Colonization,* O. Mannoni has suggested, on the basis of his own experience in the French colony of Madagascar in the 1940's, that most colonizers who go out into the overseas possessions suffer from an inferiority complex peculiar to Western civilization, while the colonized natives have dependent personality types.[6] Mannoni's *aperçù* that colonizers may be acting out a "Robinson Crusoe" or "Prospero" dream seems to ring true and points to the changes that have taken place over the centuries of European colonization in the types of men who have gone out into the colonies. From the beginning and on into the nineteenth century, these included the explorers, pioneers, and empire builders who wanted to "start from scratch," be their own rulers, and rule over thousands of others, relatively unimpeded by the complexities of Europe's past and present. The more utopian empire builders among the earlier colonizers should not be described as pragmatic but rather as legalistic and ideological personality types. Some of them wanted to construct a perfect community according to some preconceived blueprint. But even in the earlier half of the long age of colonization, there were the explorer-exploiters, who wanted to "turn a fast buck"— more appropriately, "fast bullion"— and then return home. They were willing to employ any means to attain their end. As colonization and empire building became more bureaucratic, the same was true of the thousands of government and business administrators who went out into the colonies, although it generally required a longer stay overseas before enough had been earned and saved for return and retirement at home. Here, too, very pragmatic behavior seemed best designed to speed attainment of this goal. Some European colonies attracted, among others, the human refuse of the domestic society, including potential and convicted criminals, who faced fewer legal and other restraints abroad than at home. Starting with the end of World War I,

---

[6] O. Mannoni, *Prospero and Caliban: The Psychology of Colonization* (New York: Frederick A. Praeger, 1956), *passim.*

and in mounting volume after the great economic and political catas-
trophies that then followed one upon the other in the more developed
parts of the globe—inflation, depression, revolution, World War II—
increasingly pragmatic personality types went out into the colonies.
Many of these typified the "devaluation of human values" bemoaned by
political philosophers of the period. Some, for example, went to enjoy
amenities like domestic servants that were becoming increasingly ex-
pensive in Europe and which many of these particular colonizers could
never have afforded there anyway. This trend introduced a further
push toward pragmatic style in most colonial territories.

Now, it was during this period that the leaders of independence
movements—leaders-to-be of the new states—received their formative
political experience. A number of factors, therefore, came together
which might have predisposed these politicians for the politics of pragmatism at best, and corruption and corrupt violence at worst: native
political custom and colonial administrative procedure, and native personal dependency feelings toward expatriates acting out their inferiority complexes in the colonial situation. To this we have to add the im-
portation into the colonies during their terminal stage of explicitly
"political" corruption, e.g., electoral corruption in some French possessions. In the old, but newly developing, states of Latin America, old
habits of political pragmatism brought over from Spain and Portugal
before independence, were compounded by the process of development itself and by the exploitation of these customs on the part of
European and North American commercial companies.

With this background, a bias toward pragmatism was given to the
politics of the new and developing states from their prenatal days.
Most of them have, in fact, been troubled by problems of corruption
and general unsteadiness in the pursuit of whatever goals of state
building and development they may have set themselves, although
again in this respect the variations from region to region, and within
each area, are great. Our question is about the consequences of this
bias for the contributions of the new states to world politics. A generalized answer, requiring many qualifications, would find stronger
tendencies toward pragmatism than toward ideologism in the international politics of the new states. This is related to the very newness
of these political systems and their self-professed preoccupation with
development, i.e., with flexibility among the four basic goals. Even
though a particular independence movement may have elaborated a

complete ideology precisely in reaction against the cynical corruption under which its leaders believed themselves to be suffering, and even though this ideology was designed and believed to offer solutions to *all* problems they might have to confront in the future, solution of the principal problem of dependence usually erodes commitment to the ideology. Replacement of colonialism with neocolonialism rarely suffices in order to maintain ideologism, because the countervailing tendencies are too strong. These countervailing pushes come not only from the factors discussed in this section, but also from the facts—as distinguished from the fictions—of neocolonialism and what might be called the "neocolonial situation," which contains within itself the aftermath of the psychological ingredients of the previous colonial situation.

The leaders of the developing countries, at least in the first generation after independence, generally received their academic and political education and training in the West or in Western educational systems. With rare exceptions, like President Leopold Senghor of Senegal, whom the French accept as a distinguished poet of the French langauge, these intellectuals continue to have ambivalent feelings of affinity and hostility toward their erstwhile mentors, including those white people who have been their consistent political supporters. Even where the former colonial state has agreed to let the former colony stand completely on its own feet economically and militarily, relations, including cultural relations, continue between the two systems. These cannot be based upon equality, except in the formal sense of equality between sovereign states under international law. This factual inequality heightens the ambivalence of the leaders of the new state and often leads them to oscillate frequently and radically in their attitudes and policies toward the former mother country and toward the rest of the West, of which the exmetropole is the best-known representative. Since no true "ideology" permits of this kind of erratic behavior, these partly psychological pressures lead to the ditching of the ideology and of ideologism, in favor of greater pragmatism in world politics.

Moreover, pragmatism is also encouraged—or, where the tendency already prevails, exploited—by the major parties to the Cold War. Both the communist camp and the "free world" have been trying to win the developing countries over to their side by appealing to them with their antagonistic ideologies. The communists have generally been more successful in their ideological efforts, because neither Russia nor China happen to have controlled territories in the developing areas in recent times, and because Marxism-Leninism-Stalinism, contemporary Soviet socialism, and Maoism are all ideologies of industrial development and social modernization. The anticommunist ideology or ideologies of the Western countries suffer, in competition with communism, from at least three disadvantages: They are being advanced by countries most of which were until recently colonial or imperial powers; most of which already have highly developed of even overdeveloped economies and societies; and they impress the politicians of the new states as insufficiently positive in their basic direction— which is "negative" anticommunism. However, even the communist states have not been markedly successful in their purely ideological appeals to the developing world, for reasons some of which have already been mentioned. One of these is the antiideological bias of most of the peoples of the nonwhite world. Another is the falseness of the analogy between the development problems of Russia and of China on one side, and of Ghana, Indonesia, Pakistan, Syria, and even Cuba on the other.

As a result of the failures of the ideological appeals for support, both the communists and the free world have done two things: They have tried to amend their ideologies to meet the apparent needs of the developing countries, thereby in effect to drop ideologism. And they have made purely pragmatic appeals. The United States, for instance, has given up its former insistence that only free private enterprise on the American model could propel developing countries into true economic development and now stands ready to support various types of state-owned or state-controlled economies with economic and technical assistance. While John Foster Dulles was Secretary of State, American ideology virtually forbade the United States to have moderately friendly relations with tropical developing countries that called themselves (noncommunist) socialist, because the American ideology considered this kind of socialism as the penultimate step on the road to joining the Soviet Bloc. The communists, on the other hand, have gone through a whole series of internal ideological controversies, especially between the Soviet Union and communist China, about the proper application of Marxism-Leninism to the problems of the developing countries, particularly in connection with the progressive or reactionary character of their "national bourgeoisie," and the exportability of national liberation wars on the model of either the Russian or the Chinese Revolutions. As a result of these very divisive controversies, the original monolithic communist ideology has in effect been replaced by two ideologies, at least one of which must differ substantially from the original version, so that communist ideologism in appealing to the developing states has also been reduced.

The purely pragmatic appeals from the two camps of the Cold War have generally been more effective and have also made stronger contributions toward enhancing the already present pragmatic tendencies of the developing countries in world politics. Put most crudely, these pragmatic appeals consist of attempts to "buy the support" of particular countries, and they take many different forms, all the way from almost literally buying a whole country by assuming responsibility for its economy, payment of its public services, and perhaps large payments to its leaders, to extending hospitality to diplomats in order to get them at least to abstain from voting against one's own position at the United Nations. Frequently, the two camps have outbid one another in offering development aid to developing countries, as for example for the building of the Aswan Dam in Egypt, providing steel mills for India, supplying food to India, Pakistan, Egypt, and many other developing countries, or surveying a projected railway from Zambia to Tanzania. The leaders of the new states were made keenly aware of the crude pragmatism of these appeals and of the frequent contradictions between the appeals and the professed ideology of the appellant. As a result, most of them tried their hand at the new diplomatic and strategic game of playing both ends against the middle, and many of them have gotten away with it. They would tell the United States, for example, that, if it did not supply a certain amount for economic aid or military equipment, the Soviet Union would. At the same time, the Soviet Union would be told the obverse. And in the end, both Cold Warriors would supply more than either had been asked for in the beginning.

Intelligence agencies of the superpowers, with their nearly unlimited funds not subject to normal constitutional accountability in otherwise constitutional systems, have contributed to the pragmatism of world politics, partly through their operations in developing countries. The overthrow of the Arbenz government in Guatemala in 1954, for example, was engineered by the U.S. Central Intelligence Agency, and the frustrated Bay of Pigs invasion of Cuba, prepared in the territory of other Central American Republics, was sponsored and planned by the CIA. On another occasion, when the Prime Minister of Singapore was about to reveal information obtained from an unsuccessful CIA agent in his city-state, the CIA offered him what he understood as a bribe of more than three million dollars to buy his silence. He demanded ten times the amount in development aid for Singapore and received a letter of apology from the American Secretary of State. We can imagine that, in addition to this one widely publicized incident of extreme pragmatism in the policies of a nuclear state toward a new state, many other similar affairs have happened which will never see the light of day, partly because few recipients of such munificent bribe offers will be as purposive in their refusal as was Prime Minister Lee— and even he revealed the episode only several years later, when, in the aftermath of Singapore's expulsion from the Malaysian Federation, he was accused of anti-Americanism.

Pragmatism also frequently marks the international relations among developing countries, e.g., when several in one area compete for economic and military assistance from one or more of the major powers, or when chiefs of governments in the Middle East compete for leadership within the Arab world. On such occasions, previously professed principles are often disregarded completely for the sake of transient and sometimes highly personalized gain. Inexperience and freshness of diplomats and politicians from the new states with both conventional and emergent procedures of diplomacy occasionally lend a comic twist to manifestations of pragmatism, as with the reported but evidently futile attempt by Premier Moise Tshombe, as leader of secessionist Katanga Province, to bribe with $1,000,000 an unnamed Central American country into recognizing Katanga, since a single recognition was required to lend validity to its claim to statehood.

The switch executed in the policies of the United States toward Mr. Tshombe also illustrates the pragmatism of the nuclear powers toward the new states. The United States first supported his ouster from the Congo by the United Nations, then supported the Congolese government of which he was Premier in its campaigns, led by white mercenaries, against his "Lumumbist" opposition. Similarly, the United States first participated in United Nations censure of Belgium for reintroducing and maintaining troops in the Congo, and especially in secessionist Katanga Province, and then collaborated with Belgium by flying Belgian paratroopers into Orientale Province to rescue persons said to have been threatened with execution as hostages against the advance of Tshombe's mercenary column. In previous negotiations between the United States and a representative of the Congolese rebels, presided over in Kenya by its President Jomo Kenyatta, the American Ambassador was reported to have remarked, when he broke off the talks, that the only reasonable and humane way of dealing with the rebels was the way of force.[7] African politicians, who had been trying for more than two months to settle the Congolese disputes, with Mr. Tshombe's consent, within the framework of the Organization of African Unity and its Congo Conciliation Commission, might easily have been discouraged from their attempts to find a purposive compromise by this pragmatic interference from the United States. The Congo Conciliation Commission had previously announced that it was about to dispatch a special mission to Washington to seek President Johnson's support for its efforts. The United States Department of State immediately rebuffed this self-invitation, on the conventional diplomatic grounds that it could not negotiate about the affairs of another sovereign state, the Congo, in the absence of its representatives—who could, of course, have been asked to attend by the United States. The mission nevertheless came to Washington and met informally with the Secretary, and Assistant Secretary of State for African Affairs. The episode can be taken to illustrate attempts, in this case not very successful, at innovation in diplomatic procedure. Such flexibility has come repeatedly from African states, who are less burdened than most others by inhibiting traditions.

Usually it is the Western states who criticize the developing countries for their political immaturity, instability, and resultant fickleness, and it is Western political analysts who despair of their tasks because of countries like Indonesia, where an anti-American mob burns down the American library one month, while an anticommunist mob burns down the Communist Party headquarters the next. However, if one looks at the policies of the developed countries from the viewpoint of the underdeveloped ones, they appear similarly unstable, erratic, and self-contradictory, as United States policies toward the Congo suggest. The vulnerability of the major participants in the Cold War to blackmail for aid from the new states further amplifies this appearance of

---

[7]New York *Times,* November 28, 1964. See also a letter from the author, New York *Times,* December 3, 1964.

opportunism. However, even though many politicians from the Third World have sought to exploit this vulnerability in their own immediate interest, most of them are realistically aware of their continued dependence upon the developed parts of the world, including the Soviet Union. They are realistically aware, above all, of the dependence of all of mankind, for its continued existence, upon the nuclear powers and their abstinence from nuclear war. As a result, even where precolonial and colonial experience incline them strongly toward pragmatism in world politics, this awareness often leads them to be more concerned with the stability of world politics at least on those ultimate levels of power, far above their own, where the "ultimate weapons" could be used. Such considerations lead them to participate, to an extent frequently out of proportion with their "power," in the activities of the international organizations, especially the United Nations.

Legalism of International Organizations

The Latin American Republics have always inclined toward legalism in their international relations. This is historically "fitting," because the discovery of the New World provided the major impetus for the birth of modern international law. The competing claims to territory, especially by the two great Catholic colonizing powers, Spain and Portugal, resulted in mediation of the Pope. The encounter with "savage" Indians raised the question of their humanity, rationality, and the applicability to them of "natural law." These questions were answered by Spanish churchmen, who drew in part upon the humane tradition of the classic Roman *ius gentium*. Continental Roman Civil Law traveled to Latin America with the colonizers. Following the great recodification of the Roman Law by Napoleon I, the new Latin American Republics, which had gained their independence in the wake of the Napoleonic Wars, reformed their legal systems under this progressive influence. Ever since, Latin America has contributed distinguished jurists to the study and practice of international law.

In their foreign relations as in their domestic politics, Latin American countries have tended toward violence, and their occasional surface legalism can be looked upon as an effort to stabilize the ever-shifting patterns of often personal military violence. These efforts have rarely been successful. Most of the Latin American Republics, for example, have constitutions modeled on that of the United States, which are either ignored completely or changed as frequently as day-to-day circumstantial policy is in the United States. The Organization of American States, latest in a series of regional organizations designed to stabilize relations among the Latin American countries and between them on the one hand and the giant United States on the other, has not been much more effective than similar efforts on the national level. However, even this pattern of generally pragmatic violence within and among the Republics has yielded an important advance in procedural consensus, on the right of asylum. *Coups* and palace revolutions have become so frequent in Latin American politics—even "real" revolutions, like those in Mexico and Cuba, seem to occur with greater frequency than in other regions—that the Latin American states have made greater use of seeking asylum in foreign embassies in order to escape the vengeance of successful revolutionaries or of successful defenders of the *status quo*. The prevailing, formalized agreement on the scope of the right to asylum has probably also served to keep down the level of domestic political violence, by making it unnecessary for the victors to liquidate the vanquished. On the other hand, the availability of asylum in case of failure may also have encouraged potential rebels to mount their *coup*, because asylum reduced their risks from the outset. In either case, the Latin American practice of asylum, which is not as highly developed in other regions of the world, offers a good example of the slow growth of procedural consensus, arising out of practices of violence, in the boundary areas between domestic and international politics where it is difficult and useless to define the so-called function of "boundary maintenance."[8]

The Latin American states constituted the largest "bloc" of underdeveloped countries that participated in the founding of the United Nations. Their diplomats therefore spoke, though they could be but dimly aware of this representative capacity, on behalf of the majority of developing countries that would, within two decades, have the votes to carry the General Assembly. At the time of their participation in the drafting of the Charter, they spoke consciously not so much on behalf of developing states, as on behalf of small, relatively powerless

---

[8] See Otto Kirchheimer, "Asylum," *American Political Science Review*, Vol. LIII (December, 1959), pp. 985–1016, especially pp. 1003–5; also Manuel Adolfo Vieira, *Derecho de Asilo Diplomático (Asilo Político)*. (Montevideo: Biblioteca de Publicaciones Oficiales de la Facultad de Derecho y Ciencias Sociales de la Universidad de la República, Sección III–CXVIII, 1961).

states, on the periphery of the north Atlantic center of gravity of international relations, and therefore perhaps more genuinely committed to international law in general and certain legal techniques of regional cooperation in particular. Chapter VIII of the Charter of the United Nations, on "Regional Arrangements," was written partly with the experience and the special problems of Latin America in mind. Subsequently, its provisions were put to quite different use, as legal underpinning of the military treaty organizations, some of which could be considered "regional" only by a vivid imagination; e.g., Turkey, Greece, and Italy are neither northern nor Atlantic countries, but they are charter members of the North Atlantic Treaty Organization. However, in a still later development, the Organization of African Unity was founded upon principles closer to the intentions of the Latin American international regionalists of 1945. The OAU tried also to incorporate in its Charter and structure lessons learned in the Inter-American system and, more important, in the operations of the United Nations itself.

Analogies between the Latin-American system and Africa as two continental developing areas whose countries participate at an increasing rate in international politics are valid only in a very restricted sense. The main difference arises out of the role of the United States in the Inter-American system. For this, the African states have no counterpart, since they are each others' equals much more nearly in the "facts" of power and not merely the "fictions" of international law, as *Realpolitiker* would put it. But the new African states, like the old Latin American ones, have a pragmatic interest in enhancing the effectiveness of international law in general, and of the international law of international organizations in particular, precisely because it does look upon all states as formal equals and because they have at times been able to "parlay," as it were, this formal equality into substantial equality within international organizations like the General Assembly. Those colonies which gained their independence before World War II—and this applies to all of Latin America—used international law, whenever the major powers allowed them to do so, for "negative" self-protective purposes: hence theirs is a legalism of the old-fashioned conventional European type. Those colonies, on the other hand, which gained statehood after World War II, and especially the Black African territories, have used international law in a more "positive" and expansive manner, especially in extant and newly created international organizations, and have not hesitated to try to adapt the law and add to it, wherever possible, to suit their own conceptions of the needs of the global political system and of their own roles within it.

Most of the new states of the postwar years achieved their independence somehow in connection with the United Nations. As mentioned previously, most of the postwar independence movements used the provisions of the Charter, according to which the signatory states obligated themselves to move their dependencies quickly toward self-government and independence, as weapons against their own colonial rulers. They also used the forum of the United Nations in order to gain publicity for their cause, among other means through testimony before the Trusteeship Commission and, later, the Committee on Decolonization. Apart from Trusteeship territories, several of the new states enjoyed more or less direct involvement of the United Nations in their earliest period of independence; e.g., Indonesia, Cyprus, the Congo. Most of the developing countries are recipients of various forms of UN-administered assistance from the specialized agencies, like the World Health Organization, the Economic and Social Council, and the Economic Commissions for various continental regions. Although this aid has never matched in volume that proffered unilaterally by the parties to the Cold War, the developing countries would generally prefer to have more assistance come from the United Nations than from the United States and its allies or from the Soviet Union and its allies, and for obvious reasons.

The new and developing states thus started their careers in world politics with a commitment to the UN-way of doing things relatively stronger than that of the older, developed or developing states. Their representatives became active in the politics of the various councils of the United Nations, successfully ran for the various elective offices of the General Assembly and of its committees. A diplomat from a new state, Burma, became the third Secretary-General of the United Nations. These countries made efforts to increase their share in the personnel of the Secretariat. The UN's major operations for peace keeping were conducted in the developing areas. The first amendments to the Charter to be adopted responded to the new members' demands for increased representation on the Security Council and the Economic and Social Council. The Security Council was expanded from eleven to fifteen members, consisting, in addition to the five permanent members, of five from Africa and Asia, two from Latin America, one from eastern Europe, and two from "western Europe and other states." The

Economic and Social Council was expanded from eighteen to twenty-seven members. Seven of the nine new seats went to African and Asian states, one to Latin America, and one to "western European and other states."

The numerical preponderance of the developing states in the General Assembly caused considerable concern to each of the Big Four permanently represented on the Security Council, including, that is, the Soviet Union, which used to complain that the Western bloc controlled a mechanical voting majority in the Assembly. Now a simple majority, and even the two-thirds majority required for important measures, could be marshaled in the General Assembly from states whose combined financial contributions to the upkeep of the UN amounted to a negligible percentage of the total, and whose total "power"—whether figured in terms of population, gross national product, or military potential—was a negligible proportion of the power represented in the United Nations. At the United Nations Conference on Trade and Development (UNCTAD), held in Geneva from March to June, 1964, the seventy-odd have-not states almost literally "ganged up" on the have's in order to get better terms of trade.

None of this would be feasible in its actual form if conventional international law did not accord all states equal status, regardless of their underdevelopment, backwardness, or general powerlessness. Of course, the law of an international organization like the United Nations also recognizes the real inequalities among states, e.g., in the provisions for permanent membership in the Security Council and the veto of the Big Five there. Apart from such exceptions, however, sovereign states enjoy equal rights under international law, in their relations with one another, and this applies to the relations of developing countries with both developed and other developing ones. If the new states could not have joined in the new game of world politics with these rules at hand ready-made, it is unlikely that they would have achieved the relative autonomy of some in big-time world politics, or even the modicum of stability in relations with their immediate neighbors of other less successful newcomers.

The reliance of the developing countries upon the United Nations, which is occasionally based upon excessive expectations of its capabilities, does not actually arise out of any single-minded preoccupation with the basic goal of stability. It is therefore unlikely to contribute further to the already present tendencies toward legalism in world politics. Because the developing countries are so self-consciously concerned with their own development, they would be the last in contemporary international politics to advocate, or even to believe in the feasibility of, fixing permanently the structure and the procedures of international relations. They have, in fact, been more willing to experiment with and to innovate in international law than the older European states, out of whose historic problems the corpus of international law has grown.

Politicians from the developing areas have also shown a greater willingness than those from older states to avail themselves of the possibilities of international judicial action and, beyond that, of world politics in general. The case over Southwest Africa, brought by Liberia and Ethiopia against the Republic of South Africa before the International Court of Justice, has already been mentioned. Liberia and Ethiopia, and the other African states supporting the suit and sharing its considerable expenses, did not *have* to use this additional avenue of public attack upon the policies of the South African government, and some of the foreign ministers involved apparently opposed litigation in the beginning. By using this road (in addition to resolutions in the General Assembly and Security Council, trade boycotts, and the training of guerrillas and other means), the African governments risked adverse decisions from the World Court, first on the issue of jurisdiction, later on the main issue itself. They thereby demonstrated greater commitment to the Court and to international law than any of the old states of Europe or America have shown on issues of equally vital importance to themselves as the South African issue is to the independent states of Africa south of the Sahara. In this situation as in many others, the developing countries, and especially the new states of Black Africa, have made much more balanced contributions to world politics and its style than some of the oldest practitioners of international relations. Above all, they have been willing to use the channels of world politics, to take their problems into the international stream, and to keep the flow of policy moving. They may at times seem to be overburdening the circuits of world politics with a heavier load than these can safely carry. However, a system that can carry the potential explosiveness and destructiveness of nuclear world war, should be made more flexible and stable, more efficient and effective by almost any expansion consisting of less threatening problems.

Most of the new states, because of their desire for development, have not had the opportunity to get stuck in single-minded pursuit of only one of the four basic goals. Their style has generally been closer to the politics of purposive compromise than that of the major participants in the Cold War. As a result, their contribution to world politics has on the whole been less pathological than that of the Soviet Union, the United States, or that most populous of all the developing countries, China.

Irrelevance of the Cold War

The style of world politics in the era of the Cold War differs from the style of international relations in the period before World War I, in its futile pursuit of stability, motivated by the fear of nuclear violence. In the earlier period, the incidence of issues was generally less extreme, and if the major and minor powers of Europe were preoccupied with any one of the four basic goals, it was flexibility. Violence was used, but it was limited in its effects and by the prevailing consensus on the rules of warfare and the procedures of diplomacy. Today, unlimited voilence is not used except in threats, treaty organizations are being constructed and maintained even after they have achieved their original purpose, and the pathology of world politics oscillates from legalistic ideologism to pragmatic legalism.

In this picture, the contribution of the developing states seems offhand to be a throw-back to old-fashioned European international relations, because the new states, too, are somewhat preoccupied with flexibility, capable and willing to use their merely limited means of force, and committed to the emerging mixture of old and new international procedures, especially those identified with the United Nations. In fact, however, this resemblance between the new and the old states in their international behavior is misleading. For one thing, the newcomers' preference for international organizations over a multiplicity of bilateral relations makes a big difference. It has been suggested that President De Gaulle, an advocate of conventional diplomacy, wanted to replace the North Atlantic Treaty Organization with separate treaties between all of its members, i.e., to replace the one treaty organization with many separate treaties. Some of the developing states, on the other hand, would prefer to channel all of their external relations through the UN. Moreover, the breakdown of the "hard-shelled" character of territorial boundaries of the old states, which Professor Herz has noted as a phenomenon of the Cold War,[9] is even more manifest in many new states, especially of Africa, for reasons discussed earlier. This means that the developing states and their international politicians, or at least some of them, can play a much "looser" game, that they can be more relaxed than their old-school precursors of the nineteenth and early twentieth century in their pursuit of flexibility—because they have already got flexibility. This, of course, is one reason why the newcomers are in their own way more genuinely committed to the international law of international organizations: It gives them the particular kind of stability that they need more than the flexibility they have. This flexibility extends especially to frontiers in areas where the concept and the institution of territorial boundaries was introduced and imposed from Europe, and where firm loyalties to territorially and/or culturally defined "national" states have not yet had time to jell. It is in these areas, especially in Black Africa, but also in some parts of Southeast Asia, that prospects seem brightest for the creation of wider associations among political systems.

These associations would be designed to provide a variety of (possibly overlapping) services and functions, economic, cultural, military, and other. For example, it is conceivable that two or three neighboring states retain their separate sovereignties for purposes of membership in the UN and other nonregional international organizations, but establish a joint river valley authority to cooperate in *developing* and exploiting hydroelectric power and other resources arising out of their contiguity. At the same time, one of these states might join with another, which is not included in the river valley authority, to set up a *cultural* system for those of the peoples of both states who belong to the same ethnic grouping. All of these states might join with still others in a regional system of *military* alliances, and with some of the members of this alliance but still other neighbors in a common market. All of this would look rather "messy" on maps and tables of organizations, and would cause no end of difficulties if it were attempted in Europe. (It *has* been attempted there in the complex overlapping patterns of association of the European Common Market, Western European Union, Council of Europe, European Free Trade Association, the Benelux Association among Belgium, the Netherlands, and Luxembourg,

---

[9]See p. 16, above.

cooperation between West and East Germany, among the Scandinavian countries including Finland and Iceland and neutral Sweden, and so forth. But even the "Little Six" of the Common Market have been impeded in their efforts by ancient traditions of national sovereignty.) In the developing areas, to whose politicians the concept of sovereignty is an even more alien import than territoriality or nationality, such diffuseness of political associations appears as less disturbing than to Westerners. They can intellectually accept diffusion of political systems, just as they can intellectually accept diffusion of ideological systems.

This comparatively lower need of many non-Western politicians for consistency and "pointedness" in both power and ideology is one reason why they often condemn the Cold War as irrelevant to the problems of the world, at least of their Third World. On the other hand, the two superpowers—and especially some "strategic intellectuals" in the United States—occasionally suggest the irrelevance of the weak and backward, though overpopulated and overtalkative, new states to the Cold War and, therefore, their irrelevance to the "realities" of contemporary world politics. This question of what is irrelevant to whom, or who is irrelevant to what, brings us back to the shortcomings of the prevailing approaches to the study of international politics, since the ideological commitment and power of the nuclear powers and the purposive commitment and lack of resources of the developing countries are both obviously very relevant to one another and to either the stagnation or the transformation of the Cold War.

The developing states have tried by a variety of methods to overcome what they consider the futility and unrealism of alleged irreconcilabilities between the Western camp and the communist camp. Their politicians have recognized problems arising out of the irreconcilabilities of the Cold War from both parochial and universal prospectives: parochial, because one day's military expenditures of the United States or the Soviet Union surpass many a backward country's annual gross national product; universal, because nuclear world war would destroy most of civilization, and more in the northern than the southern hemisphere, because it has more to be destroyed. In order to deal with these problems of global politics, politicians from new states have tried their hand at mediation, usually with the result that the West condemned their nonalignment as actually favoring the Soviet Union.

This was the fate of some of Prime Minister Nehru's efforts at mediation. Leaders of neutralist states have also tried to organize themselves into a third "bloc" which might then play the role of balancer in the contemporary balance of power or of terror. These attempts have also failed so far. Even when they might have had an initial success, as at the Belgrade Conference of 1961, the United States and its allies criticized the nonaligned leaders at Belgrade for failing to condemn explosion of a megaton H-bomb by the Soviet Union. Several initiatives for the creation of zones free of nuclear weapons have come from the developing areas, but these, too, have had a poor reception from Western governments. Efforts to make Africa a nuclear-free zone foundered as long as France wanted to test its first atomic devices in the Algerian Sahara Desert. Attempts to conclude a treaty eliminating nuclear weapons from Latin America have so far failed, because Cuba has refused to join unless the Panama Canal Zone and Puerto Rico, a Free State under United States control, are included—and the American government has shown little interest in such proposals.

International politicians from the developing countries have tried also to contribute to the resolution of what President Johnson called "the gravest of all unresolved human issues" by promoting test ban agreements, and arms control and disarmament, under aegis of the United Nations. Here, too, the nuclear states—probably the United States *and* the Soviet Union, though the latter has been less outspoken in public—have shown no great appreciation of these efforts to nibble away at the substance of the Cold War. Western resistance took two main lines of argument. One was the strategic conception, according to which the communists' superiority in conventional armed forces and their willingness to make unscrupulous use of so-called "national liberation" wars required the Western nuclear deterrent, to protect not only the West but all of mankind from communist world domination. The second argument was technical rather than strategic, by denying the competence of negotiators from nonnuclear states, and especially from underdeveloped countries, to understand the technology of nuclear weaponry. Frequently this kind of resistance to interference with the substance of the Cold War was coupled with the admission that representatives of nonnuclear states at disarmament conferences might be able to inform themselves on the nonclassified aspects of nuclear technology *if* they were willing to do a great deal of "homework"—and their willingness to do this was implicitly questioned, or their ability to bring themselves technologically up-to-date was denied, diplomatically enough behind their backs.

This attitude of the nuclear states can be taken as another illustration of the creeping "substantivism" of contemporary world politics. Consistency in this attitude would require that the United States and others leave the negotiation of nuclear controls and disarmament entirely to scientific experts who, as noted in Chapter 5, would have an easier time arriving at agreement. But since the nuclear powers often look upon their participation in disarmament conferences as gambits in the bigger game of strategy—to communicate one's own resolute commitment to the other side and, at the same time, to communicate reasonableness to the uncommitted states—they naturally do not let themselves be carried to any such extremes by consistency. On the other hand, continued control of disarmament negotiations by non-expert political personnel of the nuclear powers should lead the latter to acknowledge the political—in conventional terminology, the "diplomatic"—contributions that politicians from nonnuclear developing countries could make to the success of such deliberations between the irreconcilable camps, despite their ignorance of nuclear technology or perhaps because of it. Politicians from the new states may benefit from the fact that their minds are not all cluttered up with a plethora of substantive knowledge (and incidentally an overweight of substantive memories). When their domestic careers were genuinely political (rather than military, bureaucratic, religious, or economic), they usually gained the experience and authority, that now brings them to disarmament and other international conferences, in the course of moving their country out of some set of substantive ruts (like colonialism or backwardness) into development. They may therefore be well qualified to help move world politics out of the substantive ruts of the Cold War into a new stage of the development of politics.

The central thesis of this book is the universality of basic political processes no matter when or where they are taking place. If this thesis has any merit, then there is a valid analogy between the development of politics in systems of different scope and at different levels. To be more specific, we can compare the processes of the development of politics in a "developing country" and in the global political system, in Nigeria and in the world. If this analogy in turn is valid, then a politician experienced in promoting the development of politics in

Nigeria or Ceylon can apply this experience (regardless of his self-consciousness of it) to promoting the development of the politics of the world.

Most colonies, upon achieving statehood, have built up considerable "capital" of substantive consensus upon the goal of independence itself. The subsequent development of their politics can move in a number of different directions, in various combinations: The leadership may search for new substantive goals to which to transfer the old consensus, and, since these goals usually lack the attractions of negative simplicity, it may then go on to impose a new substantive consensus by means of some combination of ideologism and violence. Or the leadership may seek to keep the system operating at its preindependence pace through procedural routinization. In that case, parliament and/or the bureaucracy will try to observe rather legalistically the procedures formerly in use under colonial rule, without any regard for their relevance to all the changes, internal and external to the system, that have occurred as a result of gaining statehood. If the only thing that holds the system together is such a set of now lifeless and routinized procedures, then the preindependence consensus usually crumbles and the political system may fall to pieces and cease to be a coherent system. The third and preferable major alternative pattern of development consists of the transfer of the old substantive consensus to newly forged relevant goals, to the pursuit of which colonial, indigenous, and new procedures are flexibly adapted. Basic goals are kept in tension with one another, generating the dynamic equilibrium of the politics of purposive compromise.

The Cold War, through its focus on related substantive irreconcilabilities of antagonistic ideologies and unusable weapons systems, has gotten its major protagonists, who set the tone for world politics, stuck in procedural play-acting according to poorly adapted rules that were devised in the main in the flush of anti-Axis substantive consensus. That consensus on the desirability of winning the war crumbled very soon after its goal had been achieved in 1945. Attempts failed to transfer this consensus to new goals, including the goal of the modernization of the world's more backward areas. World politics developed in spite of these failures. The global political system could not break into pieces unless the pieces were going to be destroyed in the process. World politics therefore has continued to develop—it has expanded, there is more of it now than in 1945, 1955, or 1965.

But world politics has not developed successfully. It has not become politics of purposive compromise. The style of world politics is more pathological now than it was at the end of World War II. This condition presents international politicians from the developing countries with unique opportunities, to draw upon their experience with the more or less successful development of the politics of their own systems, both "national" and regional, to "stir up" the politics of the global system so as to get its flow of issues whirling more voluminously and more centripetally.

The active participation of certain developing countries in negotiations like those at the Geneva Disarmament Conference,[10] and a number of initiatives taken by them to "reduce the tensions of the Cold War" in such areas as Indochina, have occasionally had consequences of the type just hopefully projected.[11] They have not so far, however, resulted in persuading the United States and the Soviet Union, not to speak of Communist China, to give up—or even to admit

---

[10]Including Brazil, Burma, Ethiopia, India, Mexico, Nigeria, and the United Arab Republic.

[11]Senator Robert F. Kennedy, "In a speech before an audience of high-ranking African diplomats and members of the Organization of African Unity [delivered in Addis Ababa, Ethiopia], declared that the underdeveloped world 'can be the sword to cut the Gordian knot.' The Senator castigated both sides in the cold war for having failed to find common ground for controlling the spread of nuclear weapons. The great powers, including the United States, he said, 'are simply not doing enough; not trying hard enough; not sacrificing enough to arrive at an agreement. You must therefore assume a responsibility that others have been unable to fulfill,' he declared. 'You must now take the lead and restore the flagging energies of governments and their negotiators. In every world capital, in governments and in every international capital, in every embassy, in every international organization, you must make it clear that you regard as true world leaders only those nations which are willing to walk the last mile, take the last step, in the search for the control of the atom.' . . .

"Preoccupied with their own domestic problems, and the politics of African unity, few African states have involved themselves in the question of arms control, preferring to leave the matter to those most directly concerned. Tonight Senator Kennedy attacked this 'back seat' approach as unrealistic. 'Hundreds of millions of people, in my country, in the Soviet Union, in Europe and Asia and here in Africa, would die within the first 24 hours of a full-scale nuclear exchange, and as Chairman Khrushchev once said, the living would envy the dead,' he said. Even nations with no part in the conflict whatever, unaffected directly by such a war, would find themselves without markets for their goods, without assistance for their development, without the accumulated wisdom and experience of the world community. So your stake—Africa's stake—in a nonproliferation treaty is as great as that of any of the great powers. Your voice must be heard.' "

From a dispatch by Lloyd Garrison, "Africa Gets Call in Atom Deadlock— Kennedy Urges Developing World to 'Cut the Knot.' " New York *Times,* June 16, 1966, p. 7.

the possibility of reducing—their ideologically perceived or ideologically stated hostility. For example, even when one side or the other, or both, have admitted that technical differences standing in the way of a total test-ban agreement could be solved, they have refused to follow through on the grounds that the ideologically stated goals of the opposing side made it impossible to "let down one's guard" and to trust the professed motives of the others. Would-be mediators from the Third World have been told not to "butt into" this ideological quarrel. The Western camp has told them to stay out on the basis of partly justified charges that the Africans and Asians did not understand or, at any rate, did not sympathize with the liberal individualism of the West. The communists have told them to stay out of the ideological dispute unless the new politicians were willing to take the communists' side, since Marxism was the only true and right position one could take. In other words, politicians from the Third World, the only basically "new world" in the world today, have been told that their experience with the development of politics is irrelevant to the politics of the world, where ideological commitment had generated enormous power, or enormous power was being wielded by ideologically committed politicians. Not having such power, the politicians of development were completely unused to taking the risks that the leaders of the Cold War have to take every day. From the viewpoint of the two great competing ideologies, the ideals to which politicians of the unaligned countries *might* be committed, perhaps only half-heartedly, appeared suspect in the first place. Politicians like Nehru have often been described as "wishy-washy" and irresolute by both Western and communist ideologues. Indeed, firm ideological commitment has become a hallmark of the possession of an overkill capacity. Conversely and through the operation of a vicious circle, the leaders of the Cold War have persuaded themselves and each other of the impossibility of ideological reconciliation.

If the opposing ideologies are irreconcilable, then neither the developing countries nor the emergence of procedural consensus between the superpowers can improve the current condition of world politics. We therefore turn next to the problems raised by the ideological conflicts of the Cold War.

Chapter 9

Ideological Conciliation

The Dimension of Purpose

Protagonists of international law and organizations wish to introduce, or reintroduce, greater stability into world politics. They are concerned with improving the foreknowledge of men and women who act in international politics. Some students of strategy and bargaining are interested in the dimension of choice and in bringing greater flexibility into the rigidities of the Cold War. The school of *Realpolitik* insists upon the primacy of power in international relations. Its adherents usually advocate either an increase in the resources of their own country, or a balance of power between the Western and communist camps that would deter both from the use of their nuclear arsenals. No study of world politics—or of any other type of politics—can be satisfactory unless it has these three dimensions: foreknowledge, choice, resources—and relates them to each other and to the fourth dimension of politics, purpose.

The need for integrating consideration of purpose into any adequate picture of a political system is particularly evident in contemporary world politics, where ideological differences are sometimes said to be the major obstacles to reducing the dangers of the Cold War after other differences have approached the point of resolution. We can rephrase this proposition in terms of the discussion of the preceding chapters: If our estimate of the contribution to world politics of the developing countries has been fairly accurate; if we are right about the "softening" in the units of international politics, about its transformation, and about the possible emergence of new types of political systems, including loosely overlapping associations among them; if our analysis of the inhibitions on the use of nuclear force was sound and we were correct in suggesting the existence of a negative substantive consensus upon the need for preventing nuclear world war; if our gauging of the slow accretion of a positive procedural consensus on international organization, international law, and certain forms of strategic bargaining and communications, corresponded more or less to reality—if we can concede all of these *if's*—the danger of escalating nuclear conflict would *still* be very great, as long as the governments that control illimitable means of force are also dedicated to irreconcilable ideologies which lead them to define their goals and to recognize international problems in unrealistic and unlimited global terms.

Two questions therefore arise, one about the *degree of dedication* or commitment to the ideology, i.e., the intensity of the purpose out of which (and out of other factors) political action is generated, the other about the *extent of irreconcilability* between ideologically defined purposes. We have touched upon the first question before, for instance in the suggestion that non-Westerners who "receive" interpretations of Western ideologies like Marxism are usually less committed to these systems of knowledge than Westerners out of whose own familiar historical heritage the ideologies—and the very concept of ideology—emerged. The best method for gauging commitment is, as always, comparison, in this case of the dictates of the ideology with actual policies, at different times within one political system, and between political systems confronting comparable problems. Again, as usual, even this best of methods can never yield perfectly reliable results, because other ingredients enter into the flow of decisions besides ideological commitment: in addition to purpose, resources, choice, and foreknowledge converge in the decision process. The relative "weight" assigned to each, which can again be estimated by comparisons, gives an indication of political style.

If we compare, from this point of view, the flow of United States foreign policy in the years 1917, 1940, and 1965, considerations of purpose appear to have played a weightier role in 1965 than in the previous periods. Comparative content analysis of official American statements about foreign policy made in these three years would probably show the highest incidence in 1965 of such phrases as "our national purpose," "American honor," "the American way of life," "honor our commitments," "defense of the Free World" (compared with "defense of democracy" or of "peace" in the earlier years). Comparative analysis of government statements might also reveal the highest preoccupation in 1965 with arguments about the internal consistency of United States foreign policies toward various problem areas at that time, and over time—consistency especially over the two postwar decades of the administrations of Presidents Truman, Eisenhower, Kennedy, and Johnson. Speeches, communiques, and press releases, in 1965, probably suggest stronger efforts than in 1917 or 1940 on the part of government officials to convince their public and themselves of the accuracy of their descriptions of the enemy's behavior. In 1917 and 1940, United States administrations may have been firmer than in 1965 in their own notions of the content of the "patriotic duties" of American citizens, but they probably made fewer attempts to present their definition of patriotism as an integral and consistent part of a complete interpretation of world politics, present and future. In the earlier years, there were fewer professions of certitude about the potential enemy's future actions and reactions, and more expectation of the unexpected and unexpectable from the other side, than in 1965. In the earlier two prewar years, "interventionist" Americans were generally convinced of the threats to peace, and especially to peace in Europe, coming from the enemy-to-be, without understanding these threats in terms of a complete philosophy of history. In 1965, on the contrary, American favoring intervention—e.g., in the Dominican Republic and in Vietnam—professed to be convinced of the dangers to the free world and mankind of "appeasement" as a technique dictated by communist ideology. The danger could be averted only by equal or superior Western firmness rooted in philosophical commitment to Western values. Under the Eisenhower Administration, a Commission on National Goals was appointed, served, and presented a widely publicized report.[1] Such a commission would have been inconceivable in the years preceding 1917 or 1940.

The ideologism of Soviet and Chinese foreign policies was obviously much more marked in 1965 than in 1917, when the Russian Revolution was about to take place and China was still at the mercy of European and Japanese imperialisms. In 1940, Stalin had just concluded his nonaggression treaty with Hitler, in one of the most

---

[1]President's Commission on National Goals, *Goals for Americans* (New York: Prentice-Hall, Administered by The American Assembly, Columbia University, 1960).

dramatic pragmatic reversals of what had previously seemed ideological irreconcilability, while the Kuomintang and the communists were trying to defend China against Japanese invasion through mutual cooperation. In 1965, by contrast, no statement on foreign policy ever issued from either Moscow or Peking that did not contain elaborate ideological justifications, rationalizations, and explanations, vis à vis the noncommunist world and, more interestingly, vis à vis each other. The communist leaderships of the Soviet Union and China were engaged in what they and everyone else described as a bitter ideological struggle with each other.

None of this provides positive proof of an increase in ideologism in international politics. None of it demonstrates beyond peradventure of doubt the heightened commitment to its ideology of each major participant in the Cold War. Nothing can ever "prove" theories of historical causation. Nothing can ever demonstrate the sources of human motivation. Their false pretension to such perfect proof is precisely the main error of all comprehensive, consistent, closed systems of knowledge, i.e., of ideologies. Similarly, a major shortcoming of the more extreme versions of *Realpolitik* is their assertion that *only* the pursuit of power, realistically defined, motivates actors in international relations. On the other hand, the approach used in this book was designed to yield the benefits of comprehending ideology *and* power, institutions *and* strategy, in as systematic a relation to each other as the open-endedness of real life permits.

In the context of our present question about the degree of commitment to what might be no more than ideological verbiage and "propaganda," or deceit, realists, as well as contemporary American interventionists (who incidentally, usually consider themselves realists), often contend that the Soviet Union is in fact ruled by hardheaded realists, presumably like themselves only much more ruthless, at least in their internal policies. Communist ideology is used only as window-dressing and because it has often appealed to the populations of noncommunist countries, especially to their intellectuals. For a "realistic" understanding of communist strategy, one can disregard most ideological statements, according to this line of reasoning, though occasionally the Soviet and Chinese ideologists, presumably in unguarded moments, will make very revealing utterances, like Mao's famous dictum, "power grows out of the barrel of a gun." Unfortunately, realist students of international politics have not provided us with clear criteria by means of which to winnow the ideological chaff from the realistic wheat. Moreover, the yearning by "realist" Western intellectuals for sound "strategic doctrine" can be understood as their expression of the need for ideological certitude. Proposals of comprehensive, consistent, and closed strategic theories can be interpreted as the Western functional equivalent of communist ideology.

However, so long as the foreign policies of the United States and its allies are not being made primarily by strategic intellectuals but by politicians, we should look at official American statements about foreign policy, from the official Soviet or Chinese point of view. From such a vantage, proclamations of United States purposes and goals are "taken seriously." They are taken seriously at least in the "contextual" sense of the phrase; e.g., when the President or the Secretary of Defense asserts that the United States stands ready to use its nuclear deterrent in the defense of West Berlin, Soviet politicians are persuaded that the United States government has put the defense of West Berlin into the over-all causal context of its nuclear weapons systems, though they may not be persuaded that missiles would actually be dispatched once East German troops moved into the western sectors of the city. Similarly, Chinese politicians believe that the United States thinks of the defense of South Vietnam in the over-all causal context of its global weapons systems, including nuclear warheads, though they have repeatedly questioned the resolution of the United States by calling it a "paper tiger."

The Soviet communists were the first adherents of an unlimited ideology, global and "eternal" in scope, to come into power in a country that had always played a role in conventional European international relations. Even during the more pragmatic periods of Soviet history, including Stalin's period of pragmatic violence, they continued to use ideological language to explain policies, both their own and those of the hostile foreign world. This long tradition of ideological style, in which new "cadres" are of course trained, educated, and indoctrinated, would be bound to have some effects on the way in which Soviet politicians recognize problems and formulate issues for domestic and international politics, even if the "master minds" at the top manipulate the ideology for their own cynical purposes. However, even if this were not true, politicians in the United States and the United Kingdom—the two major Western countries that have never had to contend with important domestic communist parties—would still be affected by *their* constant exposure to ideologically couched communist (and, for more than a decade before 1945, Fascist and Nazi) interpretations of and attacks on their own foreign policies. One could almost say that the ideological vocabulary of international politics has increased so much and become so popular, that American politicians especially felt they needed an ideological underpinning, or at least an ideological facade, for their own foreign policies to make them more respectable—and, therefore, more "salable"—in the eyes of the rest of the world, especially Europe and the developing areas, if not in the eyes of the American people. Without some such explanation, phenomena like the Commission on National Goals, mentioned above, would make no sense.

There is a further, related factor pointing to the "reality" of ideological thought and action in contemporary relations between the superpowers. Apparent ideological commitment, regardless whether it was fact or fiction, lent greater "credibility" to the military power potential of a state, long before the word "credibility" came into the professional vocabulary. Nazi Germany could parlay relatively little military power up to phantom proportions vis à vis neighbors like France, Austria, or Czechoslovakia, because this power was harnessed to an evidently fanatical expansionist ideology. But Nazi Germany fortunately possessed no nuclear weapons, so that there was no need for Hitler to persuade himself, his lieutenants, and his people of their own readiness to make full use of the German arsenal of weapons on behalf of the goals dictated by Germany's national interest as ideologically perceived. The United States, by contrast, when it became the first state to control nuclear bombs, was still in a comparatively unideological stage of the evolution of its political style. It believed itself to be confronted by the ideologically motivated Soviet Union as the second nuclear power (if we disregard the United Kingdom as a traditional and declining ally of the United States). This confrontation, combined with the technological improvements in bombs and delivery systems that occurred before replacement of America's nuclear monopoly with the new duopoly, made for the infeasibility of containing or limiting nuclear warfare. The Soviet communists had always avowed their commitment to universalist, world-wide goals, ideologically justified and explained. Violence, in the form of national and international revolutions, had always been accorded a crucial function in Marxist-

Leninist philosophy of history. In the United States, on the other hand, violence had generally been viewed as a negative factor by most of the competing, more or less unideological philosophies of life and politics. And the universalist strain in Americans' conceptions of their country's role in the world had always been given strong competition from the isolationist strain. The United States, therefore, stood peculiarly in need of providing ideological explanation and justification of the possible use of nuclear weapons by its government. This ideological explanation and justification was needed as much for the American people, to confirm its resolve and purpose *to itself,* as it was needed for the Soviet communist adversary.

The communists, in terms of their ideological theory, were prepared for the use of nuclear weapons by the West and its most advanced capitalist, imperialist country, the United States. Just as the irreconcilable contradictions of capitalism inevitably bring about the violent socialist revolution, so the irreconcilable contradictions between the capitalist camp and the socialist camp were likely to lead through international violence to the world-wide victory of socialism. Capitalism was expected to dig its own grave through violence provoked by itself on the international as previously on the national plane. This, apparently, was the position taken by Stalin, who was never much impressed by the qualitative transformations wrought in world politics by nuclear weapons. Khrushchev *was* impressed by these changes and, in consequence, virtually ruled out the initiation of nuclear warfare by the Soviet Union. As a result, because of his acknowledgement of the necessity of the coexistence of antagonistic nuclear weapons systems, he emphasized the ideological differences between the socialist and capitalist camps. The United States, for reasons already discussed, has not so far ruled out the initiation of "defensive" nuclear warfare, but increased its ideologism both because of its historical needs and in response to the Soviet Union's renewed emphasis on ideological differentiation. The Chinese communists, meanwhile, denounced Khrushchev for his revisionist ideological "softness," denied any qualitative difference between nuclear and conventional weapons, expressed doubts about the resolution of the American paper tiger, and (according to reports unreliable in origin, but given much credence in the United States) may even have gone so far as to assert that China, as the most populous country on earth, could "afford" to lose half its population, because it would still be left with more people than either the Soviet Union or the United States had before a nuclear world war was launched. The Chinese thus waxed more ideological, leading the Soviet Union to reassert its continued role as the only true prophet and interpreter of the holy writ of Marxism-Leninism. The United States responded by emphasizing its counterideology of anticommunism. Ideologism is a disease that grows by what it feeds on. Since each ideology has to pretend to possess a monopoly of the truth, all ideologies have to emphasize their mutual disagreements and irreconcilability. In the present situation, ideologists in China, the Soviet Union, and the United States have to emphasize irreconcilability. Moreover, each ideology perceives the other as a mirror image of itself, tied to the nuclear weapons systems which none could use without ideological rationalization.

Our second question, about the degree of ideological irreconcilability, therefore takes on unusual importance.

Ideological Mirror Images

American politicians and publicists have frequently asserted that Soviet communism is out for world conquest. Soviet politicians and publicists constantly repeat charges of "imperialist encirclement" of the socialist camp under global leadership of the United States. The Chinese politician and interpreter of the thought of Mao Tse-Tung, Marshal Lin Piao, spoke, in 1965, of world-wide struggle between "the cities of the world," consisting of North America and western Europe, which are surrounded by "the rural areas of the world," consisting of Asia, Africa, and Latin America. He said: "In one sense, the revolutionary movement presents us with a picture of the cities surrounded by the rural masses. In the final analysis, the whole cause of the global revolution depends on the revolutionary struggles of the peoples of Asia, Africa, and Latin America, who comprise the overwhelming majority of the world's population."

Thus each corner of the ideological triangle attributes to the other global ambitions which, at the same time, it admits for itself, though the content of the self-professed ideological goals differs. If you thought of yourself as an adherent of a universal ideology to begin with, as the communists generally did, then you have to attribute equally universal reactionary goals to your adversary. If, on the other hand, you expand your own, previously merely national ambitions in response to what

you understand as an antagonistic ideology bent upon world domination, you are unlikely to stop before your philosophy in effect also
"covers the world," past, present, and future—"without end" at least
until a possible nuclear judgment day. Each side sees the other as its
own *ideological* mirror image, as distinguished from a strategic mirror
image. It is like a situation in which a man faces a mirror, standing
with his back to an opposite mirror. His position enables him to see
mirror images of himself, redoubled to infinity, but they are *only* mirror
images, that is, left appears as right and right appears as left—and he
is not communicating with another human being. Analogously, the
United States and the Soviet Union interpret each other's motivations
and actions as left- or right-wing mirror images, respectively, of the
ideological interpretation that each gives to itself of itself, infinitely
regressive, and not as the outcome of much communication between
the two. Add to this the triangle of mirrors that has been created by the
ideological divisions between the Soviet Union and China, and the
possibility of optical illusions appears to be amplified even beyond infinity!

It is a peculiar characteristic of a man's perception of relations between himself and his mirror image that, although something seems
very wrong and dissimilar about the image, he recognizes a great deal
of resemblance. The same is true of the two great hostile ideological
systems. Some Americans have advanced the slogan, "Better dead than
red!"—which sounds self-explanatory. Before we try to explain their
preference, we could list three fundamental features of both Western
and communist ideologies which resemble one another like mirror
images.

The alleged irreconcilability between the two ideologies can *not*
be attributed—as it often is—to the internationalism, the materialism,
or the majoritarianism of communism. In our discussion of the removal
of the limits which formerly "contained" international relations, we
pointed out that the United States has taken a global, universalist
stance in its foreign policies at least since its leader wanted to "make
the world safe for democracy" in World War I. Since World War II,
in reaction to its recognition of increasing Soviet internationalism, and
in response to other factors, American policy has been based upon an
understanding of reality, and geared to the pursuit of goals, both of
which are genuinely world-wide. The Soviet communists, who may
during the period of "Socialism in One Country" have temporarily sur-

rendered the internationalism of the working class which Marx and Engels imparted to their ideology, have claimed unequivocally to be speaking for all of mankind, though not all of mankind have yet recognized the identity between their own interests and the ideologically defined interests of the Soviet Union. In this sense, both the Soviet Union and the United States are dedicated to an internationalism of the future, to which they want to move over the resistance offered by the nationalisms of the present. The mirror image again comes out in the criticism that each offers of the other's position on the nationalism-internationalism spectrum. Soviet communists, who conceive of themselves as genuinely identified with "workers and peasants, and toiling intellectuals" of the world, see the United States as leader of the *international* capitalist class, which is everywhere exploiting not only the oppressed classes but also such extant nationalisms as the one which manifests itself in "revanchist West German militarism." American ideologues, whose talk about the "free *world*" cannot quite eliminate the ambivalence caused by their own partly isolationist historical background, especially in a period when the ensign of the "*national* interest*" was raised on the bow of the American ship of state, often allege that Soviet ideological "propaganda" merely serves as a cover for Soviet policies which are continuations of traditional "national" Russian foreign policies that have been pursued for centuries, regardless of the ideological complexion of a particular Russian regime. But each claims to be more "genuinely" internationalist and to have the true interests of all of mankind, especially of future generations, more at heart than the other. Internationalism, therefore, is not at the bottom of the problem of ideological conciliation.

Neither is materialism, although many American anticommunists have singled out the materialism of the opposing ideology as its most dangerous, antiliberal and anti-American component. This focus often links the materialism of communism with its avowed atheism, by contrast with the important role of religion in American life and doctrine. It was partly as a result of such anticommunist thinking that the words "under God" were added by Act of Congress to the "Pledge of Allegiance," after the phrase, "one Nation." This is not the place to review the intellectual and political role of religion in the history of the United States. It should suffice to mention the materialistic uses to which religion has been put, for example, by the so-called "Gospel of Wealth," and more recently by the very anticommunists who tried to

mobilize religion on behalf, and as an integral part, of their anticommunist ideology. In the United States at least, adherents of materialism
and religiosity have not normally constituted two hostile ways of life.
The opinion is relevant here of many western Europeans and Asians,
who are familiar with both the United States and the Soviet Union,
and find both much more materialistic than they consider their own
country. The term *materialism,* to such outside observers, generally
implies a preoccupation with the construction and production of
material goods on a mammoth scale, with the enjoyment by "the
masses" of a materially comfortable life in the here-and-now, and a
disinclination for the spiritual-intellectual side of life. The communists
have been ideologically dedicated to materialism in this sense ever
since Karl Marx. The United States was the first country in the world
and in history to realize this kind of materialism, though it has only
recently, and largely in reaction to the perceived Soviet threat, begun
to ideologize about it as the "private free enterprise system," "people's
capitalism," and the like. Some Americans have had their convictions
about this ideology of materialism confirmed by the fact that the
leaders of the Soviet Union have pointed to the United States as *the*
model of modern industrialism which their country must try to catch
up with and, eventually, to excel. To politically conscious people in
the "developing areas," both the United States and the Soviet Union
appear as paradises of material achievement, but frequently also as
spiritual deserts. Materialism, therefore, is no major cause of ideological disagreement and could, on the contrary, be used as a stepping
stone toward consensus.

The same is true of "democracy," in the most general sense of the
term. In the twentieth century, the popular vocabulary of politics has
been tremendously "inflated," and this debased currency of words has
found its way even onto the bargaining counters of political philosophers. Democracy means all things to all men, and there is not a major
country left in the world which does not claim to be devoted to democratic goals, as its leaders conceive of these. However, in any more
precise meaning, democracy must, at a minimum, have more or less
representative majoritarian connotations. Majoritarianism can tend toward the fundamental (e.g., when generations dead and generations
yet unborn enjoy some kind of "virtual representation" in the political
process, as they did through the House of Lords), or it can tend toward the circumstantial (e.g., when *any* current majority, no matter

how minute, can resolve important issues). Majoritarianism can lean toward the substantive (e.g., when the majority is thought of simply as the more numerous of competing classes in a country, as in the Soviet Union before liquidation of the "exploiting" classes), or it can lean toward the procedural (e.g., in systems usually referred to as "constitutional democracies"). In comparing Soviet and American majoritarianism in these terms, one would probably find the former more inclined toward the substantive-fundamental, i.e., the ideological, and the latter more toward the procedural-circumstantial, i.e., the pragmatic. One would also find that the two antagonists of the Cold War prefer to use majoritarian arguments in the deliberation of *different* international issues; the communists, e.g., were willing to have elections held in South Vietnam under the Geneva accord of 1954, but the United States was not. Their attitudes toward elections in both Germanys, east and west, and in West Berlin, were the reverse. These, however, are merely pragmatic deviations from the usually ideologically professed majoritarianism of both sides, which each proclaims especially as the foundation of its national government. Both claim to rest upon the consent of the majority of their adult populations. Both also claim to have governments which are broadly representative of all major groups in the population, and both claim to afford some kind of "procedural" protection to minority groups.

The mirror image again emerges in the ideological accusations that each side hurls against the other, charging it with violations of the principles of representation and of procedural protection. The Soviet communists, who think that economic class defines membership in majority or minority, accuse the United States of being controlled by the "ruling circles" of the capitalist class, and of denying representation to the working class, including Negroes whose social position has to be economically defined. Americans, who have gained "admission" to the majority *en bloc* as members of ethnic groups (Irish, Jews, Italians, etc.), accuse the Soviet Union of discriminating against *its* ethnic minorities, like Jews, Armenians, Estonians, and others. However, each side, by accusing the other of violating the principles of representative majoritarianism, only reinforces its own ideologically stated commitment to the doctrine.

The internationalism, the materialism, and the majoritarianism of the Soviet communists are not the main obstacles to ideological reconciliation between the Soviet Union and the United States. On the contrary, all three are ingredients in both their ideologies. All three posit the kind of vague long-range goals, whose inclusion in formal constitutional documents can serve the useful purpose of articulating what little consensus on positive goals may exist between otherwise antagonistic components of a newly founded constitutional system. In fact, each of these three goals was written into the constitution of the United Nations, of which both the United States and the Soviet Union were charter members. The United Nations was conceived by them as an international organization more internationalist than its predecessor the League, and its Charter, both in the Preamble and elsewhere, posits values of material welfare and majoritarian democracy for the politics of its member-states, their dependent territories, and mankind as a whole.

Ideological disagreement is the result of the mirror image misinterpretation by each side of the other's ideological intentions. For Soviet communists, Marxism–Leninism (and sometimes, –Stalinism) has for two generations served as a genuine ideology, in the sense in which the term has been used in this book: a comprehensive, internally consistent, closed system of knowledge, of which its adherents expect answers to all questions, solutions to all problems. As a consequence, when communists hear what sounds to them like the ideology of American imperialism, they expect the government of the United States to be as firmly and automatically committed to its system of knowledge as the Soviet government has been to its. Since the United States government has made its most ideological-sounding statements in connection with nuclear strategy, the possibilities of ideological conciliation appear dim to the communists. For the United States, on the other hand, ideologism is a novel political style, which has been somewhat deliberately developed, partly in response to communism, but mainly due to the need for confirming the Americans' own determination to use nuclear weapons systems. Americans, in other words, pragmatically use ideological style in order to enhance their own commitment, and they therefore believe that Soviet ideological statements about the inevitable victory of communism—e.g., Khrushchev's assertion that President Eisenhower's grandchildren would live under communism—betray the same sort of resolution that the Americans (wish they could) put into their own ideological statements about nuclear strategy. To contrast the two types of ideological style in world politics, we could call that of the Soviet Union an ideology of knowledge, that of the United States an ideology of (wished for) commitment. This contrast distorts, however, because the communists are also committed— in fact, their commitment used to be so strong, that they no longer have to worry as much about it as the Americans. And the new United States ideology, especially in its "strategic doctrine," also purports to offer a system of knowledge, but the Americans are not as concerned about systematic knowledge, because they think that their past success has been achieved by their pragmatic, trial-and-error approach.

The appearance of ideological irreconcilability has another cause, which is related to these mirror-image interpretations. This is the very real disagreement on the means by which the world can be moved toward the vaguely agreed goals of universal human material welfare, and the understanding and misunderstanding by each side of how the other intends to contribute toward reaching these goals. It is out of this type of disagreement that the slogan, "better dead than red," arose. Those in the United States who fear communism more than death evidently expect a communist victory in war or communist domination, perhaps by domestic communists, to be so horrible, that they prefer death because life would no longer be worth living. This expectation is usually linked to the communist insistence upon total planning of the economy which, it is feared, will lead to "totalitarianism" in the sense of complete regimentation, terror, the suppression of all forms of individual self-expression (including private ownership of property) and ultimately, perhaps, the "transformation of human nature." Adherents of the slogan would rather be dead human beings than live but "Pavlovian" human cattle.

It is doubtful that Pavlov's experiments, in which he got dogs to respond uniformly to repeated stimuli, regardless of discontinuation of the rewards initially offered, influenced Soviet ideology or practice. However, it is true that Marxists generally tend to be more optimistic than followers of some, but not all, other Western political philosophies about the feasibility of reaching certain types of social goals through planned collective efforts. This is related to the Marxian assertion, made by both Karl Marx and Friedrich Engels, that "human nature" could be transformed, i.e., that the "nature" of men as they lived as members of opposing classes, under the conditions of mid-nineteenth century European bourgeois capitalism, would be changed as a result of the abolition of classes. In fact, the Marxian assumption always has been that such a transformation is as necessary, in the sense of being historically inevitable, as the proletarian revolution and the successive establishment of socialism and communism. Nevertheless, just as the vanguard of the proletariat, the communist party, had to *act* in order to bring about the revolution, so the government, before achievement of full communism, had to *plan* for purposes of both current administration and movement toward the ultimate goal. The action and the planning were based upon Marxism-Leninism, the one true system of knowledge, containing the necessary "natural" laws of historical development. In the Marxist epistemology, *the* substantive truth exists, it can be known, "true" Marxists have access to this single truth, and they should therefore rule.

There are, of course, other Western philosophies that have identical or similar epistemologies, though their visions and versions of the substantive truth differ from one another and from Marxism. However, there are still *other* Western philosophies (and non-Western ones, as well) which either deny the existence of a single substantive truth, or deny (or doubt) that anyone has access to the single truth *if* it exists. As a result, even politicians who are ideologically inclined or committed, but who come from areas not dominated by Marxism-Leninism as the official ideology, are accustomed to the constant clash between philosophies that are more or less ideological. This leads most of them to understand politics as having as much to do with *issues,* i.e., with disagreement and its deliberation and resolution, as it has to do with "rule," i.e., the imposition through the use of power of the one right solution to the problem. Politics in this sense tends to be valued for its own sake. In an environment of one single ideology, on the contrary, politics in the sense of the processing of disagreements tends to be denigrated. The politics that *is* valued concerns itself with rule on behalf of realization of the single truth. For Soviet communists it has made little difference that they have lived in a global environment of contending ideological and other philosophies. On the contrary, their definition of the principal conflict as the one between Marxism-Leninism and imperialist capitalism has, if anything, tended to confirm them in their adherence to their single substantive vision of reality.

This discussion suggests that the main cause of the belief in the irreconcilability of the two great opposing ideologies may be found in the basic difference between their epistemological foundations and environments. There would be little reason to expect any important change to occur in this respect, were it not for one recent event: the conflict between Soviet and Chinese communists. Until this quarrel erupted, and at least since Stalin had established himself as the final interpreter of communist ideology, international communism was characterized by—was virtually defined by its leaders as—complete consensus on matters of substance. The content of this consensus was promulgated from time to time by the Kremlin. Whether or not people were communists depended on their acceptance of the "party line" in just this substantive sense. Because substantive agreement was taken for granted, there was no need for working out procedures for the formulation, deliberation, and resolution of issues arising out of disagreement on substantive problems recognized by international communism, regardless whether the substantive problems referred to circumstantial policy or fundamental philosophy. Sooner or later, however, substantive disagreement was bound to arise, both within Soviet communism itself and between it and other new centers of communist power. When this happened, between Peking and Moscow, international communism suffered from the same disadvantage that always afflicts political systems founded upon substantive consensus. Their members have little experience with, and less commitment to, procedures of compromise. As Melvin Croan has shown in a brilliant article,[2] one of the main difficulties in the Sino-Soviet dispute was the lack of any agreed upon procedures by means of which it could even be discussed so as to further its amelioration. In such situations, procedural "frustration" often becomes so intense, that even re-establishment of substantive consensus is followed by continuing procedural, that is, "constitutional" disputes which can, of course, be much more divisive than simple issues of "power." This may have been happening in the international communist system in the mid-1960's.

Whatever the outcome of the Sino-Soviet conflict, in terms of power, ideology, or procedure, it had already, by 1964, destroyed the impression of an *ideological* monolith which international communism used to make. It had not yet quite eroded the epistemological assumptions of either Soviet or Chinese communists, since both of them were still appealing to the same single source of the same single truth, which they interpreted differently. It had, however, pushed communists closer toward an environment of multiverity, at the same time that some

---

[2] Melvin Croan, "Communist International Relations," *Survey,* No. 42 (June, 1962), pp. 9–19.

Westerners were trying to create an environment of monoverity, with less success than rewarded their efforts to provide themselves with an anticommunist ideology.

A Contribution from Political Philosophy?

The preceding discussion warrants optimism about neither the possibilities of reducing ideological hostilities, nor, therefore, the likelihood of averting a nuclear world war. The positive developments in those directions—largely identical with the development of global politics *per se*—are proceeding at a very slow pace, in the face of great obstacles from antipolitical inertia, which consists, in the main, of unwillingness to face up to the existential necessity of disagreement and the beneficent inevitability of dialogue. The authors and elaborators of the opposing substantive ideologies want to resolve their disagreements not through dialogue and deliberation, nor even through search for a common denominator of rules of the game for such a "debate," but through imposing acceptance of their own version of the whole truth upon the other side and, indeed, all of mankind. As a result, their ideologies seem shallow and most of what passes for political philosophy today deals with relatively circumstantial problems. This comes as a disappointment to anyone who is led, by slogans like "Better dead than red," to expect that political philosophy will address itself to fundamental problems: What values are worth the risk of destroying mankind? What values should be compromised in order to avert nuclear world war? To which values, and which community, should the ultimate loyalties of individuals be tied?

If we look on politics as the process by which a community deals with its problems, and on problems as obstacles between men and their goals, then we may state the task of political philosophy as follows:[3] To define the goals toward which a community is or should be striving, in a clear way that makes possible a systematic understanding of the concrete conditions of human existence so as to be of help in solving the problems to which these conditions give rise. This is the task to which those philosophers who have been judged great in the light of hindsight did address themselves. The goals or values which

---

[3]The remainder of this section is adapted from the author's "Responsibility and the Goal of Survival," *Responsibility, Nomos,* Vol. III (New York: Liberal Arts Press, 1960), pp. 290–303.

they forged have in every case been related to the most crucial problem of the age and area in which a philosophy wielded its greatest influence: survival of the *polis;* relations between *civitas Dei* and *civitas humana* and between spiritual and secular authorities; anarchy before power had been centralized and, following solution of that problem, control of the exercise of centralized power; relations among "classes" of emergent "mass" societies; and the organization of production.

The present poverty of political philosophy has been variously noted and lamented.[4] Self-critical political philosophers admit that they are living off the capital of ideas and ideals one or two centuries old or older. They work with conventional analytical concepts, like *state, power, war,* and *peace.* When they are not writing the history of political thought, they are elaborating values, like *liberty* and *equality,* which are so well worn by use that they mean all things to all men, and certainly antagonistic things to followers of hostile ideologies. This evaluation of contemporary political philosophy may sound too harsh— but where is the John Stuart Mill or the Karl Marx of our time? The answer seems harder to find than would have been an answer to the same question, raised in the nineteenth century, about its Jean-Jacques Rousseau or its John Locke.

The relative failure of political philosophy in our age cannot be attributed to the abensce of, or to our inability to recognize, one crucial problem of overriding importance on whose solution everything depends. Quite the contrary, the existence of only *one* such problem appears much more clearly today than it could have to any generation of our forefathers at least since the Protestant Reformation. For us, *the* problem is how to prevent the extermination of mankind. Perhaps the fearful dimensions of this problem, and the possibility that it may be literally the last problem about which men make decisions, explains the reluctance of political philosophers to come to grips with it, leaving this task to politically inclined Churchmen (like Pope John XXIII and Karl Barth), psychoanalysts(like Erich Fromm), or natural scientists (like Linus Pauling and Anatol Rapoport).

The concrete nature of the threat to survival is becoming daily more evident. It involves the destructiveness of nuclear weapons, their proliferation, and the speed with which they can be delivered, dangers

---

[4]E.g., by Alfred Cobban, "The Decline of Political Theory," *Political Science Quarterly,* Vol. LXVIII (1953), pp. 321–37.

of radio-active fall-out, and the like. But the problem presented by threats to survival cannot be solved, unless the goal of survival—on the road to which these threats are our obstacles—can be defined in a way which commands nearly global consensus. For this purpose, the concept of responsibility may be of help.

Whatever the content of the goals of a community, including the global community of mankind, their definition or elaboration, or even their creation, is the task of political philosophy. Values or goals should be stated with reference to the concrete conditions of life existing in the community for which the philosopher is working. In order to be effective, the goals contained in a political philosophy should be capable of eliciting the agreement of all those members of the community whose disagreement could prevent achievement of the goals. In the past, philosophers were able to satisfy this requirement by securing the agreement only of the strongest part of the community. This is no longer true for the world community, because any nuclear state acting in it could set off a train of events which would culminate in general extermination. Conceivably, even a state not possessing nuclear weapons could do this through interference with the attack detection system of nuclear states.

The political philosopher who identifies himself with the global community of mankind must, therefore, seek to find and define goals that can command the widest possible consensus, at least among those men who could start a nuclear world war. This kind of search may be condemned as immoral ("Why should we seek to find a basis for agreement with the evil Soviet communists or imperialists?"), or rejected as futile ("Nothing will deter the Communists or imperialists from pursuing their goal of world domination!"). The burden of proving either immorality or futility rests with the critics. If they should turn out to be right, chances are that they will not be alive to tell us, "We told you so"—nor we to concede the point.

The crucial problem is the threat to the survival of mankind, and the task of political philosophy is the search for goals commanding enough agreement. Until now, most political philosophers have concentrated on defining *differences* between the values of the "free world" and the "communist world." The wide academic and popular currency of these phrases and of their communist counterslogans shows the strength of emphasis on differentiation. This emphasis had been so successful that Americans found it very difficult to visualize life behind the "Iron Curtain" in terms other than those which would be used to describe a vast concentration camp. This explains the over-reaction of many when, during the "thawing" years of the "Cold War," they discovered that Russians were human beings like themselves, with families, loves, worries, jobs, and ambitions. Political philosophy which concentrated on differences between the goals pursued by the two great camps was intended to strengthen the determination to "re-sist aggression." But such philosophy, at best, stood in the service of one of the two great alliances of states. At worst, it stood in the service of only one national community or less, like armed services competing for appropriations. Neither this kind of philosophy nor those com-mitted to it can provide any help in solving the present problem.

Still, the study of such philosophies and ideologies may be helpful in the search for a common denominator of ultimate goals capable of securing support from both major parties to the Cold War and from the Third World as well. This kind of comparative study of philos-ophies does, however, present several difficulties. Among these is the loose use of words and their mobilization for propaganda. There are few political philosophies left in the world today, and fewer poli-ticians, that do not advocate freedom, equality, democracy, constitu-tionalism, international harmony, reduction of violence, and similar causes. But it is hard to tell whether they do this because they want to win friends and influence peoples, or because they are actually committed to these goals.

Even where we can establish "genuine" commitment, through comparison, how do we know the content of the goals that are the object of this commitment? The meaning of goals is obscure, not only because they have been used for so many, often contradictory pur-poses. Terms like "freedom" and "democracy" are obscure also, be-cause they were given their original modern meanings in response to the distinctive problems of earlier ages. This applies alike to normative and analytical concepts. For example, as was mentioned in Chapter 2, *power* was defined when its consolidation was a major problem. To use the term in its conventional meaning for an analysis of current rela-tions between the United States and the Soviet Union is, therefore, not likely to be helpful. The goal of *equality* was filled with its mod-ern content at a time and in places where vast economic, social, and political inequalities constituted the single most important problem. Such inequalities no longer exist in the United States, Europe, or the

Soviet Union. But since the Industrial Revolution, equality has been put to so many uses, and in so many different contexts, that it would be very hard to redefine it in a way designed to overcome contradictory prevailing stereotypes of equality. To get agreement on the desirability of a redefined notion of equality as a goal would probably prove impossible. The same is true of similar other concepts.

If the conventional values of political philosophy are inadequate to serve as goals commanding enough agreement to prevent extermination, where else should we turn in our search? Perhaps the two opposing camps are so fundamentally opposed to each other in their ultimate goals, that they could agree, if at all, only on temporary, expedient, circumstantial policies. This attitude has been taken by those, on both sides, who favor "coexistence" only as a transient measure, e.g., on issues like the Austrian peace treaty of 1955, the partial test-ban treaty of 1963, and the United Nations intervention in the Kashmir conflict of 1965.

Those who assert that negotiations can do no harm go a little farther in their hope for the construction of layers of procedural consensus. These hopes may or may not be warranted. In either case, resignation to finding agreement only at the pragmatic level of solutions to immediate problems implies a much wider resignation. It contributes little to solution of the central problem of the survival of humanity. Since, moreover, such resignation means the failure of political philosophy to live up to its task of clarifying ultimate goals, it may involve either side in the first step on the road toward concessions which might end in surrender of its fundamental goals.

Could agreement on matters lying beyond politics proper reduce the threat to the continued existence of mankind? Since the beginning of cultural, technical, and scientific exchanges between the United States and the Soviet Union, the similarity of problems faced by members of various professions on both sides has often been remarked upon. Poets and pianists, farmers and pharmacists, architects and astronomers are all members of communities based on a commonality of problems, knowledge, and experience, and on the use of the same techniques, methods, or procedures for dealing with their problems. Except for differences in the standard of living, auto workers in Detroit and Leningrad or subway workers in New York and Moscow lead very similar lives—more similar at any rate than any of their lives are to those of a Chinese peasant or a Ghanaian cocoa farmer.

These kinds of agreement explain why it has been so much easier for scientific and technical experts to agree on solutions to problems like the control of nuclear tests, than it has been for politicians to resolve issues arising out of the same problems. This fact in turn suggests that issues about ultimate goals will always be raised, and that consensus on the level of circumstantial solutions to circumstantial problems is not enough.

If neither lip service to old values, nor pragmatic agreement on temporary policies, and on procedures for their negotiation, nor finally consensus on professional methods seems designed to help solve the problem of the threat to human survival, how can we hope for such aid from the concept of responsibility, at the level of ultimate goals?

Is it not the ultimate goal of the communists to dominate the world, and of the West to "expand the area of freedom" till *it* covers the world? The first glimmer of hope comes from assertions made by both sides to the effect that rule by itself is not the ultimate goal, but envisaged rather as means toward some further end: establishment of the global classless society for the communists, establishment of conditions favorable to the self-realization of human beings for the West. True, each side casts doubt upon, or rejects the credibility of, the other's protestations. But each side at the same time also indoctrinates its own youth—and especially its future leadership—with these ultimate goals.

The contents of these two sets of final goals are rather similar, for the obvious reason of their common roots in the values of European political systems, including the United States, in the eighteenth and nineteenth centuries. The forms of their statement also bear a great deal of resemblance, e.g., in their indefiniteness about the future. Just how useful this vagueness in the statement of ultimate goals may be, is shown by the rapid and radical changes in the content of human problems, brought about by the expansion of human knowledge about and human control over nature and the universe. It is virtually impossible to project goals in definite and substantive terms when one does not know what vast new possibilities of human achievement the future may bring.

"From each according to his ability, to each according to his need," in "an association in which the free development of each is the condition for the free development of all," after completion of the "leap from the realm of necessity into the realm of freedom"—these Marxian phrases contain statements of ultimate goals not fully accepted and not realized in either the Soviet Union or the United States today. Their emphasis on the individual, on equality, on freedom, and on reason, are derived from the common sources of Marxian and non-Marxian Western philosophy. As interpreted on each side, goals such as these might be mutually acceptable, but interpretations of the current single crucial problem derived from them would not be in sufficient agreement to produce purposive compromise for the resolution of issues generated by that problem. The reason is twofold: first, the vagueness of terms like equality and freedom, along with the propaganda use to which they have been put, as mentioned above; and second, possibilities like the conceivable future solution of problems of production and distribution and the consequent irrelevance, in a world of plenty, of both productive abilities and material needs—the same possibilities again that make the forecast of goals formulated substantively nearly impossible.

Does *responsibility,* as an ultimate goal, suffer from the same handicaps? There is hope that it might not, except for an unfortunate "legal encumbrance" on the concept of responsibility. The legal encumbrance is unfortunate, because legal philosophy in the English-speaking Common Law world has a retrospective temporal orientation, while legal philosophy in the Civil Law world has a passion for the systematic which often leads it to unrealistic and abstract ideologism. The nature of politics as the queen of the sciences demands that political philosophy look to the future, propose and define goals for it, and do so in a way that makes reference to concrete present problems easy.

The legal encumbrance was created by the claim staked by lawyers and legal philosophers to the concept of responsibility, in the sense of liability, accountability, or answerability. This is undoubtedly the sense in which it was used by Alexander Hamilton, James Madison, and others in the eighteenth century.[5] Since then, the emphasis of common usage has shifted to responsibility in the sense of "capacity to cause," i.e., to choose among alternatives, in the light of knowl-

---

[5] See, e.g., Hamilton, in *The Federalist,* No. 70: "Responsibility is of two kinds—to censure and to punishment. The first is the more important of the two. . . ." And Madison, in *The Federalist,* No. 63: "Responsibility, in order to be reasonable, must be limited to objects within the power of the responsible party, and in order to be effectual, must be related to operations of that power, of which a ready and proper judgment can be formed by the constituents."

edge about probable consequences, with resources for implementation, and in commitment to some set of fundamental values.

In the course of the democratization of constitutional governments and the opening of many and intricate channels through which citizens can contribute to central decisions, responsibility in this sense has been extended to ever more, and eventually to almost all, citizens. In the course of scientific and technological progress, human responsibility has been extended to realms previously wholly beyond its scope—like private and public health, aerial and space flight, before long the control of weather, and already the survival or destruction of responsible human beings as a species. Individuals can now become responsible, to an extent unthought of a hundred or even fifty years ago, for such matters as education, career, mate, residence, or the look of one's face (through plastic surgery). There are differences between different areas of the world, but everywhere the trend is toward the extension of responsibility.

Usually, the capacity of the political system to become responsible for its future precedes the capacity of smaller groups and of individual members to become responsible for theirs and to contribute to the central flow of policy about the common fate. But increases in communal capacity for responsibility have usually been justified as serving the ultimate goal of increased individual responsibility. The norm of individual responsibility, as noted earlier in this book, has been and is being advocated by a large number of prominent thinkers from different fields of learning and activity and with widely differing ideological convictions. It is being advocated today especially by philosophers, like the late Martin Buber, who are deeply disturbed by the inability of human beings to communicate with each other, an inability caused partly by ideologism and partly by psychologism. The possibility therefore arises that the value of responsibility, if properly conceived of, might serve as a common denominator of normative agreement.

We described the concept of the sound "situation of responsibility" in Chapter 3.[6] It requires that individuals should be given opportunities to contribute to those central decisions whose consequences will affect themselves, to an extent proportionate to their exposure to these consequences. The four ingredients of the sound situation of responsi-

---

[6]See pp. 76–80, above.

bility are foreknowledge, choice, resources, and purpose. Now, it may be feasible to elicit the kind of consensus needed for solving the problem of the threat to the survival of mankind, on the desirability of the goal of improving situations of responsibility.

This agreement could be reached most easily with regard to improvements in resources as a desideratum, especially resources for increasing human control over the nonhuman sectors of nature and the universe, for with respect to nature and cosmos men come closest to forming a true community. Collaboration for the achievement of intermediate goals, as in the International Geophysical Year or the exchange of meteorological information, may serve as illustrations. Agreement should also be easy to obtain on the desirability of improving foreknowledge of the consequences of decisions. Even if it were not "in the nature" of knowledge to become common property, increasing communication among all scientific workers of the world makes the prolonged restriction of improvements very difficult to maintain. At least no one of influence on either side of the Cold War today would make a statement like the following, made in 1938 by an official of the Spanish Ministry of Education: "All the misfortunes of Spain come from the stupid desire of the governments to teach Spaniards to read. Teaching a man to read is only to oblige him to assume a position that will cause misfortune for himself and for his motherland."[7]

It would not be as easy to get agreement on the kind of alternatives that could or should be made available for choice. Because they deny that persistent limits are set to all human foreknowledge, adherents of necessitarian ideologies like Marxism-Leninism often refuse to admit the existence of any sets of alternatives other than those of the ancient Stoic dictum: *Volentem fata ducunt, nolentem trahunt.* (Him who is willing, the fates lead; him who resists, they drag along.) By contrast, followers of more skeptical philosophies would often offer alternatives even to those people whose choice is likely to lead them to disaster. Nevertheless, Marxists would agree with them that, at least ultimately, each should have opportunities to make contributions to policies about the future of all, that is, to the central flow of politics whose consequences will affect himself, and to the extent that this will be true. The communists, after all, criticize "bourgeois democracy" because they be-

---

[7] The Marques de Lozoya, quoted by Howard K. Smith, *The State of Europe* (New York: Alfred A. Knopf, 1949), p. 241.

lieve that under it the working class, a majority of the population, are denied meaningful opportunities to make such contributions. Communist propaganda designed to stir up sentiment on behalf of cessation of nuclear tests and universal general disarmament also implied the belief that alternatives are available with regard to the most crucial problem of survival.

Political philosophies in the West and the communist orbit are in agreement that the extermination of mankind is not necessary and that its prevention is desirable. They are in disagreement in their answers to the question: What is the best solution to the problem posed by this threat? This disagreement is due to the fact that the ideologies of the two sides are committed to different ultimate purposes and, therefore, hold different visions of the content of the goal of survival. This goal is not really ultimate—it is penultimate. Neither side stops with the negative goal of wanting to prevent the outbreak of a nuclear war. Neither side is willing to resign itself to maintenance of the *status quo.* Even if they showed such willingness, technological change would make such a position untenable.

We have already tried to analyze the position of those who would prefer universal death to survival under domination of the victorious other side, with the help of the notion of the ideological mirror image. There is another related explanation for this preference of universal suicide: refusal to face up to the likelihood that the general extermination of all of mankind *is* one of the alternatives of the issue generated by the problem of the threat to human survival. The attempt to construct "substitute" alternatives, like limited nuclear war, is an example of this refusal. Both the refusal to accept the extermination of human life as one of two alternatives, and the explicit or implicit preference for general suicide, are related to thinking—again on both sides—in terms of goals relevant to problems which are no longer crucial and many of which have, in fact, come close to being solved. Among these are *security, equality, welfare,* and *democracy.* The degree to which political systems have approached realization of these goals, which are in the main substantive, differs between the two camps, and within each. But the problems, in response to which these goals were given the content they still hold today, are no longer the most serious problems faced by the citizens of these countries, nor even of the developing states (though possibly *between* the developing and the developed areas).

The most serious problem for men living in the two great hostile camps today is that presented by the threats to human survival. In order to be able to solve it, they need clarity about the nature of the ultimate goal, next to which survival itself is penultimate. One of the purposes of this book is to show that this final goal can no longer usefully be defined with the conventional values of contemporary political philosophy. The frequent and unpredictable changes in the substance of the problems confronted by mankind suggest that a definition of ultimate goals in excessively substantive terms would also be of little help. The value of *responsibility*, as here conceived, is meant to counterbalance the usual substantive bias, by tending toward the procedural: It provides guidelines for *how* communities, including the global community of mankind, should go about the solution of their problems, not *what* the solution should be in any particular case. This is another aspect of the goal of responsibility, that commends it as a common denominator capable of commanding sufficient agreement for resolving the purposive dimension of the issues raised by the problem of the threat to survival.

If political philosophers work on behalf of the emerging community of mankind, the path toward making their contribution to the solution of the crucial problem of our time may be similar to the one outlined in this section. In any case, that path must be quite different from the one which influential political philosophy on both sides of the Iron and Bamboo Curtains has been traveling in the last two decades. If we continue to follow the old path, chances are that all our paths will come to an abrupt and permanent end. Prevention or postponement cannot be guaranteed by concentration on the formulation of ultimate goals capable of eliciting the needed consensus. But if political philosophy were to address itself to this great task, responsible human beings will at least have the consolation, if worse comes to worst, of having brought about their own demise in a responsible manner.

Politics as the Highest Value

Few contemporary political philosophers have addressed themselves to the classic first question: What is the purpose of the political system? Unfortunately, they have eschewed the question for the circumstantial reason of their involvement in ideologizing, rather than for the fundamental reason that there is no single best answer to the question. There is not even a best way to ask the question. This has always been true, Plato and his intellectual heirs to the contrary notwithstanding. But it has never been as true of other political systems as it is of the system of world politics today.

We can use our imagination and envisage a variety of future conditions for the community of mankind, but technological progress is such that it is impossible for us to forecast the substantive conditions of our own life twenty years from now, not to speak of the substantive conditions of the lives of our children in fifty years. If one state or bloc of states should suddenly acquire a weapons system putting all of mankind at its absolute mercy, it would be possible also to stabilize the future absolutely and to eliminate both violence and dissent. It would not follow, however, that "world government," made perfectly stable and effective, would continue to be the best of all possible governments in the best of all possible worlds. With greater flexibility, and with the opportunity to use force on behalf of the values of the politics of purposive compromise, other alternatives for the development of mankind might have been formulated, and out of the weighing of these alternatives against absolutely effective stability a future otherwise foreclosed might have emerged.

In the future, and the not too distant future at that, almost anything will be possible, if men decide through politics that it is desirable. Men will be able to restrict their birthrate, to breed superior human beings and beings so superior or so highly specialized that they will no longer be considered human. All human beings *could* be enabled to participate daily in world-wide electronic referenda on current issues of world politics. And so forth. The only condition that seems at present to be impossible in the future, and even in the present, is the isolation of any part of mankind from the politics of the world or from the world of politics.

Since men as we know ourselves now, as individuals and as members of political systems, look upon themselves as beings capable and desirous of development, who require varying combinations of flexibility and stability, of effectiveness and efficiency, and since these combinations can be maintained and changed only through politics, politics again emerges as the most encompassing of human concerns and activities. As in the *polis* of old, politics is the master science, only that the small *polis* of Athens or Sparta has been replaced by the all-inclusive *cosmopolis* of mankind. In Athens philosophers like Plato and

Aristotle could speak with some authority of the purpose of the politics of the *polis,* because no one in their time envisaged the substantive transformation of the conditions of human existence. Even at that, no political philosophers in the *polis* spoke with sufficient authority to elicit so much consensus on his definition of *the* purpose, to prevent the *internal* disintegration of the *polis* as a type. Today, no political philosophers are speaking to this question. If they were, chances are they would meet with less success than the founders of their profession.

Plato and Aristotle and most of their contemporaries (except the Cynics) were at least committed to the primacy of politics. By contrast, there are today philosophers about politics (not political philosophers properly so called) who deny the primacy of politics in favor of the primacy of power or ideology, of economics or law. Politics deals with all of these, because men are capable of generating disagreements about all of them and the relations among them. The faculty of deliberation about disagreement with an eye to its purposive resolution is the political faculty. It is, so far as we know, uniquely human and makes man a political being. Only through politics can men, and can mankind, express their humanity. Only through politics can they develop their humanity. They could also destroy mankind through politics, but this catastrophe is more likely to follow from a rejection of politics in favor of one of its ingredients. The purpose of politics that emerges is the development of politics. The goal of world politics must be the development of world politics. Without its development, world politics would run down to its own and mankind's end.

Appendix

TREATY

*banning nuclear weapon tests
in the atmosphere, in outer
space and under water**

The Governments of the United States of America, the United Kingdom of Great Britain and Northern Ireland, and the Union of Soviet Socialist Republics, hereinafter referred to as the "Original Parties",

Proclaiming as their principal aim the speediest possible achievement of an agreement on general and complete disarmament under strict international control in accordance with the objectives of the United Nations which would put an end to the armaments race and eliminate the incentive to the production and testing of all kinds of weapons, including nuclear weapons,

Seeking to achieve the discontinuance of all test explosions of nuclear weapons for all time, determined to continue negotiations to this end, and desiring to put an end to the contamination of man's environment by radioactive substances,

Have agreed as follows:

ARTICLE I

1. Each of the Parties to this Treaty undertakes to prohibit, to prevent, and not to carry out any nuclear weapon test explosion, or any other nuclear explosion, at any place under its jurisdiction or control:

(a) in the atmosphere; beyond its limits, including outer space; or underwater, including territorial waters or high seas; or

(b) in any other environment if such explosion causes radioactive debris to be present outside the territorial limits of the State under whose jurisdiction or control such explosion is conducted. It is understood in this connection that the provisions of this subparagraph are without prejudice to

---

*United States Treaties and Other International Agreements, Vol. 14, Part 2, 1963 (Washington, D.C.: U.S. Government Printing Office, 1964), pp. 315–19.

the conclusion of a treaty resulting in the permanent banning of all nuclear test explosions, including all such explosions underground, the conclusion of which, as the Parties have stated in the Preamble to this Treaty, they seek to achieve.

2. Each of the Parties to this Treaty undertakes furthermore to refrain from causing, encouraging, or in any way participating in, the carrying out of any nuclear weapon test explosion, or any other nuclear explosion, anywhere which would take place in any of the environments described, or have the effect referred to, in paragraph 1 of this Article.

ARTICLE II

1. Any Party may propose amendments to this Treaty. The text of any proposed amendment shall be submitted to the Depositary Governments which shall circulate it to all Parties to this Treaty. Thereafter, if requested to do so by one-third or more of the Parties, the Depositary Governments shall convene a conference, to which they shall invite all the Parties, to consider such amendment.

2. Any amendment to this Treaty must be approved by a majority of the votes of all the Parties to this Treaty, including the votes of all of the Original Parties. The amendment shall enter into force for all Parties upon the deposit of instruments of ratification by a majority of all the Parties, including the instruments of ratification of all of the Original Parties.

ARTICLE III

1. This Treaty shall be open to all States for signature. Any State which does not sign this Treaty before its entry into force in accordance with paragraph 3 of this Article may accede to it at any time.

2. This Treaty shall be subject to ratification by signatory States. Instruments of ratification and instruments of accession shall be deposited with the Governments of the Original Parties—the United States of America, the United Kingdom of Great Britain and Northern Ireland, and the Union of Soviet Socialist Republics—which are hereby designated the Depositary Governments.

3. This Treaty shall enter into force after its ratification by all the Original Parties and the deposit of their instruments of ratification.

4. For States whose instruments of ratification or accession are deposited subsequent to the entry into force of this Treaty, it shall enter into force on the date of the deposit of their instruments of ratification or accession.

5. The Depositary Governments shall promptly inform all signatory and acceding States of the date of each signature, the date of deposit of each instrument of ratification of and accession to this Treaty, the date of its entry into force, and the date of receipt of any requests for conferences or other notices.

6. This Treaty shall be registered by the Depositary Governments pursuant to Article 102 of the Charter of the United Nations.

Article IV

This Treaty shall be of unlimited duration.

Each Party shall in exercising its national sovereignty have the right to withdraw from the Treaty if it decides that extraordinary events, related to the subject matter of this Treaty, have jeopardized the supreme interests of its country. It shall give notice of such withdrawal to all other Parties to the Treaty three months in advance.

Article V

This Treaty, of which the English and Russian texts are equally authentic, shall be deposited in the archives of the Depositary Governments. Duly certified copies of this Treaty shall be transmitted by the Depositary Governments to the Governments of the signatory and acceding States.

IN WITNESS WHEREOF the undersigned, duly authorized, have signed this Treaty.

DONE in triplicate at the city of Moscow the fifth day of August, one thousand nine hundred and sixty-three.

For the Government of the United States of America

(Signed)
DEAN RUSK

For the Government of the United Kingdom of Great Britain and Northern Ireland

(Signed)
HOME

For the Government of the Union of Soviet Socialist Republics

(Signed)
A. GROMYKO

Bibliography

ALKER, HAYWARD R., JR. and RUSSETT, BRUCE M. *World Politics in the General Assembly.* New Haven: Yale University Press, 1965.

ALMOND, GABRIEL A. and COLEMAN, JAMES S. (eds.). *The Politics of the Developing Areas.* Princeton: Princeton University Press, 1960.

AMERICAN SOCIETY OF INTERNATIONAL LAW–AMERICAN POLITICAL SCIENCE ASSOCIATION. *A Survey of the Teaching of International Law in Political Science Departments,* 1963.

BAILEY, SYDNEY D. *The General Assembly.* New York: Frederick A. Praeger, 1960.

BARKER, CHARLES A. (coordinator). *Problems of World Disarmament: A Series of Lectures Delivered at The Johns Hopkins University.* Boston: Houghton Mifflin Co., 1963.

BIDWELL, PERCY W. *Undergraduate Education in Foreign Affairs.* New York: King's Crown Press, 1962.

BLOOMFIELD, LINCOLN F. *The United Nations and U.S. Foreign Policy: A New Look at the National Interest.* Boston: Little, Brown & Co., 1960.

BONDURANT, JOAN V. *Conquest of Violence: The Gandhian Philosophy of Conflict.* Berkeley and Los Angeles: University of California Press, 1965.

BOWETT, D. W. *United Nations Forces.* New York: Frederick A. Praeger, 1964.

BOYD, ANDREW. *United Nations: Piety Myth Truth.* Baltimore: Penguin Books Inc., 1962.

BRAMSON, LEON and GOETHALS, GEORGE W. (eds.). *War: Studies from Psychology Sociology Anthropology.* New York: Basic Books, Inc., 1964.

BRIGGS, HERBERT W. *The International Law Commission.* Ithaca, N.Y.: Cornell University Press, 1965.

——— *The Law of Nations: Cases, Documents, and Notes.* New York: Appleton-Century-Crofts, Inc., 1938.

BURKE, EDMUND. *Reflections on the Revolution in France.* London: F. Dodsley, 1790.

BURLINGAME, ROGER. *General Billy Mitchell: Champion of Air Defense.* New York: McGraw-Hill Book Co., Inc., 1952.

BURTON, J. W., JR. *International Relations: A General Theory.* New York: Cambridge University Press, 1965.

——— *Peace Theory: Preconditions of Disarmament.* New York: Alfred A. Knopf, 1962.

CLARK, GRENVILLE and SOHN, LOUIS B. *World Peace Through World Law.* 2nd ed., rev. Cambridge: Harvard University Press, 1960.

CLAUDE, INIS L., JR. *Power and International Relations.* New York: Random House, 1962.

———— *Swords into Plowshares: The Problems and Progress of International Organizations.* 2nd ed., rev. New York: Random House, 1961.

———— *The OAS, the UN, and the United States. International Conciliation,* No. 547. New York: Carnegie Endowment for International Peace, March, 1964.

CLAUSEWITZ, KARL VON. *On War.* Trans. O. J. MATTIJS JOLLES. New York: Modern Library, 1943.

COBBAN, ALFRED. "The Decline of Political Theory," *Political Science Quarterly,* Vol. LXVIII (1953), pp. 321–37.

COMMAGER, HENRY STEELE (ed.). *Documents of American History.* New York: F. S. Crofts & Co., Inc., 1934.

Conference of Heads of State or Government of Non-Aligned Countries held in Belgrade, September 1st to 6th, 1961. Belgrade: Publicisticko-Izdavacki, 1961.

CRANKSHAW, EDWARD. *The New Cold War: Moscow v. Pekin.* Baltimore: Penguin Books, Inc., 1963.

CROAN, MELVIN. "Communist International Relations," *Survey,* No. 42 (June, 1962), pp. 9–19.

DALLIN, ALEXANDER. *The Soviet Union at the United Nations: An Inquiry into Soviet Motives and Objectives.* New York: Frederick A. Praeger, 1962.

DEUTSCH, KARL W., JACOB, PHILIP E., and others. *The Integration of Political Communities.* New York and Philadelphia: J. B. Lippincott Co., 1964.

DEUTSCH, KARL W. *The Nerves of Government: Models of Political Communication and Control.* New York: Free Press, 1963.

———— and others. *Political Community and the North Atlantic Area.* Princeton: Princeton University Press, 1957.

EASTON, DAVID. *A Framework for Political Analysis.* Englewood Cliffs, N.J., Prentice-Hall, 1965.

———— *The Political System.* New York: Alfred A. Knopf, 1953.

ECKSTEIN, HARRY (ed.). *Internal War: Problems and Approaches.* New York: Free Press, 1964.

EMERSON, RUPERT. *From Empire to Nation: The Rise to Self-Assertion of Asian and African Peoples.* Cambridge: Harvard University Press, 1960.

EPSTEIN, EON D. *British Politics in the Suez Crisis.* Urbana: University of Illinois Press, 1964.

EUROPEAN COMMISSION AND EUROPEAN COURT OF HUMAN RIGHTS. *Yearbook of the European Convention on Human Rights.* The Hague: Martinus Nijhoff, 1960.

FALK, RICHARD A. *Law, Morality and War in the Contemporary World.* Published for the Center of International Studies, Princeton University. New York: Frederick A. Praeger, 1963.

FALL, BERNARD. *The Two Viet-Nams: A Political and Military Analysis.*
New York: Frederick A. Praeger, 1963.

FINER, HERMAN. *Dulles over Suez: The Theory and Practice of His Diplomacy.* Chicago: Quadrangle Books, 1964.

FINER, S. E. *Men on Horseback: The Role of the Military in Politics.*
New York: Frederick A. Praeger, 1962.

FISHER, ROGER (ed.). *International Conflict and Behavioral Science.* New York: Basic Books, 1963.

FRANCK, THOMAS M. "Structuring Impartiality in International Third-Party Lawmaking," *Indiana Law Journal,* Vol. 39, No. 3 (Spring, 1964), pp. 446–64.

FRIEDRICH, CARL J. (ed.). *Authority: Nomos I.* Cambridge: Harvard University Press, 1958.

———— *Responsibility: Nomos III.* New York: Liberal Arts Press, 1960.

FROMM, ERICH. *May Man Prevail? An inquiry into the Facts and Fictions of Foreign Policy.* Garden City, N.Y.: Anchor Books—Doubleday & Co., Inc., 1961.

FULBRIGHT, J. W. *Old Myths and New Realities and Other Commentaries.* New York: Random House, 1964.

GALBRAITH, J. K. *The Affluent Society.* Boston: Houghton Mifflin Co., 1958.

GAMES RESEARCH, INC. *Diplomacy.* Boston, 1960.

GAREAU, FREDERICK A. (ed.). *The Balance of Power and Nuclear Deterrence.* Boston: Houghton Mifflin Co., 1962.

GILPIN, ROBERT. *American Scientists and Nuclear Weapons Policy.*
Princeton: Princeton University Press, 1962.

———— and WRIGHT, CHRISTOPHER (eds.). *Scientists and National Policy Making.* New York: Columbia University Press, 1964.

GOLDSEN, JOSEPH M. (ed.). *Outer Space in World Politics.* New York: Frederick A. Praeger, 1963.

GOLDWIN, ROBERT A. (ed.). *America Armed: Essays on United States Military Policy.* Chicago: Rand McNally & Co., 1961.

GOODRICH, LELAND M. *The United Nations.* New York: Crowell, 1959.

GREELEY, HORACE. *The American Century.* Hartford: O. D. Case & Co., 1864.

GRODZINS, MORTON and RABINOWITCH, EUGENE (eds.). *The Atomic Age.*
New York: Basic Books, 1963.

GROSS, ERNEST A. *The United Nations: Structure for Peace.* Published for the Council on Foreign Relations. New York: Harper & Bros., 1962.

GUEDALLA, PHILLIP. *Palmerston, 1784–1865.* New York: G. P. Putnam's Sons, 1927.

HAAS, ERNST B. *Beyond the Nation-State: Functionalism and International Organization.* Stanford: Stanford University Press, 1964.

———— *The Uniting of Europe.* Stanford: Stanford University Press, 1958.

HAGEN, EVERETT E. *On the Theory of Social Change: How Economic Growth Begins.* Homewood, Ill.: Dorsey Press, 1962.

HAHN, WALTER F. and NEFF, JOHN C. (eds.). *American Strategy in the Nuclear Age.* Garden City, N.Y.: Anchor Books—Doubleday & Co., 1960.

HAMILTON, ALEXANDER, MADISON, JAMES and JAY, JOHN. *The Federalist or The New Constitution.* New York: Heritage Press, 1945.

HENKIN, LOUIS (ed.). *Arms Control: Issues for the Public.* The American Assembly, Columbia University. Englewood Cliffs, N.J.: Prentice-Hall, 1961.

HERZ, JOHN H. *International Politics in the Atomic Age.* New York: Columbia University Press, 1959.

———— *Political Realism and Political Idealism.* Chicago: University of Chicago Press, 1951.

HERZOG, ARTHUR. *War-Peace Establishment.* New York: Harper & Row, Publishers, Inc., 1965.

HOFFMANN, STANLEY H. (ed.). *Contemporary Theory in International Relations.* Englewood Cliffs, N.J.: Prentice-Hall, 1960.

———— *The State of War: Essays in the Theory and Practice of International Politics.* New York: Frederick A. Praeger, 1966.

HOROWITZ, IRVING LOUIS. *The War Game: Studies of the New Civilian Militarists.* New York: Ballantine Books, 1963.

HOVET, THOMAS, JR. *Africa in the United Nations.* Evanston, Ill.: Northwestern University Press, 1963.

———— *Bloc Politics in the United Nations.* Cambridge: Harvard University Press, 1960.

HSIEH, ALICE LANGLEY. *Communist China's Strategy in the Nuclear Age.* Englewood Cliffs, N.J.: Prentice-Hall, 1962.

HURLEY, MAJOR ALRED F., USAF. *Billy Mitchell: Crusader for Air Power.* Watts Aerospace Library. New York: Franklin Watts, Inc., 1964.

JACOB, PHILLIP E. and ATHERTON, ALEXINE L. *The Dynamics of International Organization: The Making of World Order.* Homewood, Ill.: Dorsey Press, 1965.

JANOWITZ, MORRIS. *The Military in the Developing Countries.* Chicago: University of Chicago Press, 1964.

JENKS, C., WILFRED. *The Common Law of Mankind.* New York: Frederick A. Praeger, 1958.

JOHNSON, JOHN J. *The Military and Society in Latin America.* Stanford: Stanford University Press, 1964.

KAHN, HERMAN. *On Escalation: Metaphors and Scenarios.* New York: Frederick A. Praeger, 1965.

———— *On Thermonuclear War.* Princeton: Princeton University Press, 1960.

———— *Thinking about the Unthinkable.* New York: Horizon Press, Inc., 1962.

KAPLAN, MORTON A. *System and Process in International Politics.* New York: John Wiley & Sons, Inc., 1957.

———— and KATZENBACH, NICHOLAS DEB. *The Political Foundations of International Law.* New York: John Wiley & Sons, Inc., 1961.

KAUTSKY, JOHN H.   "Myth, self-fulling prophecy, and symbolic reassurance in the East-West conflict," *Journal of Conflict Resolution,* Vol. 9, No. 1 (March, 1965), pp. 1-17.

————— *Political Change in Underdeveloped Countries: Nationalism and Communism.* New York: John Wiley & Sons, Inc., 1962.

KELMAN, HERBERT C. (ed.).   *International Behavior: A Social-Psychological Analysis.* New York: Holt, Rinehart & Winston, 1965.

KELSEN, HANS.   "Collective and Individual Responsibility for Acts of State in International Law," *Jewish Yearbook of International Law* (1948).

————— *Law and Peace in International Relations.* Cambridge: Harvard University Press, 1942.

————— *Peace Through Law.* Chapel Hill: University of North Carolina Press, 1944.

KENNAN, GEORGE F.   *Realities of American Foreign Policy.* Princeton: Princeton University Press, 1954.

KERLEY, ERNEST L.   "Some Aspects of the Vienna Convention on Diplomatic Intercourse and Immunities," *American Journal of International Law,* Vol. 56 (1962), pp. 88-129.

KIRCHHEIMER, OTTO.   "Asylum," American Political Science Review, Vol. LIII (December, 1959), pp. 985-1016.

KISSINGER, HENRY A.   *Nuclear Weapons and Foreign Policy.* New Foreword by Gordon Dean. Garden City, New York: Doubleday Anchor Book, 1958.

KLINEBERG, OTTO.   *The Human Dimension in International Relations.* New York: Holt, Rinehart & Winston, 1964.

KOHN, HANS.   *Nationalism: Its Meaning and History.* Princeton, N.J.: Van Nostrand, 1955.

LARSON, ARTHUR.   *When Nations Disagree: A Handbook on World Peace Through World Law.* Louisiana State University Press, 1961.

LARSON, DAVID L. (ed.).   *The "Cuban Crisis" of 1962: Selected Documents and Chronology.* Boston: Houghton Mifflin Co., 1963.

LARUS, JOEL (ed.).   *Comparative World Politics: Premodern Non-Western International Relations.* Belmont, Calif.: Wadsworth Publishing Co., Inc., 1964.

LATHAM, EARL (ed.).   *The Philosophy and Policies of Woodrow Wilson.* Chicago: University of Chicago Press, 1958.

LAUTERPACHT, H. (ed.).   *L.F.L. Oppenheim, International Law. 7th ed.* New York: Longmans, Green & Co., 1948.

LEFEVER, ERNEST W. (ed.)   *Arms and Arms Control: A Symposium.* New York: Frederick A. Praeger, 1962.

————— *Crisis in the Congo: A U.N. Force in Action.* Studies of U.S. Policy and the U.N. Washington, D.C.: Brookings Institution, 1965.

LEGUM, COLIN.   *Pan Africanism: A Short Political Guide.* Rev. ed. New York: Frederick A. Praeger, 1965.

LERNER, MAX.   *The Age of Overkill: A Preface to World Politics.* New York: Simon & Schuster, 1962.

LIEUWEN, EDWIN.   *Arms and Politics in Latin America.* Rev. ed. Published for the Council of Foreign Relations. New York: Frederick A. Praeger, 1961.

MacArthur, Douglas. *Reminiscences.* New York: McGraw-Hill Book Co., Inc., 1964.

Mangone, Gerard J. *The Elements of International Law.* Homewood, Ill.: Dorsey Press, Inc., 1963.

Mannheim, Karl. *Ideology and Utopia: An Introduction to the Sociology of Knowledge.* New York: Harvest Books, 1936.

Mannoni, O. *Prospero and Caliban: The Psychology of Colonization.* 2nd ed. New York: Frederick A. Praeger, 1964.

Mao Tse-Tung. *Selected Works.* 5 Vols. New York: International Publishers, 1954-56.

Mason, Philip. *The Men Who Ruled India.* 2 volumes. London: Jonathan Cape, Ltd., 1953-54.

McDougal, Myres S., Lasswell, Harold D. and Vlasic, Ivan A. *Law and Public Order in Space.* New Haven: Yale University Press, 1963.

McKay, Vernon. *Africa in World Politics.* New York: Harper & Row, Publishers, 1963.

McNair, Arnold D. (ed.). *L.F.L. Oppenheim, International Law.* 4th ed. New York: Longmans, Green & Co., 1928.

McWhinney, Edward. "The 'New' Countries and the 'New' International Law: The United Nations' Special Conference on Friendly Relations and Co-operation Among States," *American Journal of International Law,* Vol. 60, No. 1 (January, 1966), p. 1–33.

Melman, Seymour. *The Peace Race.* New York: Ballantine Books, 1961.

Merton, Robert K. "The Unintended Consequences of Purposive Social Action," *American Sociological Review,* Vol. 1 (December, 1936), pp. 894–904.

Mills, C. Wright. *The Causes of World War Three.* New York: Ballantine Books, 1958.

Mitrany, David. *A Working Peace System.* London and New York: Royal Institute of International Affairs, 1946.

Morgenthau, Hans J. *In Defense of the National Interest.* New York: Alfred A. Knopf, 1951.

——— *Politics among Nations: The Struggle for Power and Peace.* 3rd ed. New York: Alfred A. Knopf, 1960.

Mullins, Claud. *The Leipzig Trials.* London: H. F. and G. Witherby, 1921.

Neustadt, Richard E. *Presidential Power.* New York: John Wiley & Sons, 1960.

Nicholas, H. G. *The United Nations as a Political Institution.* London: Oxford University Press, 1962.

Nicolson, Sir Harold. *Diplomacy.* 3rd ed. New York: Oxford University Press, 1964.

Northrop, F.S.C. *The Meeting of East and West: An Inquiry into International Understanding.* New York: Macmillan Co., 1946.

Orwell, George. *Burmese Days.* New York: Popular Library, 1958.

OSGOOD, CHARLES E. *An Alternative to War or Surrender*. Urbana, Ill.: University of Illinois Press, 1962.

OSGOOD, ROBERT E. *NATO: The Entangling Alliance*. Chicago: University of Chicago Press, 1962.

PACHTER, HENRY M. *Collision Course: The Cuban Missile Crisis and Coexistence*. New York: Frederick A. Praeger, 1963.

PLISCHKE, ELMER (ed.). *Systems of Integrating the International Community*. Princeton, N.J.: D. Van Nostrand Co., Inc., 1964.

POPE JOHN XXIII. *Peace on Earth: Encyclical Letter, April 11, 1963*. Washington, D.C.: National Catholic Welfare Conference, 1963.

PRESIDENT'S COMMISSION ON NATIONAL GOALS. *Goals for Americans*. Administered by The American Assembly, Columbia University. Englewood Cliffs, N.J.: Prentice-Hall, 1960.

PYE, LUCIAN W. *Guerrilla Communism in Malaya*. Princeton: Princeton University Press, 1956.

RAMSEY, PAUL. *The Limits of Nuclear War: Thinking about the Do-able and the Un-Do-able*. New York: Council on Religion and International Affairs, 1963.

RAPOPORT, ANATOL. *Strategy and Conscience*. New York: Harper & Row, Publishers, Inc., 1964.

REES, DAVID. *Korea: The Limited War*. New York: St. Martin's Press, 1964.

ROMULO, CARLOS P. *The Meaning of Bandung*. Chapel Hill: University of North Carolina Press, 1956.

ROSECRANCE, RICHARD N. *Action and Reaction in World Politics: International Systems in Perspective*. Boston: Little, Brown & Co., 1963.

ROTBLAT, JOSEPH. *Science and World Affairs: History of the Pugwash Conferences*. London: Dawsons of Pall Mall, 1962.

RUSSELL, BERTRAND. *Common Sense and Nuclear Warfare*. London: George Allen & Unwin, 1959.

———— *Has Man a Future?* Baltimore: Penguin Books, 1961.

RUSSELL, RUTH B. and MUTHER, JEANNETTE E. *A History of the United Nations Charter*. Washington, D.C.: Brookings Institutions, 1958.

RUSSETT, BRUCE M. *Trends in World Politics*. New York: Macmillan Co., 1965.

SCHELLING, THOMAS C. *Arms and Influence*. New Haven: Yale University Press, 1966.

———— *The Strategy of Conflict*. Cambridge: Harvard University Press, 1960.

———— and HALPERIN, MORTON H. *Strategy and Arms Control*. New York: Twentieth Century Fund, 1961.

SCHLESINGER, ARTHUR M., JR. *A Thousand Days: John F. Kennedy in the White House*. Boston: Houghton Mifflin Co., 1965.

SCOTT, ANDREW M. *The Revolution in Statecraft: Informal Penetration*. New York: Random House, 1965.

SHILS, EDWARD A. *The Intellectual between Tradition and Modernity: The Indian Situation*. The Hague: Mouton, 1961.

SINGER, J. DAVID (ed.). *Human Behavior and International Politics: Contributions from the Social-Psychological Sciences.* Chicago: Rand McNally & Co., 1965.

SMITH, HOWARD K. *The State of Europe.* New York: Alfred A. Knopf, 1949.

SPANIER, JOHN W. *The Truman-MacArthur Controversy and the Korean War.* New York: W. W. Norton & Co., Inc., 1965.

————— and NOGEE, JOSEPH L. *The Politics of Disarmament: A Study in Soviet-American Gamesmanship.* New York: Frederick A. Praeger, 1962.

SPIRO, HERBERT J. (ed.). *Africa: The Primacy of Politics.* New York: Random House, 1966.

————— *Government by Constitution: The Political Systems of Democracy.* New York: Random House, 1959.

————— *Politics in Africa: Prospects South of the Sahara.* Englewood Cliffs, N.J.: Prentice Hall, Inc., 1962.

STAMBUK, GEORGE. *American Military Forces Abroad: Their Impact on the Western State System.* Columbus: Ohio State University Press and the Mershon Center for Education in National Security, 1963.

STIMSON, HENRY L. and BUNDY, McGEORGE. *On Active Service in Peace and War.* New York: Harper & Bros., 1947-48.

STOESSINGER, JOHN G. *Financing the United Nations System.* Washington, D.C.: Brookings Institutions, 1964.

————— *The Might of Nations: World Politics in Our Time.* Rev. ed. New York: Random House, 1965.

————— *The United Nations and the Super Powers: United States-Soviet Interaction at the United Nations.* New York: Random House, 1965.

————— and WESTIN, ALAN F. (eds.). *Power and Order: Six Cases in World Politics.* New York: Harcourt, Brace & World, Inc., 1964.

STONE, I. F. *The Hidden History of the Korean War.* New York: Monthly Review Press, 1962.

STONE, JULIUS. *The International Court and World Crisis.* International Conciliation No. 536. New York: Carnegie Endowment for International Peace, January, 1962.

THUCYDIDES. *The Peloponnesian War.* New York: Modern Library, 1934.

WALTERS, F. P. *A History of the League of Nations.* 2 Vols. London: Oxford University Press, 1952.

WHITAKER, ARTHUR PRESTON. *Development of American Regionalism: The Organization of American States.* New York: Carnegie Endowment for International Peace, 1951.

WISE, DAVID and ROSS, THOMAS. *The Invisible Government.* New York: Random House, 1964.

WOLFF, ROBERT LEE. *The Balkans in Our Time.* Cambridge: Harvard University Press, 1956.

WRIGHT, QUINCY. *A Study of War.* 2 vols. Chicago: University of Chicago Press, 1942.

————— *Problems of Stability and Progress in International Relations.* Berkeley: University of California Press, 1954.

ZARTMAN, I. WILLIAM. *International Relations in the New Africa.* Englewood Cliffs, N.J.: Prentice-Hall, 1966.

ZAWODNY, J. K. *Guide to the Study of International Relations.* San Francisco: Chandler Publishing Co., 1966.

Index

This book has been set in 10 point Caledonia, leaded 3 points, and 9 point Caledonia, leaded 2 points. Chapter numbers are in 14 point Caledonia Italic; chapter titles are in 30 point Caslon True Cut Italic. The size of the type page is 26 by 44 picas.